Improving
Impact Assessment

Westview Replica Editions

The concept of Westview Replica Editions is a response to the continuing crisis in academic and informational publishing. Library budgets for books have been severely curtailed. Ever larger portions of general library budgets are being diverted from the purchase of books and used for data banks, computers, micromedia, and other methods of information retrieval. Interlibrary loan structures further reduce the edition sizes required to satisfy the needs of the scholarly community. Economic pressures on the university presses and the few private scholarly publishing companies have severely limited the capacity of the industry to properly serve the academic and research communities. As a result, many manuscripts dealing with important subjects, often representing the highest level of scholarship, are no longer economically viable publishing projects--or, if accepted for publication, are typically subject to lead times ranging from one to three years.

Westview Replica Editions are our practical solution to the problem. We accept a manuscript in camera-ready form, typed according to our specifications, and move it immediately into the production process. As always, the selection criteria include the importance of the subject, the work's contribution to scholarship, and its insight, originality of thought, and excellence of exposition. The responsibility for editing and proofreading lies with the author or sponsoring institution. We prepare chapter headings and display pages, file for copyright, and obtain Library of Congress Cataloging in Publication Data. A detailed manual contains simple instructions for preparing the final typescript, and our editorial staff is always available to answer questions.

The end result is a book printed on acid-free paper and bound in sturdy library-quality soft covers. We manufacture these books ourselves using equipment that does not require a lengthy makeready process and that allows us to publish first editions of 300 to 600 copies and to reprint even smaller quantities as needed. Thus, we can produce Replica Editions quickly and can keep even very specialized books in print as long as there is a demand for them.

About the Book and Editors

Improving Impact Assessment:
Increasing the Relevance and Utilization
of Scientific and Technical Information
edited by Stuart L. Hart, Gordon A. Enk, and William F. Hornick

As Environmental Impact Statements (EIS) become increasingly important in the policymaking process, it is vital that they be as complete and accurate as possible. The authors of this volume consider ways in which the development and evaluation of scientific and technical information for EIS can be improved. Addressing key legal, social, political, and ecological issues, they explore ways to facilitate communication between researchers and policymakers, evaluate the need for an Environmental Impact Assessment Network, and review case-study applications of new approaches.

Stuart L. Hart is assistant research scientist and project director at the Institute for Social Research at the University of Michigan and consultant to the Research and Decision Center, Medusa, New York. Gordon A. Enk is president of the Research and Decision Center, where William F. Hornick is an associate.

Improving Impact Assessment

Increasing the Relevance and Utilization of Scientific and Technical Information

edited by Stuart L. Hart,
Gordon A. Enk,
and William F. Hornick
with James J. Jordan and Paul Perreault

Westview Press / Boulder and London

The grant award by the National Science Foundation for
this project was made in 1979 to the Economic and Environmental Studies Center (EES) of The Institute on Man and
Science (IMS), Rensselaerville, New York 12147; the staff
of the EES Center initiated and conducted the project. In
the course of the project, the staff of the EES Center
left IMS and founded a new, independent organization, The
Research and Decision Center. The project and this report
were completed by the research staff at The Research and
Decision Center, Medusa, New York 12120. The final copy
of the book manuscript was prepared at the University
of Michigan's Institute for Social Research, Ann Arbor,
Michigan 48106.

A Westview Replica Edition

Published in 1984 in the United States of America by
    Westview Press, Inc.
    5500 Central Avenue
    Boulder, Colorado 80301
    Frederick A. Praeger, Publisher

Library of Congress Cataloging in Publication Data
Main entry under title:
Improving impact assessment.
    (A Westview replica edition)
    1. Environmental impact analysis. I. Hart, Stuart L.
II. Enk, Gordon A. III. Hornick, William F.
TD194.6.I55   1984   333.7'1   84-19531
ISBN 0-86531-865-4

Printed and bound in the United States of America
10 9 8 7 6 5 4 3 2 1

36701 ✓

2.3.86
3.6.87

Contents

List of Tables   xi
List of Figures   xiii
Acknowledgments   xv

Introduction: Problem Statement and Project
               Context   1

PART 1
REDEFINING THE SCOPE OF ENVIRONMENTAL ASSESSMENT

1   A Process-Oriented Approach to Human Concerns
    in Environmental Decision Making, *Stephen
    Kaplan*   21

2   Assessing Human Concerns for Environmental
    Decision Making, *Rachel Kaplan*   37

3   EIA Scoping for Aesthetics: Hindsight from
    the Greene County Nuclear Power Plant EIS,
    Carl H. Petrich   57

4   Socioeconomic Impact Assessment and Nuclear
    Power Plant Licensing: Greene County, New
    York, *Elizabeth Peelle*   93

5   The Role of Human Values, Attitudes, and
    Beliefs in Environmental Assessment, *Margaret
    S. Hrezo and William E. Hrezo*   119

PART 2
APPLYING ASSESSMENT TECHNIQUES

6   Improving Predictive Performance and
    Usefulness of Biological Environmental Impact
    Assessment: Experimental Impact Studies and
    Adaptive Impact Assessment, *Diana Valiela* . .   143

7   Preliminary Environmental Assessment
    Techniques for Soils, *Nellie M. Stark*   159

8   Land-Capability Analysis As a Planning and
    Regulatory Tool, *James J. Jordan*   171

9   The Application of Image-Based Information
    Systems for Environmental Assessment, *Ronald
    G. McLeod*   189

10 Toward a Participant Value Method for the
    Presentation of Environmental Impact Data,
    *Eric L. Hyman, David H. Moreau, and Bruce
    Stiftel*   209

11 Comparisons of Methods for Evaluating Multi-
    attributed Alternatives in Environmental
    Assessments: Results of the BNL-NRC Siting
    Methods Project, *Benjamin F. Hobbs, Michael
    D. Rowe, Barbara L. Pierce, and Peter M. Meier*   227

12 The Scoping Concept and Citizen Involvement:
    An Opportunity for Rejuvenating NEPA, *James
    R. Pease and Richard C. Smardon*   253

PART 3
KEYING ANALYSIS TO DECISION MAKERS

13 How to Write a Socially Useful EIS, *Selina
    Bendix*   271

14 The EIS and the Decision Maker: Closing the
    Gap, *Ruth-Ellen Miller*   289

15 The Impact Judgment: A Technical Impasse?,
    Robert E. Henshaw   313

16 Organizational Environmental Management: The
    Los Alamos National Laboratory and Tennessee
    Valley Authority Experience, *Shelby Smith-
    Sanclare*   325

PART 4
ANALYSIS AND CASE STUDY

17 The Costs of Environmental Review: Assessment
    Methods and Trends, *Stuart L. Hart*   339

18 The Fate of EIS Projects: A Retrospective
    Study, *Granville H. Sewell and Susan Korrick* .   359

19 Improving the EIS Process: A Case Study of
    Spruce Budworm Control, *Lloyd C. Irland* . . .   375

20 The Interface Between Federal and State EIS
    Requirements: An Overview, *Dennis Lundblad* .   393

21 The Uses of Scoping: The Massachusetts
    Experience, *Samuel G. Mygatt*   399

22 Changing the Environmental Review Procedure in
    Minnesota, *Sharon Decker*   403

PART 5
RECENT CHANGES AND CONCLUSIONS

23 The 1979 CEQ NEPA Regulations, *Nicholas
    C. Yost*   415

24 Concluding Observations and Future Directions   423

Contributors   435

Tables

1.1   Framework for portable model: human needs and public participation   30

3.1   Comparison of responses to photographs of cement plants, cooling towers and plumes, and existing landscapes by respondent groups   74

4.1   Greene County nuclear power plant licensing action: brief selected chronology   100

4.2   Mitigation of socioeconomic impacts of GCNPP at Cementon site   105

5.1   Rankings accorded pollution since 1972 . . .   131

6.1   Key uncertainties suggested by modelling the consequences of marsh habitat loss for salmon populations of the Fraser River . . .   155

8.1   Lake Tahoe basin land area classified by inherent erosion hazard   174

8.2   Geomorphic units, Lake Tahoe basin   175

8.3   Basis of capability classification for Lake Tahoe basin lands   176

8.4   Lake Tahoe basin land area classified by capability   177

8.5   Example of capability ranking by soil type .   178

10.1   Alternative descriptions   219

10.2   Alternative rankings   219

10.3   Aspects of social welfare considered in the analysis   223

14.1   Sample "organizational process" summary (focusing on generating employment)   299

14.2   Potentially relevant works of speculative fiction   302

17.1   EIS cost-accounting system   342

18.1   Number of EISs by project type, 1973   361

18.2   EIS breakdown by agency, 1973   362

18.3   Project status   363

18.4   EIS accuracy of description of environmental
       effects   364

18.5   Evaluation of EIS science content   367

19.1   Summary of past aerial spraying for spruce
       budworm control in Maine   376

19.2   Actors in the Maine spruce budworm program .   378

19.3   Timing constraints in EIS process: spruce
       budworm spray projects   381

19.4   Summary of reviews of DEIS, Maine spruce
       budworm projects, 1975-1981   386

20.1   SEPA-NEPA: eight years of environmental
       reporting in Washington (based on documents
       received in the Department of Ecology),
       January 1980   394

Figures

3.1   Computer-drawn view of the mid-Hudson River
      Valley and Catskill Mountains
      from the northeast to the southwest.   60

3.2   "Bend in the River" view from Olana looking
      to the southwest over the Hudson River. . .   80

3.3   <u>Winter Landscape from Olana</u> (c. 1879) by
      Frederic E. Church (1826-1900). Oil
      on paper, 11 5/8 x 18 1/2 inches.   81

3.4   Church's southwesterly "Bend in the River"
      view with the Greene County
      Nuclear Power Plant artistically
      superimposed at the proposed Cementon
      location.   83

4.1   NRC licensing of nuclear power plants:
      environmental and safety reviews.   97

6.1   Diagrammatic representation of the input of
      biological information into an environmental
      impact assessment.   146

6.2   Flow diagram of the oyster production
      simulation model.   147

6.3   Simulated production of oysters by bottom
      culture in British Columbia assuming present
      levels (solid line) and moderate gradual
      increases in conflicts (dashed line) with
      the forest products industry.   148

6.4   Simulated production of oysters by string
      (off-bottom) culture in British Columbia
      assuming moderate gradual increases in
      conflicts with the forest industry, other
      conditions being favorable, and no
      protective reserve status for any areas
      (solid line) and reserves in two highly
      productive areas (dashed line).   149

6.5   Simplified flow diagram of estuarine
      utilization by chum and chinook juveniles. .   154

9.1   Land-use planning and management information
      system.   192

9.2   California Desert digital mosaic.   196

9.3   The Santa Ana East 1° x 1° image.   197

9.4   Summary tabulation of biomass for selected
      grazing allotments.   199

9.5   Four data planes used in the Lake Tahoe data
      base.   201

9.6   Summary cross-tabulation report of Lake
      Tahoe data items.   202

9.7   Census tracts registered to Landsat image. .   204

9.8   Portland, Oregon, air pollution relative
      health impact by 2-km² grid cells.   206

10.1 Environmental impact assessment.   211

10.2 Analytical phase of water resource planning.   214

11.1 Generalized environmental impact assessment
      process.   229

11.2 Examples of candidate areas generated. . . .   242

14.1 Linstone's multiple perspectives on decision
      making (1981).   291

16.1 Basic components of EIS procedure.   329

17.1 Generalized dynamic of caseload.   355

Acknowledgments

This book encapsulates the diligent efforts of many persons to improve the scientific soundness, utility, scope, and usability of environmental impact statements and the process that produces them. We are indebted to a host of contributors who made the project and the symposium upon which these pages are based possible, who produced the individual essays in this volume, and who worked tirelessly in the production of the manuscript. Our sincerest appreciation is extended to Sidney Draggan and Richard Morrison of the Division of Policy Research and Analysis of the National Science Foundation, the funder of this research, symposium, and documentation effort; to the symposium participants and authors of the essays presented here; to Gerard Finin for his research and logistical support for the field study of the Greene County nuclear power plant siting case; to Judith Bayer, who served as project secretary; and to Rose Frisbee and Jeanette Lendrum, who worked many long hours in the typing of the draft manuscript. Finally, thanks must be extended to Jane Stanton for her careful yet efficient preparation of this manuscript.

Medusa, New York
July 1984

Stuart L. Hart
Gordon A. Enk
William F. Hornick
with
James J. Jordan and
Paul Perreault

Introduction: Problem Statement and Project Context

The Environmental Impact Statement (EIS) process was established as a requirement for all major federal projects significantly affecting the human environment by the National Environmental Policy Act of 1969 (NEPA). Since then, 25 states and 16 other nations have adopted some form of environmental impact review of government activities.[1]

Although the EIS process has become a widespread, multilevel phenomenon, little effort has been made to collect and synthesize the diversity of approaches and experiences of the many implementing agencies, researchers and practitioners. While a handful of efforts have attempted to improve the dialogue among those involved in the field of impact assessment, they either have been directed at a largely academic audience[2] or have addressed only a narrow set of concerns.[3] Indeed, the need to improve the utility of the EIS process has been openly acknowledged by the federal government as well as the states. Testimony of federal, state and local officials, as well as private spokespeople, at public hearings held in 1977 to review the federal EIS process resulted in significant rule changes regarding NEPA.[4]

Administrative and procedural issues are, without question, important factors in the discussion of environmental impact assessment and have necessarily received a great deal of attention by agencies, the courts, and research commentators.[5] The scientific and technical aspects of the EIS process have to date, however, received only fragmented or otherwise inadequate attention. Several factors contribute to the inadequacy of the "substantive basis" of environmental impact assessment. These include:

- The lack of basic monitoring, survey and baseline information;
- The uncertainties of descriptions, predictions, and thresholds pertaining to natural and social systems; and
- The inability to generalize the findings of most ecosystem and social analyses since most are highly site specific.

Consequently, most EISs have not contained sound scientific data.' Instead, they have characteristically contained discussions of individual species, physical parameters, and social characteristics but little consideration of ecological communities, social systems, or their systematic interrelationships. Futhermore, while initial concern was focused predominately on technical issues such as air and water quality, in the last decade the spectrum has been broadened to include more "soft" science issues such as socioeconomic and aesthetic considerations. Thus, not only are the scientific and technical aspects of the EIS process inexact at best, but the substantive base of environmental assessment has been continually broadening.'

Developing adequate scientific and technical information for the EIS process has been further hindered by several "procedural" stumbling blocks. For example, data generated by the EIS process have often been filed away and later duplicated by other studies due to nonexistent or archaic systems of information storage and retrieval.' Similarly, there has been little coordinated effort to verify the findings of past EISs--an endeavor that could provide an excellent source of baseline information.' Indeed, it is difficult to separate substantive from procedural considerations in environmental assessment since substantive criteria must have a methodological or "procedural" component just as procedural provisions (such as the EIS) must have inherently "substantive" ends in mind.

Not only are substantive and procedural issues intimately interwoven in the EIS process, so too are political considerations. This was brought into sharp relief by one of the few attempts to improve the quality, quantity, and usability of scientific information in the EIS process--The Environmental Impact Assessment Project (EIAP) of The Institute of Ecology (TIE).'° In this effort, TIE attempted to involve natural and social scientists in the environmental impact assessment process as reviewers of draft EISs. It was naively assumed that scientists would lend their expertise in a cooperative mode and their input would be accepted and incorporated into the EIS.

One important "lesson learned" was that most scientists who became involved did so because they had a personal and often emotional involvement in the particular project. They often (not always) ended up participating as activists, not scientists--they were advocates, not analysts. This meant that they often abandoned empirical research, data bases, and the scientific approach and instead viewed proposals as unacceptable and proceeded to argue against them. They left the scientific realm behind when they entered the political arena. This resulted in a situation of minimum learning (by EIS writers, decision makers, and scientists) and promoted confrontation. Thus, while the EIS process can serve many useful functions, it was not initially designed to resolve environmental disputes.[11] There is an additional problem with respect to the scientific basis of environmental impact statements: since the political world often moves on a much faster time scale than proper scientific study designs might prescribe, there is frequently pressure for release of preliminary (and often premature) results. In essence, the legal and administrative process used to collect information for decision making is inherently at odds with the nature of traditional scientific inquiry.[12] Thus, while the theoretical base for environmental impact assessment has improved substantially, the use of scientific analyses in the decision-making process still suffers serious shortcomings.

Numerous studies have been conducted to examine the way in which scientific information is used (or fails to be used) in the political process.[13] By and large, these utilization studies have identified three categories of factors involved in the apparent schism between analytical requirements and political needs:

1. Factors unique to the policy maker and policy process;
2. Factors unique to the researcher or research product; and
3. Factors associated with the interaction between two groups with different values, reward systems, and "languages."

This suggests that the quality and utility of scientific analysis in EISs can be improved only by either (1) making researchers more responsive to the needs of the political process or (2) making practitioners and political institutions more aware of and sensitive to the needs and findings of the scientist and researcher.

Recently, however, Charles Lindblom in his book, Usable Knowledge,[14] has criticized these and other "parochial" views of research utilization as confusing the parts with the whole:

> Seen as a whole, obstacles to and potentials for more useful social science and research pose profound questions about man as a problem solver, about knowledge and craft, about science, and about a complex social and political order in which knowledge and science are embedded and by which they are shaped.

Acknowledging Lindblom's insight, it is clear that the currently expressed desire to make EISs useful to decision makers is premised upon, and therefore limited by, the parochial assumption that researchers (i.e., scientists, planners, and EIS preparers) and decision makers (i.e., bureaucrats and politicians) are engaged in distinct and separate activities. Under this model, politically astute researchers should provide a flow of strategic information and analysis (knowledge) to awaiting decision makers whose information requirements are determined by the need to act in a politically constrained decision process (action).

But, by assuming a split between those who know and those who do, knowledge and action are separated, the flow of information is restricted to one direction, and the opportunities for a social decision-making process enhanced by interaction and mutual learning are greatly reduced. What is required is a process that encourages not only practical theorists but also reflective decision makers. This means that analysts must become more policy-conscious while, at the same time, decision makers must become more sophisticated in their use of scientific information of all types.

This book reports on a project initiated by the Research and Decision Center (R&D Center) that attempted to come to grips with the above situation. It attempts to collect and synthesize the experience, approaches, and insights of both project staff and project participants and should be useful to the researcher and decision maker alike. It is our contention that, while there can be no "quick fixes" to the problem, there is tremendous potential to benefit from each other's mistakes, perspectives, and experiences. For this reason, we designed the effort to deal with the issues in a nonthreatening and supportively interactive setting. Part of this effort entailed convening key members of state and federal agencies involved in the EIS process, environmental scientists, researchers, and educators for a four-day invitational symposium on "Improving the Quality and Utility of Scientific and Technical Information in EISs" (May 18-23, 1980). The overall goal of the project was to enhance the use of scientific and technical analyses in environmental impact assessment within a framework of tested yet innovative procedures drawn from the participants' experiences. Toward this goal, the project had four specific objectives.

First, to assemble and analyze the results of the *latest EIS research*. Of particular concern was the reliability and use of ecosystem analyses, predictive studies, and the retrospective verification of past EISs for accuracy of impact forecasts. Special attention was also focused on evolving categories of concern such as environmental values, human preferences, social and economic impact assessment, and community analysis. Recent legal precedents and political changes were also examined to determine their impact on the goal of improved procedural and substantive environmental impact analysis.

Second, to *review EIS program innovations*. Several

states had adopted innovative approaches to many aspects of the EIS process; however, the experience of these new approaches remained uncommunicated prior to the symposium. Thus, the project, especially in its symposium component, fostered the articulation and translation of these diverse experiences in terms of their usefulness for CEQ, EPA, and other NEPA-administrative bodies.

Third, to facilitate *interaction* and *supportive communication* among the leading researchers, scientists, policy makers, and practitioners of EIS processes. This was accomplished through numerous formal and informal group tasks and interactions.

Fourth, to assess the need for and test the viability of an *Environmental Impact Assessment Network* of national (or even international) dimension. Such a network would function as a communication medium on the problems and prospects involved in implementing novel approaches and conducting environmental impact analyses.

Additional tasks to be performed within the context of the project included the generation of a "Research Agenda" pertaining to the improved use of scientific and technical knowledge in EISs and decision making and the development of recommendations for a "Model Environmental Impact Statement Process."

In designing the project to meet the above objectives, a sequence of activities was initiated that culminated in the symposium. First, an extensive literature review and networking with leading professionals in the field were conducted. "Networking" is an extension of the traditional literature review through personal contacts with current researchers and decision makers. The process identifies people and information not yet widely known or disseminated and facilitates the "targeting" of particularly important or unique perspectives. This, combined with a "Call for Papers," provided a good sense of the state-of-the-art in the field. Various issue categories were then established enabling the many topics and analysts to be grouped and representatives of those groups targeted for participation in the project. The result was many more potential presenters and papers than could possibly be accommodated during the symposium. Proposed papers were evaluated on the basis of the following criteria: scientific soundness, practical applicability, suitability for audience, innovativeness, and replicability. Further, a detailed "profile" of potential participants and their interests was made to aid staff in selecting an appropriately diverse mix of presenters and participants. All of those papers that were accepted but not chosen for symposium presentation were retained for publication in a larger proceedings. This book contains many of these contributions in addition to the symposium papers.

Initially, approximately 70 participants were anticipated to attend the symposium. In addition to the

above criteria for selecting presenters, there was also a
desire to maintain an organizational, philosophical, and
geographical distribution among attendees. Given our
professed intent to focus on state and federal decision
makers, we envisioned 50 representatives from the states,
10 representatives from federal agencies, and 10
representatives from the scientific, research, and
professional community. In targeting government
participants from the state and federal levels, it was our
intention to attract neither the agency chief executives
nor the day-to-day implementors of agency policy. We
specifically sought to identify and involve those in the
"middle level" of the organization--people who manage and/
or make operational decisions about the environmental
impact of the agency's behavior--since certain innovations
could be operationalized almost immediately at a staff
level by such individuals while larger program or
strategic changes could be most effectively recommended to
upper management by such individuals as well. Thus, by
involving key mid-level staff in an interactive session
with the research and scientific community, it was hoped
not only that maximum learning might be encouraged but
also that the maximum potential for implementation and
innovation might be achieved.

A number of factors intervened, however, to alter the
initial image of the participant mix. By far, the most
important of these was the difficulty many practitioners
and decision makers had setting aside five days for the
symposium. Even with financial assistance in the form of
paid travel and hospitality, only 18 of the 50 states sent
representatives. Further, exigencies of government meant
that the targeted person was sometimes unable to attend,
the result being an agency-picked replacement. In the
final analysis, the symposium was comprised of the
following mix: 18 representatives of the states, 8
representatives from federal agencies, 1 representative of
local government and 14 representatives from the
scientific, research, or professional community. (See the
section on Contributors for names and affiliations of
those presenting papers.)

The symposium was therefore designed to reflect the
somewhat altered mix of participants. Formal
presentations were mixed with actual site visits and
specific small group tasks. Formal presentations were
arranged into three broad categories:

1. Broadening the Scientific Scope of Environmental
   Impact Assessment;
2. Using Environmental Impact Assessment Techniques;
   and
3. Keying Environmental Impact Assessment to
   Decision Making.

Roughly, the same organization was retained for this

book; in addition, Part 4: Analysis and Case Study serves as an umbrella for the separate evening session presentations, concurrent sessions, and analytical pieces. The site visits were made to key locations discussed in the Greene County Nuclear Power Plant EIS. This served to put some flesh on the bones of the approaches and observations discussed at the symposium. Indeed, two papers in this volume, that by Carl Petrich and that by Elizabeth Peelle, detail issues of critical importance surrounding this situation; in this case, the EIS was instrumental in the Nuclear Regulatory Commission's denial of a permit for construction of a new nuclear power plant largely on the basis of the aesthetic and socioeconomic impact analysis conducted by the two authors.

The small group tasks addressed three issues: (1) the prospects for an "Environmental Impact Assessment Network;" (2) the generation of a "Model EIS Process;" and (3) the generation of a "Research Agenda" for Environmental Impact Assessment. Because of the integrated nature of the papers and the task groups, we briefly summarize the results of these efforts below. Conclusions and reflections on the implications of these results follow each result's description.

STRUCTURING AN "ENVIRONMENTAL IMPACT ASSESSMENT NETWORK"

The comprehensive nature of the Environmental Impact Statement process has resulted in significant problems of coordination--both within and between the various levels of government involved. Problems of duplication have also arisen where a given project or proposal is subject to more than one EIS requirement (e.g., state and federal). In addition, the EIS process has generated an extensive quantity of scientific and technical information that has oftentimes led to information overload rather than to problem clarification. These problems have been compounded by a lack of access to appropriate methodologies and procedural approaches that might facilitate improved environmental decision making. Combined with widespread lack of communication among individuals and agencies involved in EIS programs, these factors have resulted in fragmentation and isolation of EIS program experiences.

As one solution to these problems, an "Environmental Impact Assessment Network" designed to foster dynamic interaction and sustained dialogue among EIS practitioners has often been suggested. Such a network could function as a communication medium on the problems and prospects of conducting EIS programs and implementing novel or adaptive approaches to environmental analysis and review. It could also function to make newly developed information immediately available to practitioners who need it, without depending upon the formal media and journals.

In order to test the need and usefulness, as well as

the structure and format, for an "EIA Network," we solicited the input of participants at the symposium. The first step in this assessment of an "EIA Network" involved completion of a one-page questionnaire by all participants to determine the general consensus as to the need and usefulness of such a network. Only one respondent to the questionnaire indicated that an "EIA Network" was not needed or useful. All other respondents (40) considered the network a potentially useful mechanism to some degree.

On the basis of the participants' consensus that an "EIA Network" was needed and would be useful, the next step in the network assessment was initiated. Symposium participants were divided into four equal-sized task teams with all major participant disciplines distributed within each group. Each task team discussed the concept and provided recommendations to the full body of symposium representatives.

The similarities in the groups' discussions and recommendations appear to reflect some universal needs experienced by most individuals participating in the EIS process. The need to save time, reduce work, and have a system "on line" as quickly as possible and at lower cost was expressed by all groups. The types of information most often requested included technical information and assistance in solving administrative or project-specific problems. Information on public involvement approaches and current research areas was also included as a need that could be satisfied by a network. Finally, the need was voiced for information on failures. By establishing a process to benefit from the mistakes of others, a "learning system" could be established that goes beyond any existing EIS information system.

All groups felt that a list of private, state, and federal resource people in the EIS process would be the most effective manner for commencing a network. Such a "living network" (including phone number, interest "key words," and affiliation) has already been initiated by the Research and Decision Center. Two mechanisms for extending such a process were offered. One suggested the utilization of existing library services, associations, and publications to obtain bibliographic information, storage of information by subject matter, and current research information. The other mechanism suggested surveying the U.S. Environmental Protection Agency (EPA) and other agencies that may already have a network in progress. If no network currently exists, the suggestion was to encourage EPA to initiate one. The financing of such a network would initially come from a seed grant from an institution such as EPA, the President's Council on Environmental Quality, or the National Science Foundation, with continued support coming from subscriptions to the networking service.

Other types of networking instruments suggested that could supplement the "living network" at a later date included:

  - an annual conference,
  - a newsletter,
  - an "EIS Hotline" 800 number,
  - a computer conferencing system,
  - on-line search capabilities, and
  - a compendium of EIS resources.

R&D Center staff conclusion:

While the need and value of an EIS Network is
generally agreed upon, the possibility of sustaining
a significant network is low.

There is ample evidence that people in the EIS field
view the potential utility of an established network
system in a very positive light; it is clear that what
people sense is needed is the establishment of a "learning
system." The interest is widespread but diverse. The
fundamental problem is that no group of persons or
institutions is apparently in a position to support such a
concept from a financial standpoint. There have been
previous attempts to set up directories or periodicals
(e.g., the Institute of Water Resources magazine Impact
published in the early 1970's and the U.S. Army Corps of
Engineers' Directory of Environmental Life Scientists
published in 1974) to address the perceived need, and none
of them had financial staying power. Futhermore, no
current institution has a clear mandate or available
resources (money and person power) for such a function.
It is very likely that, without a commitment from an
appropriate institution, the proposals for an informal,
low-keyed network will not be sustained.

GENERATING A MODEL ENVIRONMENTAL
IMPACT STATEMENT (EIS) PROCESS

The diversity of approaches to preparing and
processing environmental impact statements and the
numerous emerging methodologies and techniques of
assessment can be viewed as the raw material for a "Model
EIS Process." This model would attempt to use the most
practical or promising of the program and research
experiences in this area to provide an easily applied and
replicable tool useful at all levels of impact assessment.
The concept of a Model EIS Process is certainly not
new. However, all of the past attempts deal largely with
legislative aspects and not the intricacies of program
implementation. Serious problems have also been
encountered; the diversity of agencies and political
jurisdictions made it difficult to develop a model
applicable to all situations.
The R&D Center, therefore, sought to explore

development of a Model EIS Process that would balance
concerns for practical applicability and scientific
creativity in a context of fiscal constraint and
organizational diversity. By identifying the "core" of a
process that can be supplemented by additional adaptations
where deemed useful or appropriate, the model could be
made responsive to users with different levels of access
to expertise and resources.

Through the use of a structured group decision-making
process, it was hoped that the participants could
interactively identify (on the basis of their varied
experiences with EISs) the priority items and issues that
should be included in an effective EIS process. The
participants were again divided into four equal-sized task
teams with all major participant disciplines distributed
within each group. With R&D Center staff acting as
facilitators, each group utilized Nominal Group Technique
(NGT)[1] to identify and prioritize components of a Model
EIS Process. Addressing the question, "What are the
components of a Model EIS Process?," the technique
proceeded as follows:

Step 1: Silent generation of ideas (for
identification of Model EIS Process
components) by each group member. A time
limit of five minutes was imposed on this
step.

Step 2: Round-robin listing of all responses
prepared by the group; no evaluation was
allowed at this stage.

Step 3: Exploration of all responses by group
members to clarify, consolidate, or
otherwise revise responses by consensus of
the group.

Step 4: Voting by each group member, independent of
other members, to assign a priority to each
of the remaining responses. A scale of "0"
(not important) to "5" (very important) was
used in the voting. Tallying of group
members' votes resulted in a prioritization
of responses.

This technique, when properly employed, can help assure
that all participants have their ideas and priorities
clearly understood and seriously considered by the group.
It tends to minimize domination by a verbal minority and
helps to ensure that the group considers a comprehensive
set of options.

While the results of the NGT did not produce any
recommendations of earth-shaking originality, the exercise
did serve to clarify and prioritize many areas of concern.
First, there was a strong cluster of ideas around the
notion of "expanding the life of the EIS." In order for
EISs to become more useful evaluation tools (and not

merely static reflections of opinions and conclusions at a given time), the process must begin very early (project planning) and continue through project implementation and operation. Associated with the early initiation of impact assessment were concepts such as identification of all affected parties, scoping, and open (or "fishbowl") planning. The follow-up component included concepts such as monitoring predicted impacts and model validation. Enforcement of mitigation measures was also seen as a positive feature.

The second major cluster dealt with issues of EIS concept. The strongest suggestion was that of moving beyond project description to a more analytic, predictive, and verifiable approach. Consideration of the full spectrum of alternatives (including those beyond the scope of the agency) and the probabilities and risks associated with various impacts was also stressed.

A third cluster of recommendations revolved around the format of EISs and sought to improve document readability. Suggestions included the use of executive summaries, professional editors (to ensure consistency and clarity), and key word indexes. Strong need was voiced for writing in plain English--a document should not be considered professionally acceptable until it can be understood by the interested lay public.

Finally, many participants stressed the need for a more central role for EISs in decision making. This recommendation was complex and multifaceted and included at least the following dimensions: translation of scientific information into a form that decision makers are compelled to use, the internalization of environmental values by agency managers and project initiators, the imposition of enforcement power or "teeth" to require environmentally responsible decisions, and the use of the "decision record" approach to force decision makers publicly to display their rationale for decisions.

R&D Center staff conclusion:

There were few new suggestions for improving the content of EISs; instead, there was a strong sense that the actual use and utility of EISs needed improvement.

The recommendations resulting from the discussion of a Model EIS Process are probably most notable for their lack of new, novel, or creative elements. This suggests that those involved in the EIS process are beyond the initial stage of EIS conceptualization--the phase that observers of innovation would call "early adoption." The workshop participants were more concerned with developing a sound process that people take seriously when faced with a decision. The components suggested would result in an approach and a document that would:

- involve all the concerned and potentially impacted
  individuals (citizens, scientists, and decision
  makers) early in the process and maintain their
  participation throughout;
- contain as much sound information based on valid
  analysis as possible;
- allow room for subjective considerations that
  would be labelled as such;
- be readable; and
- be used to guide decisions.

GENERATING A RESEARCH AGENDA FOR ENVIRONMENTAL IMPACT ASSESSMENT

When considering a complex task such as generating a
research agenda for impact assessment, it is critical to
take advantage not only of the depth of an individual
participant's experience but also the breadth and
diversity of the collective group. The objective then is
an organizational design that incorporates both group and
individual contributions.

To maximize the information gained from the effort,
an idea-generation technique called "Brainwriting" was
used.[14] Brainwriting is similar to the somewhat more
familiar brainstorming technique. A group of participants
is seated around a table. One sheet of paper, with the
question to be considered by the group written at the top,
is distributed to each participant and to the group
facilitator. An extra sheet is placed in the middle of
the table. Each participant writes his/her response to
the question on the sheet. He/she then exchanges the
sheet for the one in the middle of the table. The
participant reads all the ideas written on this sheet
before adding his/her own new idea. This statement may
respond to, elaborate on, or contradict the other ideas on
the sheet or head off in an entirely new direction.

Brainwriting allows participants to interact without
disturbing one another by verbal discussion or personal
confrontation. It tends to avoid the problems, common in
unstructured discussions, of premature dismissal of ideas
and of overconcentration on one or two approaches to a
problem. It also has the practical advantage of being
self-documenting, since the brainwriting sheets
automatically record the progress of the exercise.

After some discussion, the question to be addressed
by the brainwriting exercise was determined to be, "What
research should be initiated to improve the use of
scientific and technical knowledge in EISs and the
decision-making process?" The following is an
interpretation and categorization of the brainwriting pool
results.

A. Examine what factors or characteristics of EISs result
    in better documents or decisions:

- Analyze the extent to which the "success" of certain EISs (i.e., predictive accuracy, sensitivity of project decision) correlates with certain preparation and review methods.
- Examine whether the way in which EISs are written (apart from content) and presented affects the extent of their use in decisions.
- Assess which factors (e.g., method of analysis, technical data base, political pressure, citizen participation, etc.) are most significant in influencing ultimate decisions.
- Discover how significantly decisions are influenced by people outside of the sponsoring or lead agency.
- Recommend what is (are) the most appropriate point(s) in the decision-making process at which to integrate NEPA concerns.

B. Explore techniques for making better use of already existing information and analysis:

- Assess whether a national information collection, storage, and retrieval system is desirable or if there is a greater need for better quality analysis of project-specific situations. What are the trade-offs?
- Explore how existing data collection systems (e.g., U.S. Geological Survey, Census) can be better coordinated.
- Assess what scale (e.g., local, regional, national) is most appropriate for data base development.
- Investigate how remote sensing and computerized graphics can be made more accessible to potential users.
- Examine how agencies or organizations operating on small budgets might take advantage of more sophisticated analytical processes.

C. Evaluate approaches that can be employed by practitioners to encourage more environmentally sensitive decisions (e.g., management "bonus system" funding for intervenors, informal rewards, veto power, etc.):

- Explore how decision makers can be "trained" to make better use of EISs.
- Analyze the extent to which the propensity of certain decision makers to use EISs is correlated with certain frames of reference of personal backgrounds.
- Since there is seldom a single identifiable decision maker, assess whether it is possible to identify sets of decision makers for different

       classes of EISs.
- Measure decision makers' perceptions of the usefulness of different kinds of EISs as decision aids.
- Assess whether "political realities" can be made a positive force in the EIS process.
- Make the decision process more explicit (e.g., keep records of decisions) in order to force clearer consideration of trade-offs and adequate explanation of project choices.
- Evaluate whether innovative methods for communicating environmental information to decision makers can be devised and implemented.

D. Analyze the predictive capacities and capabilities of EISs:

- Track the extent to which actual project impacts compare with those forecasted.
- Assess whether comparisons among similar natural or social systems can be usefully developed and generalized.
- Inventory and analyze the most practical post hoc evaluation methods for impact model verification.
- Isolate the causes of inaccurate predictions of impacts.
- Explore how iteration and feedback can be best incorporated into the EIS process.
- Analyze the costs and benefits of feedback and evaluation.

E. Undertake the comprehensive comparative research so as to take advantage of the breadth of existing experience:

- Compare state-level EIS processes with those of other countries. What are the practical implications?
- Analyze how the role played by EISs has changed since 1970. Has their predictive accuracy improved? Have they actually had any impact on decision making?
- Examine the relationship between the quality of information contained in EISs and their effectiveness in the political process.

F. Consider ways to systematize or standardize the approach to environmental impact assessment so as to reduce the ad hoc, uneven, and site-specific nature of analysis:

- Explore the feasibility of developing (a) set(s) of "EIS Acceptability Criteria" to include standards for data precision and accuracy, methods

employed, and team composition.
- Assess whether baseline information can be meaningfully standardized nationwide.
- Analyze whether a consistent approach to assessing trade-offs and comparing "apples and oranges" can be devised.

G. Examine the role of the expert:

- Analyze how experts' preferences affect the results of environmental impact assessments.
- Compare the values of experts systematically with those of the general public.

H. Examine the role of the citizen:

- Assess how the effectiveness of the different citizen participation modes compares according to project type and point of initiation in the planning process (timing).
- Investigate the "anatomy" of public opposition. How do people form opinions on poorly defined or unfamiliar issues?
- Explore ways in which the critical actors associated with a given proposal can be identified early enough to make the participation process more effective.

R&D Center staff conclusion:

The proposed "Research Agenda" is rich with interesting ideas and concerns.

The research suggested appears to be guided by a quest to understand how to shape better decisions using the EIS process. Central to this discussion is a desire to learn more about decision makers and what guides them as they evaluate their options. Many of the "Research Agenda" items suggested were presented in terms and language that imply an increasing sensitivity to concepts usually viewed as analytic or scientific in nature--terms such as "predictive accuracy," "validation," "trade-off analysis," and "replicability." However, most of the items recommended for research also appear to be directed at increasing actual usefulness of the EIS.
As the staff reviewed the results of the Model EIS and Research Agenda Task Teams, we were struck by the very different responses that the participants presented. The response to the first issue seemed staid and reserved, while in the second instance the suggestions were more creative and expansive. We are not sure if it was the phrasing of the question (i.e., Model EIS compared to a Research Agenda), the group process technique used (i.e., Nominal Group Technique compared to Brainwriting), or a

combination of the two. Perhaps the notion of a model EIS has been discussed so often that the participants sensed there was little to add. It is also possible that the CEQ regulations are viewed as a codification of a model EIS. At the same time, the concept of developing a research agenda is less constraining and, hence, more liberating to new ideas.

BOOK ORGANIZATION

As stated previously, this book reflects, in large measure, the organization of the symposium effort discussed in the preceding pages. The book is divided into four major sections, each reflecting a different perspective or approach to the topic.

Part 1 of the book focuses on the increasing breadth of concerns and issues that have characterized environmental impact assessment. Now much more than a statement of physical environmental conditions and constraints, the EIA process has come to embrace the total human environment. Part I reflects this expansion by addressing some of the emerging ways of assessing human preferences, values, and aesthetics as well as historical, cultural, social, and economic factors.

Part 2 shifts attention from the broadening of issues of concern to the actual application of EIA methods and techniques. Here we have a discussion of a wide range of emerging methodologies, including physical analysis techniques (for biological impact and soils), data gathering and display techniques (through remote sensing), and social decision techniques (using both citizen participation and quantitative data as inputs). It is hoped that wider awareness of such methods may aid EIS writers in better selecting appropriate analytical tools and verse decision makers in their use and interpretation of their results.

The focus of Part 3 of the book turns to the link between the analytical process and the decision maker. Here the concern is not only the selection of processes and formats that encourage use of scientific and technical information by decision makers in a political process but also the ways to enhance scientists' and analysts' awareness of the political implications of their endeavor. Ultimately, the integration of EIA is an organizational question that transcends the differences in perspectives of the different actors. Thus, we hope that this part of the book will spark critical interest and practical thought concerning the relationship between science and the political process.

Part 4 of the book contains a variety of analyses and case studies by both academic observers and practitioners. A discussion of the cost implications of EIA is supplemented by a study that analyzes the scientific quality of EISs over the past several years. Case studies

include an issue-focused analysis of the Spruce Budworm
EIS processes in Maine as well as the reflections of three
practitioners of key state-level EIS programs.
   The book closes with a summation of recent changes in
EIS regulations and their intended impact, our concluding
observations about the EIS process, a discussion of the
emerging research in the field, plus our sense of where
environmental assessment seems headed in the future and
where we would like to see it headed.

NOTES

   [1]Environmental Quality: The Ninth Annual Report of
the Council on Environmental Quality. Washington, D.C.:
GPO, December 1978.
   [2]For example: "Symposium on Environmental Impact
Statements" in Natural Resources Journal, 16(2), April
1976; the Environmental Impact Assessment Project
conducted by the Laboratory of Architecture and Planning
at the Massachusetts Institute of Technology; and the
Workshop on the National Environmental Policy Act, a
report prepared pursuant to the request of the House
Subcommittee on Fisheries and Wildlife Conservation and
the Environment by the Congressional Research Service,
Library of Congress, February 1976.
   [3]The Environmental Impact Statement Process under
NEPA; Environmental Law Institute, Washington, D.C.,
November 7-8, 1977, and November 30-December 1, 1978;
American Law Institute--American Bar Association Course of
Study: Environmental Law VIII, Washington, D.C., February
9-11, 1978 (co-sponsored by the Environmental Law
Institute and the Smithsonian Institution).
   [4]Federal Register, 55978, November 29, 1978.
   [5]Among the principal analyses and evaluations of
NEPA are: Frederick Anderson (1973), NEPA in the Courts,
Baltimore, Maryland: Johns Hopkins University Press;
Richard N. L. Andrews (1976), Environmental Policy and
Administrative Change, New York, New York: D.C. Heath and
Co., 1976; Richard Liroff (1976), A National Policy for
the Environment, Bloomington, Indiana: Indiana University
Press; The Environmental Impact Statement--It Seldom
Causes Long Project Delays but Could Be More Useful if
Prepared Earlier, report to the Committee on Environment
and Public Works by the U.S. General Accounting Office,
August 9, 1977; Environmental Impact Statements, a report
to the Commission on Federal Paperwork, Washington, D.C.,
February 25, 1977; Environmental Impact Statements: An
Analysis of Six Years' Experience by Seventy Federal
Agencies, report of the Council on Environmental Quality,
March 1976; and the following oversight hearings before
the Subcommittee on Fisheries and Wildlife Conservation of
the Committee on Merchant Marine and Fisheries:
Administration of the National Environmental Policy Act,

Parts I, II, and Appendix, 91st Congress, 2nd Session
(1970); <u>Administration of the National Environmental
Policy Act--1972</u>, 92nd Congress, 2nd Session (1972); and
<u>National Environmental Policy Oversight Hearings</u>, 94th
Congress, 1st Session (1975).

[6]Cf. Richard Andrews, Paul Cromwell, Gordon Enk,
Edward Farnworth, James Hibbs, and Virginia Sharp (1977),
<u>Substantive Guidance for Environmental Impact Assessment:
An Exploratory Study</u>, The Institute of Ecology.

[7]This has been one of the early findings of research
conducted by Dr. Thomas Gladwin of the Graduate School of
Business Administration, New York University, examining
patterns of environmental conflict. See Gladwin, Thomas,
"Patterns of Environmental Conflict over Industrial
Facilities in the United States, 1970-78," <u>Natural
Resources Journal</u>, 1980, <u>20</u>(2).

[8]See Stuart L. Hart and Gordon A. Enk (1980), <u>Green
Goals and Greenbacks: A Comparative Study of State-level
Environmental Impact Statement Programs and Their
Associated Costs</u>, Boulder, Colorado: Westview Press.

[9]An exception is the U.S. Army Corps of Engineers'
Institute for Water Resources, which has been involved in
the retrospective analysis of social impacts resulting
from water resources development projects. See, for
example, Henry Hitchcock (March 1977), <u>Analytical Review
of Research Reports on Social Impacts of Water Resources
Development Projects</u>.

[10]Several publications resulted from this project.
One important report was <u>Working Papers on Substantive
Guidelines for Improving Environmental Impact Statements</u>,
Washington, D.C.: October 1975.

[11]The emerging field of "environmental mediation"
seeks to remedy many of the problems inherent in the EIS
process by applying many of the same principles used in
mediating labor disputes. Further, the "scoping" process
is really a conflict-anticipation technique.

[12]See C. W. Churchman (1971), <u>The Design of Inquiring
Systems</u>, New York: Basic Books; and Daniel Willard (1974),
"NEPA and the Scientist," unpublished manuscript.

[13]See, for example, Nathan Caplan et al. (1975), <u>The
Use of Social Science Knowledge in Policy Decisions at the
National Level</u>, Ann Arbor, Michigan: Institute for Social
Research, The University of Michigan, and Mark Berg
(1978), <u>The Use of Technology Assessment Studies in Policy
Making</u>, Ann Arbor, Michigan: Institute for Social
Research, The University of Michigan.

[14]See Charles Lindblom (1979), <u>Usable Knowledge</u>, New
Haven, Connecticut: Yale University Press.

[15]See Andre Delbecq et al. (1974), <u>Group Techniques
for Program Planning</u>, Glenview, Illinois: Scott, Foresman
and Co., for more detail on the method.

[16]See Horst Geschka et al. (1973), "Modern Techniques
for Solving Problems," <u>Journal of Applied Behavioral
Science</u>, <u>14</u>(2), for more detail on the method.

PART 1

Redefining the Scope
of Environmental Assessment

INTRODUCTION

What constitutes the environment and, therefore, must
be examined in an environmental impact review cannot be
definitively stated in a static checklist. Not only does
the increasing sophistication of the physical and social
sciences change the process for producing an EIS, it also
changes the subject matter and enables the consideration
of issues previously ignored or insufficiently explored.
The expanding scope of environmental assessment reflects
the maturation of the EIS process, increased scientific
and technical capabilities, and, most important, the
collective skill of those who conduct the studies.
This chapter presents five papers that deal with
qualitative issues, often the most controversial items in
a proposed action. These papers cumulatively state that
the qualitative aspects of assessments need not be
subjects for despair among practitioners or decision
makers. Not only can issues concerning value,
preferences, and highly subjective judgments be
systematically approached, they can be studied and
assessed in ways that meet the muster of scientific
scrutiny and social acceptability without depreciating the
qualitative nature of the issues being examined.
Stephen Kaplan, in "A Process-oriented Approach to
Human Concerns in Environmental Decision Making," and
Rachel Kaplan, in "Assessing Human Concerns for
Environmental Decision Making," in tandem present a
methodology for determining visual preferences and an
overview of how the results of that approach have been
used in impact assessments. The papers set the stage for
Carl H. Petrich's "EIS Scoping for Aesthetics;" Petrich
explains how he incorporated an examination of aesthetic
impacts into an EIS on a nuclear power plant proposed for
a historic site in the mid-Hudson River Valley of New
York. The result was a precedent-setting decision by the
Nuclear Regulatory Commission to deny a permit for plant
construction largely because of the severe aesthetic
impacts.
Using the same Greene County, New York, example,
Elizabeth Peelle explores the process by which aesthetic
and socioeconomic issues surfaced and became paramount in

the assessment. Peèlle proffers that the long and
convoluted hearing process on the proposed plant was, in
effect, a scoping exercise that identified the major
aesthetic concerns that were not considered in the
preliminary EIS. The chapter concludes with Margaret and
William Hrezo's statement, "The Role of Human Values,
Attitudes, and Beliefs in Environmental Assessment." As a
unit, these papers testify not only that the scope of
environmental assessment has been and continues to be
redefined but also that these expanded considerations have
proven to be the pivotal issues for the interested publics
and decision makers.

1. A Process-Oriented Approach to Human Concerns in Environmental Decision Making[1]

Stephen Kaplan

The environmental impact statement process inevitably involves people. People are involved directly, both in mandated opportunities for public input and in the necessary interactions among experts. People are also involved indirectly to the extent that social, recreational, and aesthetic impacts are taken into account. While many areas of expertise are brought together in the EIS process, the "people" aspect is generally handled in an intuitive, unscientific fashion. This is not because of a lack of data and theory concerning the properties of people. In fact, an extensive empirical literature exists that describes human thought and functioning. Much of this literature, however, is undigested and fragmented. It is not in a form that would be useful to the kinds of planning and management issues that are central to the EIS process.

Making this body of knowledge available for use in on-line, applied settings is a difficult task and not one that can be carried out as a direct translation from data to practice. Rather, it is a process involving at least two distinct phases. The first phase is to generate a synthesis that integrates data into a coherent, interrelated framework. The second phase is to extract from this larger theory a subset of information particularly pertinent to the applications and problems in a given area. The desired result of this second phase is a "portable model," a small enough and intuitive enough perspective that can be carried around in the practitioner's head and brought to bear in the real-time, on-line contexts where it is needed. A model that is not portable, that resides only in a book on the shelf, may be of little practical value given the inevitable pressures experienced by decision makers in the management and planning areas.

There may seem to be a contradiction between the statement that dealings with and about people are being carried out on an uneducated, intuitive basis and the proposal to develop a "portable model" that is itself intuitive. The distinction here is between uneducated and educated intuition. Practitioners' implicit models of people are often gleaned from personal experience and from assumptions about people made in economics courses. Neither of these sources is fully satisfactory; however, given more adequate information, it is possible to develop a perspective that is equally intuitive but in far better accord with the facts.

The first phase of this process, the development of a synthesis, a framework that integrates across the different domains of human functioning, is particularly challenging because of the tendency within psychology to concentrate on limited theories. A systematic effort to put together such a larger framework has been underway at The University of Michigan for some twenty years now. It is based on advances in cognitive psychology, with particular emphasis on human information processing. It has been extended through use of physiological data and evolutionary information and through a concern to interrelate motivational and cognitive processes. A number of published papers detail portions of this synthesis (S. Kaplan, 1973, 1976, 1978; Pomerantz, Kaplan, and Kaplan, 1969; Weisman, 1979). Several recent dissertations have used computer simulations and formal analyses in testing and extending this framework (Booker, 1981; Weiser, 1979; Whitehead, 1977). A recent volume provides further explication of this developing position (Kaplan and Kaplan, 1982).

The purpose of this paper is to extract from this larger framework a few key principles of particular pertinence to the EIS process. The "portable model" uses as a central theme the role of evolution in the shaping of human information processing. This is done for several reasons. First, our understanding of basic human process is greatly enhanced by an understanding of evolutionary constraints (Campbell, 1974; S. Kaplan, 1972), a perspective now beginning to be appreciated within the information-processing approach (Lachman and Lachman, 1979). Secondly, the evolutionary perspective has great advantages in terms of the "portability" of the model. People tend to find that evolutionary material makes intuitive sense; further, it provides a coherence for the proposed principles.

The paper is organized around three rather simple questions. The issues they raise are quite general; at the same time, these are questions that persons in charge of public hearings have been known to ask (sometimes accentuated by expletives that have been omitted in the present version). Perhaps the frequency and intensity of frustration resulting from public participation can be mitigated by a better understanding of the participants involved.

Suspicions about human irrationality on the part of veterans of public hearings are certainly understandable. It is, however, no more accurate a characterization of human nature than is the "rationality" model one learns in economics courses. It is probably a mistake to view humans as either rational or irrational. Humans are reasonable under certain circumstances and, at the same time, highly unreasonable under others. Since they are so responsive to circumstances, it pays to devote some attention to what these circumstances might be.

THE QUESTIONS

The first of these questions is at least as much an expression of exasperation as it is a question: *do people understand what one tells them?* It is not just educators who are inclined to wonder if their words are more often than not wasted. How often is the careful explanation of the planner or designer met by noncomprehending expressions? Moreover, it seems pointless to listen to the comments of people who have not understood what they were told in the first place.

The second question also expresses no small amount of exasperation: *do people know what they want?* There are indications that people's responses to certain choices posed to them are quite unreliable even within a relatively short period of time. There are also innumerable cases where no objections were raised to plans but great contention became evident when the plans were executed. It has also been observed that even asking people directly what they want provides little or no useful clue to what they really want. It is not difficult to understand where the suspicion comes from that people may not even know what they want.

The third question reflects the common observation that people often stay away from public meetings in droves and that many of those who do come never say a word. Hence the question: *do people want to participate?* When given no chance, they raise such a fuss that it makes participation seem absolutely essential. On the other hand, they take such limited advantage of the opportunities afforded them.

SOME ASPECTS OF HUMAN NATURE

Clearly there is a reasonable argument for answering each of these questions with "no." But there is more that needs to be said. There are, of course, circumstances when people have excellent comprehension, know what they want, and participate effectively.

Do people understand what one tells them?

The first of the three questions must at least superficially be answered in the negative. Much talk often produces little enlightenment. This does not mean, however, that people are stupid or in any sense incapable of understanding. Rather, much of the problem lies on the "telling" side of the fence. While people tend not to do well being "told" (deCharms, 1968), there is ample evidence that they are capable of absorbing and managing information rapidly and with considerable sophistication (Dreyfus, 1972). Thus, the difficulty may be with how the information is presented more than with the information-handling capacity per se.

There are a number of factors of importance in the transfer of information and a number of other places where we deal with this issue (R. Kaplan, this volume; Kaplan and Kaplan, 1978, 1982). For present purposes, I would like to emphasize one particular aspect that is directly pertinent to so much of the planning process. In contrast to all the telling that people are exposed to, to all the verbal material that is heaped on them, people are exceptionally facile in dealing with visual/spatial material (Bower, 1970, 1972; Kaplan, Kaplan, and Sampson, 1968; Shepard, 1967).

Perhaps a comment or two is called for with resect to the expression "visual/spatial." Much of our experience is based on visual information and, in many instances, we rarely even talk about it. For many years, visual imagery was thought to subsume spatial components of thought as well. Now, however, there is growing awareness of the spatial aspect of the thought process (Attneave, 1972; Robinson and Petchenik, 1976; Wickelgren, 1979). While the visual mode is the most common one for obtaining spatial information, it is by no means the only one. One can explore space by touch and by hearing as well. Some people who lack extensive visual imagery turn out to use space extensively in their thought process.

Tables and diagrams (as illustrated by the relief they provide in this volume) aid in the understanding of text by taking advantage of our spatial capability. The spatial component is often the easiest to reconstruct, even when it may be of little practical value. How often we can remember where on the page the pertinent information was--without being able to remember what it was. Thomas (1977) has argued that in the context of evolution this was most useful. Remembering where one found a patch of blackberries or other foodstuff could be highly adaptive in the long run.

While it is increasingly evident that space plays an important role in human thought, the specific ways it does this are not yet understood. Problems of comparison (e.g., George is wealthier than Sam, Fred is wealthier than George . . .) seem to be solved spatially by most people (Huttenlocher, 1976). Understanding complex sentences (Luria, 1973) and mathematical calculations (Kinsbourne, 1971) both suffer when there is damage to the spatial part of the brain; perhaps even these processes have a spatial component.

The implication here is that there is something

rather basic and deeply human about the handling of visual/spatial material (Campbell, 1974; Posner, 1973). This runs directly counter to the old literature on cross-cultural differences in perception, which claimed to have found that nonliterate people do not comprehend photographs or simple pictures. This material has received a thoughtful re-analysis by Kennedy (1974), who finds it to be without merit. Perhaps one of the most striking attempts to explore this issue was reported by Collier (1967). He showed photographs to New Mexico Navajos, a group quite untouched by the vast quantities of photographic images that surround most Americans.

> After the first round of interviews, we had our initial answer: there was no doubt at all that the Navajos could interpret two-dimensional images . . . . The Navajos read photographs as literally as we urban Westerners read books or mariners read charts. A typical example: we handed a panoramic view to Hosteen Greyhills, a Navajo farmer. He held the photograph firmly with both hands, studied it with some apparent confusion, then began moving in a circle, 'til finally his face lit up. "That's how he was standing. There is the East. Sun has just risen; it's early in the morning. The picture is in the spring; it was made at Many Farms the first year of farming." The picture was laid down emphatically. "How do you know it is Many Farms?" Greyhills raised the picture again with some irritation. "See . . . those head gates. Nowhere else do they have head gates like that. See . . . it's the stubble of the first cover crop. No hogans. People living over there." He gesticulated out of the picture. "Spring--nothing growing." The picture was laid down for good and a second photograph was studied. Greyhills' analysis of the panorama seemed uncanny. With a magnifying glass, shapes could be made out that might be head gates. There certainly were no hogans. To our amateur eyes the cover crop was unrecognizable. But the reading was 100 percent correct. The photograph had been made five years earlier, at Many Farms, 80 miles to the southwest in the first year of this agricultural project from a mesa looking over the valley at perhaps 7:30 in the morning.[2]

Do people know what they want?

The second of our three questions cannot be answered in any simple fashion. Much depends upon what one asks and what one means by "know." Fortunately, a convergence of several areas of research makes it possible to point to a better way of discovering what people want. This way of asking makes it possible for people to provide confident and reliable indications of what alternatives they do and do not prefer.

"Preference" is, in fact, the central concept here. It has been shown that people are able to indicate their likes or dislikes with great speed. Further, people have considerable confidence in their judgments and arrive at them without conscious calculations of any kind (Bargh, 1981; Zajonc, 1980). In fact, they may be hard put to come up with a line of reasoning that supports their conclusion. Thus, people often know what they like without knowing why they like it.

Related findings have been obtained in studies of people's reactions to different kinds of landscapes. People can indicate their preference for different settings easily and confidently. We have found photographs highly effective for this purpose. They provide the visual means for comprehending--a necessary condition for meaningful responses (R. Kaplan, 1979).

Our research on preference has indicated that such judgments, far from being erratic of idiosyncratic, reflect something far more basic about the way people respond to different landscapes. Even though people often cannot explain their reactions, preferences turn out to be closely related to what it seems possible to see and do in that particular setting. People are, in other words, making some very rapid (and unconscious) assessments of the possibilities that would be available to them (S. Kaplan, 1979a). Thus, this research supports the conclusions made by Gregory (1969) and Gibson (1977) that the process of perception is intimately connected to determining what is offered by whatever it is one is looking at. Casting this type of automatic, unconscious analysis in terms of what an object "affords" the individual, Gibson (1979) has coined the term "affordance."

While many ways of asking people about what they want have not yielded meaningful, reliable indications, the straightforward preference ratings of visual scenes have generated consistent, interpretable patterns for a wide range of different settings and for diverse groups of people (S. Kaplan, 1979a, b). It must be remembered, however, that people will likely be unable to explain or analyze the bases for these reactions in any useful fashion. Thus, asking people for explanations or calculations will not necessarily reveal the same insights as can be obtained through analysis of preference rating.

An unfortunately typical example of the sorts of calculations often required of people in efforts to determine their "wants" involved information collected for the cost-benefit analysis of the proposed third London airport. People were asked, "What price would be just high enough to compensate you for leaving your home (flat) and moving to another area?" Eight percent of those asked said that there was no price high enough to induce them to move. Their responses were recorded as £5,000 (Mishan, 1970).

Do people want to participate?

The third of our questions provides another case where the answer is a definite "yes" although, once again, there are many ways to ask or even undermine this human concern. People wish to play a part in what goes on around them (Cantril, 1966; Seligman, 1975), but not at the cost of comprehension (cf. Antonovsky, 1979). Unfortunately, many ostensible opportunities for participation are circumstances where people are likely to be overwhelmed and confused. Since it is unlikely that people could participate effectively in such circumstances anyway, their avoidance of them may not be inappropriate.

The importance of comprehension, both in the context of participation and otherwise, cannot be emphasized too much. The centrality of this human concern is particularly well illustrated by what is in many ways a rather artificial, even trivial, psychological experiment. The study was a fairly typical exploration of the human perceptual process. In this sort of study, an image is flashed on the screen and the task is to identify it. If the image is not identified at the initial duration, say 1/100 second, then it is projected for a slightly longer duration, and so on until it is correctly identified. In this particular study (Bruner and Postman, 1949), the images were playing cards; to make the task a bit more challenging, they were printed in the opposite color from the usual pattern. In other words, spades were red and hearts were black.

The performance of one particular individual on this task was especially striking. The duration had to be increased steadily until the image was presented for 0.3 seconds, quite a long time for a study of this kind. The response to this extended duration was as follows:

> I can't make the suit out, whatever it is. It didn't even look like a card that time; I don't know what color it is now or whether it's a spade or heart. I'm not even sure now what a spade looks like! My God!

One must admit this is a rather trivial situation. Nothing terrible is going to happen if the pattern is not correctly identified. Yet, the concern to comprehend, to make sense out of the world around one, is urgent no matter what the situation.

People do not take confusion lightly. They will avoid it if they can, but this is not always possible. When comprehension fails, or when the time for action arrives before comprehension does, people may be driven to take rather extreme actions or positions (Frankl, 1963;

Fromm, 1961).

One way of dealing with the threat of confusion is the "us vs. them" paradigm (Wilson, 1978). This sort of polarization is conveniently simplifying even if it is rarely productive. Under more extreme pressures, people may retreat to an "us vs. everyone" paradigm. This is very simplifying and very effective in creating order out of chaos, although at terrible cost in terms of contact with reality. The popularity of this rather extreme solution to threatened confusion is evident in the fact that group-supported paranoid views are available in this country in several flavors. One can choose a "capitalist plot" or a "communist plot" as the explanation for all the otherwise perplexing events that constantly threaten to overwhelm us.

AN EVOLUTIONARY PERSPECTIVE

The various characteristics of people that we have been considering may not be merely peculiar foibles, limitations of an otherwise rational animal. Rather, these characteristics may represent deep and enduring themes in the human makeup (cf. Foa, 1971; Kates, 1962; Simon, 1979). In other words, they may be essential components of human nature. Humans are not, after all, a recent invention. They are the product of a long and challenging past. To survive what our ancestors survived required an animal not only highly capable but capable in rather particular ways. Let us return to our three themes, this time with the perspective of the sort of survival issues that might have fostered each of these characteristically human ways of functioning (see Table 1.1).

The kind of world humans had to deal with during much of their evolution was filled with information vital to their survival. This was a complex and uncertain world, requiring great skill at information processing (Laughlin, 1968; Washburn, 1972). Further, these pressures were operating well before humans had developed elaborate language systems (Peters, 1980). The capacity to recognize and predict, to assess the conditions and to act, all depended on visual and spatial information (S. Kaplan, 1972). Thus, for millions of years the survival of our ancestors depended upon skillful handling of nonverbal information. It is hardly surprising, then, that humans do this with great efficiency.

The inclination to prefer certain environments over others is by no means unique to humans. Most animals are best adapted for a certain range of environments; the fact that they demonstrate a preference for those for which they are adapted (Hilden, 1965; Partridge, 1978) would seem not only reasonable but essential for any animal with substantial mobility. The fact that such preferences in humans are quick and automatic, apparently occurring without conscious reflection, suggests that they have been an element in the human survival pattern for a very long time. People seem to be using (without generally being aware of it) information about how well they would function in a given environment as the criterion for how much they like it. Thus, central predictors of preference turn out to be such factors as how readily could one locomote here, how much could one learn, and how safe could one be (S. Kaplan, 1979a). Appleton's (1975) analysis of the role of prospect and refuge in environmental aesthetics provides further support for such an approach. Here, too, what people like is critically linked to what would have been vital to functioning in the environment in which people evolved.

In the complex and dangerous world in which humans evolved, much depended upon clear understanding and prompt action based on that understanding. Our ancestors were not particularly formidable animals; they could not overwhelm potential enemies by fang and claw or by sheer size. On the other hand, they were not small enough to hide in cracks and pass unnoticed. Survival turned out to depend on being able to act in anticipation of events that had not yet happened and anticipation, in turn, depended upon understanding. Given the urgency of "keeping ahead of the game," survival required that our ancestors live by their wits (Pfeiffer, 1978). It is hardly surprising that confusion (Midgley, 1978) and helplessness (Seligman, 1975) are not well tolerated by this species. Had there been humanoid individuals milling around on the African savanna a few million years ago who did not in the least mind being confused, they would not have become our ancestors.

Table 1.1 provides a summary of the framework I have presented. Each of the questions raises some particularly salient properties of people rooted in our long history. Of course, humans have many other characteristics as well. But even if we limit the discussion to these three domains, it should be possible to approach the "people" side of the EIS process in a more professional and more satisfactory fashion.

THE EXPERT AND THE PORTABLE MODEL

People's perceptions, their thought patterns, and ultimately their behavior are greatly influenced by their model of the world--or their model of the particular aspect of the world they are trying to cope with at any particular moment. People are indeed resistant to attempts that tell them what to do (Brehm, 1972) or, even, to facts that they have no idea what to do with. But people are eager for information that helps them understand and relate to the world more effectively. Thus, information that aids in model building is likely to have far more impact than information that may seem more

TABLE 1.1
Framework for portable model:
human needs and public participation

Perplexing Questions	Characteristics	Larger Picture
Do people understand what one tells them?	Visual and spatial vs. verbal in handling information	Millions of years of nonverbal information processing
Do people know what they want?	The immediacy of preference judgments	Vital role of habitat selection
Do people want to participate?	People want to comprehend and they want to play a part	Survival through acquiring knowledge and avoiding helplessness

directly related but fails to speak to that agenda of
implicit questions they have about the world.
     The environmental planner or decision maker fits this
characterization as much as anyone. In other words,
"people" here refers to all of us. But there is a growing
body of evidence (cf. DeGroot, 1963; S. Kaplan, 1977;
Langer and Imber, 1979) that indicates that experts are
different from other people. More accurately, it is not
that experts are different from other people but, rather,
that all of us in the areas in which we have expertise are
different from those who do not share it. Experts differ
in how they perceive; situations they know a great deal
about look different to them, although they seldom are
aware of the difference. Not surprisingly, what the
expert prefers might differ from what other people prefer
(Anderson, 1978; Gifford, 1980; R. Kaplan, 1973). And how
they explain something they understand very well is likely
to be very different from what a nonexpert needs to hear.
     An expert's effectiveness often depends on the
capacity to communicate information to people who are
amateurs with respect to that particular expertise.
Assuming that another's perceptions, interests, and
concerns are similar to one's own is a great mistake.
Assuming that the other is stupid because one's insights
are not being comprehended is probably an even greater
mistake. An expert urgently needs a model of other people
in order to know what to do. The thought that one can use
oneself as this model is a popular, but probably
disastrous, solution.
     Experts and others share a dependence on information

for building models that help them understand particular issues. Experts, more than others, however, must in addition have models that help them understand the way in which their own way of looking at a situation is necessarily different because of their greater knowledge. The intent of the material presented here is to provide a basis for such a "portable model," that is, a framework that is sufficiently sensible and coherent so that it can be taken out on the job and used in practical settings. It provides a perspective of how ordinary people behave: what enhances comprehension, why comprehension matters, and how people can express their desires given an understanding of the situation.

In the EIS context, the implications are clear. Meaningful public input, either direct or as translated into social, recreational, or aesthetic impacts, cannot take place without careful attention to the participants' understanding of what is occurring. This will require not only more care in developing ways to inform people but also a great sensitivity to indicators of whether the material is doing the job. The appropriate format for soliciting reactions, too, must be worked out with more consideration of how humans function. As we have seen, the human facility for reacting in terms of preference can be a great help in solving this problem. From one perspective, these considerations only make the entire process that much more difficult. On the other hand, current practices cannot be said to yield uniformly satisfactory results. There is no reason that the domain of people—like any other domain within the purview of the EIS process—should not be approached on the basis of the best scientific information currently available.

REFERENCES

Note: Some of the references listed below are reprinted or excerpted in S. Kaplan and R. Kaplan (Eds.), Humanscape: Environments for People. These are preceded by an asterisk.

Anderson, E. (1978), "Visual Resource Assessment: Local Perceptions of Familiar Natural Environments." Unpublished doctoral dissertation, The University of Michigan.
Antonovsky, A. (1979), Health, Stress, and Coping. San Francisco: Jossey-Bass.
Appleton, J. (1975), The Experience of Landscape. London: Wiley.
Attneave, F. (1972), "Representation of Physical Space." In A. W. Melton and E. Martin (Eds.), Coding Processes in Human Memory.
Bargh, J. A. (1981), "Automatic Information Processing and Social Perception." Unpublished doctoral

32

dissertation, The University of Michigan.
Booker, L. B. (1981), "A Distributed Processor Model of Knowledge Representation and Acquisition." Unpublished doctoral dissertation, The University of Michigan.
Bower, G. H. (1970), "Analysis of a Mnemonic Device." American Scientist, 58, 496-510.
Bower, G. H. (1972), "Mental Imagery and Associative Learning." In L. W. Gregg (Ed.), Cognition in Learning and Memory. New York: Wiley.
Brehm, J. W. (1972), Responses to Loss of Freedom: A Theory of Psychological Reactance. Morristown, N.J.: General Learning Press.
*Campbell, B. G. (1974), Human Evolution: An Introduction of Man's Adaptation. Chicago: Aldine.
*Cantril, H. (1966), The Pattern of Human Concerns. New Brunswick, N.J.: Rutgers University Press.
Collier, J., Jr. (1967), Visual Anthropology: Photography as a Research Method. New York: Holt, Rinehart, and Winston.
deCharms, R. (1968), Personal Causation. New York: Academic.
DeGroot, A. D. (1965), Thought and Choice in Chess. The Hague: Mouton and Co.
Dreyfus, H. L. (1972), What Computers Can't Do: A Critique of Artificial Reason. New York: Harper and Row.
*Foa, U. G. (1971), "Interpersonal and Economic Resources." Science, 171, 345-351.
Frankl, V. (1963), Man's Search for Meaning. New York: Washington Square Press.
Fromm, E. (1941), Escape from Freedom. New York: Rinehart.
Gibson, J. J. (1977), "The Theory of Affordances." In R. Shaw and J. Bransford (Eds.), Perceiving, Acting, and Knowing. Hillsdale, N.J.: Erlbaum.
Gibson, J. J. (1979), The Ecological Approach to Visual Perception. Boston: Houghton Mifflin.
Gifford, R. J. (1980), "Judgments of the Built Environment as a Function of Individual Differences and Context." Journal of Man-Environment Relations, 1, 22-31.
Gregory, R. L. (1969), "On How Little Information Controls So Much Behavior." In C. H. Waddington (Ed.), Towards a Theoretical Biology, Two Sketches. Scotland: Edinburgh University Press.
Hilden, O. (1965), "Habitat Selection in Birds." Ann. Zool. Fenn., 2, 53-75.
Huttenlocher, J. (1976), "Language and Intelligence." In L. B. Resnick (Ed.), The Nature of Intelligence. Hillsdale, N.J.: Erlbaum.
Kaplan, R. (1973), "Predictors of Environmental Preference: Designers and Clients." In W. F. E. Preiser (Ed.), Environmental Design Research. Stroudsburg, Penn.: Dowden, Hutchinson,

and Ross.
Kaplan, R. (1979), "Visual Resources and the Public: An
    Empirical Approach." In Proceedings of Our National
    Landscape Conference. USDA Forest Service General
    Technical Report PSW-35.
Kaplan, S. (1972), "The Challenge of Environmental
    Psychology: A Proposal for a New Functionalism."
    American Psychologist, 27, 140-143.
Kaplan, S. (1973), "Cognitive Maps in Perception and
    Thought." In R. M. Downs and D. Stea (Eds.), Image
    and Environment. Chicago: Aldine.
Kaplan, S. (1976), "Adaptation, Structure, and Knowledge."
    In G. T. Moore and R. G. Golledge (Eds.),
    Environmental Knowing. Stroudsburg, Penn.: Dowden,
    Hutchinson, and Ross.
Kaplan, S. (1977), "Participation in the Design Process: A
    Cognitive Approach." In D. Stokols (Ed.),
    Perspectives on Environment and Behavior. New York:
    Plenum.
*Kaplan, S. (1978a), "Perception of an Uncertain
    Environment." In S. Kaplan and R. Kaplan (Eds.),
    Humanscape: Environments for People. Belmont, Cal.:
    Duxbury.
*Kaplan, S. (1978b), "Attention and Fascination: The
    Search for Cognitive Clarity." In S. Kaplan and
    R. Kaplan (Eds.), Humanscape: Environments for
    People. Belmont, Cal.: Duxbury.
Kaplan, S. (1979a), "Concerning the Power of Content-
    identifying Methodologies." In Assessing Amenity
    Resource Values. USDA Forest Service General
    Technical Report RM-68.
Kaplan, S. (1979b), "Perception and Landscape: Conceptions
    and Misconceptions." In Proceedings of Our National
    Landscape Conference. USDA Forest Service General
    Technical Report PSW-35.
Kaplan, S., and Kaplan. R. (1978) (Eds.), Humanscape:
    Environments for People. Belmont, Cal.: Duxbury.
    [Ann Arbor, Mich.: Ulrichs, 1982.]
Kaplan, S., and Kaplan. R. (1982), Cognition and
    Environment. New York: Praeger.
Kaplan, S., Kaplan, R., and Sampson, J. R. (1968),
    "Encoding and Arousal Factors in Free Recall of
    Verbal and Visual Material." Psychonomic Science,
    12, 73-74.
*Kates, R. W. (1962), Hazard and Choice Perception in
    Flood Plain Management. University of Chicago:
    Department of Geography Research Paper No. 78.
Kennedy, J. M. (1974), A Psychology of Picture Perception.
    San Francisco: Jossey-Bass.
Kinsbourne, M. (1971), "Cognitive Deficit: Experimental
    Analysis." In J. L. McGaugh (Ed.), Psychobiology.
    New York: Academic.
Lachman, J. L., and Lachman, R. (1979), "Theories of
    Memory: Organization and Human Evolution." In C. R.

34

Puff (Ed.), Memory Organization and Structure. New York: Academic.

Langer, E. J., and Imber, L. G. (1979), "When Practice Makes Imperfect: Debilitating Effects of Overlearning." Journal of Personality and Social Psychology, 37, 2014-2024.

*Laughlin, W. S. (1968), "Hunting: An Integrating Biobehavior System and Its Evolutionary Importance." In R. B. Lee and I. DeVore (Eds.), Man the Hunter. Chicago: Aldine.

Luria, A. R. (1973), The Working Brain. New York: Basic Books.

Midgley, M. (1978), Beast and Man: The Roots of Human Nature. Ithaca: Cornell University Press.

Mishan, E. J. (1970), "What Is Wrong with Roskill." Journal of Transport Economics and Policy, 4, 221-234. (Reprinted in R. Layard (Ed.), Cost-Benefit Analysis. Middlesex, England: Penguin, 1974.)

Partridge, L. (1978), "Habitat Selection." In J. R. Krebs and N. B. Davies (Eds.), Behavioral Ecology: An Evolutionary Approach. Sunderland, Mass.: Sinauer.

Peters, R. (1980), Mammalian Communication: A Behavioral Analysis of Meaning. Monterey, Cal.: Brooks/Cole.

Pfeiffer, J. E. (1978), The Emergence of Man (3rd ed.). New York: Harper.

Pomerantz, J. R., Kaplan, S., and Kaplan, R. (1969), "Satiation Effects in the Perception of Single Letters." Perception and Psychophysics, 6, 129-132.

Posner, M. I. (1973), Cognition: An Introduction. Glenview, Ill.: Scott, Foresman.

Robinson, A. H., and Petchenik, B. B. (1976), The Nature of Maps. Chicago: University of Chicago Press.

Seligman, M. E. (1975), Helplessness. San Francisco: Freeman.

Shepard, R. N. (1967), "Recognition Memory for Words, Sentences, and Pictures." Journal of Verbal Learning and Verbal Behavior, 6, 156-163.

*Simon, H. A. (1979), Models of Thought. New Haven: Yale University Press.

Thomas, J. C. (1977), "Cognitive Psychology from the Perspective of Wilderness Survival." IBM Research Report RC 6647 (#28603).

*Washburn, S. L. (1972), "Aggressive Behavior and Human Evolution." In G. V. Coelho and E. A. Rubinstein (Eds.), Social Change and Human Behavior. Washington, D.C.: National Institute of Mental Health.

Weiser, M. D. (1979), "Program Slices: Formal, Psychological, and Practical Investigations of an Automatic Program Abstraction Method." Unpublished doctoral dissertation, The University of Michigan.

Weisman, G. D. (1979), "Way-finding in the Built Environment: A Study in Architectural Legibility." Unpublished doctoral dissertation, The University of

Michigan.
Whitehead, B. A. (1977), "A Neural Network Model of Pattern Recognition." Unpublished doctoral dissertation, The University of Michigan.
Wickelgren, W. A. (1979), Cognitive Psychology. Englewood Cliffs, N.J.: Prentice-Hall.
Wilson, E. O. (1978), On Human Nature. Cambridge, Mass.: Harvard University Press.
Zajonc, R. B. (1980), "Feeling and Thinking: Preferences Need No Inferences." American Psychologist, 35, 151-175.

NOTE

[1]Acknowledgment: Work on this paper was supported, in part, by Cooperative Agreement 13-655, Urban Forestry Project, U.S. Forest Service North Central Forest Experiment Station.
[2]Reprinted with permission of the author, John Collier.

2. Assessing Human Concerns for Environmental Decision Making[1]

Rachel Kaplan

> We assume that the welfare of human beings,
> interpreting welfare in the broadest sense, is the
> main preoccupation of environmental planning. If
> this is so, the wisdom of a decision maker must be
> judged in relation to areas of human concern.

This statement in the SCOPE volume "Environmental
Impact Assessment" (Munn, 1979) gives one pause. It could
be argued that our capacity to assess air, water, climate,
plant life, fish, and wildlife has made far greater
strides than our capacity to anticipate human concerns.
In dealing with environmental issues, one is repeatedly
confronted by the paradox that the biggest obstacle to a
more humane world for people--is people. Unfortunate and
unanticipated consequences all too often accompany
attempts to improve existing conditions. Such unwelcome
experiences are by no means limited to particular
geographic regions or socioeconomic groups. The losses
that are discovered only in retrospect are all too
frequently in the realm of human values.
      Collecting information about people is not a strong
point of the Environmental Impact Statement (EIS) process
as it is currently practiced. This is not due to a lack
of available procedures. Lists of methods and social
indicators are included in many volumes on impact
assessment.[2] But even with diligent attention to
inventorying numerous aspects of social impacts, the
"wisdom of the decision maker" remains largely unaffected.
It would seem that the assessment of human concerns does
not lend itself to a cookbook approach. As with so many
other domains, wisdom comes from understanding. In the
case of assessing human concerns, users of various
procedures must understand the rationale and capabilities
of these approaches, as well as some of the psychological
issues that underlie the processes of collecting
meaningful environmental information about people.
      Achieving such understanding presents a difficult,
perhaps insuperable, problem. One could send potential
users of the procedures back to school to acquire the

necessary background. Alternatively, one could hire a consultant to do one's assessments. The purpose of this paper is to provide yet another alternative, albeit a risky one. This involves creating an intuitive synthesis of the most urgently needed background issues and providing a practical framework for using it and adapting it to one's circumstances.

The riskiness of this approach lies in its unconventionality. To accomplish such a mission, the document cannot get into technicalities (which necessarily require a background different from that of most readers). Nor can it include extensive citations since it is dealing at a rather high point in the knowledge chain. Most of the statements, in other words, are based on whole courses rather than on individual studies. In psychology, as in many other fields, knowledge is acquired in small bits and applied in large chunks.

The approach to assessing human concerns that is presented here constitutes a series of applications of a theory of human functioning. Even if one were to return to academia and learn the latest in sampling theory, statistics, research design, and data collection methods, one would be unlikely to gain this perspective. Yet these applications have been used extensively in diverse environmental arenas, yielding results that have been useful both in a practical sense and in furthering theoretical understanding of human concerns.[3]

A WORD ABOUT PEOPLE

Consider for a moment what is important to people. What do they care deeply about? What gets them upset if it is withdrawn or absent? How about one's own concerns and priorities? It is not difficult to generate a long list of items in answer to these questions. It is also likely that certain items will appear frequently as different people construct such lists, while others will be more idiosyncratic.

Many of the listed items are likely to be "things." People care about their homes and gardens, parks and open spaces, schools, neighborhoods, friends, and many other categories. We have called such categories "contents." But in addition to the content domain, humans also care deeply about activities and arrangements that cut across contents. These we have termed "process" concerns. Freedom of choice, for example, expresses itself as a human value in various situations. So do the desires to be heard, to be challenged, and to know what to expect.

Many of the processes that are important to people involve information. From a psychological point of view, it is reasonable to postulate that information (or knowledge), rather than money, is the common human coin. The exchange of information is basic to human interaction, and the processing of information is the cornerstone of human functioning.

The theoretical framework that we have been developing for well over a decade involves the elaboration of these points.[4] The informational needs that are critical to people we have grouped into two major categories: <u>making sense</u> and <u>involvement</u>. Being able to recognize and identify what is going on around one and being able to predict or to know what to expect are all aspects of the "making sense" needs. The inability to accomplish these tasks readily leads to frustration and even to hostility. At the same time, however, the fulfillment of this set of needs is insufficient. While people express a desire for predictability, they also cherish situations where there is a measure of uncertainty. Many are the jobs and hobbies that are direct expressions of this pull. The scientist explores the unknown; the gambler is intrigued by odds. Fishing and gardening, and many other activities, would lose much of their satisfaction if the outcomes were totally in one's own hands.[5] Involvement, then, depends on the promise of further information and on a richness of possibilities to create a situation that is not totally predictable.

The combination of these informational needs expresses itself in many ways and in numerous settings. Preferred environments can be viewed from this perspective, and so can effective communication. It is, after all, the pervasiveness of these needs across many situations that defines them as process concerns.

SOME REQUIREMENTS OF USEFUL INPUT

To assess human concerns, one must collect information about people. Some of this can be done indirectly through available records and archives, and some can be accomplished by observation of people's activities or the consequences of the activities. But there are many aspects of human concerns that are difficult to determine without some more direct approach. Interviews, surveys, workshops, advisory groups, public hearings, and "open-house" hours for citizens to appear before officials all constitute methods that can be used for such relatively direct assessments. The purpose of this section is not to evaluate these methods.[6] Regardless of the particular approach one selects, there are certain issues that must be considered in order to increase the likelihood of useful input.

The brief account of the informational analysis of human needs serves as a basis for understanding what is important to people and as an introduction to the process of obtaining useful information from them. In particular, three requirements of useful input will be discussed here. One of the most important issues involves the need to provide information that is understandable. If people are to participate effectively, they must comprehend the issues, the context, the questions. Unfortunately, this is difficult to achieve. Comprehension is enhanced by presenting alternatives; given alternatives, people can more readily provide meaningful responses. Finally, a third essential component to consider involves the response format, the particular way in which participants are asked to provide their reactions.

Comprehension

It may not be self-evident that collecting information by these more direct methods necessarily involves providing information as well. Sometimes this is minimal, amounting to little more than the context the question provides. In public meetings, however, the provision of information can assume a primary focus and the citizen input may play a secondary role. But the provision of information is no guarantee that the information will be understood. There may be too much information, or it may be too technical or uninvolving. In other cases, so little information is provided that people's concerns are assessed in a vacuum. It is no wonder that officials often find information they get from citizens of little use. What has been obtained is an expression of fear, frustration, or a stereotypic response to a looming event. Where participants have had no opportunity to understand the context or issues, their contribution will be of minimal utility. To prevent this situation, citizens must be presented with information that is compatible with their cognitive requirements.[7] How can this be accomplished?

Amount of information. There is no "correct" answer to the issue of how much information to provide to enable participants to supply useful input. It is possible, however, to present too much or too little. Perhaps stemming from a fear of biasing the respondent, surveys frequently offer very little context or basis for understanding the issues about which answers are sought. The interviewer's objectivity and the randomness of the sample are important concerns, but neither reduces the importance of providing information. References to a legislative act by its official name and number may not be sufficient for participants to recognize it. Comparably, inquiring about their attitudes toward "selective cutting," "line service," or "siting" are instances where more information would yield more meaningful responses.

In the public hearing or workshop context, it is more likely that too much information would be offered. The more one knows about something, the harder it seems to be to recognize what and how much someone else needs to know about it to "just have a sense for it." In areas we know well, we are tempted to provide much too much information, to get into the complexities and technicalities. The

effects of overloading participants with information can
be dire.' Not only will the recipients fail to grasp all
the details, they may not even retain any of the
essentials and, instead, acquire only a negative attitude
about the entire effort. The amount of information people
can comprehend depends in part on their prior knowledge
with resect to that topic. One way to reduce the
likelihood of presenting too much information is to permit
people to pace themselves rather than to force them to
follow the material in a prescribed time period (such as a
formal presentation).

Information participants already have. If more
information can be provided in areas where participants
have prior knowledge, then it would be useful to have a
sense for what they already know and to begin with that.
Planners are sometimes disgruntled by people's tendency to
try to find their own home or location on an aerial
photograph or map even though the purpose of presenting
the material has no relationship to the areas where these
people reside. While one can interpret such behavior as
selfish or foolish, it is just as true that these people
are establishing some known location as a starting point.
Starting from "where they're at" is an important way to
take advantage of existing cognitive structures. Thus,
relating the problem under discussion to known conditions
and places, to the recent history that the participants
might know about, or to analogous situations that are
widely known is likely to increase comprehension of the
material.'

How to present information. Of course, there is no
single "right way" to present information most
effectively. There are, however, several ways that make
it likely to be less effective. The way we have all been
subjected to all too often is to be "talked to." Someone
in the front of the room goes on and on telling us things
that we are supposed to want to know about. There are
people who can do this well and there are circumstances
where this may be appropriate. Much of the time, alas,
neither is it involving nor does it provide sufficient
imagery. It is these two conditions that are particularly
important to consider; in many cases they can be
accomplished simultaneously.

Visual and spatial information is particularly
salient in the way people experience the environment.'°
That is not to say that any presentation that is visual
will work. One must bear in mind the consideration of the
amount of information and its relation to what
participants already know regardless of the method of
presentation. But visual imagery is particularly
effective at evoking a range of experiences that people
already have; it can provide information about things that
are difficult to portray in words alone. While
photographs, slides, physical simulations, graphics, and
other visual material have a direct tie to the issue of

imagery, they also can be effective ways to increase involvement.

The vividness and concreteness of the information, however presented, enhance imagery and involvement.'' Vivid material is particularly effective at holding people's attention; without attention, all else is lost. On the other hand, using material just because it is vivid, although otherwise irrelevant, can be a serious error. In such cases it becomes a distraction, calling attention to itself and away from the intended content.

Concreteness is often introduced into domains whose very abstractness may make them difficult to think about otherwise. Thus, an example or a "case in point" is easier to relate to than the underlying principle or plan. While specific instances are often helpful in communicating the pertinent issues, they can also become the objects of participants' reactions along directions that are not particularly related to the issue at hand. This makes it all the more important to choose one's concrete example carefully.

One of the most basic of human concerns is the concern to comprehend, to make sense of what is going on. The assessment of human concerns thus requires that information be given to the participant in order to make the process useful. In the absence of sufficient information to place what they are being asked to do in context, people may devote a substantial portion of their effort to trying to figure it out, to creating a sensible story that relates the aspects that are accessible to them. Since human processing capacity is limited, the quality of the effort devoted to the investigator's task is likely to suffer. It is rare in the environmental domain that hiding the intent of the project is necessary. On the contrary, the ability to participate--to be a "part of" and to be "party to"--is greatly enhanced by informed input.

Alternatives

In many environmental situations, the attempt to measure human values and concerns is not borne of a general, broad-gauged interest but, rather, from a particular set of events. Even more specifically, the need is to anticipate people's requirements with respect to events that have yet to occur, at least as much as with respect to existing situations. To know how people feel about the current pattern when this is likely to change necessarily provides only part of the story. So the need becomes one of portraying possible futures and determining what problems might arise.

Developing comprehensible material to present various futures is potentially expensive and complex. Certainly the models that are often constructed to inform people, even about a single building, cost huge sums. It would hardly be reasonable to invest in such beautiful models for each possible design for the proposed building, not to mention large projects, merely to determine people's concerns and desires. Thus, it might appear more reasonable to take advantage of the designer's expertise to develop the best possible alternative and to then get people's reactions to that solution. After all, if done before it is too late, people would still have the opportunity to provide their input.

Presenting only one alternative for people's consideration, however, has serious drawbacks. When the multiplicity of dimensions of an environmental decision are combined in a single formulation, citizens have neither comprehension of what is possible nor a concrete basis for differential expression. Further, by presenting various facets of the situation, there is less temptation on the part of the planner to become prematurely committed to one or another of the alternatives. By reducing the inclination toward polarization, areas of common agreement can be identified. Ideally, the ultimate solution is a new synthesis incorporating preferred features of the various alternatives.

The requirement of presenting more than one model, and of doing it at an early enough state in planning so that the input can be used, suggests that the cost of preparing such material must be kept to a minimum. Fortunately, this is not difficult, as long as what is presented is not in a form that is intended to elicit pleasure with the beauty of the model but, rather, comprehension with respect to the decisions that must be made. While such material must meet the requirements discussed earlier (e.g., visual/spatial, vivid, and concrete), it does not have to be highly detailed or "polished." In fact, the lack of detail can be helpful in directing attention to the issues being considered, and the lack of "polish" can help communicate that the input is being sought at an early enough stage so that it can affect decisions.[12]

Simulation models provide only one way to meet the requirements of presenting alternative solutions. They have the advantages of presenting information in a visual and spatial format and of portraying possible renditions of not-yet-existent settings. But there are other approaches to presenting alternatives that should also be considered.

Environmental sampling. When citizens voice concern about the proposed solution to an environmental problem, it is difficult to determine whether their displeasure is with the solution as a whole. It is possible, of course, that any solution would be dismissed. But it is also possible that the objections are to some relatively minor aspects of the whole that could be altered, although the disgruntled citizens have no way to identify these portions as separate components of the larger solution.

By providing people with images of possible approaches to the various components of the project, these difficulties can be avoided.

The underlying issue here is one of providing sufficient examples to make one aware of the categories they exemplify. If one wishes to choose a tree for one's garden, seeing only one tree is unlikely to be satisfactory. If one wishes to know how citizens would respond to an issue, knowing the reactions of one citizen would be insufficient. In fact, in many such cases, even two or three examples may be too few. While many professionals are quick to raise concerns about the need for a large enough sample to draw meaningful conclusions, the need for adequately sampling the environment is generally ignored. But the argument is essentially identical. When assessment is based on poor sampling of the environment, it is impossible to know to what settings the results can be applied in much the same way that a limited sampling of people limits the ability to generalize to other populations. Multiple instances of the kind of environment in question are the necessary antidote. Environmental sampling is thus important both for methodological reasons and on substantive grounds as well.[13]

Conscientious sampling of the environment raises other problems, however. First, there is the issue of collecting enough examples and finding ways to present these that are in keeping with the comprehension needs of the participants. In many cases, this can be achieved by the use of slides[14] or photographs.[15] The examples can be drawn from comparable solutions that have been tried in other locales or by altering photographs of existing conditions to reflect possible new alternatives.[16]

A further problem with conscientious environmental sampling is that it can generate large quantities of data. By looking at participants' responses to each of the examples, one can quickly generate more analyses than anyone can handle effectively. If the data that are collected cannot or will not be processed meaningfully, they should not have been collected. The desirability of adequate environmental sampling thus calls for data reduction procedures that help one understand the results.

Dimensionalization procedures. Fortunately, there exists a variety of analytical procedures that help in this process. These procedures make it possible to start with many instances (such as participants' responses to each of 40 photographs) and proceed to a smaller set of composites that capture the basic categories of people's reactions to these instances. In other words, these procedures generate underlying themes or groupings by examining the patterns in the responses.[17]

The computer-generated identification of these categories or groupings is in itself a major step in understanding human concerns. Rather than assuming that

one's a priori classification of the environment is shared
by the citizenry, these results permit one to discover
patterns of perception or experience that are shared by
the participant sample. The notion of discovery is very
important here. Many times such groupings would be
difficult to determine by more direct means. The fact
that people respond similarly to certain examples is not
necessarily something they are aware of; nor is it
something that they could easily explain.[18]

Response Format

To ask people what they want or why they want it is
in many instances unproductive and frustrating.[19] Our
inability to explain things that are important to us seems
surprising. The basis of much experience, even for
humans, is not verbal. We perceive the world around us by
visual means and depend on a great deal of spatial
information in the way we take in the information. Having
the knowledge and sharing it with others are hardly the
same. To tell others about it requires a translation from
the way we have stored the experience. As is so
frequently the case with translations, the proper
expression is unavailable. In the case of many
environmental problems, the use of visual/spatial material
to elicit the responses circumvents some of these
difficulties. In fact, such material is doubly useful.
The very same photographs or slides that are the basis for
the participants' input can at the same time provide the
information that participants need to be able to make
informed judgments.[20]
But the problem remains as to what the participant is
to "say" with respect to the visual/spatial material.
Clearly, it would be foolish to depend on a visual
response form--say, to ask participants to draw pictures
of some kind. To ask for an explanation of the visual
material gets right back to the verbal problem. So we
need to find some way that minimizes dependence on
explanation but provides an indication of the
participants' reactions.
One approach is to ask participants to take the
visual material--say, photographs--and to sort them into
groups that are meaningful to them. One could repeat the
task and ask people to try a second sorting, using some
other basis. One can prescribe the number of categories,
or a minimum number of photographs that must be used to
form a category, or simply let the participant decide.
Such a free-category sort is not only a doable task but
one that participants often enjoy. By examining both the
photographs that constitute a category and the range of
categories that was formed, the investigator can gain
insight into the salient issues for the participant and
into the agreement about these issues for the sample as a
whole. It is often useful to ask the participants to try

to name the categories or indicate the basis for their decisions. While these verbal responses might be similar across the group of participants, the instances that were used to characterize the categories may be quite different. Conversely, a group of photographs that are frequently categorized into one group may receive a wide range of labels.

The free-category sort is a useful approach for assessing human concerns. It is particularly appropriate for relatively small groups of participants and in situations where each person can work individually with the photographs.[21] The comparison of categories across many participants is a time-consuming task. Even with a limited set of photographs (say, 20-40), there are innumerable possible combinations. We have found that the procedure is useful in two kinds of situations: early in the process and for certain specific groups. When one uses free-category sorts as a pre-test, it can provide information about how some of the photographs are interpreted and whether there are enough examples of different settings. This permits adjustments in the set of pictures, thus improving the sampling of environments for the study proper when a different response format will be used. In the case of particular groups, the free-category sort can, for instance, tell one whether different professional groups perceive the problem similarly.[22]

An entirely different approach to the problem of minimizing the need for verbal responses involves preference reactions.[23] Participants are simply asked to indicate how much they like, or prefer, each of the visual items presented as slides or photographs or sketches. A convenient format for this purpose is a five-point rating scale that either uses verbal tags for each of the five points or only anchors the extreme scale points with verbal equivalents (e.g., "not at all" and "a great deal").[24] Among the major attractions of this procedure are that it is efficient, taking participants little time to do, that it is enjoyable, and that it generates meaningful information. There is good reason for these advantages: the decision as to what we like and do not like tends to be fast and automatic. It is the basis for many of our actions and activities.[25]

There are, of course, other ways to approach preference than to use a rating scale. One procedure, in particular, is used quite widely and deserves some discussion. Participants are asked to rank their preferences or to indicate which alternative they like the most. This has several disadvantages that a rating procedure avoids. Putting several examples in rank order is time consuming. Implicit in ranking is a series of comparisons of all possible pairings; and the more items in the group, the greater the number of pairs. But even more important than that is the problem of raising false

hopes. Once people have declared their favorite choice--
that is, voted--they are more likely to want their
solution to be the "winning" choice. More likely than
not, the ultimate solution to the environmental problem
will not be in that form. Such a referendum model may
thus be totally inappropriate and damaging. It can lead
to divisiveness when hard stances are not helpful. At the
same time, little knowledge has been gained about the
acceptability of the other choices. By having a rating of
each alternative, it is possible to determine the relative
attractiveness of all the choices.

Verbal measures. The advantages of using visual
material do not preclude using questions requiring verbal
responses as well. Of course, there are many questions
and issues that depend on participants' verbal responses
and the verbal material, together with the visual,
provides checks on one's interpretations.[24] In fact, many
of the points made about responses to the pictures also
apply to verbal items. The problem of ranking as opposed
to rating, the advantage of a rating scale over long
answers, and the benefit of many brief items that are
efficient to handle pertain equally to pictures and words.

While people not trained in producing visual
questionnaires recognize that they might need some advice
from experts in this area, the same is not always true
about questionnaires in general. But, alas, there is much
advice that could be offered on this topic. We have found
particularly useful a format that involves many, very
brief examples of a common domain. For instance, one
might want to know about people's concerns with respect to
increased development of an area. Rather than asking
about major categories of development (industrial,
institutional, recreational, residential, etc.), the
question would include several examples of each of the
categories. While involving more items, they are quick to
do and they make it possible to determine whether what a
planner considers to fall within a particular category is
comparably perceived by the citizen. A bank and a post
office may have more in common than do a gas station and a
grocery store--when these are to be placed across the
street from one's house.

The appropriate response format will differ with the
circumstances, but its compatibility with the participants
must not be ignored. The most sophisticated procedures
for drawing samples will not generate useful information
if what these randomly chosen individuals are asked to do
makes no sense to them. Their failure to comprehend the
context and the questions, their inability to respond to
the material, and their hostility to the entire process
are all real problems that must be considered, regardless
of the sampling procedures.

SOME CONCLUSIONS

Public meetings can bring out the worst in people, produce little useful information, and generate a sense of futility for all involved. Survey research also has the potential for antagonizing (as many cartoons suggest) and generating voluminous data that go unheeded. The suggestions made in this paper are attempts to avoid some of these problems. There is no fail-safe method that can solve all the difficulties of measuring human well-being,[27] but there are ways to improve the current situation.

The approach we have taken is guided by a framework about humans and their characteristics. People are not at their best when angry and suspicious. They are more helpful, however, when approached as participants, as human beings with curiosity and considerable knowledge. The purpose of studies of human concerns is to generate useful information without raising false hopes, to help people deal with impending change, and to provide an opportunity for citizen involvement that is productive and unthreatening.

While approaching participation through the simple devices discussed here may seem simplistic, the results have been far reaching. They have served to inform the public while, at the same time, also informing the planners and managers. In addition to the practical benefits, the studies have helped us gain an understanding of concerns that people have with respect to environmental problems. While the specific details vary greatly, time and again we find that people want to understand. They want some order and predictability, but not to the exclusion of opportunities to explore and to learn new things. They want to have choices and they appreciate the opportunity to have input into decisions that affect their lives.

REFERENCES

Anderson, E. (1978), "Visual Resource Assessment: Local Perceptions of Familiar Natural Environments." Unpublished doctoral dissertation, The University of Michigan.

Bailey, K. D. (1978), Methods of Social Research. New York: Free Press.

Blumenthal, A. L. (1977), The Process of Cognition. Englewood Cliffs, N.J.: Prentice-Hall.

Bransford, J. D. (1979), Human Cognition: Learning, Understanding, and Remembering. Belmont, Cal.: Wadsworth.

Brunswik, E. (1956), Perception and the Representative Design of Psychological Experiments. Berkeley: University of California Press.

Campbell, A. (1976), "Subjective Measures of Well-being."
American Psychologist, 31, 117-124.
Christensen, K. (1976), Social Impacts of Land
Development. Washington, D.C.: The Urban Institute.
Cohen, S. (1978), "Environmental Load and the Allocation
of Attention." In A. Baum, J. E. Singer, and
S. Valins (Eds.), Advances in Environmental
Psychology, Vol. 1. Hillsdale, N.J.: Erlbaum.
Dee, N., Baker, J., Drobny, N., and Duke, K. (1973), "An
Environmental Evaluation System for Water Resource
Planning." Water Resources Research, 9, 523-535.
Dreyfus, H. L. (1972), What Computers Can't Do. New York:
Harper and Row.
Finsterbusch, K. (1980), Understanding Social Impacts.
Beverly Hills, Cal.: Sage.
Finsterbusch, K., and Wolf, C. P. (1977) (Eds.), The
Methodology of Social Impact Assessment.
Stroudsburg, Penn.: Dowden, Hutchinson, and Ross.
Foa, U. G. (1971), "Interpersonal and Economic Resources."
Science, 171, 345-351.
Frey, J. E. (1981), "Preferences, Satisfactions, and the
Physical Environment of Urban Neighborhoods."
Unpublished doctoral dissertation, The University of
Michigan.
Gallagher, T. J. (1977), "Visual Preferences for
Alternative Natural Landscapes." Unpublished
doctoral dissertation, The University of Michigan.
Glass, A. L., Holyoak, K. J., and Santa, J. L. (1979),
Cognition. Reading, Mass.: Addison-Wesley.
Golledge, R. G., and Rushton, G. (1972), Multidimensional
Scaling: Review and Geographical Applications.
Washington, D.C.: Association of American
Geographers.
Grant, M. A. (1979), "Structured Participatory Input."
Master's thesis in Landscape Architecture, The
University of Michigan.
Hammitt, W. E. (1979), "Measuring Familiarity for Natural
Environments through Visual Images." In Proceedings
of Our National Landscape Conference. USDA Forest
Service General Technical Report PSW-35.
Hammond, K. R. (1966) (Ed.), The Psychology of Egon
Brunswik. New York: Holt.
Heberlein, T. A. (1976), "Some Observations on Alternative
Mechanisms for Public Involvement." Natural
Resources Journal, 16, 197-212.
Herbert, E. (1981), "Visual Resource Quality: Prediction
and Preference in Oakland County, Michigan."
Master's thesis in Landscape Architecture, The
University of Michigan.
Herzog, T. R., Kaplan, S., and Kaplan, R. (1976), "The
Prediction of Preference for Familiar Urban Places."
Environment and Behavior, 8, 627-645.
Herzog, T. R., Kaplan, S., and Kaplan, R. (1982), "The
Prediction of Preference for Unfamiliar Urban

50

Places." Population and Environment, 5, 43-59..
James, W. (1892), Psychology: The Briefer Course.
    (Collier Books, 1962.)
Kaplan, R. (1972), "The Dimensions of the Visual
    Environment: Methodological Considerations." In
    W. J. Mitchell (Ed.), Environmental Design: Research
    and Practice.
Kaplan, R. (1973), "Some Psychological Benefits of
    Gardening." Environment and Behavior, 5, 135-162.
Kaplan, R. (1974), "A Strategy for Dimensional Analysis."
    In D. H. Carson (Ed.), Man-Environment Interactions:
    Evaluations and Applications. Stroudsburg, Penn.:
    Dowden, Hutchinson, and Ross.
Kaplan, R. (1975), "Some Methods and Strategies in the
    Prediction of Preference." In E. H. Zube,
    R. O. Brush, and J. G. Fabos (Eds.), Landscape
    Assessment. Stroudsburg, Penn.: Dowden, Hutchinson,
    and Ross.
Kaplan, R. (1977a), "Preference and Everyday Nature:
    Method and Application." In D. Stokols (Ed.),
    Perspectives on Environment and Behavior. New York:
    Plenum.
Kaplan, R. (1977b), "Down by the Riverside: Informational
    Factors in Waterscape Preferences." In River
    Recreation Management and Research Symposium. USDA
    Forest Service General Technical Report NC-28.
Kaplan, R. (1978), "Participation in Environmental
    Design." In S. Kaplan and R. Kaplan (Eds.),
    Humanscape: Environments for People. Belmont, Cal.:
    Duxbury.
Kaplan, R. (1979), "A Methodology for Simultaneously
    Obtaining and Sharing Information." In Assessing
    Amenity Resource Values. USDA Forest Service General
    Technical Report RM-68.
Kaplan, R. (1983), "The Role of Nature in the Urban
    Context." In I. Altman and J. F. Wohlwill (Eds.),
    Behavior and the Natural Environment. New York:
    Plenum.
Kaplan, R., Kaplan, S., and Deardorff, H. L. (1974), "The
    Perception and Evaluation of a Simulated
    Environment." Man-Environment Systems, 4, 191-192.
Kaplan, S. (1973), "Cognitive Maps, Human Needs, and the
    Designed Environment." In W. F. E. Preiser (Ed.),
    Environmental Design Research. Stroudsburg, Penn.:
    Dowden, Hutchinson, and Ross.
Kaplan, S. (1975), "An Informal Model for the Prediction
    of Preference." In E. H. Zube, R. O. Brush, and
    J. G. Fabos (Eds.), Landscape Assessment.
    Stroudsburg, Penn.: Dowden, Hutchinson, and Ross.
Kaplan, S. (1977a), "Tranquility and Challenge in the
    Natural Environment." In Children, Nature, and the
    Urban Environment. USDA Forest Service General
    Technical Report NE-30.
Kaplan, S. (1977b), "Participation in the Design Process:

A Cognitive Approach." In D. Stokols (Ed.),
Perspectives on Environment and Behavior. New York:
Plenum.

Kaplan, S. (1979), "Concerning the Power of Content-
identifying Methodologies." In Assessing Amenity
Resource Values. USDA Forest Service General
Technical Report RM-68.

Kaplan, S., and Kaplan, R. (1978) (Eds.), Humanscape:
Environments for People. Belmont, Cal.: Duxbury.
[Ann Arbor, Mich.: Ulrichs, 1982.]

Kaplan, S., and Kaplan, R. (1982), Cognition and
Environment. New York: Praeger.

Kerlinger, F. N. (1973), Foundations of Behavioral
Research. New York: Holt.

Lachman, J. L., and Lachman, R. (1979), "Theories of
Memory Organization and Human Evolution." In
C. R. Puff (Ed.), Memory Organization and Structure.
New York: Academic.

Leopold, L. B., Clarke, F. E., Hanshaw, B. B., and
Balsley, J. R. (1971), "A Procedure for Evaluating
Environmental Impact." Geological Survey Circular
645. Washington, D.C.: Government Printing Office.

Mandler, G. (1975), "Consciousness: Respectable, Useful,
and Probably Necessary." In R. L. Solso (Ed.),
Information Processing and Cognitive Psychology.
Hillsdale, N.J.: Erlbaum.

Michelson, W. (1975) (Ed.), Behavioral Research Methods in
Environmental Design. Stroudsburg, Penn.: Dowden,
Hutchinson, and Ross.

Midgley, M. (1978), Beast and Man: The Roots of Human
Nature. Ithaca, N.Y.: Cornell University Press.

Miller, G. A. (1956), "The Magical Number Seven, Plus or
Minus Two: Some Limits on Our Capacity for
Processing Information." Psychological Review, 63,
81-97.

Miller, G. A. (1962), Psychology: The Science of Mental
Life. New York: Harper and Row.

Munn, R. E. (1979), Environmental Impact Assessment:
Principles and Procedures. Chichester: Wiley.

Nicoll, G. (1981), "Pattern Language as an Approach to
Pedestrian Design: A Participatory Analysis."
Master's thesis in Landscape Architecture, The
University of Michigan.

Norman, D. A. (1970), (Ed.), Models of Human Memory. New
York: Academic.

Nunnally, J. C. (1978), Psychometric Theory. New York:
McGraw-Hill.

Petrich, C. H. (1979), "Aesthetic Impact of a Proposed
Power Plant on an Historic Wilderness Landscape." In
Proceedings of Our Natural Landscape Conference.
USDA Forest Service General Technical Report PSW-35.

Pick, A. D. (1980), "Cognition: Psychological
Perspectives." In H. C. Triandis and W. Lonner
(Eds.), Handbook of Cross-cultural Psychology, Vol 3:

Basic Processes. Boston: Allyn and Bacon.

Pitt, D. G., and Zube, E. H. (1979), "The Q-sort Method:
Use in Landscape Assessment Research and Landscape
Planning." In Proceedings of Our National Landscape
Conference. USDA Forest Service General Technical
Report PSW-35.

Posner, M. I. (1973), Cognition: An Introduction.
Glenview, Ill.: Scott, Foresman.

Sewell, W. R., and Coppock, J. J. (1977) (Eds.), Public
Participation and Planning. London: Wiley.

Shields, M. A. (1975), "Social Impact Studies: An
Expository Analysis." Environment and Behavior, 7,
265-285.

Van Dyke, H. (1903), Fisherman's Luck and Some Other
Uncertain Things. New York: Charles Scribners.

Warner, M. L. (1973), "Environmental Impact Analysis: An
Examination of Three Methodologies." Unpublished
doctoral dissertation, The University of Wisconsin.

Warwick, D. P., and Lininger, C. A. (1975), The Sample
Survey: Theory and Practice. New York: McGraw-Hill.

Webb, K., and Hatry, H. P. (1973), Obtaining Citizen
Feedback. Washington, D.C.: The Urban Institute.

Weber, W. M. (1980), "A Comparison of Media for Public
Participation in Natural Environmental Planning."
Unpublished doctoral dissertation, The University of
Michigan.

Wickelgren, W. A. (1979), Cognitive Psychology. Englewood
Cliffs, N.J.: Prentice-Hall.

Zeisel, J. (1981), Inquiry by Design: Tools for
Environment-Behavior Research. Monterey, Cal.:
Brooks/Cole.

Zube, E. H. (1980), Environmental Evaluation: Perception
and Public Policy. Monterey, Cal.: Brooks/Cole.

NOTES

[1]Acknowledgment: Work on this paper was supported,
in part, by Cooperative Agreement 13-655, Urban Forestry
Project, U.S. Forest Service North Central Forest
Experiment Station.

[2]Table 3.3 in Munn (1979) is particularly thought
provoking. Munn also includes a chapter on using
socioeconomic methods. Dee, Baker, Drobney, and Duke
(1973), Leopold, Clarke, Hanshaw, and Balsley (1971),
Shields (1975), and Warner (1973) all discuss pertinent
indicators. Finsterbusch (1980) provides an entire volume
on social impact indicators, and Finsterbusch and Wolf
(1977) include many applicable methods. Christensen
(1976) takes the reader through many of the steps in
carrying out social impact analyses and provides useful
information about sources of data for different categories
of questions.

[3]The chapter notes provide extensive, although by no

means exhaustive, references for further reading.
Included are examples of our own research to highlight the
variety of settings in which the proposed approaches can
be applied as well as citations to theoretical and
methodological works.

⁴Kaplan and Kaplan (1978, 1982), S. Kaplan (1973,
1975, 1977a), and R. Kaplan (1977a, b) provide further
discussion of human concerns in an environmental context.

⁵Van Dyke (1903, p. 5) recognized the importance of
uncertainty to the angler. R. Kaplan (1973, 1983)
presents some pertinent empirical support in the gardening
context. The role of making sense and involvement in
environmental preference was studied in many of the
projects cited in Notes 13 and 14.

⁶Comparisons of methods in the context of citizen
participation are available in various sources, including
Heberlein (1976), Sewell and Coppock (1977), and Zube
(1980). Books on research methods (e.g., Bailey, 1978;
Kerlinger, 1973; Michelson, 1975; and Zeisel, 1981)
provide extensive discussion of particular approaches to
direct assessment procedures. Warwick and Lininger (1975)
and Webb and Hatry (1973) are particularly useful with
respect to surveys and related issues.

⁷Knowledge concerning human cognitive capacities and
inclinations has grown rapidly in recent years.
Stimulated by developments in the machine processing of
information, the study of human information processing
made great strides both empirically and theoretically.
One of the best introductions in the area is still Posner
(1973). Among the more recent texts in the area,
Blumenthal (1977), Bransford (1979), and Wickelgren (1979)
are particularly helpful. An important statement on the
limits of the computer analogy as a model of human thought
is provided by Dreyfus (1972).

⁸Current thinking concerning the limitations on how
much information humans can process effectively at any one
time has been greatly influenced by the classic paper by
Miller (1956). A readable and engaging discussion of this
and related issues can be found in Miller (1962). For an
update on this issue, see Mandler (1975). While these
references deal with the human inability to handle
information beyond certain limits, they do not address the
issue of costs. A perceptive analysis of the linkages
between too much information and stress is provided by
Cohen (1978).

⁹Being able to use one's prior knowledge in
interpreting new material can play a decisive role by
providing essential context (cf. Bransford, 1979).
Another way in which people use prior knowledge is in
organizing and structuring the new material (Glass,
Holyoak, and Santa, 1979). In addition, there is the
long-studied role of familiarity (cf. Norman, 1970).
Hence, connecting new information to prior knowledge calls
on various powerful information processing factors, all

54

likely to contribute to enhanced comprehension.
[10]S. Kaplan's chapter in this volume provides further discussion of the salience of visual and spatial processing. Lachman and Lachman (1979) also examine the centrality of visual processing from an evolutionary perspective.
[11]In psychological research, "vividness" usually refers to material that is striking, distinct from surrounding material, or otherwise noteworthy. William James (1892) pointed to a number of the critical issues here in his discussion of what he called "involuntary attention." Some things are inherently interesting to people while others, through learning, have come to be recognized as important in one way or another. Midgley (1978) provides a useful analysis of many of the things that people find inherently interesting. In certain economic circles, there is a tendency to believe that what is in the long run the most vivid kind of information boils down to dollars and cents, or "the bottom line." A helpful antidote to the belief that there can be any single bottom line is provided by Foa (1971). For a general discussion of what matters and, hence, what is likely to be experienced as vivid by people, see Kaplan and Kaplan (1978, 1982).
[12]Kaplan, Kaplan, and Deardorff (1974) and S. Kaplan (1977b) discuss the use of simple, low-detail simulation models in research and applied settings. Zube (1980) devotes a chapter of his book to the evaluation of alternative futures using simulation models. R. Kaplan's (1978) study for the city of Ann Arbor used photographs of models as a means of providing citizens with information about possible designs for a vest-pocket park. The same low-cost procedure was used by Grant (1979) and Nicoll (1981).
[13]Brunswik (1956) introduced the concept of "ecological validity" to reflect the importance of the representativeness of the environments that are sampled. Hammond (1966) provides further discussion of this concept. R. Kaplan (1972) discusses some approaches to selecting pertinent examples.
[14]Much of the research we and our students have carried out falls into the categories of slides and photographs. Weber's (1980) dissertation addresses the issue of the effectiveness of different means of visual presentation. He found color slides to be superior in a number of respects to the more costly color video procedure. The studies by Herzog, Kaplan, and Kaplan (1976, 1982) involve slides of various urban contexts, while Herbert (1981) studied the feasibility of extending the procedure to a countywide scale.
[15]Black-and-white photographs have proved to be a particularly effective and inexpensive format for providing participants with a range of alternative scenes. By printing eight photos to a page, such

photoquestionnaires can readily include 24 to 40 instances. Examples of pertinent studies are provided in Anderson (1978), using forest practices in a national forest as the context; Frey (1981), in a study of urban residential settings; Gallagher (1977), for prairie restorations and ornamental landscapes in an institutional context; Hammitt (1979), in exploring bog settings; and R. Kaplan (1977a), for proposed changes to a storm drain system, and (1983), for multiple-family housing.

¹⁶Petrich's (1979 and this volume) photoquestionnaire provides an excellent example of combining actual scenery with simulated plumes. In many cases, such procedures are quite expensive and require greater expertise than needed for photographing examples of existing situations.

¹⁷As a class, these procedures are known as dimensional analyses. Factor analyses constitute one family of programs under this heading, but there are various other approaches to extracting clusters or themes as well. Kerlinger (1973) and Nunnally (1978) include chapters on these procedures that are less technical than most of the volumes specifically addressed to dimensional approaches. While the applications in many treatments of this subject are generally psychometric (e.g., concerned with individual differences in personality), Golledge and Rushton (1972) provide a useful overview in a geographic context. All the studies cited in Notes 13 and 14 used both a nonmetric factor analysis and a form of cluster analysis to determine the underlying themes. The rationale for these choices is provided in R. Kaplan (1974, 1975).

¹⁸Use of these dimensional procedures is reliably instructive. The empirical studies cited earlier provide an indication of the insights that this approach permits. S. Kaplan (1979) offers a comparison of some of the thematic groupings that have emerged across a variety of studies. Although the environmental contexts are widely different, the emergence of strong similarities in groupings has been an important step in learning about characteristic patterns of preference.

¹⁹Open-ended questions--where the respondent must formulate the answer--are useful in many situations; guidelines for their use are provided in various research methods books (cf. Note 5). In the environmental context, however, such items also have serious drawbacks. In many cases, participants are "at a loss for words" to state their reasons or choices and feel incompetent or ignorant when they fail to respond. Those who do find the words may provide a stereotypic response, leaving the investigator with the job of interpreting what is meant. Thus, for instance, the expressed concern for "safety" may include a variety of other unstated considerations (e.g., comfort and aesthetics). The noncomparability of responses offered by many participants presents a further difficulty.

[20]R. Kaplan (1979) deals with the issue of simultaneously obtaining and sharing information.

[21]Categorization tasks of this kind have also been used in cross-cultural research to study bases of classification of objects (cf. Pick, 1980).

[22]An example is provided by Anderson (1978), who asked professional foresters to sort pictures showing different forest practices to see whether their categories would be similar to each other and to the kinds of categories generated by the approaches discussed in Note 16.

[23]Q-methodology has many similarities to preference ratings. While it is physically similar to the free-category sort in as much as the participants are asked to array the photographs into piles, the basis for the sort is a preference response. Pitt and Zube (1979) provide a useful discussion of this approach.

[24]There is nothing magical about a five-point Likert scale. The literature is ambiguous as to the advantages of an odd vs. an even number or categories, as to how many categories to use, and also about the use of verbal anchors (cf. Nunnally, 1978). We have found five levels with a label for each to work very well. While our lowest scale point indicates that the participant does "not at all" like the scene, the Likert scale is flexible as to the definition of the scale points.

[25]See S. Kaplan's chapter in this volume for further discussion.

[26]R. Kaplan (1977a, 1983) provides examples of such internal checks.

[27]Campbell (1976) presents a useful general discussion of the problems of "subjective measures of well-being."

3. EIA Scoping for Aesthetics: Hindsight from the Greene County Nuclear Power Plant EIS[1]

Carl H. Petrich

OVERVIEW

Scoping in the environmental impact statement (EIS) process commands sensitivity to a wide range of potential environmental impacts. This paper suggests and justifies a process for scoping aesthetic impacts. It is based on the author's experiences and insights gained from assessing the aesthetic impacts of the proposed Greene County Nuclear Power Plant. This facility was to be located on the west bank of the Hudson River at the foot of the Catskill Mountains in an area that was the geographic center of and inspiration for the country's nineteenth-century romantic movement. A brief, general background of approaches to aesthetic analysis is given to provide a framework for considering the scoping suggestions. The research concluded that building the power plant in the proposed location would entail an unacceptable negative aesthetic impact. This finding was the primary basis for the issuance of a final environmental statement by the U.S. Nuclear Regulatory Commission staff recommending that the utility's application for a construction permit to build this plant be denied, an action unprecedented in the history of the nuclear power industry.

The adoption in 1979 of the new Council on Environmental Quality (CEQ) regulations for scoping in the EIS process has brought much consternation among managers as to how they might best estimate the most important impacts accompanying proposed actions or developments. In the field of aesthetics, an impact area of great subjectivity and normally of low consequence and/or of mitigable dimensions, an early assessment of potential importance is quite difficult. Based on my experiences in working on the precedent-setting Greene County Nuclear Power Plant EIS, in which aesthetics played the critical role, I offer in this paper an approach for managers to employ in assessing aesthetic impacts in the scoping stages. Before discussing this approach, it is necessary to understand a little of the nature of power plant

siting, aesthetic analysis approaches in general, and the
Greene County analysis in particular.

INTRODUCTION

The timely development of a regional or national
electrical generation system powered partially by nuclear
fission depends, among other things, on selecting sites
for new reactor facilities that meet stringent safety and
environmental standards. For most areas of projected high
future electrical demand, utilities or other industrial
users have already claimed the most desirable sites for
large generating plants. Consequently, utility planners
must look to less suitable areas and, therefore, to sites
more likely to conflict with factors that constrain power
plant siting.

From an analysis conducted at the Oak Ridge National
Laboratory (ORNL) of the impacts on one factor,
aesthetics, I concluded that the construction and
operation of the proposed $1.8 billion Greene County
Nuclear Power Plant in New York State would result in an
unacceptable aesthetic impact. Staff at ORNL and at the
U.S. Nuclear Regulatory Commission (NRC) endorsed this
finding. On February 9, 1979, the NRC published the Final
Environmental Statement (FES) for the Greene County
Nuclear Power Plant (NRC, 1979). Primarily on the basis
of the unmitigable negative aesthetic impacts, the NRC
staff recommended in the FES that a construction permit
for the plant be denied.

This was the first time in the history of the nuclear
power industry that the NRC (or its Atomic Energy
Commission predecessor) had recommended the rejection of a
proposed nuclear power plant site for environmental,
nonsafety reasons (Spangler, 1980). That the
recommendation was based primarily on aesthetic impacts as
well as other serious socioeconomic impacts made this
event particularly unusual. On January 18, 1980, the
Power Authority of the State of New York (PASNY) formally
withdrew its application for a construction permit from
the New York State Board on Electric Generation Siting and
the Environment, and on October 20, 1980, PASNY withdrew
its application for a construction permit from the NRC.

The 1191-MW(e)(net) nuclear generating unit was to be
located 64 kilometers (40 miles) south of Albany at the
foot of the Catskill Mountains on the west bank of the
Hudson River near the hamlet of Cementon (Figure 3.1).
PASNY proposed an alternative site 15 kilometers (10
miles) to the north and just west of the river-front town
of Athens. PASNY's engineering designs called for a 137-
meter (450-foot) tall natural-draft cooling tower and a
62-meter (205-foot) domed reactor containment structure.
PASNY, a state-owned, tax-exempt utility, planned to
transmit most of the electricity to the New York City
metropolitan area, where its principal customer was to be

the subway system.

A conflict arose because of the plant's location in the cradle of the nineteenth-century American romantic movement--the cultural, religious, and political current that asserted the validity of the subjective and spawned this country's still-growing love affair with nature. In the first quarter of the nineteenth century, the mid-Hudson River Valley and the Catskill Mountains were perceived throughout the nation as the country's wilderness. The American West, the Adirondacks, and the southern Appalachian Mountains were for the most part inaccessible and largely unknown. When European visitors came to the young nation during the early nineteenth century, it was to the mid-Hudson River area that they were taken to see America's wild lands. By the middle of the century, the Catskills and mid-Hudson River Valley areas were the geographic center of and the inspiration for this country's romantic literature and art. From this area and from similar European antecedent counterparts evolved the American perception of what we call "beautiful" landscapes.

It was in this context that I assessed what impacts might be expected should PASNY construct and operate the proposed plant. This assessment became, in part, the determination of the dimension of intrusion of a quintessential symbol of the twentieth century into a landscape still decidedly nineteenth century in character and meaning. The following sections present, first, the relevant portions of the federal law that prompted this study. An investigation of the historical and cultural context for the assessment is a background prerequisite to defining and explaining the approach to aesthetic impact analysis that I used. Because aesthetics deals, in part, with the subjective attachments people may have for a given landscape, it was essential to understand and try to measure the strength of these attachments before trying to assess the potential aesthetic impact of the plant. Ascertaining the historical importance of this area to laypeople and to art and cultural historians as well was, therefore, critical to the total effort. It is sensitivity to elements such as these that give direction to the scoping process.

NEPA AND AESTHETICS

As part of its federal responsibilities under the National Environmental Policy Act of 1969 (NEPA), the NRC performs independent environmental assessments of each application for a license to construct or operate a nuclear power plant. The NRC contracted with ORNL to conduct the environmental assessment for this plant. In March of 1976, the NRC issued a Draft Environmental Statement (DES) in support of the license application. During the comment period on the DES, readers criticized

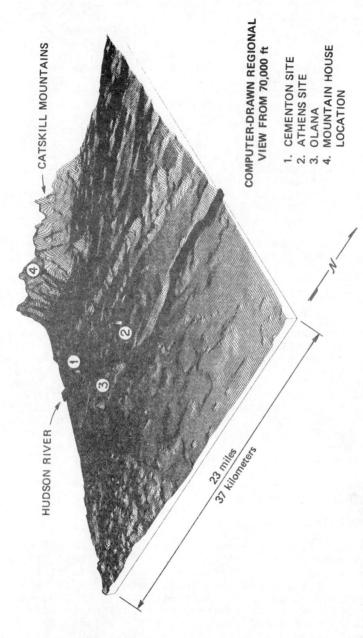

ORNL—DWG 79-11538

CATSKILL MOUNTAINS

HUDSON RIVER

COMPUTER-DRAWN REGIONAL
VIEW FROM 70,000 ft

1. CEMENTON SITE
2. ATHENS SITE
3. OLANA
4. MOUNTAIN HOUSE
   LOCATION

N

23 miles
37 kilometers

Figure 3.1   Computer-drawn view of the mid-Hudson River Valley and Catskill Mountains from
the northeast to the southwest. Topography and cooling towers have been
exaggerated five times in the vertical dimension.

the inadequacy of the analysis of the plant's possible
visual impact. No one experienced in aesthetic analysis
was involved with the NRC project until I joined the ORNL
assessment team in April of 1977.

The ORNL task group for assessing the environmental
impacts of the Greene Country facility performed two
functions. First, each member did an assessment in the
corresponding disciplinary area (aquatic or terrestrial
ecology, social impact, thermal diffusion, etc.).
Subsequently, the whole group weighed the importance of
each assessment. Through this group process, we reached a
final conclusion and reviewed our conclusion with the NRC
regarding the suitability of the plant for a permit and
the superiority of at least one alternative site.

Central to this second group function were several
pertinent aspects of NEPA. The act requires the

> Federal Government to use all practicable means . . .
> [to] . . . assure for all Americans safe, healthful,
> productive, and aesthetically and culturally pleasing
> surroundings . . . [and to] . . . preserve important
> historic, cultural, and natural aspects of our
> national heritage, and maintain, wherever possible,
> an environment that supports diversity and variety of
> individual choice. (NEPA Sect. 101[b][2, 4])

To this end, federal agencies are directed to

> utilize a systematic, interdisciplinary approach that
> will insure the integrated use of the natural and
> social sciences and the environmental design arts in
> planning and in decision making that may have an
> impact on man's environment. (NEPA Sect. 101[2][A])

AESTHETICS IN THE SITING PROCESS

General power plant siting methodologies are guided
and constrained by the necessity to give appropriate
consideration to engineering, economic, and environmental
factors. In current practice, a geographical hierarchy,
coupled with a hierarchy of data variables, points to
suitable sites through some manual or automated screening
algorithm (Dobson, 1980). In most schemes, availability
of fuel, land, and water, along with suitability of
population density, geology, and seismicity, plays a
dominant role for the first-cut (regional-scale) site
selection for nuclear power plants. Meteorological, land-
use, social, and aquatic and terrestrial ecological
suitability, along with accessibility, is the normal
consideration at the second-cut (intermediate or
candidate) level of site selection. At a third level,
individual sites are judged for availability of community
services; proximity to sensitive historic sites or natural
features; competition for land and water; compatibility

with adjacent land uses and master plans; and the social, economic, engineering, and environmental impacts associated with transmission line right-of-way acquisition and development. Most unsuitable power plant sites are eliminated at the first or second level. Conflicts appear at the second level when utilities, regulatory agencies, and citizen groups differ on the relative importance of given variables. Indian Point, Diablo Canyon, Bodega Head, Seabrook, and the proposed Sun Desert power plants, among others, typify these conflicts.

When a candidate site overcomes the first two levels of siting constraints, utility planners move to the third level fairly confident that there are economically feasible trade-offs to reduce the environmental impacts through engineering design. At the best site among the candidates, problems are assumed to be manageable. Aesthetic impacts normally enter the process at this third level in the site selection process under the assumption that such impacts are cosmetic and can be ameliorated through changes in the design of buildings, plantings, facades, and/or basic site plans. Changing the selected plant location is normally not considered a feasible option at this level. The problem in the Greene County case was that, in the final opinion of the NRC staff, the feasible engineering or design modifications could not satisfactorily mitigate the negative aesthetic impact (both physical and symbolic) of the massive cooling tower and its plume. (While large cooling towers occur with many fossil-fueled plants, I found that the lay public generally sees a tower as a symbol of nuclear power and twentieth-century technology.)

Because aesthetics is normally considered so late in the siting process, a situation may result in which any negative impact must be weighed against the substantial investment already committed to the project. It is not surprising that insurmountable mitigation problems can result from failure to consider socioeconomic impacts earlier in the assessment of the costs and benefits of alternative sites while there is still ample flexibility in plant location as well as in plant design (McCoy and Singer, 1980). Aesthetic impacts of large energy facilities are closely related to the appropriateness of location and may not be easily amenable to mitigation through design modifications. In the following sections, I describe my general approach to aesthetic analysis and the nature of the aesthetic impacts in Greene County that were deemed beyond feasible mitigation.

ASSESSMENT OF THE VISUAL RESOURCE AND
AESTHETIC IMPACT ANALYSIS

NEPA has provided much of the motivation for developing tools to assess impacts on the visual resource. In one of its lesser-known clauses, the act explicitly calls for more work in these areas:

> To the fullest extent possible . . . all agencies of
> the Federal Government shall . . . identify and
> develop methods and procedures in consultation with
> the Council on Environmental Quality established by
> Title II of this Act, which will insure that
> presently unquantified environmental amenities and
> values may be given appropriate consideration in
> decision making along with economic and technical
> considerations. (Sect. 102[2][B])

Since the passage of the law in 1969, researchers in a
variety of assessment tasks developed many methodologies
for incorporating these unquantified values into local,
state, and national decision-making processes (Elsner and
Smardon, 1979; Zube, Brush, and Fabos, 1975). Most
methodologies attempt to provide systematic and objective
information concerning the assessment of the visual
quality of landscapes and of the visual impacts resulting
from proposed land-use activities.

Aesthetic Analysis Defined

Aesthetic analysis, as used here, means analysis of
the quality of the visual resource. Aesthetics is more
than visual, but the majority of our sensory information
regarding the impact of a nuclear power plant is visual in
origin. Aesthetics has to deal with how people feel
(consider "anesthesia," the lack of feeling) about their
environment. In assessing the impact of a proposed
nuclear power plant, separating attitudes about the health
and safety of nuclear power per se from public concerns
(feelings) about visual impacts was a major problem. I
tried to isolate those attitudes through preference
testing, but I recognized that these attitudes are beyond
present testing techniques and do ultimately affect how
the visual environment is perceived and interpreted.

The assessment of landscape visual quality is more
than an inventory of its scenic amenities. First,
amenities imply something agreeable--enjoyable "extras"
where and when they can be found. We live in the visual
landscape. It is the stage for our daily activities, not
just a passive backdrop for them. We are the central
participants, not the peripheral observers. The quality
of that stage actively interacts with the quality of our
lives. Second, scenic resources imply more than just the
value of certain selected, limited views from fixed
viewpoints. The visual experience appreciated while
driving along a scenic highway is more than enjoying the
designated scenic overlooks. A third concern is quality.
To professional aesthetic analysts in a formal sense and
to lay observers in an informal, nonconscious way, scenic
quality relates to the analysis of design relationships--

principles of scale, proportion, unity, harmony, color, form, and texture. Because there is no ultimate scientific or reductionist way to determine whether something is well designed, there is no purely objective way of inventorying those landscapes that are beautiful. The state of the art (and it is most certainly partially an art) is, however, well beyond the idiosyncratic "beauty is in the eye of the beholder." Visual resource analysts have documented surprising uniformity in landscape preferences.

Traditional Approaches

The analytical approach I used in the Greene County case modified and incorporated aspects of four traditional methodologies used to assess landscape quality for application in decision making. These approaches have evolved over the past ten to fifteen years, with the narrowness, shortcomings, and general dissatisfactions of the early approaches stimulating the development of improved methodologies. Aspects of each general approach have survived, and their simultaneous application as a comprehensive set of landscape assessment tools increases the credibility of the conclusion of a study when congruence of findings occurs among the different approaches. Overreliance on any one approach betrays the very complexity and subjectivity of the assessment of the visual resource. The nature and origin of the four approaches are briefly described in the following.

Expert opinion. Lacking models to assess landscape quality and at the same time not trusting the general population to make aesthetic judgments, decision makers turned first to the opinions of experts in visual quality: environmental planners, landscape architects, and architects. The use of expert opinion as representative of or as surrogate for public preference has been empirically supported in a few studies but, more frequently, questioned in others (Bukyoff et al.., 1978; S. Kaplan, 1979; Posner, 1973; Zube, Brush, and Fabos, 1975). Experts are inclined and trained to see the landscapes differently from other people; presumably this is an important aspect of their expertise. Professionally, the expert is caught in a bind between merely reflecting public values and leading those values. This is not to say that professional judgment has no place in landscape assessment. That judgment needs to be clearly labeled as personal and subjective, however, and, as such, combined with other sources of information to give the decision maker a comprehensive perspective of the problem at hand.

Modelling analysis. Distrust of the high subjectivity and possibly elitist nature of this intuitive, expert approach led decision makers to encourage the development of supposedly more objective

modelling approaches that are based on precise
measurements of landscape attributes and analyzed with
sophisticated statistical techniques. This was an attempt
by researchers in landscape quality to remove entirely
their own biases from their analyses. The analyses, based
on attempts to model or quantify the landscape's values,
rely chiefly on assessing those landscape features that
reflect the public's assumed preferences. These
preferences can be empirically derived and generalized
from sample population groups. For example, the public
prefers strong differences in relative topographic relief
within a landscape, a rather obvious conclusion. Some
models are more subtle and heuristic; others, although
they can be supported empirically through regression
equations, lack theoretical foundation (S. Kaplan, 1979).
     Procedures to assess landscape quality by use of
modelling techniques frequently are misnamed "quantitative
evaluations." As such, they carry an aura of objectivity.
Although we can measure and scale many features and
relationships of the landscape and can use the results
effectively in a comparative, qualitative sense, we must
remember that analysis of the visual resource is
subjective at its heart: we cannot escape that and should
not feel compelled to try. The ordinal numbers
researchers attach during their analyses are merely
convenient, useful labels for the landscape aesthetic
variables they represent. The researcher experiences
problems when he or she forgets the qualitative,
comparative application of these assumed numbers and
begins to draw conclusions by multiplying, differentially
weighting, or summing numbers reflective of disparate
elements in varied landscapes. Another problem is that
such studies do not normally deal with the ephemeral
landscape--the changing clouds, sky colors, seasonal
vegetation and color, weather, animal life, or other
dynamic aspects of the landscape. Often it is these
changes in an otherwise common landscape that make it so
endearing.
     Preference approach. Currently, aesthetic analysts
are moving toward public preference approaches because of
the increasing emphasis on decision makers to consider
public opinion and because it is believed that complex
models merely point out the obvious, justify previous
conclusions, and hide the inescapable subjectivity of the
field behind a curtain of statistics. The preference
approach employs techniques for eliciting preferences of
lay individuals for differing landscapes and for project
alternatives in a given landscape (Kaplan and Kaplan,
1978).
     This third approach bespeaks a basic respect for
people. It recognizes that people are forced daily to
assimilate huge quantities of information from their
visual world and act according to that processed
information. People know and care about their immediate

surroundings. They have feelings and opinions about changes that might affect them directly. They want, therefore, to understand and to be involved in decisions regarding proposed changes in their environment. The researcher need only be creative and sympathetic with the layperson to extract this information for use in decision making. Techniques need to be efficient, brief, and simple. The participant should not have to wrestle with abstract concepts of aesthetics. Well-designed research strategies need to be nonthreatening and can be enjoyable for a large cross-section of participants. Preference techniques do capture underlying expectations, biases, cultural norms, perceptual abilities, past experiences, etc. but do not capture them explicitly.

Not all researchers in landscape assessment have enthusiastically embraced preference testing. Many feel that expressed judgments are arbitrary, idiosyncratic, and even random. To hold what they deem a plebiscite, a search for popular consensus, would debase the theoretical underpinnings of aesthetic analysis. S. Kaplan (1979) responds to this criticism:

> Hidden in this fear is a profound irony. It implies that there is no basic consistency, no underlying pattern characteristic of preference judgments. Without such an underlying basis, however, aesthetics becomes trivialized. If aesthetics is not an expression of some basic and underlying aspects of the human mind, then it is hard to see why it is of more than passing significance. It is reduced to mere decoration as opposed to being something with pervasive importance. In the concern to preserve aesthetics untarnished, it makes it at the same time inconsequential . . . . Perception and preference, for that matter, are no more variable than any other aspect of human experience and human behavior. As with everything else, there is regularity and there is variability. As with anything else, identifying and understanding that regularity is crucial to appropriate policy and decision making.

A variation of the preference approach gaining acceptance among some researchers is the "bidding game" (Adams et al., 1980). In this technique, a questionnaire is used to determine the aesthetic impact by measuring the maximum amount people would be willing to pay to avert (or the minimum they would be willing to accept in compensation for) those changes a project would bring to their visual environment. A basic philosophical problem surrounds the use of bidding games: a rational, economic approach based on pricing commodity resources is used to price noncommodity resources whose value and essence are derived not from their scarcity but from their context and the way they are perceived. This philosophical problem is compounded further because bidders are being asked about hypothetical payments (i.e., their hypothetical behavior). Assessment of "placeness." Emerging is a fourth general approach, a move toward techniques that elicit from the public the reasons for valuing even common landscapes as special. Most researchers would agree that a first step in landscape assessment is to identify those areas of unique scenic quality, the landscapes of national value. This is conceptually analogous to the protection of endangered species. In the sense of preserving diversity, the argument is normally sound and fairly well-grounded legally. Uniqueness, per se, however, does not make a landscape necessarily worth special protection. In terms of value and importance through scarcity alone, the protection of unique landscapes again reduces aesthetic analysis to an economic pricing system (Kaplan, 1979). People can imbue commonplace landscapes with special personal or community values just as they can do so with heirlooms, neighborhoods, or even old oak trees. Standard economic analyses do not readily capture these special and noneconomic values. People respond with equal fascination to relatively common puppies, kittens, and bunnies as to rarer lion cubs or progeny of unique, exotic species. Similarly, humans have a noneconomic need for certain common landscapes, such as the English garden or park.

Uniqueness is intimately tied to several other ideas. Bosselman (1979) and others (Gussow, 1972) have suggested that the most important quality of a landscape is its holistic "specialness" rather than any combination of discrete scenic attributes. It is this sense of special place that people, with some uniformity, say they experience there that they cannot experience in other places. People are responding to some combination of complex characteristics of their past personal, social, and cultural experience that, when coupled with the landscape at hand, elicits an appreciation and attachment beyond the observable features of the landscape. Normally, these feelings are not closely related to the visual scarcity of the landscape. These special local places can form an integrated image or pattern at the regional scale that expert judgments or complex landscape attribute models can miss completely.

Another related aspect of uniqueness is specialness in terms of accessibility. A seemingly commonplace landscape can still be unique by being the only one available given certain constraints (normally, time or money). (The opposite can also make a place special--a park valued not solely for its beauty but also for its difficult accessibility.) In most conventional scenic landscape inventories, neither situation would be considered in qualifying a given area for inclusion. These examples underscore the need for sensitive research strategies to dissect the intuitive public preferences in ways that reveal how people function or would like to

68

function in the landscapes under question.

AESTHETIC IMPACT ANALYSIS OF THE GREENE COUNTY NUCLEAR POWER PLANT

The following recounts my application of the aforementioned tools of visual analysis in assessing the aesthetic impact of the proposed Greene County Nuclear Power Plant. The framework for their application centers on the idea that the aesthetic experience depends on an environmental stimulus (the landscape that is there to be seen) and the background (ethnic and demographic characteristics, expectations, past experiences) and context (physical and behavioral) of those doing the seeing. The analysis encompassed the viewer's immediate geographical setting, expectations, attitudes about nuclear power, and degree of affinity for and familiarity with the local landscape as well as a more detailed study of the historical and cultural context to assess the sense of place--the perceived uniqueness of the mid-Hudson River Valley. From this case study a generalized scoping procedure will be suggested and implications and applicability for more common landscapes will be explored.

Evaluation of the Extant Scenic Quality

This facet of the aesthetic impact analysis examined the scenic quality of the area--the landscape to be seen-- surrounding the two proposed sites, Cementon and Athens. It was an attempt to identify quality and to assess the values placed on what exists in the area; this meant discovering the landscape's overall integrity, the fabric that holds it together holistically for inhabitants and other users. Only by understanding this integrity can decision makers determine where something best fits into the landscape or whether it fits at all. The analysis used a combination of expert opinion, assessment of the sense of place, and modelling of the landscape's scenic quality.

To varying degrees, all landscapes are both resilient and adaptive. By understanding the landscape's integrity, we can assess how well it can absorb change without losing its essential sensory character. As a stage for human life, the landscape changes and expresses the new values and tastes of its changing users. I tried to determine what changes would occur in the mid-Hudson River Valley landscape as it accepted the addition of the proposed plant.

I turned first to identify those things both natural and man-made in this landscape that enhanced its coherence, its legibility, and its sense of harmony. I identified those areas of scenic distinction that were clearly of national importance. This relatively small landscape is unusual because of several nationally

significant vistas. In addition, the basic elements of
the nineteenth-century American landscape that give the
area its charm and grandeur remain intact. These elements
include historic homes, neighborhoods, and buildings;
village industries; scenic mountain streams, waterfalls,
forests (some virgin), and roads; unique rural and village
ambience; strong topographic enclosure in the valley of a
major American river; and many impressive panoramic views
of the Catskill Mountains and the Hudson River Valley. As
an integrated whole, the valley-mountain-river system
dominates the visual experience. At a more intimate
scale, the remnants of the nineteenth-century character
and ambience prevail, although they have been severely
damaged in places.

Using the criteria developed in the Connecticut River
Valley studies of lay preferences for varying landscapes
(Zube, 1973a, 1973b, 1974, 1976; Zube, Pitt, and Anderson,
1974), ORNL colleagues and I developed a computer-assisted
model of the scenic quality surrounding the two sites in
order to quantify, in part, the scenic quality of the
landscapes where potential viewers would stand. The
findings of the modelling efforts were inconclusive in
suggesting which plant location might be preferable.

To simulate the changes in the landscape that would
occur with the construction of the proposed plant at
either site, an artist at ORNL superimposed the plant and
its visible plume (both appropriately scaled and
positioned from calculations) on photographs from critical
viewing locations. A computer model (Dunn et al., 1978)
of a broad variety of visible plume possibilities provided
the artist with appropriate wind directions and dimensions
for a typical plume (not a worst case, yet still highly
visible). Visible plumes consist of water droplets; and
their presence depends on hourly, as well as daily and
seasonal, variations in the meteorology of a site. The
output of the model also helped to characterize the
frequency and extent of the visible plume throughout the
year. On these same photographs, the artist simulated the
impacts with alternative cooling tower and plume
configurations. These simulations included the use of two
116-meter (380-foot) natural-draft towers, four 52-meter
(171-foot) fan-assisted, natural-draft towers, and three
18-meter (59-foot) circular, mechanical-draft towers. The
aquatic ecologists at ORNL believed that there would be
unacceptable impacts if once-through cooling were used as
an option (NRC, 1979). Environmental Protection Agency
constraints that were in effect during PASNY's application
also precluded the use of once-through cooling technology.

With the help of the simulated plant and plume
combinations and alternative cooling tower and plume
configurations, I assessed and described from each
critical location around the two sites the projected
aesthetic impacts of the project as designed, including
the engineering changes for mitigating the size of the

tower and the plume. I used traditional criteria for visual analysis such as changes in scale, proportion, form, color, balance, and unity. I also described the changes I believed likely to occur in the area's cultural and historical ambience from each plant location and design alternative. Based solely on my professional judgment, this analysis using traditional aesthetic criteria clearly pointed to the Cementon location as being more vulnerable than Athens to disruption from the construction of the power plant under any of the design options. The FES contains the complete assessments and the details and maps of the computer-assisted scenic quality modelling study (NRC, 1979).

Visual Preference Survey

The landscape is more than the aggregation of its component parts. The variations in individual scenic preferences could never be totally explained, even by a more exhaustive set of relevant landscape variables than I used in the scenic quality modelling study. Landscape is a social resource, and direct social appraisals of landscapes yield greater analytical validity than the sole use of expert opinion and/or graphic or computer simulations of proposed landscape changes. To assess the perceived whole, therefore, I combined a visual preference approach with modelling and descriptive techniques. I based the approach on a methodology developed by Rachel and Stephen Kaplan, environmental psychologists at The University of Michigan. They and their colleagues have successfully applied variations of this approach to a wide array of respondent groups in different environmental situations (Gallagher, 1977; Hammitt, 1978; Herzog, Kaplan, and Kaplan, 1976; Kaplan, Kaplan, and Wendt, 1972; Levin, 1977) and found it to be reliable, valid, and theoretically meaningful. The important point to policy makers and decision makers was that the approach offered opportunities not only to measure the preferences of people but also to begin to understand the underlying perceptual patterns and processes contributing to their preferences.
The approach was modelled, in part, after Hammitt's (1978) study of visual preferences of recreationists in bog environments. The survey consisted of a photoquestionnaire of eight pages: a cover sheet of brief instructions, five pages of black-and-white photographs, and two pages of textual questions. Research studies in perception (Daniel and Boster, 1977; Kaplan, 1972, 1974; Kaplan, Kaplan, and Deardorff, 1974) support the use of black-and-white photographs as valid representations of real landscapes. There are obvious logistical problems with taking subjects to the sites if one could (and the weather, lighting, subject energy and enthusiasm, etc. never changed); however, the respondents still would not

have a power plant to look at in the proposed locations.
Researchers have tried tethering weather balloons at the
height of the top of proposed cooling towers and stacks,
but this hardly replicates the bulk of a tower or even
suggests the presence and dynamics of a visible plume. In
this age of photojournalism and television, people are
used to two-dimensional pictures as portrayals of their
three-dimensional world. Using photographs as surrogates
for the landscape, Clamp (1980) found that

>ordinary people make inferences far beyond the
>information that is immediately apparent visually.
>The photographs were always described as real places
>rather than visual patterns, and individuals usually
>disregarded the specific choice of camera viewpoint
>and considered each view as an example of a
>particular kind of landscape.

Herzog, Kaplan, and Kaplan (1976) similarly found that

>when one does present photographs of familiar places,
>the effect is to trigger the individual's concept or
>internal representation of that place. Thus, the
>reaction is not to the presented stimulus per se but
>to a distillation of experience and knowledge about
>the place depicted.

With these insights in mind, it is not surprising that
R. Kaplan (1979) also found that the size and quality of
reproduction or resolution of the photographs are not all
that critical in preference testing.
     The power plant at the Cementon site was to be
nestled in among three existing cement plants. It is this
industrial setting that the utility used as its argument
in support of the compatibility of the power plant in the
Cementon location. I wanted to see if people viewed the
cement plants differently from how they might view the
proposed power plant. Using middle- to long-distance
photographs of local landscapes in the mid-Hudson River
Valley, an artist superimposed either cooling towers and
plumes or cement plants on 16 photographs.[2] We included
the Cementon and Athens sites in this treatment, along
with other plausible but not proposed locations. The
result was eight groups of three photographs each (the
actual scene as photographed, the same scene with a
cooling tower and plume superimposed, and the same scene
with a cement plant superimposed) and 16 other
photographs. The 40 photographs were reduced to 5 x 7.5
centimeters (2 x 3 inches), randomized, placed eight
photographs to a page, and printed by an offset process.
The power plant was represented by a cooling tower and
plume because, at the distances represented in the
photographs, they would be the dominant sources of visual
impact.

I chose cement plants as a comparable intrusion into
various local environments because they represent heavy
industry, make sense in terms of the actual local economic
base (e.g., oil refineries or steel factories would have
been inappropriate), and represent a taxable industry
(whereas a fossil-fueled power plant might not, just as
the proposed nuclear plant did not). Although a fossil-
fueled plant probably would also have a cooling tower, I
assumed that laypeople might not readily discern the
difference between a nuclear plant and a fossil plant with
both portrayed at the pictures sizes used and the
landscape distances represented.

By using the "cement plant"/"cooling tower and
plume"/"existing scene" triads, I was partially able to
control for biases regarding nuclear power. Responses to
the textual comments showed that from the valid responses
to the photoquestionnaires, nearly 80 percent of the
people answering the relevant questions were opposed to
the construction of a nuclear power plant at either
Cementon or Athens. Nearly 60 percent opposed a fossil-
fueled plant at either site. The cover page of the survey
informed respondents that "some [pictures] have been
retouched by artists to suggest possible future
developments such as the operation of new cement
facilities or cooling towers like those associated with
electrical power generating plants" (NRC, 1979). I made
no mention of nuclear power on the cover page. The
significance of a cooling tower as a symbol of nuclear
power was, of course, made abundantly clear (if not
already perceived) to any observer of the mass media after
the accident at Three Mile Island. It should be noted
that the visual preference survey in Greene County was
completed before this hypersensitization occurred.

Respondents were instructed to preview the
photoquestionnaire quickly to get a feel for what the
photographs were about and then to indicate their opinion
of each photograph by circling one of five numbers below
each photo. I used a five-point rating scale (1 = "not at
all," 5 = "very much") and asked each respondent to "rate
each photograph as to how much you like it." During June
of 1978, a colleague and I approached potential
respondents on the local streets, in restaurants, in
stores, and in parks. A women's club and workers at a
cement plant constituted two large groups that were
interviewed. We found respondents willing to participate,
especially once they realized the survey contained mostly
pictures. This enthusiasm for photographs is consistent
with the other applications of this approach by the
Kaplans and their colleagues. This preference-testing
technique was neither too difficult for the young nor too
demeaning for the mature. As R. Kaplan (1979) reported,
the positive reactions to it are not restricted to "the
lazy, uneducated, disenfranchised, or otherwise excluded
groups."

With 154 valid responses, the survey had a balanced distribution of respondents by age, sex, income, occupation, education, duration of residence in the region, location of childhood residence, and present residence. The survey responses were divided into 24 respondent subgroups (included among these, for example, were "strongly antinuclear," "weakly antinuclear," and "not antinuclear") from the original sample by using the demographic information supplied by each individual or from the nature of the answers to specific questions. I made statistical cross-tabulations of subgroup pairs on all the photographs and on the pairs of responses in the case of picture triads (e.g., "as is" landscape rating vs. "with cement plant" rating, "with cooling tower" vs. "with cement plant," and "with cooling tower" vs. "as is").

A serious concern was that the respondents might be reacting to more than the mere presence in the photograph of the cooling towers and plumes or the cement plants. A factor analysis of responses to the eight photographic triads confirmed my hypothesis that the respondents considered the existing landscapes and the cooling tower scenes unidimensionally, i.e., when a cooling tower, for example, was in a picture, it appeared to be the major influence on the respondents' ratings. The hypothesis was null for a comparable analysis regarding the cement plants. One can assume that multiple influences probably affected preference ratings for the cement plants. Responses to photographs of real cement plants were approximately the same as those to the superimposed photographs, suggesting that the superimposition process itself did not influence the responses. That the cement plants (real and superimposed) were rated consistently and significantly higher than the cooling tower pictures by all subgroups strongly suggests a distinct tolerance of or aesthetic preference for the presence of the cement plants. One hypothesis that, in part, may explain this difference in ratings is that local people are familiar with the cement plants and have learned to accommodate them. In some cases, the people are employed or have relatives employed at the plants. Cooling towers and plumes represent something totally unfamiliar in the landscape. Whether cooling towers are less preferred because of their size, their lack of scenic attributes, their nonfamiliarity, or all of these is impossible to infer from this survey. Because the "not antinuclear" subgroup (Table 3.1) responded with a significantly higher preference for cement plants, too, one can assume that more than an antinuclear power stance contributed to the lower preference ratings. Details and a discussion of the visual preference survey results can be found in the FES (NRC, 1979).

As a further check on the results of the survey, I interviewed local officials and residents and searched

TABLE 3.1
Comparison of responses to photographs of cement plants, cooling towers and plumes, and existing landscapes by respondent groups

Group	Number of Respondents	Statistical Measure	Photograph Subject			
			Existing Landscape	Landscape with Superimposed Cement Plant	Real Cement Plant	Landscape with Cooling Tower
All respondents	154	X^1	3.575^2	2.924	2.722	1.891
		Range³	4.641-1.900	4.395-1.706	4.313-2.007	2.132-1.464
Not antinuclear respondents	27	X	3.453	3.212	3.184	2.644
		Range	4.462-1.840	4.346-1.889	4.115-2.423	3.280-2.115
Antinuclear respondents	105	X	3.601	2.865	2.626	1.604
		Range	4.683-1.823	4.405-1.667	4.355-1.919	1.992-1.315
Strongly antinuclear respondents	42	X	3.615	2.632	2.406	1.235
		Range	4.857-1.667	4.405-1.381	4.512-1.690	1.476-1.048

[1] X = mean of each photograph's mean recorded by that respondent group for that subset of photographs.

[2] Numbers are responses to instructions to "rate each photograph as to how much you like it," with 1 = "not at all" and 5 = "very much."

[3] Range = derived from the range of the respondent group's mean for each photograph within that subset of photographs.

newspaper files for indicators of attitudes toward the
local visual environment. From this information and the
survey, I concluded that the people most likely to view
the proposed nuclear power plant can be described thusly:

1. They are likely to be strongly opposed to large,
   natural-draft cooling towers and plumes in their
   landscape.
2. They have apparently adjusted through familiarity
   or other means to the presence of cement plants
   in their landscape.
3. They perceive their area of the Hudson River
   Valley as having the highest scenic quality of
   any area between New York City and Albany.
4. They value and frequent the historic and cultural
   sites of the area.
5. They perceive the proposed facility at Athens to
   have less aesthetic impact than would the
   facility at Cementon.

Historical and Cultural Context

In this analysis, it quickly became apparent that the
mid-Hudson River Valley was of special aesthetic
significance because of its historical and cultural
context, in addition to the aesthetic factors that persist
today. I used an analysis that covered the period from
colonial times to the present and incrementally narrowed
in scale from the larger New England landscape to the
actual importance and quality of one specific view. In
each focal step, the emphasis was on uniqueness and
special qualities integrated into the general landscape.
A cumulative pattern of unique cultural qualities of
pivotal historic importance emerged in the analysis.
    The early colonists considered nature as something to
fear and subdue. Jeffersonian America viewed nature as
something to embrace and transform in order to cultivate a
new agrarian country-gentleman lifestyle. Into this
idyllic view rushed the Erie Canal, the steamboat, and the
locomotive (all reaching their earliest maturity in the
commercial activity of the Hudson River Valley). Romantic
America in the second decade of the nineteenth century had
to deal with a new force--rapidly increasing
industrialization. It seemed to make both the cities less
livable and the agrarian ideal achievable; it made the
hinterlands accessible for both escape and exploitation.
These two opposing effects of technology were a chief
source of the tension pervading the immediate antebellum
decade and the source of the county's first indigenous
fine art: the writings of Emerson, Thoreau, Whitman, Poe,
Bryant, Dana, Melville, and Hawthorne; the photography of
Watkins and O'Sullivan; the landscape designs of Downing
and Olmstead; and the landscape paintings of the Hudson
River School. This corpus of art gave America its first

cultural identity to complement its emerging industrial
identity.

James Fenimore Cooper's Leatherstocking Tales and
Washington Irving's Tales of Sleepy Hollow and Rip Van
Winkle, this country's first reputable novels, were
inspired by and permanently grounded in the Catskills'
wilderness setting. Artist Thomas Cole was the first to
record this landscape in a vivid, bold new style on his
realist canvases that became the foundation of the Hudson
River School. New York City grew with the nation and by
the 1840s had become a business community capable of
providing the patronage needed to support artistic
endeavors. The romantic movement that William Cullen
Bryant and Thomas Cole catalyzed in 1825 helped America
break both from European themes in its art and from
considering nature as a liability. For the next 50 years,
romanticism dominated the art, politics, and religion of
America. We still feel its influence in novels,
subdivision layouts, park and residential landscape
designs, photography, poetry, wilderness preservation, and
back-to-the-land movements. The conceptual theories
behind all these attitudes found their initial inspiration
and development in the mid-Hudson River Valley in the mid-
nineteenth century. A 16-kilometer (10-mile) radius
around the proposed power plant at Cementon would take in
dozens of the scenic views and picturesque areas that were
eventually transferred to canvases now hanging in the
country's major museums and art galleries.

Portraying nature's newly perceived glories and
discerning and interpreting nature's part in the
revelation of divine plans for the country's immediate
future consumed artists' spirits throughout the romantic
period. The artists saw the American landscape as a New
World landscape, one unavailable as an inspirational
source to European artists. Although the romantic
movement in America had the same philosophical source as
it did in Europe, the visual manifestations of it were
quite different and were directly related to this
country's boundless forests and unnamed mountains. A
nationalistic and religious mythology infused the Hudson
River School paintings (Powell, 1980). The cardinal
belief of the romanticist was that technology and the
country's vast land resources would coalesce into a unique
civilization--the climax of Western civilization--that
would spread across the continent as America's "Manifest
Destiny." It was the mid-Hudson River Valley that
provided the combination of natural splendor and
technological advances that inspired the leading figures
of the romantic movement. The New World people would live
in a land not of the Jeffersonian country gentleman's
dream but of a middle area, a compromise between agrarian
ideal and technological reality (Marx, 1964). Few, if
any, at the time truly foresaw what the dimensions of that
technological reality might encompass only 10 to 20 years

later (robber-baron capitalism, mass production, and urban
blight). The tension between the agrarian dream and
emerging industrialism spawned a romantic motif given
image by the landscape painters. This image was one of an
Arcadian middle ground where man blissfully lived part in
the city and part in the country (a suburban illusion many
still pursue).

The public was looking for leaders to explain the new
meaning of a nation dividing itself politically and of a
paradise being invaded. The landscape painters arose as
the popular cultural leaders of the day, giving the public
what they wanted to hear and see. Civilization was not
merely stable but was beginning to flower into a "New
Eden," and all Americans were the "New Adams" (Huntington,
1966, 1980). The American nation, as they popularized it,
was on the threshold of a "New Genesis."

From this group of Hudson River School painters
emerged one crucial leader in this critical decade.
Frederic Edwin Church (1826-1900) was the most popular and
best-known painter in the country in the 1850s and 1860s.
Americans today who were not familiar with Church learned
of him in October of 1979, when his painting Icebergs,
which had been lost for over a century, was sold for $2.5
million, the most money ever paid at an auction for a
painting by an American artist and, at the time, the
third-highest amount ever paid for any painting.

John Wilmerding, Curator of American Painting and the
Senior Curator at the National Gallery of Art, claims
Church was "intellectually most representative of American
cultural attitudes in the middle decade of the century
. . . [and he] distilled the national vision and gave it
visibility" (Wilmerding, 1978b). Life magazine called
Church "the Michelangelo of landscape art."

Church put his considerable talent into painting the
icons of his time--archetypal New World images such as
South American volcanoes (through trips inspired by Von
Humboldt's Cosmos), the wilderness of the north woods
(through trips suggested by Thoreau), North Atlantic
icebergs, Niagara Falls, and pyrotechnic sunsets. He was
a cousin of Frederick Law Olmstead (co-designer of Central
Park and the father of landscape architecture in America)
and was Thomas Cole's only pupil. He learned landscape
painting at Cole's home and studio (a National Historic
Landmark) in Catskill, 8 kilometers (5 miles) from the
proposed facility at Cementon.

Church's paintings and wise investments brought him
enough wealth (while still in his early thirties) to buy
some choice land atop a steep hill above the east bank of
the Hudson River, opposite Catskill. On this site he
applied his design genius for the next 30 years in
constructing a mansion and grounds that exist today as one
of the few surviving Victorian estates still in a setting
comparable to its nineteenth-century environs. Art and
architectural historians have called it the most

spectacularly sited mansion in the country and termed it the best site in the eastern United States (NRC, 1979). Even though the estate, known as Olana (Persian for "our place on high"), is located 10 kilometers (6 miles) from the Cementon site, the proposed plant would have been very visible directly in the center of the major view from Olana. The New York Times (1966) editorially referred to Olana as "the essence of the Hudson River School of painting . . . the authentic aesthetic expression of a unique moment in art and time." An article in Saturday Review (Kuh, 1965) referred to the Olana site as a "symbol, even the apotheosis, of all Hudson River landscapes." Theodore Stebbins (1978) said that now Olana "is the best place to feel the spirit of the artist coming together with nature as it was in the nineteenth century." Its uniqueness is like the recently restored gardens of Claude Monet at Giverny in that the whole environment of the painter, as he experienced it, is still intact: home, furniture, setting, views, library, and landscape. In a word, the ambience still survives.

Of the setting and ambience at Olana, Barbara Novak (1978), art historian at Barnard and Columbia Universities, said that

> the Cementon-Athens area is the heart of American nineteenth-century culture. If anyone were to ask me to pinpoint on the entire continent . . . one area of landscape that the nation as a whole and the federal government specifically should designate as a national landmark, as a step toward the preservation of our American past and culture, I would choose this area. (Novak, 1978a)

Wilmerding (1978a) joins Novak in this regard: "portions of the Hudson should be kept as pure as Yosemite and this is one of them. There are some crucial places which should be forever wild--one can fairly argue that this is one."

An aspect of the ambience of Olana is its landscaped views--the southwesterly view in particular. Architectural historians Goss (1973) and Scully (1965) believe that Church's efforts to take advantage of this view with masterly landscaping according to the theories of picturesque design rank second only to his paintings in Church's creative legacy. Architectural Digest columnist and former Harper's editor Russel Lynes called it "the finest view in the eastern United States" (Huntington, 1978). Because of the southwesterly view, Olana was sited atop its particular hill and oriented directly toward the view. Scully (1978) says, simply, "The whole point of Olana is the view." Contemporary landscape artist Alan Gussow (1979a) summarizes,

Suffice it to say that Frederic Church had travelled

the world over and selected the vista from the Olana
Hill as the emblematic scenic view. In other words,
it was the archetypal nineteenth-century idea of what
was beautiful in landscape.

Church has named this view "Bend in the River" (Goss,
1973). The Church family oriented their daily lives to ·
the enjoyment of it. Because of the bend in the river, it
is as if the house were floating over the river; one can
look directly downstream (Figure 3.2). Church painted
this view at least 35 times and commissioned a local
painter, Arthur Parton, to do three paintings of it.
Church also built a lake, in part, to enhance this view by
providing the classical middle-ground water accent. He
created the total landscape architectural sequences and
the architectural sequences of the house to climax at the
framing of that view. One painting of that view (an oil
sketch, Figure 3.3) has emerged today with the critical
blessing of John Howat, the Curator of American Painting
at the Metropolitan Museum of Art: "[it] comes as close
to perfection as anything done by American artists
painting in the field" (Howat, 1972).
     Church did not merely find a beautiful site and build
his house there. He found a beautiful site and created a
three-dimensional painting with stone, wood, glass, trees,
bushes, and lawn. It is in the highest romantic tradition
to create the views you wish to emphasize--to enhance the
natural. When rheumatoid arthritis left Church unable to
paint for the last 18 years of his life, he turned to
landscape architecture, designing in three dimensions at
Olana, with the aesthetic sensibilities, passion, and
genius of one of the country's greatest landscape
painters. This fact alone makes Olana a unique treasure
to the landscape architecture profession.
     Of course, the Cementon site has not entirely escaped
the effects of modern technology. The power plant there
was to be nestled among three existing cement plants.
This setting was the basis of the utility's argument that
the power plant was compatible with the Cementon location.
In spite of the cement plants, the editors of Outdoor
World (1978) saw fit to use a photograph of the present-
day southwesterly view from Olana as the dustjacket of
their 1978 book, Rivers of North America. Through my
analysis, I found that most people interviewed (local
residents as well as art historians and representatives of
the mass media) acknowledge the presence of the cement
plants as unfortunate but praise the area's pastoral
intactness relative to the rest of the present-day quality
of the Hudson River Valley. Repeated mention of the
Hudson Highlands and the view from Olana as being superior
to any other stretches of the Hudson River Valley clearly
suggest that this area of the river is an endangered
survivor of the past century's urban and industrial
development. The Hudson River's diversity, the source of

Figure 3.2   "Bend in the River" view from Olana looking to the southwest over the Hudson River. Church painted this view at least 35 times. A 37-room mansion, Olana, is a National Historic Landmark and a New York State Historic Site open to the pubic since 1967 under the supervision of the New York State Office of Parks and Recreation.

Figure 3.3 Winter Landscape from Olana (c. 1879) by Frederic E. Church (1826-1900). Oil on paper, 11 5/8 x 18 1/2 inches. By permission of the New York State Office of Parks and Recreation, Division for Historic Preservation, Bureau of Historic Sites, Olana State Historic Site, Taconic Region.

its charm, depends on such threatened cultural remnants
being protected against insensitive development. Art
historians and laypeople who were queried voiced a clear
"devastating" to the plume and tower of the power plant as
depicted in Figure 3.4[3] and in alternative schemes they
were shown.

There are other quite notable views in the area. The
panorama from the escarpment of the Catskills, for
example, can be seen at the site of the Catskill Mountain
House (Figure 3.1), the country's first mountain resort
and hub of the country's first scenic hiking trails. The
proposed power plant and its cooling tower plume would
have been 11 kilometers (7 miles) away; but when seen from
an elevation nearly 970 meters higher, they would have
become the focus of the panorama. This view, too, is
steeped in historic and romantic tradition; James Fenimore
Cooper used Natty Bumpo and Hawkeye to praise its
splendor.[4]

The area landscape would also be affected in a more
general way. Hudson River Valley residents for the past
three centuries have displayed at least a tacit
understanding of and sensitivity to scale and balance
between natural landforms and man's physical changes on
the landscape. One can see this in the integration of
small farms, orchards, estates, and picturesque riparian
hamlets and towns. It is a visually resilient landscape
that has absorbed some industrial development while
maintaining a definite, almost archetypal, pastoral
romantic ideal. The charm and the dignity of this
landscape are reflections of this balance and diversity.
The integrity of the area is tied to ensuring that any
development is reflective of this harmonic sense of
balance and scale.

The effects on the broader landscape were significant
and important. In terms of NEPA requirements, however,
impacts on the southwesterly view from Olana became
increasingly crucial. Olana's importance lies in giving
the visitor the ability to understand Church's world--
America in one of its most critical decades. The
floodgates of technology opened after the Civil War and
the nation and the land were transformed. Finance
capitalism, the robber-barons, the telegraph, and the
railroads became symbols of the new era. In addition to
these blows to their Arcadian middle-ground conceptions,
the romantics were ignored in the wake of Darwin's
revolutionary concepts. It appeared to society that no
deity had a grand plan for America. The romantic suddenly
had an empty philosophy and no audience.

At Olana, however, the romantic world still lives.
One can see and try to understand the vast panorama of the
American nation looking confidently westward across the
continent with great expectations. To the art historians
who were queried, the construction of the power plant at
the Cementon location would narrow the blinds on this

Figure 3.4 Church's southwesterly "Bend in the River" view with the Greene County Nuclear Power Plant artistically superimposed at the proposed Cementon location.

window to the "minds of our ancestors" (Huntington, 1966, 1980). Art historians emphasize that not many of these windows are left. Jefferson's Monticello, as a window to the federalist period, or the view from Louis XIV's bedroom at Versailles, as a window to the eighteenth-century French monarchy, are in the same category. Church's "window" at Olana appears to be one of the largest and clearest anywhere. Without its nineteenth-century ambience, Olana becomes merely a pretty museum and another historic estate.

The making of views, of creating two-dimensional scenes with a three-dimensional landscape, is historically the essence of the landscape architect's craft. The proposed power plant would severely inhibit the appreciation of one of the few remaining American landscape prototypes, original source material for understanding the beginning of the landscape design profession, and a living embodiment of popular American landscape taste. The human preference is for controlled vistas--tamed nature (Kaplan and Kaplan, 1978). We need wilderness for raw inspiration; but in our art, and for our front yards, local parks, and the daily refreshing of our spirits, we prefer the romantic American landscape prototype: the nineteenth-century Hudson River estate and its derivatives.

Conclusions from the Greene County Analysis

In the aesthetic impact analysis of the Greene County Nuclear Power Plant, vivid symbols of modern technology--a domed reactor containment structure and a monolithic natural-draft cooling tower--played the dominant roles in the conflict with a remnant landscape of America's romantic past. I concluded, and the NRC concurred, that the proposed plant would entail an unacceptable aesthetic impact, beyond mitigation, on certain important local, regional, and national historic, scenic, and cultural resources. In large part, the conclusions are an amplification of these thoughts by John Wilmerding (1978b) of the National Gallery of Art:

> I think there is a subtle but important contrast between preserving the views from Olana and other well-known scenic vistas in this country, related to artistic images or otherwise. While it would have been desirable to save intact the views of Niagara Falls, Kaaterskill Clove, the Catskill Mountain House, the Schuylkill River of Eakin's Max Schmidt, for example, the Olana landscape is unique in being a total synthesis of distinctive scenic beauty and an important artist's original house, studio, collection, and grounds. In other words, we ought to preserve not merely a beautiful view in its own right, but one integrally fused with an extant

embodiment of the very artist's vision which helped to define for Americans a century ago the significance of our national panorama. What I am urging is saving both the view of as well as the view from something. To disrupt one, in my opinion, irrevocably damages the other. What is supremely important here, I believe, is that you preserve an American landscape not just to be seen, but to be understood.

In its proposed location along the mid-Hudson River Valley, the plant fell into conflict with at least four major facets of the area landscape (Dearden, 1980). (1) The towering height and mass of the cooling tower became a man-made focus in a landscape noted for its scenic quality and natural landmarks. With no definite decommissioning plans for dismantling the cooling tower and containment building and returning the site to the preplant landscape, the panoramic natural splendor could in essence be exploited as a nonrenewable resource. Being a threatened and remnant landscape (visually) makes this conflict even more critical. (2) The construction of the plant would have greatly diminished the recreational opportunities abundant in the area. High scenic quality strongly correlates with outdoor recreational satisfaction (Dearden, 1976; Lucas, 1979). One study (Shafer and Meitz, 1979) indicated that recreationists rate the aesthetic experience highest, above even emotional, educational, physical, and social experiences. (3) Construction of the plant would have greatly diminished (physically and symbolically) the opportunity to appreciate the mid-Hudson River Valley landscape as a spiritual resource. A remnant of the nineteenth-century landscape has survived at the foot of the Catskill Mountains. The sunsets and the broad panoramas touched only by sky meeting mountain or water are strong attractions. Residents of the country's largest metropolitan area are only several hours by train or car from this unique area with its potential for solitude, contemplation, and meaning in a grand pastoral setting. (4) The construction of the plant would have greatly diminished (again, physically and symbolically) the opportunity to understand the mid-Hudson River Valley landscape as a historic resource.
Panoramic, uninterrupted views are critical in understanding the romantic designs as manifested at Olana and other estates, at North Lake near the Catskill Mountain House site, and in the Hudson River School paintings. Boundless views in the mid-Hudson River Valley are essential in this twentieth-century period to be able to understand the boundless vision of a generation of mid-nineteenth-century Americans and their antebellum Manifest Destiny.

SCOPING FOR AESTHETIC IMPACT

The basic issue in scoping for aesthetic analysis is the initial estimation of significance. The Greene County analysis demonstrates an extreme in terms of significance; by examining such extremes, however, generally applicable principles are more clearly perceived. These principles underlie an approach quite suitable for analyses of a variety of proposed projects in common as well as unique landscapes.

The Greene County Nuclear Power Plant EIS was produced before the CEQ's scoping requirements became effective. Traditional NRC procedures, however, incorporated much of what the regulations eventually required. The environmental impact assessment (EIA) scoping process, as such, failed in many respects (Peelle, 1979). Early open hearings that the NRC held did not elicit aesthetics as a high-priority impact that concerned the local public (although it was mentioned). Publication of the NRC's DES elicited some public concern over the cursory treatment of potential aesthetic impacts but, again, it was not a high priority. Concern seemed to build during the hearings as PASNY, the prospective developer, presented its supporting arguments. This was very late in the EIA. Yet, aesthetics turned out in the long run to be the critical issue. When the public and the EIA experts fail to identify an issue as critical, what are managers to do in investigating and allocating limited funds and time to the most important environmental concerns?

I suggest an approach that can be used; it was inspired, in part, by artist Alan Gussow (1979b). The best solution is, first, the leadership of a sensitive, broad-minded manager. Ideal would be a person, for instance, who could identify the potential importance of a conflict between a nuclear power plant site and nineteenth-century romanticism. Lacking such a Renaissance manager responsible for scoping the EIA, the systematic employment of the following approach should suffice.

The first step in assessing the potential impacts a proposed project may have on the landscape is to try to understand what is of special value in the general landscape. What is it that holds together the integrity of the landscape? What is the landscape's intrinsic character? In the detailed Greene County analysis, I did this through the mapping of scenic quality by use of models, through the visual preference survey, through my own professional judgment, through discussions with art historians, and through an assessment of the historical and cultural context of the mid-Hudson River Valley. I discovered the area to be rich in variety and historical and symbolic meaning, to have a special sense of place operating at several scales, and to be a landscape quite

intact as a harmonious whole in an otherwise highly
fractured regional landscape. In this initial stage of
scoping, it is important that the manager not turn
prematurely or in a knee-jerk fashion to overreliance on
the belief that strategies for mitigating any impacts on
such a low-priority item as aesthetics will surely evolve
when needed. An attitude of "dealing with them later" can
produce multibillion-dollar impasses, as the Greene County
case established. As stated earlier, the sheer physical
scale of larger energy facilities makes many mitigation
strategies for aesthetic impacts meaningless. The impacts
appear to be best dealt with at the alternative-sites
stage. Alternative cooling options are some of the few
mitigation strategies that make any sense.
    The second step in scoping for critical aesthetic
impacts is the identification of those features in the
landscape that are in need of special protection.[5] What
scenic features have been called out by public designation
or by artistic, folk, or special interest group attention?
In my analysis, the historical and cultural context study
and the visual preference survey addressed this issue
directly. Besides the strong emotional ties to the Hudson
River per se and the valley environs, I discovered the
importance attached to Olana, the Catskill Mountain House
site, a highway bridge over the Hudson River, and to
special historic neighborhoods and districts. This whole
step is analogous to identifying endangered species and
the critical habitats that foster their survival.
    The third step is determining how much change the
landscape in question can undergo without losing the
intrinsic character identified in the first step or
endangering the critical elements identified in the second
step. Is the landscape adaptable enough or resilient
enough to visually absorb a given project? Will the
proposal render the landscape more coherent and
harmonious, or more chaotic? Again analogous to doing an
ecological assessment, the better we understand the
behavior of a given system (in aesthetics, the quality of
the landscape as estimated from the first two steps), the
better we can assess the consequences of perturbations to
it (the visual addition of a proposed project). In the
Greene County case, the NRC staff believed that a
threshold would have been crossed in terms of aesthetic
impact. Licensing the proposed plant would jeopardize the
protection of national scenic treasures and the intrinsic
nineteenth-century character of the mid-Hudson River
Valley landscape.
    What has been suggested in this three-step approach
is fairly obvious and simple. Its successful application
depends on sensitive managers who stress the importance of
early site visits by staff personnel who have the ability
to rely on reconnaissance-level information and
intuitions. Assuming the scoping process has pointed to
aesthetic impacts in a given project as being important,

at the conclusion of the studies the manager needs to evaluate how well the assessments have been conducted and to ascertain that sufficient documentation is available to support the conclusions in an adversary legal process. A fugitive literature plagues aesthetic analysis, but Duffey-Armstrong (1979) has pulled together criteria for assessing the appropriateness and soundness of an analysis. Congruency of conclusions from disparate analytical techniques is a basic objective. Murray and Newman (1979) round out the story with an account of those factors crucial to a sound defense should the assessment be headed for an adversary hearing.

By using the Greene County Nuclear Power Plant EIA as a case study and by giving the background of a little-known discipline, I have presented an approach for scoping aesthetic impacts of proposed projects. My experiences in the Greene County analysis, both through hindsight and precedent, suggest a more confident and facile use of aesthetic assessments in the environmental decision-making process.

The basic intent of NEPA--the importance of considering man's whole environment in decision making--became quite clear in this unprecedented action regarding the licensing of a multibillion-dollar power plant. Beyond boosting the status and recognition of visual resource assessment as an integral component of comprehensive impact analyses, this study demonstrated the necessity for cooperation and communication between the harder and softer sciences. The conclusions demonstrated the importance of addressing "softer" factors earlier in the site selection process. Postponing consideration of their implications may ensure a major and expensive conflict. In evaluating scenic beauty or other "soft" attributes of the quality of life, there is a place for the systematic application of scientific rigor through analyses that are primarily subjective in nature.

REFERENCES

Adams, R. C., et al. (1960), The Visual Aesthetic Impact of Alternative Closed Cycle Cooling Systems. Washington, D.C.: U.S. Nuclear Regulatory Commission.
Bosselman, F. P. (1979). In R. N. L. Andrews (Ed.), Land in America: Commodity or Natural Resource? Lexington, Mass.: Lexington Books.
Bukyoff, G. J., et al. (1978), "Landscape Architects' Interpretations of People's Landscape Preferences," Journal of Environmental Management, 6, 255-262.
Clamp, P. (1976), "Evaluating English Landscapes--Some Recent Developments." Environment and Planning, 8, 80.
Daniel, T. C., and Boster, R. S. (1977), "Measuring Landscape Aesthetics: The Scenic Beauty Estimation

Methods." USDA Forest Service Research Paper RM-167,
    Rocky Mountain Forest and Range Experiment Station,
    Fort Collins, Colorado.
Dearden, P. (1976). In P. Dearden (Ed.), Landscape and
    Habitat Survey. Saanich Municipality, British
    Columbia.
Dearden, P. (1980). Environmental Conservation, 7, 153.
Dobson, J. E. (1980). Geographical Review, 69, 224.
Duffy-Armstrong, M. (1979), "The Generation of Criteria
    for Selecting Analytical Tools for Landscape
    Management." In G. H. Elsner and R. C. Smardon
    (technical coordinators), Proceedings of Our National
    Landscape: A Conference on Applied Techniques for
    Analysis and Management of the Visual Resource.
    Washington, D.C.: U.S. Department of Agriculture.
Dunn, W. E., et al. (1978), Mathematical Modeling of
    Plumes from Proposed Cooling Towers at Seabrook and
    Alternative Sites. Argonne, Ill.: Argonne National
    Laboratory.
Elsner, G. H., and Smardon, R. C. (technical coordinators)
    (1979), Proceedings of Our National Landscape: A
    Conference on Applied Techniques for Analysis and
    Management of the Visual Resource. Washington, D.C.:
    U.S. Department of Agriculture.
Gallagher, T. J. (1977), "Visual Preference for
    Alternative Natural Landscapes." Unpublished
    doctoral dissertation, The University of Michigan.
Goss, P. (1973), "An Investigation of Olana, the Home of
    Frederic Edwin Church, Painter." Unpublished
    doctoral dissertation, Ohio University.
Gussow, A. (Ed.) (1972), The Sense of Place: The Artists
    in the American Land. New York: Saturday Review
    Press.
Gussow, A. (1979a), Prepared Testimony for Case 80006 and
    Nuclear Regulatory Docket 50-549, Power Authority of
    the State of New York, Greene County Nuclear
    Generating Facility. Submitted to the New York State
    Board on Electric Generation Siting and the
    Environment and the U.S. Nuclear Regulatory
    Commission, March 2, 1979.
Gussow, A. (1979b), "Conserving the Magnitude of
    Uselessness: A Philosophical Perspective." In G. H.
    Elsner and R. C. Smardon (technical coordinators),
    Proceedings of Our National Landscape: A Conference
    on Applied Techniques for Analysis and Management of
    the Visual Resource. Washington, D.C.:
    U.S. Department of Agriculture.
Hammitt, W. E. (1978), "Visual and User Preference for a
    Bog Environment." Unpublished doctoral dissertation,
    The University of Michigan.
Herzog, T. R., Kaplan, S., and Kaplan, R. (1976).
    Environment and Behavior, 8, 627.
Howat, J. K. (1972), The Hudson River and Its Painters.
    New York: Viking.

90

Huntington, D. C. (1966), The Landscapes of Frederic Edwin
    Church: Vision of an American Era. New York: George
    Braziller.
Huntington, D. C. (1978), personal communication, January
    5.
Huntington, D. C. (1980). In J. Wilmerding (Ed.),
    American Light, the Luminist Movement 1850-1875.
    Washington, D.C.: National Gallery of Art.
"An Imperiled American Treasure" (1966). Life, 60, 64.
Kaplan, R. (1972), "The Dimensions of the Visual
    Environment: Methodological Considerations." In
    W. J. Mitchell (Ed.), Environmental Design: Research
    and Practice. Proceedings of the Environmental
    Design Research Association, University of
    California, Los Angeles.
Kaplan, R. (1974), "A Strategy for Dimensional Analysis."
    In P. K. Mautz and R. Kaplan, "Residential
    Modification as Mode to Self-expression." In ERDA
    Five, Proceedings of the Fifth Environmental Design
    Research Association Conference. Milwaukee, Wis.
Kaplan, R. (1979), "Visual Resources and the Public: An
    Empirical Approach." In G. H. Elsner and
    R. C. Smardon (technical coordinators), Proceedings
    of Our National Landscape: A Conference on Applied
    Techniques for Analysis and Management of the Visual
    Resource. Washington, D.C.: U.S. Department of
    Agriculture.
Kaplan, R., Kaplan, S., and Deardorff, H. L. (1974), "The
    Perception and Evaluation of a Simulated
    Environment." Man-Environment Systems, 4, 191-192.
Kaplan, S. (1979), "Perceptions and Landscape: Conceptions
    and Misconceptions." In G. H. Elsner and
    R. C. Smardon (technical coordinators), Proceedings
    of Our National Landscape: A Conference on Applied
    Techniques for Analysis and Management of the Visual
    Resource. Washington, D.C.: U.S. Department of
    Agriculture.
Kaplan, S., and Kaplan, R. (Eds.) (1978), Humanscape:
    Environments for People. Belmont, Cal.: Duxbury.
Kaplan, S., Kaplan, R., and Wendt, J. S. (1972),
    Perceptual Psychophysiology, 23, 354.
Kuh, R. (1965). Saturday Review, 48, 46.
Levin, J. E. (1977), "Riverside Preferences: On-site and
    Photographic Reactions." Master's thesis, The
    University of Michigan.
Lowenthal, D. (1978), personal communication, October 3.
Lucas, R. C. (1979), User Evaluation of Campgrounds in Two
    Michigan National Forests. Washington, D.C.:
    U.S. Department of Agriculture.
Marx, L. (1964), The Machine in the Garden: Technology
    and the Pastoral Ideal in America. New York: Oxford
    University Press.
McCoy, H. A., and Singer, J. F. (1980). International
    Journal of Environmental Studies, 15, 95.

Murray, B. H., and Niemann, B. J. (1979), "Visual Quality
    Testimony in an Adversary Setting." In G. H. Elsner
    and R. C. Smardon (technical coordinators),
    Proceedings of Our National Landscape: A Conference
    on Applied Techniques for Analysis and Management of
    the Visual Resource. Washington, D.C.:
    U.S. Department of Agriculture.
Novak, B. (1978a), personal communication, February 27.
Novak, B. (1978b), personal communication, May 15.
"Olana" (1966). New York Times, June 10, p. 44.
Peelle, E. (1979), "Socioeconomic Impact Assessment and
    Nuclear Power Plant Licensing: Greene County, New
    York." Paper presented at the session "Environmental
    Sociology: A Government Approach," American
    Sociological Association Annual Meeting, Boston,
    Mass., August 29.
Posner, M. I. (1973), Cognition: An Introduction.
    Glenview, Ill.: Scott, Foresman.
Powell, E. A. (1980). In J. Wilmerding (Ed.), American
    Light, the Luminist Movement 1850-1875. Washington,
    D.C.: National Gallery of Art.
"Rivers of North America" (1978). Outdoor World.
"Preservation Leaps the Garden Wall" (1981). Landscape
    Architecture, 71, 1.
Scully, V., Jr. (1965). Progressive Architecture, 46,
    185.
Scully, V., Jr. (1978), personal communication, January
    10.
Shafer, E. L., and Meitz, J. (1970), It Seems Possible to
    Quantify Scenic Beauty in Photography. Washington,
    D.C.: U.S. Department of Agriculture.
Spangler, M. B. (1980), United States Experience in
    Environmental Cost-Benefit Analysis for Nuclear Power
    Plants with Implications for Developing
    Countries. Washington, D.C.: U.S. Nuclear Regulatory
    Commission.
Stebbins, T. E. (1978), personal communication, January
    10.
U.S. Nuclear Regulatory Commission (NRC) (1979), Final
    Environmental Statement for Greene County Nuclear
    Power Plant Proposed by Power Authority of the State
    of New York. Washington, D.C.
Van Zandt, R. (1966), The Catskill Mountain House. New
    Brunswick, N.J.: Rutgers University Press.
Wilmerding, J. (1978a), personal communication, January
    13.
Wilmerding, J. (1978b), personal communication, May 23.
Zube, E. H. (1973a). Landscape Architecture, 63, 126.
Zube, E. H. (1973b). Landscape Architecture, 63, 371.
Zube, E. H. (1974). Environment and Behavior, 6, 69.
Zube, E. H. (1976). In I. Altman and J. G. Wohlwill
    (Eds.), Human Behavior and Environment: Advances in
    Theory and Research, Vol. 1. New York: Plenum.
Zube, E. H., Brush, R. O., and Fabos, J. G. (Eds.) (1975),

Landscape Assessment: Values, Perceptions, and Resources. Stroudsburg, Penn.: Dowden, Hutchinson, and Ross.

Zube, E. H., Pitt, D. G., and Anderson, T. W. (1974), Perception and Measurement of Scenic Resources in the Southern Connecticut River Valley. Amherst, Mass.: Institute for Man and Environment.

NOTES

[1]The research supporting this paper was sponsored by the Division of Site Safety and Environmental Analysis, U.S. Nuclear Regulatory Commission, under Interagency Agreement IA-544-75 with the U.S. Department of Energy under contract W-7405-eng-26 with the Union Carbide Corporation. The U.S. Government retains a nonexclusive, royalty-free license in and to any copyright covering this article.

[2]A concern in any survey of this nature is how fairly and accurately the simulation of the proposed project communicates the true visual impact of the project, were it to be built. In a review of my work, David Lowenthal (1978), a cultural geographer at University College, London, directed comments to this issue: "the highly negative response elicited by pictures of cooling towers constitutes as good evidence as one can get without actually building them on the site."

[3]The plume is portrayed in a "worst-case" position in terms of direction but not in terms of length, height, or opacity. A computer model (NRC, 1979) of projected plume dimensions, directions, and frequencies for the time of year shown in the photograph demonstrated that an observer at Olana could reasonably expect to see a plume similar to this one at least 0.4 percent and no more than 19.3 percent of the time.

[4]The view from the Catskill Mountain House has been acclaimed the finest in the Catskills, the Hudson River Valley, and the Eastern Seaboard, depending on author and time period. In its heyday, the house was one of the most famous sites within the Atlantic states. Washington Irving's opinion was that the view from this site affords "one of the finest prospects in the world." James Fenimore Cooper suggested that it offered a panorama of "all creation" (see R. Van Zandt, 1966). Van Zandt found it not at all surprising that Cooper's Natty Bumpo commented to Hawkeye that the view of the Hudson River extended for 70 miles. Accolades for this view abound in current literature on regional travel and hiking.

[5]Examples of general aesthetic impact analyses can be found in Elsner and Smardon (1979). Examples of aesthetic impacts associated with historic landscapes can be found in a special edition of Landscape Architecture entitled "Preservation Leaps the Garden Wall."

4. Socioeconomic Impact Assessment and Nuclear Power Plant Licensing: Greene County, New York

Elizabeth Peelle

OVERVIEW

The Final Environment Statement (FES) for the proposed Greene County Nuclear Power Plant (GCNPP) on the Hudson River below Albany, New York, is unique among Nuclear Regulatory Commission (NRC) impact statements in containing an extensive socioeconomic analysis and an unprecedented aesthetic analysis. It was the first Nuclear Regulatory Commission FES ever to recommend denial of a construction permit on aesthetic and socioeconomic grounds.

Adverse and unmitigable impacts upon local cultural, scenic, and historic resources of national importance were the prime reason for the FES conclusions. Additional adverse socioeconomic impacts supported the finding, which also depended on the identification of several preferable alternate sites. The main socioeconomic impact issues arose from the tax-exempt status of the utility, the Power Authority of the State of New York (PASNY); the possible displacement of an existing tax-paying industry with potential losses in taxes, jobs, and opportunity costs for local jurisdictions; serious impacts from an elaborate but inadequate series of road access improvement proposals; and visual and secondary impacts on the numerous historic properties in the 10-mile impact area. These conclusions reversed those of the 1976 Draft Environmental Statement (DES) because of the development of extensive new information, enlargement of the appropriate impact area to include off-site impacts, and recognition of the need for an aesthetic analysis.

This paper reviews the setting, participants, and history of the joint federal-state hearings, the findings of the FES, the problems of conducting social impact assessment (SIA) for the GCNPP, the effects and outcomes of the joint hearing process, the interplay of internal and external pressures for NEPA compliance, and the nature and effect of public participation in the formal, legalistic hearing process.

Suggestions for improving future joint hearing

processes, public participation, and the technical adequacy of SIAs are given. The GCNPP FES is seen as representing the increasing independence, scope, and relevance of SIA in NRC environmental statements. While improving, the quality of SIAs lag behind what is technically possible because of continuing administrative, time, and resource constraints. Outcomes of individual statements are strongly affected by random and accidental factors, such as timing and delays, characteristics of the utility, competing agency priorities, availability of experienced staff with needed skills, and the presence of knowledgeable intervenors. The valuable informational resource created by the hearings remains largely inaccessible because of its formidable volume and fragmentation. Public participation serves a vital role in setting the agenda for technical assessments, but it fails to meet other important needs.

The Greene County FES demonstrates the key importance of the process of assessment and evaluation in determining content and outcomes. The joint hearing process introduced huge quantities of additional information two years after the DES was issued, thus raising new issues. The joint hearings functioned as a gigantic scoping operation. The interaction of the state and federal agencies in the time-consuming and frustrating process was, nonetheless, synergistic in some respects and resulted in broadening the scope of the NRC analysis and, ultimately, in reversing the conclusions of the earlier environmental statement.

INTRODUCTION

Since the passage of the National Environmental Policy Act of 1969, the revolutionary mandates of NEPA have been the cause of intense activity in public agencies, private industry, activist groups, and impacted areas and among those professionals charged with evaluating impacts of proposed actions through the Environmental Impact Statement (EIS) process. The 12,000 EISs produced through 1979 also resulted in 1,200 lawsuits (CEQ, 1978, 1980) and innumerable meetings and supporting studies and have greatly expanded whole disciplines such as social impact assessment. This activity is carried out by hundreds of professionals and supporting staff in a variety of working environments (universities, institutes, government agencies, national laboratories, and consulting firms), some of which were expressly created or expanded for this purpose.

In the evaluation being widely conducted in NEPA's second decade, it is appropriate to ask whether NEPA's objectives and promises are being fulfilled, and how. Is agency decision making being affected? Are noneconomic factors included in assessments? How are social and aesthetic factors treated relative to the technical and

economic factors that have historically determined
development decisions? Are social impacts being
adequately defined and dealt with? Are those who bear the
burdens of development involved in the decision making
that ultimately affects their quality of life and life
options? How are social impact issues and assessments
defined and conducted within differing agencies? How do
interactions between cooperating agencies with different
goals and procedures affect NEPA outcomes? What is the
relative importance of scientific excellence in assessment
vs. process factors (i.e., how the particular
organizational context affects the assessment) in
determining NEPA outcomes? What is the role and
importance of internal vs. external pressures on agencies
for NEPA compliance?

These questions will be addressed in varying depth in
this paper, depending on experience and information
availability, by reviewing the precedents set by the
content and decisions of the Nuclear Regulatory
Commission's final environmental statement in the
licensing action of the proposed nuclear plant for Greene
County, New York. The outcomes of the licensing process
are reviewed in terms of problems in conducting the social
impact assessment and in terms of the effects of the joint
hearing process. The latter was undertaken midstream in
the separate licensing actions underway in the NRC and the
New York State Board on Electric Generation Siting and the
Environment. Some observations of the role of public
participation in nuclear licensing actions are made. The
main thesis of this paper is that the EIS process itself
as a major determination of the scope and adequacy of
assessment outcomes.

THE SETTING OF THE GREENE COUNTY NUCLEAR
POWER PLANT LICENSING ACTION

As background to the subsequent discussion of social
impact assessment evolution within environmental impact
statements, the organizational setting, history of the
Greene County EIS, and joint hearings in New York State
will be reviewed here, and the findings of the NRC EIS
will be presented in the following section.

As the second major joint state-federal nuclear
licensing action,' the organizational milieu included
several large public bureaucracies as well as affected
local governments, private organizations, and a local
industry. The large bureaucracies and their respective
roles were: the U.S. Nuclear Regulatory Commission
(federal regulator and licensor); Oak Ridge National
Laboratory (providing technical assistance for NRC); and
various New York State agencies providing technical
expertise to the New York State Board on Electric
Generation Siting and the Environment (NYSBEGS&E) (state
regulator and licensor). The New York State agencies

included the Public Service Commission, the Department of
Environmental Conservation, the Department of Parks and
Recreation, and the Power Authority of the State of New
York, the applicant for the power plant license.
    The U.S. Nuclear Regulatory Commission is empowered
by Congress[2] to issue construction permits and operating
licenses for nuclear power plants following the
independent evaluation of impacts of the proposed project
as required by NEPA. The NRC issues an increasingly
detailed series of environmental impact statements that
culminate in a final EIS (FES). The NRC subcontracts
major portions of the technical analyses and impact
statement writing to various national laboratories
(currently Argonne or Oak Ridge) while retaining control
over all policy, scheduling, budgetary, and legal matters
involved with statement publication and the licensing
hearing. This involves review and veto power relative to
all technical analyses and conclusions. NRC appointed
project managers for the two licensing actions:[3] the
safety and engineering assessments and the environmental
assessments. Internal staff from at least three divisions
are involved in the review and approval of any EIS:
technical, licensing, and legal. All of these staff and
their managers interact during the course of statement
preparation and hearings with the laboratory technical
staff who actually analyze the data, write the EIS, and
testify in subsequent hearings before the Atomic Safety
and Licensing Board (ASLB). Figure 4.1 depicts the usual,
unilateral NRC licensing process steps and the order of
the various environmental reports, drafts, and statements.
    Oak Ridge National Laboratory (ORNL) is likewise a
large and complex bureaucracy, but one devoted to
research, development, and assessment rather than
regulation (current staff: 5,000, including 50 social
science professionals). Within ORNL, EISs are produced by
multidisciplinary task forces of 4-10 professionals. Each
member of the GCNPP task group was responsible to a home
division or group (environmental sciences, social impacts,
economics, thermal hydraulics, etc.), while she/he
received task assignments from the EIS management within
the laboratory. In a high-priority, controversial EIS
like that of Greene County, the analyses and findings of
the ORNL staff are given extensive cross-disciplinary and
management review before they are sent to the NRC for
further review. The Social Impact Assessment Group within
which the author works was created in 1975 and now
includes 10 professionals representing the disciplines of
political science, psychology, planning, sociology,
demography, and communication. The aesthetic analysis on
which the rejection of the licensing application was in
part based was conducted by a landscape architect in the
ORNL Resources Analysis Group (also including cultural and
physical geographers, a systems analyst, and computer
support personnel).

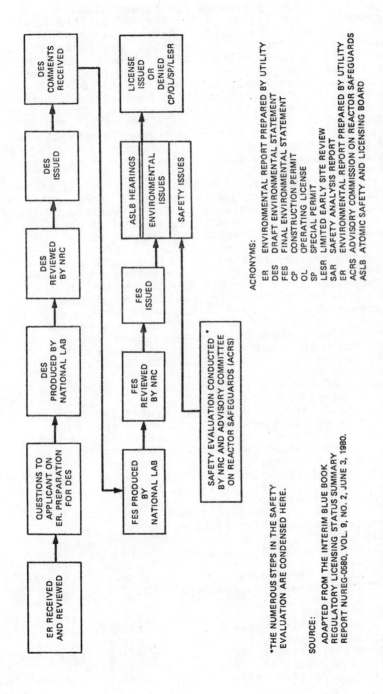

Figure 4.1 NRC licensing of nuclear power plants: environmental and safety reviews.

ACRONYMS:

ER   ENVIRONMENTAL REPORT PREPARED BY UTILITY
DES   DRAFT ENVIRONMENTAL STATEMENT
FES   FINAL ENVIRONMENTAL STATEMENT
CP   CONSTRUCTION PERMIT
OL   OPERATING LICENSE
SP   SPECIAL PERMIT
LESR LIMITED EARLY SITE REVIEW
SAR   SAFETY ANALYSIS REPORT
ER   ENVIRONMENTAL REPORT PREPARED BY UTILITY
ACRS ADVISORY COMMISSION ON REACTOR SAFEGUARDS
ASLB ATOMIC SAFETY AND LICENSING BOARD

*THE NUMEROUS STEPS IN THE SAFETY
EVALUATION ARE CONDENSED HERE.

SOURCE:

ADAPTED FROM THE INTERIM BLUE BOOK
REGULATORY LICENSING STATUS SUMMARY
REPORT NUREG-0580, VOL. 9, NO. 2, JUNE 3, 1980.

Boxes in the flowchart:

ER RECEIVED AND REVIEWED

QUESTIONS TO APPLICANT ON ER. PREPARATION FOR DES

DES PRODUCED BY NATIONAL LAB

DES REVIEWED BY NRC

DES ISSUED

DES COMMENTS RECEIVED

FES PRODUCED BY NATIONAL LAB

FES REVIEWED BY NRC

FES ISSUED

SAFETY EVALUATION CONDUCTED BY NRC AND ADVISORY COMMITTEE ON REACTOR SAFEGUARDS (ACRS)

ASLB HEARINGS
ENVIRONMENTAL ISSUES
SAFETY ISSUES

LICENSE ISSUED OR DENIED
CP/OL/SP/LESR

    In 1975, PASNY presented its three-volume
Environmental Report (ER) to the NRC and applied for a
construction permit to build a one-unit 1,200 MW(e)
pressurized-water reactor at Cementon, New York, on the
Hudson River about 40 miles south of Albany. One 450-foot
natural-draft cooling tower was proposed for the plant.
The tower and plume would have been visible 6 miles
downstream from Olana, the hilltop home of the nineteenth-
century landscape painter Frederic Church. The home and
grounds are now a National Historic Landmark. The house
and its setting were designed to frame the view of the
"Bend of the River" that Church painted at least 35 times.
These oil sketches now hang in Olana as well as in various
national galleries.
    The site for the $1.8 billion nuclear plant included
most of the plant and property of one of three rather
ancient cement companies that provide a noticeable share
of the employment, tax, and economic base of the
neighboring towns of Catskill and Saugerties and
surrounding counties. The only road access to the plant
was to be a narrow, no-shoulder, blind-curve section of
U.S. 9W, noted for two very narrow railroad underpasses.
    Under the joint hearings protocol signed by the NRC
and the New York State siting board, a joint hearing on
most issues was to be held before a joint hearing board
composed of three NRC commissioners and two New York State
Public Service Commission examiners (USNRC and NYSBEGS&E,
1976). Beginning in May 1977, hearings were conducted in
Albany, New York, in a Public Service Commission hearing
room until suspension of the proceedings in April 1979,
two months after the NRC FES was issued. Because of
differing procedures and objectives of the two licensing
boards, the joint hearings as structured led to
proceedings of extraordinary diffuseness and length
(22,000 pages of testimony during the first round of
hearings involving witnesses for only one of the six
parties to the licensing action). Thousands of pages of
supporting exhibits, studies, and documents were also
involved. For instance, while the New York State Board
and its supporting agencies concentrated upon the
question, Which of two sites (Cementon or Athens) and of
two methods of generation (nuclear or coal) is most
suitable for construction of a PASNY generating plant?,
the NRC was considering two questions: Is Cementon an
acceptable site for construction of this particular
nuclear plant? And do any obviously superior alternative
sites exist? Other significant differences included the
differing staff roles and hearing functions for the two
licensing agencies: since the New York State agencies do
not prepare a full-fledged EIS, they normally use hearings
to generate, discover, and verify information for the
testimony they prepare for hearing commissioners at the
end of the proceedings. For the federal licensing
process, laboratory staff normally assess the applicant's

ER and other relevant information in order to prepare
their FES, which becomes part of the information base for
hearings before the NRC licensing board (ASLB).
Recommendations of the NRC staff in the FES are usually
adopted by the ASLB with occasional additions of modifying
or mitigating conditions following testimony by all
parties about the validity and intensity of the expected
impacts. Because large quantities of new information were
being introduced into the proceedings via the hearings,
the NRC FES was delayed for almost two years after the
start of the hearings while new issues and information
were analyzed and included. The FES in this case was a
result of the joint hearings, rather than a prime input to
hearings. It would have undoubtedly had a major effect
upon subsequent hearings had the process continued. A
brief chronology in Table 4.1 summarizes the Greene County
nuclear plant licensing process before the federal and
state agencies.

More than most other licensing actions with which the
ORNL staff is familiar (60 since 1971),[4] the GCNPP
licensing issues evolved, changed, and grew over the four-
year licensing period. New issues were developed as a
result of extensive new information and the increased
depth of analysis. A succession of technical staff was
involved (as principal author of the FES SIA sections, I
was the fourth SIA staff person). The net result was an
unprecedented reversal of the conclusions of the Draft
Environmental Statement of 1976 (where impacts were deemed
acceptable) by the FES in February 1979 (impacts deemed
unacceptable since several alternate sites had been
identified). The new issues in the FES included aesthetic
impacts upon Olana and the area, effects of the elaborate
system of transportation and road alternatives proposed to
handle construction traffic, and impacts resulting from
the possible closing of the Lehigh Portland Cement
Company. Because very little had been included in the
utility's ER about these impacts, the relative importance
of that document to the final outcome was much less than
usual.

Dozens of contentions about anticipated adverse
impacts were submitted by the several intervenor groups,
the cement company, and the local governments. Those
contentions that were accepted by the licensing board as
germane to the proceedings were subsequently addressed
either in the FES or in separate testimony by ORNL or NRC
staff. These concerns included possible adverse effects
of (1) the cooling tower upon land use and aesthetics,
property values in adjacent areas, and neighboring apple
orchards, (2) the radiation releases upon the health of
the public, (3) a large, inmoving work force demand upon
community services and housing (a possible "boom-bust"
situation), (4) the proposed road modifications upon
traffic safety and the Lehigh Cement Company, and (5) pre-
emption of cement company land upon local employment and

TABLE 4.1
Greene County nuclear power plant licensing
action: Brief selected chronology

	1975
July	PASNY submits Environmental Report to NRC, initiating licensing
	1976
March	USNRC Draft Environmental Statement recommends licensing (aesthetics not mentioned)
June	PASNY applies to New York State Siting Board for Certificate of Environmental Compatibility and Public Need
November	Joint Hearing Protocol signed by NRC and NYPSC
	1977
February	Draft FES sent to NRC by ORNL; very similar to DES in content
April	N.Y. Board allocates funds for municipal parties (Greene and Columbia Counties)
May	Joint hearings begin in Albany, N.Y.; PASNY begins testimony (first of six parties)
September	PASNY applies for LWA
November	PASNY socioeconomic testimony and cross-examination by other parties begins
December	Late intervention granted for three intervenor groups on aesthetic issues
	1978
July	Hearings recess temporarily at conclusion of PASNY testimony
October	Draft FES reviewed internally at ORNL

1978	
December	Revised draft FES reviewed by NRC

1979	
January	Revised draft FES reviewed by NRC
February	NRC FES is published stating that (1) building GCNPP at Cementon would cause unacceptable impacts, (2) other more acceptable sites exist, and (3) therefore CP should be denied
March 16	PASNY chairman suggests cancellation to PASNY Board because of cost escalation of proposed plant
March 20	PASNY asks suspension of immediate hearing dates
March 29	TMI accident begins
April 5	PASNY Board announces decision to sell GCNPP nuclear assets and to seek approval of coal-fired facility at Athens; joint hearings suspended until October
October 15	PASNY requests continuance to February 1980

1980	
January	PASNY withdraws from New York State proceedings
October	PASNY withdraws NRC construction permit application

tax base, among others.

The utility's response to the negative findings of the FES included the submission of 560 interrogatories to NRC about the nature, background, and history of staff assessment. Shortly before the Three Mile Island accident, the PASNY chairman suggested the "sale of the assets" of the plant because of the extensive escalation of the cost of the proposed plant to $3.1 billion. The PASNY board delayed action on this proposal until April 9, shortly after the Three Mile Island accident, when it decided to proceed with sale of the assets (reactor and steam supply elements on order). No mention was made of the FES and its findings by the utility. However, PASNY's cost escalation estimates included estimated relocation costs for moving the plant from Cementon to Athens, a preferable site (Nuclear News, 1979). PASNY opposed termination of the proceedings despite its announced intention to sell. The joint hearing was suspended indefinitely (with PASNY required to report back in October 1979 as to the status of its application and the proposed sale of the Babcock and Wilcox reactor unit) and then cancelled altogether in January 1980, at the applicant's request. The NRC license application was withdrawn in October 1980, concluding the chronology in Table 4.1.

CONTENT AND FINDINGS OF THE EIS

Because other alternate sites could be identified without the severe and unmitigable aesthetic impact of the cooling tower and plume upon the National Historic Landmark Olana and other local cultural, scenic, and historic resources of national importance, the FES recommended denial of a construction permit at the Cementon site (Greene County NRC FES, 1979). Additional serious-to-severe socioeconomic impacts contributed to the unfavorable rating of the site. Seven alternate sites were deemed preferable on the basis of reconnaissance-level data.

Because of the subjective nature of aesthetic analysis, three separate analyses were done by Carl Petrich, ORNL landscape architect. The studies involved objective measures of visual quality and visibility, subjective measures of local values using comparative evaluation of local scenes (through a visual preference survey), and a historical-cultural evaluation of the mid-Hudson River Valley in American history. All studies pointed to the same conclusion of severe aesthetic impact (Petrich, 1979). (Also see the preceding article in this volume by Petrich.) Petrich spent two years doing the studies once it was decided by ORNL and NRC that the importance of the possible aesthetic impacts warranted special analyses.

Our socioeconomic analyses showed the major probable impacts at Cementon not to be the "boom and bust" feared by local governments but to be the effects of the work force upon roads, selected schools that were already overcrowded, and the large number of unprotected historical structures in the region, as well as the impact of the possible loss of the cement company. The anticipated effects from the closing of the cement company included possible Lehigh job loss (223 workers) and opportunity costs (if Lehigh were prevented from expanding its operations as it claimed it intended to do and the

$200,000 yearly tax loss to Greene County if the tax-exempt Power Authority displaced a tax-paying local industry). An extensive analysis of the socioeconomic effects of the six proposed road alternatives uncovered serious defects with the new and temporary roadway solutions and found only the "soft" solution of busing from selected peripheral parking lots to be acceptable under additional mitigating conditions.

Although we found the applicant's estimate of a 2,100-person work force to be seriously outdated by 1979 (we suggested 3,000 instead), we found the ER estimate of 14 percent inmovers to be reasonable when adapted to a more credible range of 14-20 percent. We anticipated that most workers would commute from nearby (in this case, Albany or Kingston) laborsheds, as is the pattern for most northeastern nuclear labor forces. Baseline estimates showed selected schools in the two most desirable (to inmovers) nearby towns would still be overcrowded in the proposed peak work force period. Because of these school estimates and because of the unavoidable uncertainty surrounding estimates of this type, we required that the applicant devise an acceptable (to NRC) mitigation plan for all community services in a three-county impact area for the construction period. Few other impacts on services were foreseen at the expected inmover rates, although the locally tight housing market would be strained in the worst case and more serious impacts would begin to occur if our inmover estimates were exceeded. These impacts were not ranked as serious in the overall evaluation of plant effects because a satisfactory fall-back mitigation plan could be devised.

The analytical approach to the 12 major social impact areas (roads, housing, public services, relocation, historical and archeological resources, local government finances, recreation, economic activity, Lehigh displacement, mitigation, and impact distribution) involved a variety of methods and relied heavily on the experience of the analysts. In all cases, we characterized the social resource, projected impacts upon that resource at the time of impact, used available criteria of impact (relocation and historical resources) or devised our own as needed, and characterized or quantified the impacts that might result. For instance, the community services and housing analyses were keyed to the work force inmigration estimates, since levels and rates of most worker inmovement have been shown to be the source of most community impacts. Using our knowledge of recent worker inmigration patterns, we estimated that most of the 300 inmovers would move close to the site (Catskill and Saugerties). Then we compared existing and planned services and housing capacity in each area with the expected additional demand. We recommended monitoring and mitigation of the new demand in the schools and police areas since there were no existing excess capacities.

Results of the extensive mitigation analysis done for each impact are shown in Table 4.2 (Table 4.17 of the FES). In some cases, institutional authority did not exist to require needed mitigation (Lehigh tax loss); while in others, only unwieldy solutions existed (required retraining or other compensation for Lehigh workers who would lose jobs). In these instances, a voluntary commitment by PASNY would have provided a basis for negotiation and possible solutions. The partial mitigation of incompatible land use changes affecting the many historical properties was beyond the authority of the federal government: the FES suggested that local governments could exercise their authority through protective land use and zoning changes. No apparent solution existed for the Olana aesthetic impacts, the highly adverse local opinion, or project-induced inflation. The tax-exempt status of the utility was identified as the source of certain intractable mitigation dilemmas since it resulted in a lack of resources to deal with difficult compensation and equity problems.

Another unusual feature of the social impact assessment was the discussion of distribution of impacts. While several important regional benefits were identified (employment, regional economic stimulus in an economically depressed area, state tax payments, plant purchases, etc.), only modest local benefits could be identified. Since many adverse local impacts were found, we observed that the relationship between local costs and benefits appeared to be adverse overall. In our judgment, regional benefits cannot be used to justify uncompensated losses for a local area.

PROBLEMS OF SOCIAL IMPACT ASSESSMENT IN ACTION

The serious problems confronting social impact assessors have remained remarkably similar over time and in different institutional settings (cf. Friesema and Culhane, 1976; Jobes, 1976). As seen again in the GCNPP statement, they are lack of adequate time and resources to do the task,[5] administrative and organizational conflicts that hinder the pursuit of the analysis, and occasional lack of autonomy on critical substantive questions. Nonetheless, significant gains were made in procedural, substantive, and policy matters on the GCNPP SIA, when problems are viewed on a relative basis and in a broader perspective.

One common problem that was blessedly absent in the Greene County case was interdisciplinary misunderstanding or conflict. The entire ORNL task force was supportive of the ongoing aesthetic and socioeconomic work as it gradually became obvious that these issues would be predominant. In an unusual development organized by the task force leader, the task force reviewed the completed work of all task group members and then voted unanimously

TABLE 4.2
Mitigation of socioeconomic impacts of GCNPP at Cementon site

Socioeconomic Impacts at Cementon	Mitigable?	Possible Solution
Road alternatives		
1B	No	
1BR	No	
2TB	No	
2T	Yes	Saugerties solution: require removal of temporary driveways and regrading
2TR	Yes	Require measures to prevent increased number of deficient roadway links
Park and Ride	Yes	
VII	Yes	
Tax loss		
Lehigh site and road properties	No[1]	Replacement payments for life of plant
Community opportunity cost (site use)	No	None
Lehigh plant costs	Yes	Through court action
Lehigh site taking	No mitigation available for community	Equivalent site found
Lehigh job loss (223 workers)	Partially	Estimate 50 percent find jobs; PASNY-supported job assistance and retraining

Socioeconomic Impacts at Cementon	Mitigable?	Possible Solution
Aesthetics View from Olana, etc.	No	None
Other historical resources	Partially	Historical and cultural area designation, local zoning
Local legal positions (Road 1B)	Yes	Select different road alternative
Local opinion	No	No siting
Relocation Site + 1B + transmission lines	Partially	Only owners will be compensated
Site + Park and Ride + transmission lines	Yes	Adequate taking and relocation payments
Public services	Yes	Monitoring and mitigation plan—schools, police, etc.
Transmission lines	Partially	Visual screening, selective routing
Inflation if Inmovers > 300 Work force > 2,100	No	None

[1]Not mitigable under present laws.

Source: Table 4.17, Greene County Nuclear Plant FES, p. 4-47.

that several obviously superior alternate sites existed.
Most of the task force also viewed the Cementon site as
unacceptable.

The usual low-priority status of SIAs was gradually
altered over the years of this statement, rising
dramatically in the final year with the assignment of
additional staff until 2-4 analysts were involved
simultaneously, instead of the previous 1/4-1/3-time
person. Adequacy of resources to do assessment must be
measured against the size of the task, however. For
Greene County, as in most impact statements, social impact
assessment was defined by EIS management to include roads
and traffic, noise, land use (nonecological aspects), and
historical and archeological resources, as well as the
usual services and community and fiscal impacts.
Fortunately, the aesthetic analysis, which is usually also
assigned to the catchall SIA bin, was removed halfway
through the analysis period and assigned to a specialist
in that field (see previous discussion). Since four of
these areas proved to have major impacts requiring
extensive independent analysis, the task was a very large
one, requiring numerous technical skills not normally
possessed by social impact analysts. Clearly, if social
impact assessment often looks more like civil engineering
in its emphasis on services, sewers, and roads (Cortese,
1977; Wilke and Cain, 1977), this is in part the result of
being overloaded with nonsocial subjects in addition to
standard community effects, something still outside the
control of SIA staff.

The two most serious problems impeding SIA assessment
on Greene County were somewhat rare: the huge volume of
relevant material from the hearings that had to be
reviewed and its diffuse and haphazard organization.
Approximately 12,000 pages of material were relevant to
our broadly defined SIA tasks (one-third of the 22,000
pages of testimony plus 6,000 pages of road studies, ERs
and amendments, interrogatories, cement company business,
intervenor-funded studies, and numerous secondary sources
concerning the mid-Hudson River Valley). After nearly two
months on the stand and two rounds of cross-examination by
all parties, the testimony of a key PASNY socioeconomic
witness was scattered and fragmented in the record. The
attempt of one of the New York State agencies to bring
order out of chaos resulted in a 46-page index of this
testimony. The information-gathering task was transformed
into an arduous, frustrating search for the latest version
of a particular fact and a continuing sifting and
evaluation of contradictory "facts" and conflicting
assertions. Much needed information was omitted
altogether in the record and the ER and had to be
independently secured, generated, or estimated. Thus, the
entire time allotted for assessment could have easily been
consumed in the mere seeking and organization of
information; a full-time information specialist would have

been invaluable. The inevitable deadline pressures mean
that shortcuts are made and there is premature pressure to
come to conclusions before the analysis is truly complete.
   The "moving-target" syndrome also plagued assessment
efforts on the GCNPP. Road proposals changed at least
three times in the four years we worked on Greene County,
from no road proposals to a preferred new road to six road
alternatives among which the applicant declined to choose.
This entailed about six times as much assessment work.
New transmission line routings were submitted in the third
year, requiring major reassessment.
   The administrative and organizational conflicts
involved lengthy, iterative discussions over whether
certain subject matter deemed important by the SIA staff
should be included. NRC managers finally agreed to the
inclusion of an appendix documenting 20 local government
actions concerned with (mostly opposed to) the GCNPP.
Extended negotiation was also necessary to achieve
inclusion of a small section that discussed
preconstruction effects in the community using four
quantitative measures: local government expenditures in
opposition to the plant, increased historical preservation
activity, increased polarization of local opinion, and the
structuring of the opposition effort by the seven local
jurisdictions involved (NRC FES, 1979, pp. 2-8). Part of
the compromise involved retitling the section as
"preconstruction activity" and shifting it from the impact
chapter to the profile chapter. As interpreted by NRC
management, "preconstruction impacts" are not germane to a
construction permit since they have already occurred and
will be unaffected by judgments on whether or not to build
the plant. "Impacts" could not exist, by this definition,
if they occurred prior to the issuance of a permit to
construct. Inclusion of the substantive concerns of local
governments (NRC FES, 1979, pp. 2-9) was also a matter for
discussion with NRC management, who argued that inclusion
would merely duplicate the contentions of intervenors that
were already recorded in the legal proceedings. The
argument over impact definition was subsequently used by
NRC in deleting (over ORNL staff protest) the item of
"preconstruction impacts" from the FES's Table 4.17.
Numerous other NRC-ORNL staff discussions were held on the
Lehigh question and treatment of distribution of impacts.
These arguments typically involved definitions of
appropriate subject matter, scope, and analytical
treatment. While NRC clearly has the right to determine
what goes into its statements, the basic desires and
judgments of the SIA analysts usually prevailed (sometimes
after extended discussions). Deletion over staff protest
occurred in only the single case mentioned above, where
legalistic definition prevailed over substantive technical
judgment--a remarkable record for one of the most
controversial and precedent-setting EISs ever issued by
the NRC.

The complex interplay of internal and external pressures for NEPA compliance (Liroff, 1976) was also illustrated in the Greene County case. Clearly, the introduction of the aesthetic issue by outside parties (Greene County, Friends of Olana, and several New York State agencies in the hearing) contributed to raising this issue from no mention in the DES to one of overriding status in the FES. Even at this point, the issue might have remained at the level of "visibility analysis" as initially defined by ORNL and NRC in mid-1977 had not qualified internal staff been available to address the issue. Staff shifts and replacements at ORNL in 1977 made available different personnel in social impacts, aesthetics, and task group leader positions. Without continuing internal pressure by the social impact analyst, the scope of the treatment of other historical sites besides Olana would have remained at the most cursory (required) level, however. After extensive discussions, agreement with NRC to expand the scope of the analysis was received at the eleventh hour--September 1978. Thus, the entire analysis of historical sites (260 potentially eligible' sites in a 10-mile radius in addition to the legally required mention of 18 sites listed in the National Historic Register) was hastily conducted in the final few days of the allotted assessment period.

SOME OBSERVATIONS ON PUBLIC
PARTICIPATION IN THE GAME OF EXPERTS

Public interest and concern over the potential impacts of the Greene County Nuclear Power Plant were high from the very beginning, as evidenced by the four-year record of the Greene County Legislature (USNRC FES, 1979, Appendix J), a review of local newspaper files, and the initial presence of 80 intervenors in the proceedings (later condensed to six intervenor groups).

Because of the formal, legalistic framework of the joint hearings, however, only those concerns that fit this framework and that were accepted by the two boards could be considered. As certain concerns were repeated and reiterated by group after group, they were highly effective in setting the agenda for the written FES and agency testimony, however. Considerable additional information was generated and assessment conducted by both the applicant and the reviewing state and federal agencies on aesthetic impacts, effects on property values, Olana, and road alternatives, among others, as a result of this definition of issues. The process was lengthened, complicated, delayed, and, finally, significantly altered because of these public inputs.

The hearing testimony, however, reveals a significant hidden agenda of additional concerns that kept bursting out and for which no provision could be made. Some such unaddressed local concerns were clearly visible in other settings (newspapers or conversations with local residents) but remained invisible in the hearings. For example, local residents resented the fact that the power to be generated by the GCNPP was destined for New York City, 90 miles away, while they would sustain the impacts from its construction and operation. While these issues will not be examined in detail here, some observations follow: local needs may include the desire for meaningful consultation with the utility about local concerns of equity and mitigation and needs for reassurance. In the absence of the above, feelings of outrage develop and the intent to delay may emerge.

Considerable frustration of intervenors occurred as they attempted to question PASNY witnesses on technical details of aesthetic and socioeconomic matters. Without technical background in these areas, they were unable to complete (or sometimes even to pursue) a fruitful line of questioning despite their frequent probings of PASNY "weak spots." Without technical support of their own, they were at a considerable disadvantage in playing the hearings game, which recognizes the expert with credentials. In addition to access to existing technical information, local participants also require resources to interpret and use such information effectively and the capability to generate additional or alternative data and analysis as needed (Herschberger, 1980). Thus, the modest funding given to Greene County to fund its own studies of roads and socioeconomic and aesthetic effects was very significant in attempting to redress a highly uneven balance of power in the hearing room. Most of these studies were not completed until the first two years were past or about the time of FES completion. The suspension of the licensing action came after only one party (the utility) had been heard and cross-examined. The most obvious effect of the intervenor funding would probably have been seen later in the direct testimony of these parties as they used the additional information and analyses to enhance their claims or to evaluate the utility and NRC studies.

EFFECTS AND OUTCOMES OF THE JOINT HEARING PROCESS

The most important effect of the joint hearing process was to broaden the information-gathering and validation stage by infusing vast quantities of new and often untested information into the process. The prolonged struggle of agency staff, managers, examiners, and intervenors to process and evaluate this nearly overwhelming load of information (more than 30,000 pages of testimony and supporting documents) led to repeated delays in the hearings schedule and a stretch-out of the licensing process.

The resulting outcomes were delay of the NRC FES and, ultimately, reversal of its conclusions from those of the

Draft Environmental Statement of 1976. The chronology of
the hearings in Table 4.1 suggests the critical effect of
the new contacts and hearings arrangements. For instance,
the preliminary FES put together by ORNL staff in late
1976 (delivered to NRC in February 1977) preceded any
significant effort in the aesthetic area and included few
significant changes from the earlier DES. The PFES
conclusions still favored NRC issuance of a construction
permit. With the opening of the joint hearings in May
1977, the new information led to the development of new
issues and expansion of old ones. The importance of the
aesthetics issue and possible impacts upon Olana were
significantly increased in December 1977, when three new
intervenor groups were granted late entry to the
proceedings solely on these issues. In addition to the
aesthetic issue, the road analyses proliferated as Greene
County organizations and government rejected the preferred
1B alternative and the Lehigh pre-emption issues rose into
prominence.

The interactive nature of the joint hearings effort
produced synergistic results that neither agency was
likely to have produced independently. Although the
different approaches and goals of the federal and state
agencies produced many complications and lengthened the
proceedings because of the mismatch, the interaction was
also productive and critical to the outcome. The New York
State Siting Board's use of the hearings to collect and
evaluate information provided a broader range of facts and
permitted raising more issues earlier than that which
occurs in the usual NRC procedure in which the analytical
document (the FES) is produced before hearings commence.
Conversely, the NRC emphasis on analysis early in its
usual assessment process permitted more in-depth analysis
of the aesthetic issues than that which New York State
agencies were prepared to do at that stage of the process.
The net effect was to broaden the focus of the NRC FES to
include major new impacts (mostly off-site) that, upon
analysis, were judged to be unmitigable.

In effect, the joint hearings process became a
gigantic scoping operation. By raising new issues and
considering new information, the narrow scope of NRC's
earlier DES assessment was broadened. Thus, four years
before CEQ's official guidance on scoping environmental
assessments for NEPA review (CEQ, 1981), more appropriate
scoping of the relevant issues was occurring in this
lengthy and arduous manner in the Greene County licensing
action through the mechanism of the joint hearings.

SUGGESTIONS FOR IMPROVING THE EIS AND LICENSING PROCESS

How can things be made to work better? Several
important changes have since been suggested or mandated by
the Council on Environmental Quality (CEQ, 1978, 1981)
aimed at improving the focus and increasing the analytical

content while decreasing the ponderous, descriptive nature of many previous EISs. In addition, our experience in assessment and licensing suggests three areas for improvement: public involvement, joint hearings' structuring, and the social impact assessment process within government.

While public involvement has served important functions in agenda setting as discussed here, there are obvious public participation needs not being met by the highly structured, legalistic framework of existing hearings. Many public concerns cannot be addressed in the existing framework. These needs could be better met through (1) earlier public involvement in the process as in the new CEQ scoping guidelines, (2) allowing a wider range of questions to be addressed, perhaps in tiered or hierarchical sequence, and (3) equalizing public interest group and local government resources if the process is to be continued as one requiring "expert" credentials.

The several advantages foreseen' for the joint hearing process have yet to be realized, if the Greene County joint state-federal hearings are an example. Enormous amounts of technical and agency staff time were consumed by the two-and-a-half year hearings, and a decision was nowhere in sight when the proceedings were stopped in midstream. The procedures used resulted in a highly fragmented and disorganized record, impeding the use of the record. At least one state agency whose participation was essential to resolution of a key issue was not involved in the process, apparently by its own choice. While cooperation between federal and state technical staff was excellent in the social impact area (in accord with the directives of the joint protocol), this was apparently the exception rather than the rule. Some of these problems might be addressed through:

- better coordination of goals and objectives when different agencies are involved so that the same question is being addressed;
- requiring all relevant decision makers to participate in licensing actions (certainly all with veto power over decisions);
- cleaner separation of information and assessment functions in hearings so that shifting from one function to another is less common;
- stronger encouragement of interagency cooperation and sharing of information in all technical fields; and
- proceeding on a subject-oriented rather than a party-oriented basis or grouping treatment by party so that the continuing merry-go-round of subjects is avoided.

Improvements in the technical adequacy and relevance of social impact assessment could result from:

- more attention to defining critical assessment issues early in the process (the CEQ scoping guidelines [CEQ, 1981] now address this issue);
- focusing on assessment, rather than description (requiring data before assessment can begin);
- primary evaluation of technical issues and content by technical, rather than legal, solely economic, or administrative criteria;
- more input and decision-making power over procedural issues by technical working group staff;
- use of outside technical review groups to evaluate the adequacy of social impact analysis; and
- more time and resources to conduct assessment-- allotting time and money in accord with the difficulty of the task rather than using only the amount of money available.

CONCLUSIONS

The Greene County case demonstrates the key importance of process factors (e.g., organizational context and procedural requirements, etc.) in determining the outcomes and content of the FES. The conclusions of the DES and PFES were reversed in the final statement largely as a result of the joint federal-state hearing process. By introducing new information into the hearings before the NRC FES was completed, new issues were raised for the latter document. The hearing process functioned as a gigantic scoping operation during its 19-month existence. The two-year delay in the issuance of the FES (which was of intense concern to NRC) was essential in enabling the processes of information sifting and issue development to proceed far enough so that a more adequate assessment could be conducted. It was the process of preparing the environmental statement in the context of the joint hearings that was critical. This process shaped and enlarged the scope, set bounds on the analysis, and ultimately determined the content of the FES.

Similar findings are emerging from one of the few retrospective examinations of FES content and implementation in various federal agencies. Sewell's evaluation of 200 FESs filed in 1973 and 1980 concludes that EIS procedures (rather than scientific content in most cases) are forcing consideration of environmental factors and are significantly affecting federal decision making (Sewell, 1981).

In substantive and procedural terms, the Greene County final environmental statement is unique and/or important in that it:

- was the first NRC FES to recommend denial of a construction permit;
- was the first NRC FES to make "unacceptable

aesthetic impacts" the basis of that denial;
- advanced the state of the art in aesthetic impact analysis, especially with the inclusion of local attitudes and behavior;
- reversed the major conclusions of the DES;
- found major adverse socioeconomic impacts in the areas of roads and transportation, possible loss of local industry with subsequent employment and tax loss impacts, and secondary effects upon the area's numerous historical structures;
- established additional major factors that must be considered in power plant siting;
- advanced the state of the art in mitigation analysis for socioeconomic impacts;
- represented the increasing scope and relevance of SIAs in NRC FESs, despite its remaining flaws; and
- illustrated the increasingly independent assessment role for SIA.

The significance of the Greene County FES can also be judged in relation to past social impact analyses of large energy facilities. This landmark statement can be seen as the outgrowth of a long evolutionary process begun at ORNL in 1972 with the Mendocino nuclear power plant assessment (Peelle, 1974). High points along the route included the Hartsville FES that required social impact monitoring as a condition of the license (NRC, 1976; Peelle, 1979), increasing analytical independence in the Blue Hills early site review (NRC, 1978), social costs identified in the San Onofre operating license review (NRC, 1981), and the analytical completeness of the Solvent Refined Coal-1 (SRC-1) FES in 1981. This progression illustrates the growth in scope, analytical sophistication, and technical independence of social impact assessments, reaching a high point in the Greene County analysis.

Lest we give the mistaken impression of inevitability or "onward and upward forever" in this discussion of the evolution of SIAs, we also note the following: outcomes of individual statements are strongly affected by assorted accidents and random factors such as timing, delays, characteristics of the utility, competing agency priorities, availability of particular staff and relevant skills, and the presence of knowledgeable intervenors, as well as the nature and severity of the impacts. The complex interplay of internal and external pressures for NEPA compliance was demonstrated in the aesthetics, social, and historical impact assessment areas.

While the state of the practice is improving, the quality of SIAs in EISs continues to lag behind what is currently possible because of the continuing administrative, time, and resource constraints. Precedents may continue to be set in community impact mitigation and aesthetics analysis (Greene County) or requirements (Hartsville), but enforcement is neglected.

Turning from the problems and progress of social impact assessments to the broader questions of the public purposes served by the licensing process, we note the following: public participation plays a vital role in setting the agenda for issues to be considered in SIAs but still falls far short of meeting goals of public involvement in decision making. Many public concerns are not addressed in the formalized procedures set up for licensing nuclear power plants. Furthermore, public groups and local governments are at a severe disadvantage in these licensing actions because of their formal, legalistic structuring as a game of experts to be played only by those with the proper chips (technical studies) and certain credentials. These disadvantages were partially offset in the Greene County case by the New York State power plant siting procedures that supplied local governments with modest funding for technical studies.

In the interest of improving future joint federal-state licensing proceedings, more attention needs to be given to establishing common objectives, more efficient and inclusive procedures, and better interagency cooperation and information sharing. The enormous amount of information made available by the joint licensing process is a distinct public and assessment benefit only if it is well organized and accessible. The volume, diffuseness, and fragmentation of the Greene County record hindered effective use by all parties, especially the public interest and local government intervenors.

The long-term significance of the Greene County FES is yet to be determined, of course. It is not clear whether Greene County will be a unique signpost along a continuing route to more independent and thorough SIA in federal decision making or whether it will be a high watermark unequalled in the future.

REFERENCES

Cortese, C., and Jones, B. (1977), "The Sociological Analysis of Boom Towns." Western Sociological Review, 8, 76-90.

Council on Environmental Quality (1978), "Regulations for Implementing Procedural Provisions of the National Environmental Policy Act." Federal Register, November 29, 43, 55978-56007.

Council on Environmental Quality (1978), Environmental Quality, p. 407.

Council on Environmental Quality (1980), Environmental Quality, pp. 383-384.

Council on Environmental Quality (1981), CEQ Scoping Guidelines, April 30.

Friesema, H. P., and Culhane, P. J. (1976), "Social Impacts, Politics, and the EIS Process." Natural Resources Journal, 16, 339-356.

Herschberger, J. (1980), A Comparative Assessment of
    Repository Siting Models with Respect to
    Intergovernmental and Public Relations. Report IGS-
    RW-003. Berkeley, Cal.: Institute of Governmental
    Studies, University of California.
Jobes, P. (1976), "Practical Problems Facing Sociologists
    Preparing Environmental Impact Statements." Social
    Impact Assessment, 8, 12-17.
Liroff, R. (1976), A National Policy for the Environment:
    NEPA and Its Aftermath. Bloomington, Ind.: Indiana
    University Press.
"PASNY Cancels Plant" (1979), Nuclear News, May, 43-44.
Petrich, C. (1979), "Aesthetic Impact of a Proposed Power
    Plant on an Historic Wilderness Landscape." In
    G. Elsner and R. Smardon (technical coordinators),
    Proceedings of Our National Landscape: A Conference
    on Applied Techniques for Analysis and Management of
    the Visual Resource. Washington, D.C.:
    U.S. Department of Agriculture.
Peelle, E. (1974), "Social Impacts of a Remote Coastal
    Nuclear Power Plant: A Case Study of the Mendocino
    Proposal." Unpublished manuscript, Oak Ridge
    National Laboratory, Oak Ridge, Tenn.
Peelle, E. (1979), "Mitigating Community Impacts of Energy
    Development: Some Examples for Coal and Nuclear
    Generating Plants in the U.S." Nuclear Technology,
    44, 132-140.
Sewell, G. (1981), The Quality of Scientific
    Considerations in Decisions Affecting the
    Environment. Report to the National Science
    Foundation. New York: Columbia University.
U.S. Nuclear Regulatory Commission (1976), Partial Initial
    Decision in the Matter of Tennessee Valley Authority
    (Hartsville Nuclear Plant, Units 1A, 1B, 2A, and 2B).
    April 20.
U.S. Nuclear Regulatory Commission (1978), Final Site
    Environmental Statement Related to the Determination
    of Suitability of Site G for Eventual Construction of
    the Blue Hills Station, Units 1 and 2, Gulf States
    Utilities Company. Docket Nos. 50-510 and 50-511,
    NUREG-0449, July.
U.S. Nuclear Regulatory Commission (1979a), Final
    Environmental Statement Related to Construction of
    Greene County Nuclear Power Plant, Power Authority of
    the State of New York. Docket No. 50-549,
    NUREG-0512, January.
U.S. Nuclear Regulatory Commission (1979b), Draft
    Environmental Statement Related to Construction of
    New England Power Units 1 and 2 (NEP I and II).
    Docket Nos. STN50-568 and 50-569, NUREG-0529, May.
U.S. Nuclear Regulatory Commission (1981), Final
    Environmental Statement Related to Operation of San
    Onofre Nuclear Generating Station, Units 2 and 3,
    Southern California Edison Company, San Diego Gas and

Electric Company. Docket Nos. 50-361 and 50-362, NUREG-0490, April.

U.S. Nuclear Regulatory Commission and New York State Board for Electric Generation Siting and the Environment (1976), Protocol for the Conduct of Joint Hearings, November 6.

Wilke, A. S., and Cain, H. R. (1977), "Social Impact Assessment under NEPA: The State of the Field." Western Sociological Review, 8, 105-108.

NOTES

[1]Douglas Point in Maryland was the first joint federal-state nuclear licensing action.

[2]NRC's principal authority to license nuclear installations comes from the Atomic Energy Act of 1954 and is supplemented by NEPA and various judicial and administrative decisions.

[3]This process has now been combined by NRC (1980) so that both functions are conducted under one licensing project manager.

[4]Only the Indian Point licensing actions exhibited comparable evolution and change in issues over time.

[5]An exception was the aesthetic analysis task, where the two years (full time) allocated and the considerable resources allocated were considered adequate by the analyst.

[6]Four previously published listings were used in compiling the list of eligible sites.

[7]These include, at least, reduction of duplication and paperwork by avoiding separate licensing actions by state and federal parties, improving coordination and understanding by requiring all relevant parties to participate in the same proceedings, thereby saving time and resources for all concerned, and speeding up the licensing process (USNRC and NYSBEGS&E, 1976). The (unexpected) effects and outcomes of the joint hearing process were described in Section VI.

5. The Role of Human Values, Attitudes, and Beliefs in Environmental Assessment

Margaret S. Hrezo and William E. Hrezo

INTRODUCTION

The National Environmental Policy Act of 1969 (P.L. 91-90) calls for the use of "a systematic, interdisciplinary approach which will ensure the integrated use of the natural and social sciences . . . in planning and in decision making which may have an impact on man's environment." Moreover, both the Environmental Protection Agency and most state guidelines consider citizen participation an essential ingredient in the assessment of a proposed project's environmental impact. However, research on and the actual use of environmental impact statements have focused on the technical, physical, and scientific implications of proposed projects much more than on the role of human values, attitudes, and beliefs in the environmental assessment process.

Thus, the officials responsible for researching and assessing the environmental impact of public policies often seem unaware that environmental choices are political choices and that political choices--choices involving how society allocates advantages and disadvantages--are based on more than quantitative analysis of the costs and benefits of available alternatives. Political choices also involve, although often unconsciously, beliefs about human nature, about how people can and should relate to one another, about what actions or ideas should receive social priority, and about the definition of good, acceptable, or just conduct within that society. For example, national and state environmental regulatory boards and agencies often receive public criticism. Much of this criticism relates to philosophical and value differences among the individuals or groups involved and, in turn, the fate of environmental policies is often more a political than a technical decision.

While the previous point is perhaps evident to the majority of those involved in the development and review

of Environmental Impact Statements (EISs), its
implications are often overlooked. Sewell and O'Riordan
(1976) commented concerning this type of situation that an
important "factor underlying pressures for greater power
sharing has been the failure of past plans or policies to
identify correctly the desires of the public." Perhaps
this results from disciplines such as political science.
Legally and practically, such an oversight is no longer an
option. Political acceptance is a major factor in the
preparation of and deliberation on environmental impact
statements; therefore, knowledge of the source and
direction of environmentally related political activities
has become a necessity. The authors contend that the
public's understanding and acceptance or rejection of
environmental impact statements can often be anticipated
by thoughtfully considering the sociopolitical values
important to American society and the relationship of
these values to public beliefs about the environment.
Insight of this sort should facilitate the development of
an approach that would enhance the probabilities of
gaining public support for environmental impact
statements.

Toward this end, this paper will undertake the
following objectives in the hope of promoting the
inclusion of information related to political beliefs,
values, attitudes, and opinions into the formulation and
assessment of environmental impact statements:

1. Outline some of the basic value assumptions of
    the American sociopolitical culture and the
    relationship of these values to public opinion
    theory;
2. Attempt to discover some of the consequences for
    the environment of the political culture by
    outlining the results of public opinion research
    concerning the environment;
3. Explore some of the effects that values may have
    on projects affecting the environment and some of
    the effects that such projects, in turn, may have
    on social, political, and economic assumptions;
4. Explicate some potential strategies, based on an
    understanding of important values and attitudes,
    that can enhance public understanding,
    acceptance, and participation in the
    environmental assessment process.

THE FORMATION OF PUBLIC OPINION

The major question raised by this paper is, How do
beliefs, values, and attitudes affect opinions on the
environment and especially citizen reaction to
environmental impact statements? Its premise is that
knowledge of how opinions are formed is an essential step
in the provision of an answer. Milton Rokeach (1968), for

instance, has found that individuals with different value systems differ in both their attitude structures and their behavior. Theories of attitude change posited by social psychologists such as Hovland, Sherif and Sherif, Osgood, Newcomb, and Festinger center on the assumption that inconsistency between attitudes and between attitudes and behavior creates stress and generates pressure to reduce the inconsistency. Their results point to the conclusion (Zajonc, 1967) that "thoughts, beliefs, attitudes, and behavior tend to organize themselves in meaningful ways." Finally, the foundation of survey research is the contention that opinion and behavior are the expression of attitudes. Thus, an exploration of the process of opinion formation will help explain the interrelationship of the elements involved (beliefs, attitudes, and values) and their effect on the expression of citizen opinion on the environment.

According to Bernard Hennessy (1970), "public opinion is the complex of preferences expressed by a significant number of persons on an issue of general importance." This paper will focus on one aspect of Hennessy's definition. Where does the "complex of preferences" originate and wherein lies its motivating force? Are preferences inherent or do we learn them? Are they influenced by our social institutions and shared group relationships? Evidence suggests that opinions are learned (Campbell et al., 1960; Jennings and Niemi, 1968; Langton, 1969; Nimmo and Bonjean, 1972). They represent patterns of behavior acquired over a period of time and structured by the social groups, culture, and institutions with which the individual interacts.

The authors believe that a broad theoretical conceptualization of ideology is fundamental to this study because it provides the means of linking together all of the major elements. In this sense, it differs from Rokeach (1973, 1975), who argues that ideologies are institutionalized and are derived from external authority. It is the contention of this study, however, that ideologies define the nature of the external authority and relate it to the individual and his or her world. Instead of external authority dictating the content of the ideology, the ideology is an attempt to explain perceived reality. It contains some factual information, usually as much as is available, but it also depends on emotional, irrational, or even illogical ideas to unify and supplement the empirical aspects. Ideology is closely aligned with the Greek meaning of "myth"--a story or parable. Parables embody as many facts as possible and explain them in a loosely knit framework that allows the individual to operate comfortably without fully understanding each detail or subtle implication. This is necessary because one can neither fully understand nor cope with all of the intricacies and complexities of reality. Yet such complexities are inescapable.

These externally generated stresses and complexities motivate the formation of an ideology and help to dictate its content. Most early theories of motivation assumed that drive states are uniformly annoying or unpleasant experiences. However, there is a growing trend, one espoused by Abraham Maslow (1968) and basically accepted in this research, that there is more to motivation than "techniques for reducing discomfort." There is also a drive to grow, to become self-fulfilled or, to use Maslow's terms, to self-actualize. Maslow believes that there are specific relationships involved between deficiency motivations and growth motivations. These relationships form a hierarchical order so that "gratification of one need and its consequent removal from the center of the stage brings about not a state of rest . . . but rather the emergence into consciousness of a 'higher' need" (Maslow, 1968). The hierarchical concept is related, at least in part, to survival since an individual who fails to meet the needs of food and shelter is unlikely to live long enough to become concerned with self-esteem or beauty. The hierarchy established by Maslow (1954) includes the following sources of motivation:

1. Physiological needs
2. Safety needs
3. Belongingness and love
4. Importance, respect, self-esteem
5. Information
6. Understanding
7. Beauty
8. Self-actualization

Less potent sources of motivation (beauty and self-actualization) do not cease to exist when an individual is operating on a more basic level. Growth-oriented motivations are present and exert some influence, their strength varying in relation to the energy necessary to cope with the needs at the bottom of Maslow's hierarchy. Further, no growth-oriented person ever becomes totally independent of safety-related drives. The result is an interdependent safety-growth dynamic.

It is obvious from Maslow's hierarchy that cultures as well as individuals experience drive states. Again, some of these stresses motivate the society to relieve an unpleasant or threatening situation while others encourage cultural growth. At both the individual and societal levels, however, they dictate the conditions under which the ideology is formed.

This conceptualization of ideology is applicable at various levels. Following Rokeach (1975), it will be called a belief system at the individual level. A belief system "represents the total universe of a person's beliefs (expectations) about the physical world, the social world, and the self." However, it will be called the pattern of social norms (instead of ideology) at the societal level. The authors feel that this change is necessary because Rokeach's theory omits any generalized formulation of the individual's relationship with the entire external world. At the same time, the term "social norms" retains the connotation of summarizing expectations about the society and its relation to the environment.

These ideas are not new. Numerous psychologists, organization theorists, and political scientists have used variations of the ideological concept in a similar fashion. Perhaps the work that most closely follows the proposed meaning and function of ideology is Sigmund Freud's The Future of an Illusion. Freud's "illusions" closely parallel the idea of a pattern of social values. His discussion of religion suggests the explanatory nature of ideology and the authoritative position voluntarily attributed to it by the society or individual. Freud also stressed the interaction between fact and fantasy that is an integral part of the ideology's capacity to explain:

> When I say that these things are illusions, I must define the meaning of the word. An illusion is not the same thing as an error; nor is it necessarily an error . . . . What is characteristic of illusions is that they are derived from human wishes. (Freud, 1964)

The combination of the additive power of irrational needs with observable facts generates a potent force. This strength is essential to this conceptualization of ideology. A large portion of the ideology's influence on behavior is grounded in its ability to explain all of the aspects of a particular situation and to explain them in a manner that provides a comfortable, comprehensible picture of the environment. Individuals become very dependent on their belief systems (and societies on their pattern of social norms) because of their explanatory power. In deference to this explanatory/conceptual strength (and also because of fear of being cut off from its psychic comforts), the ideology is often raised to unassailable heights. Its elements, whether they describe civilization as a whole or some component of it, are "credited with a divine origin" and are "extended to nature and the universal" (Freud, 1964). Beliefs, then, become dogmas.

Freud believed that religion was an example of a larger conceptual process. He maintained that illusion was the central idea and that religion was only an example of such an illusion. Freud raised the possibility of their widespread use when he wrote:

> Having recognized religious doctrines as illusions, we are at once faced by a further question: may not other cultural assets of which we hold a high opinion

and by which we let our lives be ruled be of a
similar nature? Must not the assumptions that
determine our political regulations be called
illusions as well? (Freud, 1964).

These questions seem to be the basis for much of
Murray Edelman's investigation in The Symbolic Uses of
Politics. He both accepts the idea of ideology and
demonstrates its extension into the political realm. "In
contemporary society as well, certain political beliefs
are socially communicated and are unquestioned" (Edelman,
1964). He cites the Constitution as one example of an
unquestioned political dictum that combines both rational
and irrational aspects.

At both the individual and societal levels, the
ideology generates certain values. Further, the values of
individuals tend to parallel those of society. First, the
individual may totally accept both the culture's pattern
of social norms and its accompanying values and ideals.
Second, one might use these ideals as the foundation of a
personalized variation of the cultural myth. Finally,
even if the individual attempts to reject completely the
social norms of his or her culture, socialization tends to
ingrain the society's values and set certain parameters
within which the individual will operate as he attempts to
develop a new belief system.

In Beliefs, Attitudes, and Values, Rokeach (1975)
defined a value as a type of belief that dictates that "a
specific mode of conduct or end-state of existence is
personally and socially preferable to alternative modes of
conduct or end-states of existence." Donald Super and
Martin Bohn (1970) agreed that values are "objectives that
are considered desirable and that are sought in action."
Finally, Freud (1964) argued that values are those
"estimates of what achievements are the highest and the
most to be striven after." These ideals, Freud
maintained, arise from the resolution of the challenges
presented to the culture by its unique and particular
situation and are usually incorporated into the ideology.
Values, then, are the reflection and enshrinement of
humanity's success in coping with the environment and
guarantee the continuation of those things designated as
desirable by that society's justification of its birth and
growth--its myth or pattern of social norms. These values
possess affective, cognitive, and behavioral aspects.
Once they are consciously or unconsciously internalized,
they become the standard for action and for the
development and maintenance of attitudes (Rokeach, 1975).
The ideology explains and clarifies the ends or objects
that can fulfill the person's needs. These ends become
values because of their ability to perform this
utilitarian function.

This usage of value differs in some respects from
Maslow's. Following Rokeach, the authors do not believe

that needs and values are synonymous. Values express
needs and explain, through the ideology, the ends or
objects that can fulfill needs--that is, reduce threats
from or dependence on the external world. The needs of
the individual are the source of values but these values
are defined and explained by the ideology. The critical
role of ideology, then, is its linkage of values and
needs.

This discussion also helps in the differentiation of
values from attitudes. First, values serve as a guide for
attitudes and actions. Further, values guide actions past
specific objects or immediate situations to ultimate end-
states of existence while attitudes relate only to the
object or situation at hand. Rokeach (1975) views
attitudes as "relatively enduring organizations of beliefs
around an object or situation predisposing one to respond
in some preferential way." Kretch and Crutchfield call
them "an enduring organization of motivational, emotional,
perceptual, and cognitive processes with respect to some
aspect of the individual's world" (Kiesler and Collins,
1969). Finally, Gordon Allport defines them as
"neuropsychic states of readiness for mental and physical
activity" (Jahoda and Warren, 1973). All of these
definitions highlight the relationship between ideology,
values, and attitudes. All three attempt to render the
world more comprehensible and psychically comfortable for
the individual. Katz's formulation of the four functions
of attitudes further emphasizes the complex relationship
among these three concepts. To him, attitudes perform:

1. An instrumental function;
2. An ego-defensive function in which the individual
    "protects himself from acknowledging the basic
    truths about himself or the harsh realties of his
    external world;"
3. A value-expressive function; and
4. A knowledge function "based on the individual's
    need to give adequate structure to his universe"
    (Katz, 1960).

These functions relate directly to Maslow's safety-growth
continuum and to the key role played by ideology in
linking needs and motivations to values and attitudes.

The real importance of attitudes, however, lies in
their conative or behavioral element. While values
contain a conative aspect in the sense that they lead "to
action when activated," attitudes move beyond the belief
that a goal or object is preferable to an active
predisposition to respond to that object or to achieve
that goal (Rokeach, 1973). As M. Brewster Smith (1975)
suggested, expressed opinions are overt behaviors that
reflect attitudes. This is true even where there appears
to be a contradiction between attitude and behavior. As
Rokeach points out, an attitude reflects not one

predisposition but at least two and possibly several.
Thus, behavior (either physical action or expressed
opinion) expresses the interaction between the
individual's attitude toward the object and his or her
attitude toward the immediate situation (Rokeach, 1975).
The following diagram helps to elucidate the elements
discussed:

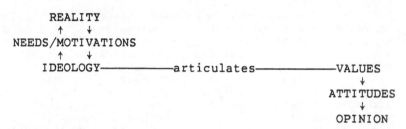

An individual's perceived reality is a function of
personal needs and motivations. The frustration of need-
related motivations, which can also result from the
failure to achieve or maintain values, generates a state
of stress. The ideology or myth clarifies the
interrelationship of these elements and suggests behavior
to reduce that stress. It expreses needs and motivations
in a comprehensible manner, develops values that reflect
and idealize them, and explains the sources of and
strategies for reducing tension. Attitudes reflect these
values and predispose the individual to action in
conformity with them. Opinion is the bridge between the
internal, psychological world of ideology, values, and
attitudes to the external world of behavior and choice.
Opinions are specific reactions to external stimuli that
provide a window to the core of the personality.
Backstrom and Hursh-Cesar (1981) provide an excellent
summarization:

> We distinguish opinion from attitude in that opinion
> is focused and expressed. Questions about opinions
> try to learn what people think or feel at a
> particular point in time about a particular subject.
> Their thoughts and feelings are, however, the fruits
> of an underlying, deeply ingrained attitude system.
> Questions about attitudes, then, tap the respondent's
> basic personality orientation.

THE CONTENT OF THE AMERICAN IDEOLOGY

It is important to understand the function and
relationship of each of the factors that affect the
formation of a "complex of preferences." However, it is
obvious that the core element is myth or ideology. Thus,
in order to understand public opinion in the United

States, it is essential to explicate the values inherent in the American ideology.

Classical liberalism provides the pattern of social norms for the values, attitudes, and opinions of the American public. According to Devine (1972),

> a consensual political culture has existed in the United States, essentially unchanged during its entire history. Its roots are in the republican principles of Locke and were reinforced and adapted to American circumstances by Madison and the other "Founding Fathers" of the Constitution.

Louis Hartz (1955) and C. B. MacPherson (1962) also support this contention. American society is so pervaded by the tenets of liberal philosophy that citizens no longer think about or question either its assumptions or its implications. What, then, are the basic assumptions of liberalism about the individual and his or her relationship to his or her social and physical world and into what values are these assumptions translated?

Classical liberal philosophers shared four key postulates. Reality, they believed, is external. The real is what the individual can see, touch, or count. The mind has no independent creative power or subconscious activity and its function is to add and subtract the evidence of the senses. Second, the natural condition of the world is scarcity. There has never been and will never be enough to supply the wants and needs of everyone. This condition makes competition among individuals endemic. Further, liberalism perceives human beings as isolated, discrete, autonomous individuals. Each individual is totally responsible for his or her position in life. Finally, the early liberal philosophers all attempted to discover some objective, external standard that would end the social, political, and private discord of their era and that would provide some means of settling conflicting demands over the allocation of the limited amount of material goods. Ultimately, all of the liberal theorists settled on some formulation of possession as the foundation of their objective standard (MacPherson, 1962).

Several values emerge from their theoretical systems. These include beliefs in limited government, liberty, equality, private property, and an emphasis on achievement (Devine, 1972). These values fit easily into the outline devised for the formation of an ideology. The liberals' view of the nature of man and the stresses posed by his social, historical, and physical reality led to a search for an unassailable standard that would settle all arguments about the worth of individuals, religions, ideas, and governments. They found their standard (ideology) in possession, and possession became the touchstone for all other social, political, and individual values.

There has been some softening of American adherence
to the most extreme aspects of classical liberalism as the
nation has become more affluent and, therefore, less
restricted to the physiological safety/needs end of
Maslow's continuum. However, poll results still
demonstrate widespread belief in individualism, private
property, and limited government.

Individualism

Americans still believe strongly that the individual
is responsible for his or her own fate and that hard work
and will power will result in success. The Political
Beliefs of Americans by Lloyd Free and Hadley Cantril
(1968) documents this credo. Consider, for instance, the
following results of their survey:

> Generally speaking, any able-bodied person who really
> wants to work in this country can find a job and earn
> a living.
> Agree   76%
> Disagree   21%
> Don't know   3%

This represents the opinions not only of the affluent who
have enjoyed all the benefits of the economic and
political system but also of 70 percent of those
respondents with incomes of less than $5,000 per year.
Further, at a time when the black unemployment rate was 15
percent, 60 percent of the black respondents also agreed
with this proposition (Free and Cantril, 1968). Sixty
percent of those interviewed (and 60 percent of those with
incomes of less than $5,000) agreed that "the relief rolls
are loaded with chiselers and people who just don't want
to work" (Free and Cantril, 1968). Finally, 79 percent of
those sampled agreed that "we should rely more on
individual initiative and not so much on government
welfare programs" (Free and Cantril, 1968).
Results from the Center for Political Studies' 1976
Election Study (1977) reinforce these findings. Forty-
five percent of the sample tended to agree that most poor
people are brought up without drive and ambition. The
survey asked for responses to the statement "the poor are
poor because the American way of life does not give all
people an equal chance." Over 50 percent of the
respondents disagreed with this statement. The Michigan
study also asked respondents to place themselves on the
following scale:

1. 14% Government should see to it that
2.   6% everyone has a job and a good
3.   9% standard of living.
4. 21%
5. 13%

6.   13%   Government should let each person
7.   21%   get ahead on his own.

While these percentages are far from conclusive, 47 percent of the sample tended to emphasize individual initiative. Only 29 percent placed themselves on the government intervention end of the scale. (These percentages do not add up to 100 percent because "don't know" and "no answer" responses are omitted.)

Private Property

Polls also demonstrate continuing confidence in the free enterprise system. A January 1976 Times poll revealed that 96 percent of the respondents believed Americans should be prepared to make sacrifices in order to preserve the free enterprise system. A February 1977 Roper survey in which 50 percent of the sample considered the American system of business and industry basically sound further demonstrated support for American capitalism. Another 19 percent of the Roper sample felt no changes at all were needed in the American economic system. Further support for this position comes from a 1979 survey by Cambridge Reports in which 58 percent of the respondents agreed that the free market system is essential to freedom. Taxes traditionally have been considered an infringement on property. In June 1978, 70 percent of the respondents in a Harris poll stated that federal income taxes were too high. Finally, 58 percent of those surveyed for a January 1978 CBS News/New York Times poll indicated that the government has gone too far in interfering with the free enterprise system.

Limited Government

In its 1976 Election Study, The University of Michigan's Center for Political Studies asked its sample whether they thought the government was getting too powerful. Seventy-six percent agreed that it was. Only 24 percent felt that it was not becoming too strong. A November 9, 1975 Gallup poll found that 67 percent of its sample agreed that cutting taxes and spending by similar amounts was a good idea. Another Gallup poll (April 8, 1976) reported that 78 percent would favor a constitutional amendment that would require Congress to balance the federal budget each year. Further, 51 percent of the respondents in a September 1978 Gallup poll felt that the government was the most to blame for inflation and an Associated Press/NBC News survey taken in December 1978 reported that 63 percent of their sample favored a substantial cut in federal spending. These results demonstrated a belief in limitations on governmental power because government action hinges on adequate funding. They also expressed the belief that government is unable to solve societal problems no matter how much money it gets. Finally, according to a 1978 Gallup survey, 47 percent of the respondents cited big government as the greatest threat to this country in the future.

IDEOLOGY AND CITIZEN OPINIONS ON THE ENVIRONMENT

Poll results, however, tend to be unidimensional. Individuals and their belief systems, values, and attitudes are not. Expressed opinions reflect the interaction of several attitudes. The salience of the attitude to the individual, and the particular motivational need each attribute satisfies, helps to determine which attitude dominates and, therefore, what opinion the individual expresses. At the same time, for instance, that three-quarters of those surveyed agreed that the government is too powerful, 57 percent favored a return to wage and price controls. While citizens indicate mounting frustration with government interference, 26 percent feel there should be more government regulation (Opinion Roundup, 1980). Results such as these support the need for an understanding of the origins and function of ideology and of the values and attitudes that it generates. An important part of the study of public opinion, then, is the investigation of the salience of attitudes and of the motivations that they reflect.

An overall conceptualization of ideology offers a particularly valuable insight into citizens' opinions concerning the environment. The values embodied in the classical liberal political philosophy suggest that the public would not demonstrate support for protection of the environment--especially if such protection conflicted with private property values or necessitated an expanded governmental role. Survey results, however, do not uniformly point in this direction. For instance, an ABC News/Lou Harris poll conducted in October 1978 reported the following results:

Would you enforce the toughest environmental standards possible, even if they increased the costs of things to both business and the consumer, or would you be satisfied with a somewhat lower level of environmental standards if this turned out to be less costly?

Enforce toughest standards	48%
Satisfied with somewhat lower standards	39%
It depends	13%

The Roper organization posed a similar question to its sample and found that 50 percent were not willing to cut back on pollution and safety regulations that raise the cost of products--if the cutback would slow progress on pollution and safety. Finally, in 1978, 53 percent of the respondents in an Opinion Research Corporation survey agreed that "protecting the environment is so important that requirements cannot be too high and continuing improvements must be made regardless of cost" (Mitchell, 1979). These findings have led one author to conclude that the environment is now "one of our more enduring social concerns" (Mitchell, 1979).

On the other hand, Gallup polls conducted over a long period of time reveal an apparently contradictory trend. For over 18 years, the Gallup organization has asked respondents to name the most important problems facing this country. Table 5.1 lists the rankings accorded pollution since 1972.

TABLE 5.1
Rankings accorded pollution since 1972

Year	Ranking	Percentage
1972 (August)	6	5%
1972 (October)	6	4
1973 (March)	6	14
1973 (May)	5	9
1973 (September)	7	8
1974 (January)	NM'	
1974 (July)	NM	
1974 (September)	NM	
1974 (October)	NM	
1975 (August)	NM	
1975 (November)	NM	
1976 (May)	NM	
1976 (November)	NM	
1976 (May)	NM	
1976 (November)	NM	
1977 (April)	8	4
1977 (August)	NM	
1977 (November)	NM	

'NM indicates that pollution was not mentioned.

In February 1976, the Gallup poll asked individuals to rank the areas that should be given first, second, and third priority "if and when more federal money from Washington is available." Pollution and conservation were mentioned by 24 percent of those interviewed and received an overall ranking of sixth. Rated ahead of environmental concerns were health care, education, law enforcement, welfare and aid to the poor, and public housing. A similar Gallup poll asked citizens to rate the most important election issues in the 1976 campaign. The sample ranked pollution fourteenth out of the twenty

concerns listed. Yankelovich asked people to rate the
severity of listed social problems according to a five-
point scale. Pollution placed eighth in this rating
system (Yankelovich, Skelly, White, 1977). Finally, in
both 1976 and 1979, the Roper organization asked citizens
to indicate which one or two things from a long list "are
the most important to be done right now." Respondents
ranked improving and protecting the environment eleventh
(8% percent) in 1978 and tenth (9 percent) in 1979.

An investigation of several projects where economic
and environmental demands clashed also demonstrates the
existence of conflicting public attitudes. The location
and construction of the trans-Alaska pipeline, for
instance, created environmental problems such as
construction-related oil spills, sewage treatment
violations, and infringement on wildlife habitats
(Virginia Water Resources Research Center, 1976). Yet
public opinion supported its construction. Congress
passed special legislation in 1979 to allow construction
of the Tellico Dam despite its violation of the Endangered
Species Act, the National Environmental Policy Act, the
Historic Preservation Act of 1966, and the Federal Water
Pollution Control Act.

Within Virginia, citizens have supported several
projects that have generated environmentally related
controversy. Although the plan has stirred some
opposition, most citizens of Rockingham County support the
Board of Supervisors' decision to rezone 236 acres of land
for the construction of a brewery. This plant,
environmentalists charge, will endanger the county's
agricultural base and pollute the water (Virginia Water
Resources Research Center, 1980a).

Coastal resources potentially are threatened by
shoreline development, the construction of refineries, and
the operations of off-shore oil wells. Proponents of the
proposed refinery in Portsmouth, Virginia, cite the need
to decrease American dependence on foreign oil and to
provide additional employment opportunities. However,
dredging, oil spills, and air pollution caused by such
plants do have an adverse effect on at least some aspects
of the surrounding environment. Further, Virginia has no
comprehensive plan to protect its coastal resources. The
state does not participate in the federal coastal zone
management program and the governor recently vetoed three
wetlands protection measures that he felt unduly
restricted development. Instead, he signed a group of
bills designed to aid individuals and localities whose
waterfront property is threatened by tidal erosion. Yet
beach replenishment and the construction of seawalls and
levees are often destructive of the fragile coastal
ecosystem.

On March 4, 1980, the Virginia General Assembly
passed popular legislation that created the Virginia Coal
Conversion Authority. This authority will seek $4 million

from the Department of Energy for a feasibility study on
the construction of a synthetic fuel plant in the state.
The state believes such a plant will provide jobs and
energy. At the same time, however, a synfuel plant
presents environmental problems such as water pollution
and the disposal of between 3,500 and 5,400 tons of solid
wastes (some potentially hazardous) every day (Virginia
Water Resources Research Center, 1980b).

Finally, Virginians have offered little opposition to
the construction of new water impoundments within the
state. In 1977, several areas asked the General Assembly
to downplay scenic river designations that might interfere
with the building of impoundments needed for water supply
or pumped-storage hydroelectric projects (Virginia Water
Resources Research Center, 1977). Hydroelectric dams are
also sources of nonpoint pollution that may disturb water
quality and kill fish.

STRATEGIES

What effects, then, do all of these findings have on
this paper's thesis that an understanding of citizen
opinion should rely on a broad theoretical
conceptualization of ideology. Have environmental
concerns overridden or undermined the traditional American
concerns for individual liberty and private property? Do
they weaken or invalidate the explanatory power of
ideology as a theoretical concept? The authors believe
that it is impossible to understand fully citizens'
opinions on environmental issues without using the total
ideology concept. Apparent contradictions in
environmental opinions may be caused by fluctuations among
the elements of the explanatory framework.

It appears that citizens do agree that water and air
pollution pose serious threats. It also appears that most
citizens define environmental problems as water and air
pollution and that, to most individuals, a quality
environment means breathable air and drinkable water. At
the same time, attitudes toward the environment possess
relatively low salience for the individual. America's
ideological base, liberalism, does not define the
environment as a central concern because it does not have
a known, or easily calculable, economic value. Citizens
are willing to pay for breathable air and drinkable water
because these issues represent unknown economic costs that
do not appear to threaten any other basic liberal values
or any high-priority drive state (e.g., food, safety, and
shelter). Citizens feel they can support clean air and
water programs and still satisfy what the ideology defines
as higher-priority needs. Moreover, the evidence suggests
that, when there is an immediate conflict between the
environment and a known economic value (such as new energy
sources or greater employment opportunities), the economic
value will triumph. It will triumph because it is defined

by the ideology as valuable and because it satisfies what the ideology considers to be a more basic human need.

Most citizens appear to consider wildlife habitats, coastal ecosystems, and floral phenomena as unrelated to the environment. The American relationship to the land has viewed the land as a resource to be used without external restraints and for private gain. Land does possess an economic value. The aesthetics of flora and fauna do not. There is little question who will emerge victorious in the battle between the snail darter and economic advantage.

In Public Perception of Water Resource Problems, Charles A. Ibsen and John A. Ballweg (1969) write that

> the acceptance of action programs by the public is largely determined by the extent to which the public:
> 1. is aware that a problem exists;
> 2. believes that the problem represents a threat to the continuity or well-being of the community:
> 3. believes that corrective action is possible and practical.

Survey results demonstrate that citizens are aware of environmental problems and consider them a threat. They also know that corrective action is often possible. However, one question remains. Do they perceive protection of the environment as practical? This question depends on ideology for an answer.

Practicality is a complex notion. Its complexity stems from the dual components of capability and salience. Are the technical, strategic, and emotional means available to treat the situation? Is the issue important enough to mobilize the resources required to solve the problem? This is essentially a political question in which the public will have an important role.

The increased desirability (and at times necessity) of citizen input into the preparation and evaluation of statements that address such questions makes the treatment of practicality strategically important to public officials. As environmental issues become more politicized, the successful development, assessment, and implementation of environmental policies will require increasing levels of citizen support. Practicality, especially in terms of political feasibility, will be a major consideration for environmental impact statements, and thus the ability to understand and anticipate public opinion and behavior concerning environmental issues will be recognized as an essential skill. The explanatory value of viewing public opinion from the combined perspective of ideology and liberalism may provide the foundation for the development of such a capability. Indeed, it is already possible to suggest certain general strategies for gauging and gaining public support.

The first alternative is simply to accept liberalism and capitalism, which is its historical and philosophical counterpart, as the dominant political/economic ideology. This ideological base can provide both a means of and a direction for involving the citizen in environmental decision making. The means come from a relatively new, but growing, body of public choice theory that incorporates the tenets of liberalism. Public choice theory assumes individual rationality and the related ability of citizens to establish priorities and to make choices based on their values. The direction of such decisions also can be anticipated to reflect the liberal values of private fulfillment and materialism. The implication is evident--let economic incentives or disincentives serve as the foundation for practical environmental decisions.

This is certainly not a new idea. Governments at all levels have long threatened polluters with economic penalties. However, rational calculations have often convinced those involved that inconsistent or nonexistent enforcement practices and lenient penalties made pollution economically advantageous. In addition, individuals generally have been willing to accept lower product prices and unwilling or unable to expend the time and energy necessary to calculate hidden or long-range costs.

However, such a situation is not inevitable. Congress has recently passed the Toxic Substances Control Act, which suggests a stronger commitment to penalizing polluters. It is also becoming increasingly evident to individuals, especially after the publicity attending the loss of homes at Love Canal, that pollution is so pervasive that it represents an economic threat to everyone. Allen Kneese (1980) has concisely summarized the importance and position of this alternative:

> One cannot say that study of the role of economic incentives in hazardous materials policy is in its infancy; it is not yet born. It is, however, one of the most important, even urgent, areas for research by environmental economists.

A second strategy evolves from an awareness of motivation in the conceptual framework. Opinions and behavior reflect motivation. Therefore, if citizens can be convinced that their basic needs are threatened, they will respond. If environmental issues can be redefined to emphasize their physical and/or ideologically determined psychological safety and security aspects, behavior related to environmental policies can be affected. To accomplish this, it is necessary both to inform the public of the conditions involved and to convince them that such conditions are threats to their fundamental, motivationally influenced values.

There is some evidence that these conditions exist

and that such a shift has begun. The Kepone incident in
Virginia posed serious health hazards to humans and has
had disastrous economic effects on the regional seafood
industry. PCBs, which have been found in dairy and beef
cattle, have caused the disruption of local farming
economies and have threatened the health of producers and
consumers. Moreover, a recent Environmental Protection
Agency survey found that "nearly one-third of industrial
surface impoundments are unlined and situated in areas
where permeable soils would not prevent wastes from
leaching into underground aquifers" (Bureau of National
Affairs, 1980).

Such issues are gaining increased public attention.
In addition, the public is beginning to perceive them as
genuine threats to its physical and economic well-being.
As this change occurs, the salience of environmental
problems and the drive to solve them increases. This
drive can be used as an effective tool in increasing the
public role in the environmental policy process.

The third alternative is simultaneously the most
difficult and, perhaps, the most promising for those whose
primary concern is the environment. It involves a
reorientation of the ideological base of American
political thinking. Liberalism has been the dominant
ideology since the founding of the regime. The
Constitution codified it and it has been incorporated into
virtually all aspects of the American lifestyle. However,
this does not mean that the doctrines of liberalism are
unassailable.

We no longer live in the world of liberal theorists
such as Hobbes, Hume, and Locke. The United States, as it
approaches the twenty-first century, may be faced with the
necessity of updating its ideology to reflect the modern
world. Kenneth and Patricia Dolbeare (1976) referred to
just such a re-evaluation in their writings on the
emergence of reform liberalism. Reform liberalism is, in
effect, a new ideology. It is based on liberalism but
reorients liberal values to fit contemporary society.

A reorientation of this type and scale necessitates
changes in the existing order. For the reform liberal,
this entails using the new ideology to alter public
attitudes and then modifying the governmental personnel
and policies that implement them (Dolbeare and Dolbeare,
1976). Practicality thus becomes a matter of changing the
public consciousness and thereby influencing governmental
policy.

While classical liberalism has not been eclipsed, a
significant segment of the American population seems to be
finding reform liberalism a more reasonable or accurate
explanation of reality. The environment has demonstrated,
throughout this period of ideological flux, the potential
to activate the process of change. A Washington Post
article concerning Earth Day 1980, commenting on a decade
of environmental awareness and activism, mirrored the

reform liberal ethic. The last ten years have seen the involvement of millions of Americans in a wide range of environmental issues, and this large-scale participation has elicited governmental response. This period has seen the passage of approximately eighty pieces of environmental legislation by the federal government. Yet, movement in public opinion concerning the environment is at best a slow, gradual process. Reform liberalism has not replaced classical liberalism, and the environmental battle has not been won. Addressing the Earth Day audience in Washington, D.C., Edmund Muskie called "for a national commitment to energy conservation to ensure that environmental ideas are not eclipsed by economic pressures" (Washington Post, 1980).

CONCLUSION

This paper has attempted to demonstrate the potential for the application of sociopolitical theories to the area of environmental policy. Such notions may seem foreign to some. However, it should be remembered that the intent of the interdisciplinary approach suggested by the National Environmental Policy Act is to stimulate interaction between those with different perspectives based on different areas of expertise. To ignore another's perspective because it seems strange or overly theoretical causes the loss of valuable insights and information. Such a loss, in terms of gaining an understanding of the basis of political decisions to support or reject environmental policies, will inevitably prove to be counterproductive.

Public opinion has become and will continue to be a vital component in the development and assessment of environmental policy. This need not vex officials involved with environmental impact statements. Rather, by using an interdisciplinary approach, it is possible to use public opinion for the successful preparation and promotion of environmental policies.

Public opinion does not develop in a vacuum. It is reflective, either in an individual or in a group, of certain attitudes and value-oriented preferences. As described in the discussion of ideological development, such values and attitudes tend to be persistent. In addition, the majority of citizens of the United States demonstrate an adherence to an ideology based on classical liberalism, making many attitudes both comprehensible and predictable. Thus, the social sciences offer a medium for analyzing public opinion by which the environmental officer can improve the political acceptability of environmental impact statements.

While various general strategies have been suggested for approaching or dealing with the public on environmental issues, no single course of action can be offered here. No one plan would be appropriate for the

138

technical and political conditions encountered in the
process of developing and assessing each individual
environmental impact statement. However, a basis for
making such judgments has been offered. Also, by applying
the overall conceptual framework presented in this paper,
the environmental officials concerned with public opinion
should be in a position to begin to accomplish
successfully the following:

1. To understand the source, meaning, and strength
   of public opinion;
2. To interpret public opinion data concerning
   environmental issues;
3. To anticipate public reactions to policies and
   ways to head off problems:
4. To identify alternative ways of presenting
   policies to the public and the various groups to
   which such alternatives would appeal; and
5. To mobilize support for policies by recognizing
   the hierarchy of values described by a particular
   ideology.

REFERENCES

Backstrom, C. H., and Hursh-Cesar, G. (1981), Survey
    Research. New York: John Wiley and Sons.
Bureau of National Affairs (1980), Environment Reporter,
    10, 2330.
Campbell, A., et al. (1960), The American Voter. New
    York: John Wiley and Sons.
Center for Political Studies (1977), 1976 American
    National Election Study. Ann Arbor, Mich.: Inter-
    University Consortium for Political and Social
    Research.
Devine, D. (1972), The Political Culture of the United
    States. Boston: Little-Brown.
Dolbeare, K., and Dolbeare, P. (1976), American
    Ideologies. Chicago: Rand-McNally.
Edelman, M. (1964), The Symbolic Uses of Politics.
    Urbana: University of Illinois Press.
Free, L., and Cantril, H. (1968), The Political Beliefs of
    Americans. New York: Simon and Schuster.
Freud, S. (1964) The Future of an Illusion (translated by
    W. D. Robinson-Scott). Garden City, N.Y.: Anchor
    Books.
"A Fine Earth Day" (1980). Washington Post, April 23,
    p. C3.
Hartz, L. (1955), The Liberal Tradition in America. New
    York: Harcourt, Brace, and World.
Hennessy, B. (1970), Public Opinion. Belmont, Cal.:
    Duxbury Press.
Ibsen, C. A., and Ballweg, J. A. (1969), Public Perception
    of Water Resources Problems: Bulletin 29.

Blacksburg, Va.: Water Resources Research Center.
Jahoda, M., and Warren, N. (Eds.) (1973), *Attitudes*. Baltimore: Penguin Books.
Jennings, M. K., and Niemi, R. G. (1968), "The Transmission of Political Values from Parent to Child." *American Political Science Review*, 62, 169-184.
Katz, D. (1960), "The Functional Approach to the Study of Attitudes." *Public Opinion Quarterly*, 24, 163-204.
Kiesler, C. A., and Collins, B. E. (1969), *Attitude Change*. New York: John Wiley and Sons.
Kneese, A. V. (1980), "Toxic Wastes and Economic Incentives." *Resources*, 64, 16.
Langton, K. P. (1969), *Political Socialization*. New York: Oxford University Press.
Maslow, A. (1954), *Motivation and Psychology*. New York: Harper and Row.
MacPherson, C. B. (1962), *The Political Theory of Possessive Individualism*. Oxford: Clarendon Press.
Mitchell, R. C. (1979), "Silent Spring/Solid Majorities." *Public Opinion*, 2, 19.
Nimmo, D. D., and Bonjean, C. M. (1972), "Political Socialization Research in the United States: A Review." In R. J. Cook and F. P. Scioli (Eds.), *Political Attitudes and Public Opinion*. New York: David McKay and Co.
"Opinion Roundup" (1980). *Public Opinion*, 3, 21.
Rokeach, M. (1968), "The Role of Values in Public Opinion Research." *Public Opinion Quarterly*, 32, 547-559.
Rokeach, M. (1973), *The Nature of Human Values*. New York: Free Press.
Rokeach, M. (1975), *Beliefs, Values, and Attitudes*. San Francisco: Jossey-Bass.
Sewell, W. R. D., and O'Riordan, T. (1976), "The Culture of Participation in Environmental Decision Making." *Natural Resources Journal*, 16, 2.
Smith, M. B. (1975), "Comment on the Implications of Separating Opinions from Attitudes." In R. O. Carlson (Ed.), *Communications and Public Opinion*. New York: Praeger.
Super, D., and Bohn, M. (1970), *Occupational Psychology*. Belmont, Cal.: Wadsworth.
Virginia Water Resources Research Center (1976), *Water News*, April, p. 13.
Virginia Water Resources Research Center (1977), *Water News*, December, p. 2.
Virginia Water Resources Research Center (1980a), *Water News*, February, p. 1.
Virginia Water Resources Research Center (1980b), *Water News*, April, p. 3.
Zajonc, R. (1967), *Social Psychology*. Belmont, Cal.: Wadsworth.

PART 2

Applying Assessment Techniques

INTRODUCTION

The redefined scope of environmental impact assessment has been accompanied by the emergence of new, more sophisticated, more useful, and more comprehensive techniques for analysis, data gathering, citizen participation, and social decision making. This chapter presents seven papers that explain recently used and still emerging techniques that have served well as analytical tools to make assessments true aids to decision makers.

Diana Valiela presents the experimental approach she has used in improving the predictive performance and usefulness of biological impact assessment in complex estuarine environments. Nellie M. Stark offers preliminary environmental assessment techniques for soils in determining the impacts of various agricultural and forestry practices. James J. Jordan recounts the use of land-capability analysis as a planning and regulatory tool in the Lake Tahoe Basin; he explains how land-capability criteria have successfully been used as primary determinants of the decisions concerning land development and use in the Tahoe area. The application of image-based information systems for environmental assessment is presented by Ronald G. McLeod; the remote-sensing technology of space satellites is shown to be an effective and comprehensive means of gathering data on land form, use, and condition.

The complexity of EIA issues, the great amount of information, and the varying interpretations of both based on differences in interests, values, and perspectives often conspire to present a prodigious task of evaluation to decision makers. Techniques for the management of this complexity, for the use and weighting of different data, and for securing the input from various publics are explored in the last three papers. Eric L. Hyman, David H. Moreau, and Bruce Stiftel summarize the status of their research to establish a participant value method for the presentation of environmental impact data. The paper by Benjamin F. Hobbs, Michael D. Rowe, Barbara L. Pierce, and Peter M. Meier presents comparisons of methods for evaluating multi-attributed alternatives in environmental assessments. James R. Pease and Richard C. Smardon examine the scoping concept and citizen involvement as an opportunity for rejuvenating NEPA.

Collectively, this part's papers convey both the variety and richness of tools for both physical analysis and social decision making. EIS practitioners have the opportunity to tailor select such tools and adapt them to their specific assessment needs. Moreover, decision makers have the opportunity, with guiding assistance from practitioners, to interpret and use the results of these techniques.

6. Improving Predictive Performance and Usefulness of Biological Environmental Impact Assessment: Experimental Impact Studies and Adaptive Impact Assessment

Diana Valiela

OVERVIEW

Environmental impact studies attempt to predict effects of impacting factors on a biological system by examining the system in its present unimpacted state. Consequently, the biological studies produced have poor predictive capabilities and are generally lengthy descriptions of the existing biological system. Simulation modelling can be used to focus selectively on important relationships between possible impacting factors and ecosystem variables. A number of methods can be used to simulate or perform the proposed development changes on an experimental basis (e.g., on simulation models, on physical model systems, on parts of the real system, in comparative studies, and in monitoring of actual developments) and, thus, improve the capability to predict impacts. Incorporation of Environmental Impact Assessment (EIS) into the management/decision-making process and its time horizon allows for revisions and re-evaluations of assessments as development proceeds and research results are produced. Examples of these approaches will be drawn from studies on effects of a variety of coastal activities on biological resource systems, including salmon and oysters in British Columbia.

Assessment of biological impacts is perhaps the most emphasized aspect of current Environmental Impact Statements (EISs). Assessment usually attempts impact identification, magnitude estimation, and evaluation of importance. Whether those identification, estimation, and evaluation functions are performed at a qualitative or a detailed and/or quantitative level, the process is essentially one of prediction since it describes future states of the system being considered. EISs generally make predictions based on knowledge of the unimpacted system. That is, in fact, the objective of current Environmental Impact Assessment: to predict impacts before they actually occur.

Two critical issues must be raised about the

prediction function of EIA. The first issue that must be
recognized is that there will always be (perhaps
substantial) uncertainty. Therefore, EISs cannot make
sure predictions; that must be planned for by interfacing
impact assessment with management and decision making,
thus providing for revisions of the EIA. The second issue
is that the major approaches presently used to predict
biological (and other) impacts are based on examination of
the unimpacted system: they must be improved upon by
using approaches that examine a simulation or other form
of the post-impact system--which is a new and different
system whose behavior is difficult or impossible to
predict even with perfect knowledge of the unimpacted
system. Examination of such simulated and/or experimental
developments can be made for a number of different
development alternatives within the same environment.
Thus, it is possible to assess provisionally ways to
enhance the desired positive effects of developments while
diminishing the negative impacts.

IMPROVING IMPACT ASSESSMENT BY
ADAPTING IT TO ONGOING MANAGEMENT

     No form of study or analysis will allow certain (or
even near-certain) impact prediction for most systems.
There will be residual or major uncertainties in all
situations as a result of biological complexity and the
unknown nature of impact interactions. It is important to
recognize and describe that uncertainty, to try to
understand the basic functioning of the new (impacted)
system, and to revise predictions as the system responds.
Thus, EIAs that are one-time, pre-impact studies have
little chance of contributing predictions that are
reliable or useful for decision making on an ongoing
basis. Unfortunately, existing institutional and
decision-making arrangements (NEPA, CEQ, EARP, and many of
their state/provincial and municipal counterparts) assume
such a temporal arrangement for EISs and, thus, do not
provide for incorporation of impact assessment into
development and post-development phases of the management
and decision-making process. There are opportunities
within current arrangements, however, for special efforts
and provisions to be made that incorporate monitoring
programs and revised assessments into post-development
management. These opportunities include specification of
post-development monitoring and reassessment requirements
in the terms of reference of an EIA, or in contractual
arrangements, and efforts to incorporate impact assessment
into management processes by working with government
agencies and development proponents outside the formal EIA
process. These efforts relax the (unattainable)
requirement of certainty in EIA predictions and allow us
to learn from our decisions and the system's responses
(see Figure 6.1). Most of our efforts at the University

of British Columbia have been directed at incorporation of impact assessment into management programs of government agencies. For example, we assessed the impacts of the activities of the forest products industry, including transport and storage of logs in coastal waters, on the oyster resource and industry in British Columbia (Valiela, 1979a, 1979b). The assessment used a simulation model (see Figure 6.2) to make initial predictions of oyster growth and survival and oyster industry production depending on levels of log activities in oystering areas. Figure 6.3 is one of the scenarios examined. It illustrates the effect on the British Columbia production of oysters, using bottom culture, of gradually increasing the conflicts with the forest industry. As shown by the solid line, if conflicts remain at their present levels, and we assume that the rate of seeding is increased and good market demand continues, then production from bottom culture could be expected to double in the next twenty years. However, if there is a gradual increase in the conflicts with the forest industry, there would be no increase in production, as shown by the dashed line, in spite of other favorable conditions. On the other hand, concentration of oyster production in areas that might be given a protected-reserve status has considerable potential even in the face of generally increasing conflicts with the forest products industry. Figure 6.4 shows how oyster production by string culture might be increased over the next twenty years even with increasing conflict if just two highly productive areas (Baynes Sound and Malaspina, in this example) are protected by a reserve status.

The initial impact predictions discussed above were accompanied by management suggestions (e.g., make deals for selected high-priority oystering areas) and selected research suggestions (e.g., measure growth rate of oysters in a log storage area). As management and system responses proceed (e.g., some high-priority oystering areas are reserved; others are lost to forest-industry uses) and results of research emerge (e.g., growth of oysters to commercially usable sizes takes, let us suppose, six years in certain affected areas as opposed to four years in similar but unaffected areas), the prediction of impact on the productivity of the oyster industry can be reformulated or revised. Thus, the initial predictions of impact need not be highly certain but are useful in suggesting immediate management and research strategies leading to future improvements in predictive and planning performance. At the same time, the results of the research and the revised impact predictions can be used for evaluation of the initial EIA.

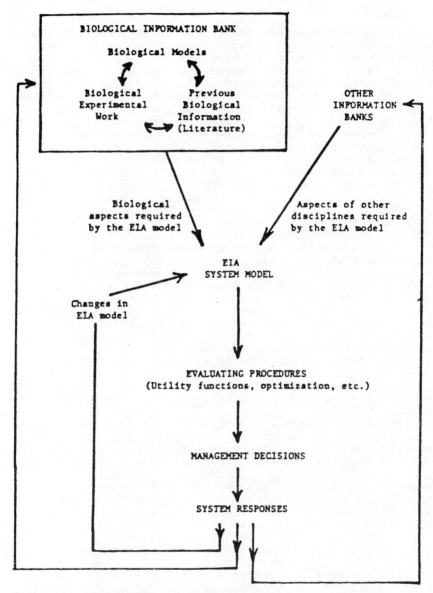

Figure 6.1   Diagrammatic representation of the input of
biological information into an environmental
impact assessment. Note that the term
"information bank" is used in the general
sense to designate the total information
available from that discipline for use by the
EIA. Note the direction of information flow
indicated by the arrows and the various
feedback loops. (Source: Ward, 1978)

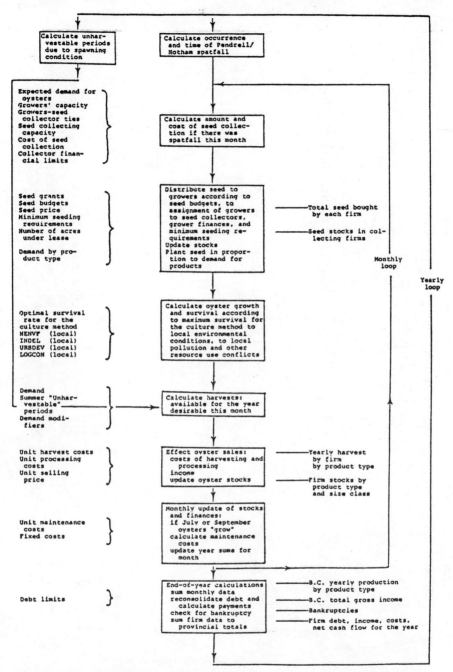

Figure 6.2 Flow diagram of the oyster production simulation model. The main inputs are on the left of the calculation boxes; the main outputs are on the right. The center of the diagram portrays the impacts of log-handling activities (LOGCON) on oyster growth and survival and, thus, on oyster production outputs further down. The effects of a range of alternative policies can be explored by varying the actions taken. (Source: Valiela, 1979b)

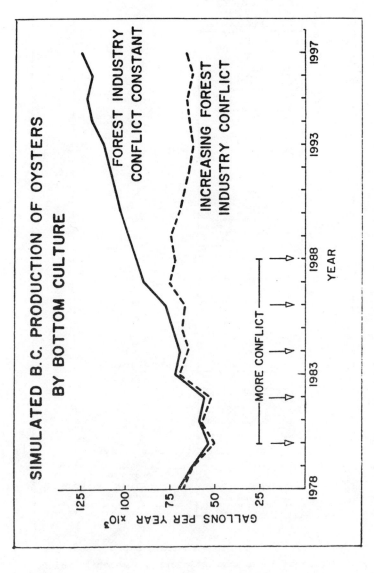

Figure 6.3 Simulated production of oysters by bottom culture in British Columbia assuming present levels (solid line) and moderate gradual increases in conflicts (dashed line) with the forest products industry. Other conditions are assumed to be favorable within realistic limits. (Source: Valiela, 1979b)

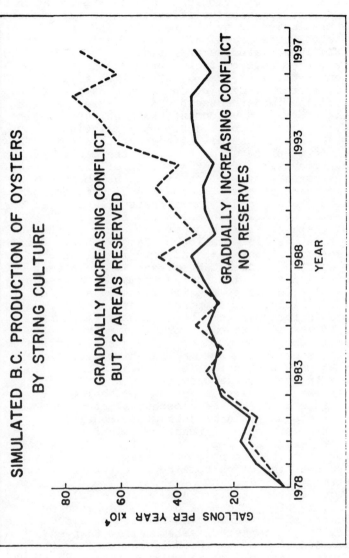

Figure 6.4 Simulated production of oysters by string (off-bottom) culture in British Columbia assuming moderate gradual increases in conflicts with the forest industry, other conditions being favorable, and no protective reserve status for any areas (solid line) and reserves in two highly productive areas (dashed line). (Adapted from Valiela, 1979b.)

IMPROVING ASSESSMENT OF IMPACTS BY
STUDYING THE IMPACTED SYSTEM

The major approaches currently used to predict
biological as well as nonbiological impacts are based on
the assumption that descriptive information in the present
state allows prediction of system behavior in changed
(impacted) states. The principal terms of reference for
most biological impact studies are usually of the form(s):
"What will be the effects of factor or development X on
biological components A, B, . . ., N?" or "What will be
the effects of factor or development X on ecosystem Y?"
The response of the impact assessor is to review various
aspects of the proposed development, examine the existing
biological system, and prepare a report presenting
speculations as to the possible effects of development X,
or of several forms of development X, on the described
components or ecosystem. The examination of the existing
biological system usually employs either the "busy-
taxonomist" approach or the "information-broker" approach.
In both, literature and other researchers are surveyed to
obtain descriptive information about the biological
components of the ecosystem in question. This is the
major emphasis in the "information-broker" method. For
the "busy taxonomist," the next and most important step is
field-survey sampling, often carried out to the extent
allowed by the time specified in the terms of reference.
The survey sampling examines the distribution and
abundance of the biological components and the values of
physiochemical factors present in the ecosystem. Often a
considerable volume of taxonomic work is involved. In
some of these studies, there is an attempt to investigate
functional characteristics--but in the unimpacted state of
the system. Voluminous descriptions and data tabulations
often result. In both approaches, a (lengthy) report is
prepared, containing guesses as to how the ecological
system might respond to each development alternative.
These guesses are based on some conceptual model of how
the new (impacted) system will function. There are often
suggestions for (expected) impact mitigation, but seldom
provisions for post-monitoring or reassessment of impacts
either at a future time or on some representation of the
impacted system.
Even within current EIA arrangements, usefulness and
predictive ability of EISs can be greatly improved by:
(1) beginning the EIS by rapid construction of a much more
explicit model of the impacted system rather than ending
the EIS by construction of an ill-defined model of the new
system; (2) using the model to formulate hypotheses about
biological effects of the proposed development;
(3) performing the proposed development on an experimental
basis (on simulation models, on physical-model systems, on
parts of the system, or in comparative studies) to test
the impact predictions generated by the initial model; and

(4) modifying the model and proposing expected impacts, along with important assumptions, key data, or analysis needs, and applicability limitations.

MODELLING AND HYPOTHESIS FORMULATION

As previously mentioned, all approaches to impact assessment involve some conceptual (mental, implicit) model of the impact system and involve a large number of implicit assumptions. The mental models are usually not sufficiently explicit to discriminate effectively the relevant vs. the irrelevant issues or to recognize and examine assumptions, certainties, and uncertainties. Further, the conceptual models tend to be constructed at the end of the EIS. Meanwhile, the bulk of the EIS effort and time has been devoted to examination of the unimpacted system.

Explicit modelling performed early in the EIS can be used to focus the study on the impacted system, to discriminate relevant from irrelevant or less crucial questions that may be pursued in the EIS, to focus selectively on important relationships between impacting factors and ecosystem variables, and to identify clearly assumptions, uncertainties, and important future information needs. A large assortment of modelling activities and types is available. (Some are compared and discussed in Holling, 1978.) In general, the more explicit (explicit does not mean detailed) we are forced to be by the modelling activity, the better. The model may be at the conceptual, verbally descriptive level, a fully computerized simulation model, or something between these two categories (e.g., matrix methods for impact identification). The model should include the proposed development factor(s) as one interacting component. This involves guessing at development effects, but in an explicit systematic framework and in the context of causal and functional pathways in the biological system. Based on this analysis, we can list predicted biological effects of the development factor(s) and identify processes and variables likely to be crucial to model outcome and to the function of the biological system.

The question of whether to attempt a computerized simulation model for a specific situation is a complex one that arises with each new (and always different) environmental impact study. A full discussion of decision criteria for computerization is given in Munn (1975). In general, matrix impact identification methods are useful for screening but not for generating predictions. Qualitative simulation models can help to construct a trial dynamic model and sometimes to experiment with alternative policies, but they are not useful for guiding research to be done in an EIS whether or not the data are good--unless there is no way to describe the basic features of the assessment (impacting factors and biological elements) and the relationships between the basic features--and are good for making predictions when the data are good (Holling, 1978). In some cases, the data (or, rather, the information, since qualitative aspects are often most important) are far better than initially suspected and can be utilized by bringing experts or managers familiar with the system into a workshop situation. In such situations, we can extract unpublished data and experientially aided guesses as to alternative functional pathways.

Application of simulation modelling to examine effects of developments and management actions on salmon systems in British Columbia provides examples of the benefits that can be derived from explicit modelling even when the data are poor and the model is essentially qualitative (whether or not it is computerized) and of the benefits that can be derived from making numerical predictions of effects even if (sometimes, especially if) the predictions are in error. One simulation model was constructed to examine consequences of marsh habitat loss through developments for salmon populations of the Fraser River (Dorcey et al., 1978; Valiela and Kistritz, 1979). It was known that juvenile salmon migrating to sea were sometimes found in Fraser marsh areas. Would the disappearance of all or some of those marsh areas affect the salmon productivity of the Fraser? It was clear from the outset that the biological system was too complex (there are five species and numerous races of salmon in the Fraser; they have a complex life history utilizing many habitats; they are affected by human activities in many ways and many places; and they number in the hundreds of millions of fish as juveniles) and the existing information inadequate to describe the major functional attributes of the marsh-salmon system. However, decisions on developments affecting or removing marshes must be made now and we cannot expect the mammoth investment in research that would be involved in understanding the entire salmon system.

As a result of explicit modelling, even at this level of information deficiency, we were able to isolate two critical research priorities, from a huge domain of possible questions, that are of greatest immediate use in evaluating the importance of marsh habitats to salmon. One important question emerged from what was included in the model (see Figure 6.5). In describing the utilization of marsh habitats by young salmon, we had only guesses on whether the fish actually resided in the marsh or simply passed through: in addition, we could not describe whether other estuarine or coastal habitats could be used by the marsh residents if they were deprived of marsh habitats. Thus, a first research priority was to determine residence time in marsh and nonmarsh habitats. Without residence, it is unlikely that survival of the fish would be greatly affect by marsh disappearance. We have now determined that chinook, and to a lesser extent chum, show significant marsh residency in the Fraser (Levy et al., 1979).

The second research priority was identified by what was excluded from the model. We realized we could not model the entire life history of the salmon, since such a model would be very large and complex and the features of marine stages are even less well known than are those of estuarine phases. However, it was also realized that, even if numerous juveniles had extended residence periods in marsh habitats, those habitats would still not be vital to stock production unless the marsh residents constituted a significant proportion of successful returning adults (i.e., their marsh residency contributes to survival until they return to spawn). Thus, the second research priority indicated was feasibility of growth-pattern analysis (in otoliths or in scales) to differentiate marsh residents from nonmarsh residents when returning as adults. Thus, even though the salmon-marsh model produced predictions of juvenile salmon numbers that were no doubt grossly in error because of the number of assumptions made in the absence of data, the modelling effort clearly identified major areas of data deficiencies (see Table 6.1) and allowed specification of high-priority questions from a huge set of possible questions.

Another modelling effort on a salmon system in British Columbia showed that making numerical predictions with a model can be of value even if the predictions are in error. The model was an attempt to predict salmon stock sizes under different fishing regimes in Georgia Strait, British Columbia (see Argue et al., in preparation; Holling, 1978, Chapter 12). The model included assumptions and data-based estimates of the catches of various fishing fleets as well as of other relationships. When model predictions of populations of chinook and coho salmon were examined, there was consistent overestimation when compared to available data. Going back to assumptions and parameters and calculating new predictions for alternative assumptions showed that the estimate of the sport catch for these two species must have been seriously underestimated (Walters, personal communication). This discovery led to recommending data collection on that issue; data recently collected show that for some stocks the sport catch of chinook and coho may be twice as high as previously thought. This information is very important to develop new management regulations for sport and commercial fishing in the area. Thus, both the modelling activity and examination of model predictions can help identify very specific high-priority data needs and eliminate general, nondirected, expensive, and time-consuming data collection programs.

It should be noted that equally expensive, time-consuming, and overly complex modelling programs can result if conscious efforts are not made to restrict

154

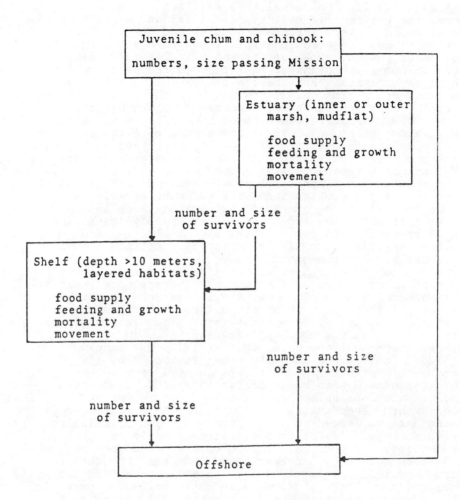

Figure 6.5 Simplified flow diagram of estuarine
            utilization by chum and chinook juveniles.
            (Source: Valiela and Kistritz, 1979)

TABLE 6.1
Key uncertainties suggested by modelling the consequences
of marsh habitat loss for salmon populations of the
Fraser River (from Valiela and Kistritz, 1979)

Distribution and Migration

1. Residence time by habitat and cues for movement
2. Size and weight of downstream migrants
3. Timing of downstream migration
4. Determinants of habitat selection
   - food supply
   - osmoregulatory limitation
   - predation avoidance
   - estuarine holding
5. Density-related behavior

Food Supplies

1. Approach to conceptualization of the complex community
   of food groups
2. Selected baseline seasonal patterns for food groups
3. Major factors used in food selection by salmon
   juveniles
4. Effects of changes in salmon predation on dynamics of
   major food organisms

Feeding and Growth

1. Perception and rate of effective search
2. Importance of fish-to-fish interactions
3. Determinants of maximum rations
4. Effects of water quality parameters on feeding rates,
   prey selection
5. Short-term feeding periodicities: time budgets

Mortality Agents

1. Behavioral implications of stress situations
2. Size-selective mortality by agent type
3. Effect of vulnerability to mortality agents relative
   to feeding-time budgets
4. Survey of actual and potential predators and estimates
   of their potential ingestion rates of salmon fry;
   aggregation behavior of predators
5. Switching of prey onto salmon

models to reasonable sizes. (The number of assumptions
increases much faster than the number of relationships
represented; the compounding-of-errors effect can thus be
very large.) In general, it should be possible to
construct initial models for impact assessment analysis
and hypothesis generation in less than a week of
concentrated effort by a team of experts and modellers
(for techniques, see Munn, 1975; Walters, 1974). If a
smaller or less-diverse group is involved, and if accurate
predictions are desired, longer periods may be necessary.
If qualitative, explicit models are constructed, usually a
day or two will suffice. Generally, even the most
ambitious models of well-known systems should be limited
to, at most, a few hundred relationships; generally much
less than that is desirable for environmental impact
purposes. There also exist mechanisms to help delimit
what is included in a model (see Munn, 1975, pp. 74-79).

EXPERIMENTAL STUDY OF IMPACTED SYSTEMS OR THEIR MODELS

So far I have attempted to show a variety of useful
aspects (e.g., conceptualization, explicitness of
assumptions, and identification and ranking of
uncertainties) of explicit modelling to examine the
impacted system in an EIS. Prediction generation is only
one of these aspects, although it is commonly assumed to
be the only objective of mathematical modelling.
Nevertheless, models will generate predictions in an EIS
and it is a valid question to ask, "How good are these
predictions?" One useful approach is to test them
empirically and, depending on the outcome, to use the
experimental results to modify our models and predictions
or to gain confidence in our conceptualization of the
system and expected impacts.
Having used explicit systematic modelling to focus
selectively on important relationships between possible
impacting factors and ecosystem variables, we should have
a set of hypotheses or predictions to test (and a set of
variables to measure as outcome indicators). A number of
methods can be used to simulate or perform the proposed
and alternative development changes on an experimental
basis: on simulation models, on physical model systems,
on parts of the real system, in comparative studies of
systems already affected, and in monitoring of actual
developments. In many situations, controlled experimental
versions of developments can be performed on mathematical
or physical models, on limited parts of the real system,
and in comparative studies. These experimental impact
studies, in combination with modelling analysis to guide
the experimentation and selected laboratory studies to
test specific hypotheses, can be very powerful and
efficient and have been discussed and exemplified
elsewhere (Ward, 1978).
An appropriate issue to discuss here is the set of

situations in which, because of the all-or-none nature of
the project (e.g., construction of a dam) or because of
the large size and complexity of the system affected
(e.g., disappearance of marsh habitats from the Fraser
estuary), it is difficult or impossible to create
appropriate (realistic) experimental environments without
simply allowing the full-scale development to proceed. In
the case of marsh disappearance in the Fraser estuary, it
is unlikely that this experiment will be made. The risks
involved are, in my opinion, seen as too great and too
costly for such a decision to be made. There will
probably be, however, some limited but further marsh loss
due to developments.
     An immediate challenge that we face in our research
is to design a marsh-loss experiment in some much smaller
system (perhaps capitalizing on an actual development) and
to show that the results are extrapolatable to the
situation in the Fraser estuary. Confidence in the
extrapolation can only be bolstered by congruent evidence
from a variety of sources. For example, if otolith
pattern analysis shows marsh residents are an important
component of returning chum and chinook populations in the
Fraser, if simulation models indicate dependency on marsh
residence for survival of some stocks of chum and chinook,
and if a marsh-destruction experiment in a smaller
estuarine system leads to reduction or disappearance of
chum and chinook stocks in that system, we could be fairly
confident that destruction of marsh habitats in the Fraser
estuary would have a similar effect. On the other hand,
lack of consensus among these various sources of evidence
would indicate that we must revise our models about the
marsh dependency of Fraser chum and chinook.

CONCLUSIONS

     The challenge for developing technologies for
biological EIA is not necessarily to develop increasingly
complex and sophisticated methodologies, although some of
these can be profitably used in combination with other
approaches if guided by the needs of the EIA rather than
by the technician's fondness for the methodology. The
challenge is, rather, to have at our disposal a variety of
methods and approaches that can be used according to the
needs of the EIA and that help us to streamline, increase
the predictive power, and enhance the management and
decision-making usefulness of biological EISs. At the
heart of such a strategy are the issues of concentration
on system conceptualization before any empirical efforts
are made, study of the impacted system in some form,
experimental vs. descriptive empirical efforts,
simultaneous use of a variety of approaches to enhance
consensual confidence, and incorporation of EIA into the
management/decision-making process to allow for revisions
and re-evaluations of assessments as developments proceed

158

and new decisions must be made. All of these issues also
emphasize our recognition that we cannot produce EISs that
are perfect predictors of impacts but, rather, assessments
that help us make decisions while we continue to explore
the limitations and uncertainties of those assessments.

REFERENCES

Argue, A. W., Hilborn, R., Peterman, R. M., Staley, J. J.,
    and Walters, C. J. (in preparation), "An Analysis of
    the Gulf of Georgia Fishery for Chinook and Coho
    Salmon." Submitted to the Bulletin of the Fisheries
    Research Board of Canada.
Dorcey, A. H. J., Northcote, T. G., and Ward, D. Valiela
    (1978), "Are the Fraser Marshes Essential to Salmon?"
    Westwater Research Centre Lecture No. 1, University
    of British Columbia.
Holling, C. S. (Ed.) (1978), Adaptive Environmental
    Assessment and Management. New York: Wiley.
Levy, D. A., Northcote, T. G., and Birch, G. J. (1979),
    Juvenile Salmon Utilization of Tidal Channels in the
    Fraser River Estuary, British Columbia. Westwater
    Research Centre Technical Report No. 23, University
    of British Columbia.
Munn, R. E. (Ed.) (1975), "Environmental Impact
    Assessment: Principles and Procedures." SCOPE
    Report No. 5. ICSU-SCOPE, Toronto.
Valiela, D. (1979a), "Oyster ecology and culture in
    British Columbia." Vol. 1 of The British Columbia
    Oyster Industry: Policy Analysis for Coastal
    Resource Management. Westwater Research Centre
    Technical Report No. 19, University of British
    Columbia.
Valiela, D. (1979b), "Policies for Development of the
    British Columbia Oyster Industry: Analyses Based on
    a Computer Simulation Model." Vol. 3 of The British
    Columbia Oyster Industry: Policy Analysis for
    Coastal Resource Management. Westwater Research
    Centre Technical Report No. 21, University of British
    Columbia.
Valiela, D., and Kistritz, R. U. (1979), Dependence of
    Salmon on Fraser Estuarine Marsh Ecosystems: A
    Simulation Analysis. Westwater Research Centre
    Technical Report No. 18, University of British
    Columbia.
Walters, C. J. (1974), "An Interdisciplinary Approach to
    Development of Watershed Simulation Models."
    Technological Forecasting and Social Change, 6,
    299-323.
Ward, D. Valiela (1978), Biological Environmental Impact
    Studies: Theory and Methods. New York: Academic
    Press.

7. Preliminary Environmental Assessment Techniques for Soils[1]

Nellie M. Stark

OVERVIEW

Environmental impact statements have traditionally provided soil profile descriptions and information on erosion and compaction hazards. Some studies have examined the deterioration of stream water quality associated with land uses, but little attention has been paid to the impacts of land use on long-term soil productivity. If we can accept that soil provides a significant resource for the growth of plants, then we must also accept the responsibility for ecologically sound soil management in ecosystems. It is essential to recognize that different land uses make varying demands on the soil resource.

Research in temperate and tropical forests over the last eight years has developed a new technology for easily assessing the long-term impacts of logging, burning, and fertilizing soils. Logging or burning may accelerate nutrient losses, resulting in a reduction of the long-term productive capabilities of the soil. Burning that is too frequent or too hot on chemically fragile, young soils can cause losses of immediately available elements needed for growth, resulting in either deficiencies or nutrient shock. Nutrient deficiencies result in slow tree growth, whereas nutrient shock will render a soil unsuitable for tree growth for a number of years, until weathering and other inputs can return the soil to productive levels. If a soil is old, heavily weathered, and leached, burning may destroy or shorten the remaining biological life of that soil. It is possible to calculate how long a particular treatment can be applied to any soil at a specified rate and time interval before that soil will no longer be able to support trees. Young soils in the Rocky Mountains have long remaining biological lives (50,000 years or more) under moderate burning treatments, whereas some depleted tropical soils can support cut-and-burn agriculture on a 50-year rotation for less than 275 years.

Harvest removes nutrients from the ecosystem that can influence long-term productivity. A means of measuring the impact of nutrient losses from harvest on forest soils has shown that conventional logging will not seriously damage the production of trees on young, fertile soils. It is possible to use simple soil measurements to predict how much fertilizer of any type can be applied to a soil of known texture under known precipitation rates to avoid excessive nutrient losses from the root zone.

These new technologies are pertinent to measuring the impacts of land use on soil fertility and should become a part of environmental impact assessment.

INTRODUCTION

Responsible use of natural resources requires the development of quantitative means of evaluating the impacts that result from the use of resources. The survival of man and all forms of life depends on the use but not abuse of natural resources. It is not adequate to guess or philosophize about man's impacts on resources when so much is at stake. One important task of the Environmental Impact Statement is to quantify the influence of land uses on soil productivity as a means of maintaining renewable natural resources. Renewable resources such as wood are renewable only as long as soil degradation does not occur. The authors of impact statements need to be able to predict what land uses will accelerate soil degradation for different soils and climates.

This need to know and predict the implications of land-use practices on the health of natural systems has resulted in legislation that requires Environmental Impact Statements (EISs). The EIS forces man to take a long, hard look into the future to prevent costly and irreversible mistakes.

All too often, quantitative results relative to soils are lacking in Environmental Impact Statements. Some things such as aesthetic considerations cannot be easily quantified. "Experience" often eludes the finite number. Other information, such as erosion hazard, can be quantified, with a grain of salt.

The soils data included in Environmental Impact Statements are often semi-quantitative or descriptive. Soil profile descriptions are frequently used with the express purpose of describing the apparent physical features of soils, with some inferred chemical information. Analysts can combine information such as annual precipitation, soil moisture, and infiltration-percolation characteristics with soil texture and estimate slump, erosion, and compaction hazards. In some cases, soil chemical data are included and the soil is rated in terms of low, medium, or high fertility. However, the interpretation of the potential impacts of management on soil stops at this point. It is or is not fertile; it will or will not erode or compact under specified

treatments. Although these are important concerns, other
impacts such as the loss of fertility have been neglected.
Perhaps one of the main environmental concerns should be
the loss of soil fertility.
     Research over the last eight years has produced some
quantitative techniques that can help evaluate objectively
the impacts of land use on soil. Although these methods
are no panacea for evaluating soil use, they provide a
beginning in the prediction of long-term nutrient impacts
on soil. The use and limitation of these methods are the
subject of this paper.

NEW TECHNOLOGY

     The loss of nutrients from soil through excessive
leaching, erosion, excessive burning, or harvest can
produce nutrient deficiency, nutrient shock, and reduced
biological life. The following pages examine each of
these categories.

Nutrient Deficiency

     This is an old and long-recognized phenomenon. Low
levels of one or more biologically essential ions limits
growth. This is the least severe nutrient loss and can be
remedied by fertilizer, for a price, or by time to allow
the system to replace the deficient element through
weathering. If the deficiency is for biologically fixed
nutrients like nitrogen, unfavorable temperature or
moisture conditions may prevent the system from overcoming
the deficiency until there is climatic change.
     If the deficiency is for an ion derived from a
geologic source and if there are appreciable amounts of
that element in mineral form, time for weathering and
further release of the ion can reduce the deficiency. The
problem is that man cannot wait hundreds of years to allow
the soil to recover from unwise use.
     The essence of deficiency is that growth is slower
than the maximum expected for the species and climate.
Deficiency is often hard to detect, especially in trees,
and it can only be verified if the plants begin to grow
better when the right nutrient is added. Deficiencies in
forests can be caused by too intense logging, erosion, or
too frequent or too hot burning on young, thin, or poor
soils.
     The proof of the existence of a deficiency of an ion
occurs if the rate of growth of the tree or the stand in
question responds positively to an addition of that ion to
the system. Change in the concentration of the problem
ion in the foliage or water in the xylem should correlate
with the treatment and with the growth response. The
proof of single-factor deficiency lies in obtaining
improved growth with the existing levels of the other
factors that influence growth. Interactions among

environmental factors often confound the effects of single
factors acting alone. Interactions among two or more
agents that influence growth may result in greater or
lesser growth than if each factor operated separately.
Interactions of ions are poorly understood; so the
prediction of their effects is limited. Usually one
factor can be found in the natural system that will
improve growth if it is increased or reduced. A model
useful in calculating deficiency is presented in Note 2.[2]

The limiting factor for growth does not have to be an
ion. It can also be water, sunlight, temperature of the
soil during the growing season, and the total grams of
water present in the root zone at the beginning and end of
the growing season, for water-limited and nonwater-limited
sites with comparable species. The trick for any area is
to determine what ion or environmental factor is most
limiting to growth while realizing that changing one
factor will influence a host of other factors. In some
cases, there may be several limiting factors interacting
simultaneously. Once the limiting factor(s) has(have)
been identified, then an EIS should specify that no
treatment should be applied that will unfavorably alter
the amounts of the factors most important to growth
control on that soil. For example, if a treatment is
likely to accelerate erosion and the soil is limited by
PO_4 that occurs at 90 percent of available soil PO_4 in the
upper six inches of soil, the treatment should be either
disallowed or carefully tested before application.

Toxicity levels of ions, rather than low ion
concentration, may limit growth on a soil. Proper
nutrient balance may be more essential to growth than
absolute amounts of the ions. The level of the suspect
limiting factor may need to be increased or decreased in
the case of toxicity. Any land treatment that will upset
the existing nutrient balance, or shift from a marginal
balance to an imbalance, must be predicted through the
EIS. An example would be the addition of an alkaline soil
amendment to an already alkaline soil that, to begin with,
was marginal for growth.

The loss of biologically essential ions below the
root zone can also be measured for similar treated and
untreated areas using lysimetry and soil water quality
after different types and intensities of land-use
treatment. Thus, it can be estimated which treatments are
more likely to produce deficiency for those ions derived
from soil minerals and which soils are most fragile in
terms of ability to withstand nutrient loss. Those soils
that are lowest in one or more biologically essential ions
are considered to be "chemically fragile" or unable to
withstand heavy ecosystem nutrient losses. The problem is
that it is not known where to set deficiency levels for
different soils. Trees sometimes grow well on soils that
chemically appear to be quite deficient. Good growth is
probably the result of the abilities of resourceful fungal

root associates to extract ions that are not apparently
available (based on soil extraction techniques). Ion
interactions that reduce the seriousness of the apparent
deficiency may allow better growth than expected in
apparently deficient soils. However, enough is known to
permit cautious deficiency predictions for agricultural
land. The other part of the problem is that it is not
known how much of each ion a tree species needs at
different ages. Most nutrient work has been done with
seedlings.

The laboratory of the School of Forestry of the
University of Montana has developed a system for examining
the quality of xylem sap in trees growing on good vs. poor
sites as a means of defining what ion levels constitute
adequate availabilities for good growth. This technology
is in the pioneering stage, but once perfected it will
define how much of each ion is needed for maximum growth,
what ion levels and balances are associated with poor
growth, if water stress if occurring, and how to recognize
easily soils were the trees are barely able to obtain
nutrients sufficient to support growth. These latter
soils can then be classed as "chemically fragile." It
would be safe to say that almost any consumptive use of
resources containing the limiting element from such soils
would constitute an unfavorable and unwise impact. The
difficult task for the author of Environmental Impact
Statements is to recognize which soils are likely to be
chemically fragile. Studies are presently in progress
that will aid in defining chemically fragile soils.

Nutrient Shock

This occurs when too intensive use or burning
followed by leaching or erosion depletes one or more
biologically essential ions to levels too low to support
tree growth. Some (but by no means all) western brush
fields in forested land are thought to be the result of
nutrient shock. Loss of vegetation may influence water
availability, creating a condition of moisture stress
coincident with nutrient shock.

Shock has the same symptoms as deficiency, except
that trees fail to grow back with shock. Shock conditions
require longer periods of time for natural recovery. Once
the limiting ion(s) is(are) restored to the system through
fertilizer or long-term weathering, the soil will again be
able to support trees. The calculation of nutrient shock
hazard is similar to that for deficiency but requires data
on the thresholds of ion levels necessary to grow trees.
These data are not yet available. The main difference is
that, once the limiting factor is known, it must be
determined how much it takes of that factor to make trees
grow again.

The potential for nutrient shock is greatest in the
thinnest, youngest soils. On soils with low levels of

available calcium, for example, any losses of calcium below the root zone as a result of land use are potentially serious. Losses below the root zone are measured by lysimetry and soil water quality. The seriousness of ion losses below the root zone has to be judged against the total content of the limiting ion present in the soil in weatherable form, how fast weathering is expected to occur, and what the needs of trees are in that area for an ion. The total chemical content of rock can be quite easily determined. Nutrient losses below the root zone can be estimated within one water year, but weathering cannot be measured accurately. Cooler and drier climates have slower weathering rates, whereas minerals in wetter and warmer climates tend to deteriorate faster. That is about all that is known, except for the relative susceptibility of different geologic materials to weathering. With the new technology of analyzing xylem sap, it should be possible to estimate how much of each ion is needed for maximum growth of tree species.

At present, the potential for nutrient shock is evaluated by the ion concentrations and total loading in soil water below the root zone compared to total soil ion levels that are available through weathering (Stark, 1977). Any land use that accelerates phosphate loss is not a good treatment in terms of soil fertility and potential shock. Given the present state of knowledge, a 25 percent reduction in the post-treatment ion content of soil water as compared to the original concentration should be considered a potential threshold for nutrient shock.

Biological Life

The biological life of a soil is the time on the geologic scale for which a soil can chemically support trees regardless of climate. Another definition is that, when each gram of soil no longer has enough available and unavailable ions to grow a tree, the soil has ended its biological life. Any reduction in the remaining biological life of a soil as a result of improper land use means significant loss of long-term soil fertility. Although the reduction of the biological life of a soil is largely a theoretical construct spanning long periods of geologic time, it can be calculated and used to compare the relative severities of different land uses on the same land.

The calculation of the remaining biological life requires a knowledge of the annual return of nutrients from bulk precipitation, pollen and dust, the quality, quantity, and annual load of soil water below the root zone of control plots, and the same for similar soil under intensive use. Surface nutrient losses from erosion, logging, or other sources need to be known in some cases.

There are measurements of precipitation quality for much
of the United States. This leaves specific site
measurement of ion losses from harvest, erosion, and in
soil water below the root zone. These are not difficult
to measure. Pollen, rain, and dust bring in fairly small
amounts of ions and these can be ignored if data are not
available.

A reduction of the biological life of the soil is not
recognizable by any immediate response in the vegetation.
Unlike conditions of deficiency or shock, the soil will
not recover to its former productive level. Return of
fertility to the site can come about only if the depleted
soil is washed away or fertile soil is deposited on top of
it. The loss of biological life occurs gradually, a
little excess nutrient disappearing with each use cycle or
rotation. Some productivity loss is inevitable with
harvest, but accelerated losses sustained for a number of
rotations from harvest in excess of natural ions will be
damaging, particularly on old, highly weathered soils.
Because the calculations allow comparisons of severity of
nutrient loss relative to the potential fertility of the
parent material, it is possible to choose the least
damaging land-use treatments in favor of prolonged
fertility (see Note 3 for the model).[3]

Studies of the remaining biological life of soil
after burning (Stark, 1977, 1981) have shown that
relatively young mountain soils in Montana can support
tree growth for from 30,000 to 55,000 years under either
burning at surface soil temperatures of 300 to 500 degrees
Celsius or with clear cutting and burning all slash on a
50- to 70-year rotation. These are moderately fertile
soils in Douglas fir forests. Some ions will remain
considerably longer than 55,000 years. We can expect
glaciation, geologic change, soil development, speciation,
migration, evolution, and other natural forces to change
the sites so much in 55,000 years that lost productivity
is not significant. Thus, the calculations for two local
forests have shown that burning can occur every 50 years
(with temperatures about 300 degrees Celsius) or clear
cutting with conventional bole removal every 70 years
without doing significant damage to the long-term
productivity of these soils. The data cannot be
extrapolated to any soil, however. This is when the
authors of Environmental Impact Statements need to be
ready to interpret the impacts of various uses on long-
term fertility.

Limited studies by the author in several South
American rain forests on old, weathered sands of very low
productivity have shown remaining biological lives of 75
to 275 years with burning and harvest. This means that
for these areas one or two more cut-and-burn operations
will destroy the ability of these soils to grow trees
until some catastrophic removal or replacement of soil
occurs. The same process of "wearing out" supposedly

occurs all over the world, but at slower rates in cooler or drier regions. Land use in the tropics on depleted soils must be viewed carefully or fertility will be lost and tropical wastelands produced (Stark, 1969; Went and Stark, 1968). Mycorrhizal root systems or beneficial fungi associated with roots are natural nutrient-conservation mechanisms. Destruction of the natural vegetation that is adapted to direct nutrient cycling from dead organic matter to living roots (bypassing the soil) reduces the ability of the site to maintain forest growth. A model describing how the remaining biologic life of a soil can be calculated is presented in Note 4.[4] Fogel and Hunt (1978) provide quantitative data on soil fungi, and Brown et al. (1977) and Faurot (1977) have listed data on volumes and weights of western coniferous species.

SITE RECOVERY AFTER HARVEST

Another concern is the impact of intensive or even conventional logging on long-term soil productivity. Studies in Montana show that, if good data exist on nutrient ranges for most above- and below-ground ecosystem compartments, including available soil and total nutrients, it is easy to subtract the nutrient levels expected to occur in the harvested material and calculate if the amount of each ion removed will be replaced from precipitation, recycling of ions from decay, or immediately available soil ions. (See Note 5[5] for a model of site recovery after harvest and Note 6[6] on when to use the various models.) Studies have shown that it is ecologically sound to have three to four times the levels of readily available or recyclable, biologically essential ions on a forest site as are needed to grow one rotation. This safety factor is needed until there is enough data on weathering rates to specify how long it will take weathering to replace the nutrients removed in harvest. If each rotation is subsidized by nutrients weathered during the present rotation and these are removed in the next harvest, the site will never mature or become more productive (Stark, 1980). The compaction hazard of soil and its nutrient and water implications have not reached the prediction stage.

Other soil considerations concern their screening abilities for nutrients. A study recently completed (Stark and Zuuring, 1981) provides regression equations for predicting the nutrient-screening power of texturally different soils: the equations are too long to be included here, but they are available in the study.

The combined analysis of nutrient screening by soil, deficiency hazard, susceptibility to nutrient shock, loss of biological life, and lost productivity from intensive harvest or burning is called IMPACS, or the Impacts of Management on Productivity and Capabilities of Soils. Erosion studies by Stark and Biggam (1979) indicate

that soils with over 13 percent silt and under 12 percent
clay are potentially erosive. The U.S. Forest Service is
modifying the universal soil loss equation for use on
forest soils (Warrington, personal communication).

WHEN TO USE THE EVALUATION OF LOST FERTILITY

Clearly, not every Environmental Impact Statement
needs to employ all of these concepts. Some evaluations
will be costly until a data base is built for each area of
the country. Very young soils are subject to deficiency
or nutrient shock. Old, highly weathered soils may be
subject to lost biological life under too severe
treatment. Many intermediate soil types pose no serious
threat for lost fertility, except from erosion or
excessive harvest. Whenever the proposed use will be
likely to produce accelerated nutrient losses, then
significance of that accelerated loss should be evaluated
against potential soil fertility and long-term effects.
With funding, the remaining tools needed to evaluate the
impacts on nutrient status as a result of use can become
available. Specifically, there is a need to determine how
much of each nutrient and what nutrient balances are
needed to support growth of large trees in different
climates.

REFERENCES

Brown, J. K., Snell, J. A., and Bunnell, D. L. (1977),
    "Handbook for Predicting Slash Weight of Western
    Conifers." USDA Forest Service General Technical
    Report INT-37.
Faurot, J. (1977), "Estimating Merchantable Volume and
    Stem Residue in Four Timber Species: Ponderosa Pine,
    Lodgepole Pine, Western Larch, Douglas Fir." USDA
    Forest Service Research Paper INT-196.
Fogel, R., and Hunt, G. (1978), "Contribution of
    Mycorrhizae and Soil Fungi to Biomass and Its
    Turnover in a Western Oregon Douglas Fir Ecosystem."
    Paper 1271, Forest Research Laboratory, Oregon State
    University, Corvallis, Oregon.
Stark, N. (1969), "Nutrient Cycling in the Amazon Basin."
    Proceedings of the Association for Tropical Biology.
    Columbia, South America.
Stark, N. (1977), "Fire and Nutrient Cycling in a Larch/
    Douglas Fir Forest." Ecology, 58, 16-30.
Stark, N. (1978), "Man, Tropical Forests, and the
    Biological Life of a Soil." Biotropica, 10, 1-10.
Stark, N. (1981), "Nutrient Losses from Harvest in a
    Larch/Douglas Fir Forest." USDA Forest Service
    Research Paper INT-231.
Stark, N., and Biggam, P. (1979), "Erosion and Logging
    Roads." Final report to Five Valley's Council,

168

Missoula, Montana. University of Montana Library
Archives.
Stark, N., and Zuuring, H. (1981), "Nutrient Retention
Capabilities." Soil Science, 131, 9-19.
Went, F. W., and Stark, N. (1968), "Mycorrhiza."
BioScience, 18, 1035-1039.

NOTES

[1]Acknowledgment: The work discussed in this paper
has been supported by the U.S. Forest Service,
Intermountain Forest and Range Experiment Station,
Northern Forest Fire Laboratory, McIntire-Stennis funds,
the Smithsonian Institution, and the National Science
Foundation over the last 12 years.

[2]Deficiency or toxicity for ions essential to growth
can be quantified through the use of the following
equation: $D_i : \pm I_i = > g$, where D_i = deficiency of ith
ion; I_i = increase[1](+) or decrease[1](-) of ith essential or
toxic ion; and > g = increased growth.

[3]The equation used for estimating nutrient
deficiency can be modified so that the desired end product
is growth of a tree species rather than increased growth:
$PS_i = A_i/B_i \times 100$, where PS_i = the potential for nutrient
shock of loss of tree growth for a species; A_i = ionic
content of the soil solution at some point after treatment
(using ion analysis of extracted soil water, not
artificial extracts); and B_i = ionic content of the soil
solution before treatment.

The results are a percentage of ion content in the
soil solution after harvest. In order to interpret this
percentage, it is necessary to know how much of the ion in
question is needed to grow the size and species present
(through xylem sap analysis) per growing season and how
rapidly new additions of the ion are occurring through
decay, precipitation, and weathering. Since weathering
cannot accurately be measured, concern should be with
precipitation, dust and pollen additions, and ion release
through decay.

[4]The remaining biological life (RBL) of a soil can
be calculated for any ion by the following equation: RBL_i
= $R_i \times$ rotation length, where RBL_i = the remaining
biological life of a soil for a particular ion; $R_i = S_i/$
Ir, the number of rotations the particular ion (i) can be
supplied from the soil total and available resources; and
S_i = total potentially available amount of the ion (i)
above the level that will produce nutrient shock.

$$Ir = \sum_{j=1}^{r} P_j - \sum_{j=1}^{r} L_j$$

where r = rotation length; j = year in the rotation; P_j
= ion input from precipitation in the jth year of the
rotation, and L_j is the loss of the ion from the system in

the jth year; and Ir = net loss of the ion during a full rotation. All measurements are relative to liquid losses of the ion in question below the root zone. The next equation on harvest includes measurements of harvest and other above-ground losses.

The final figure from this equation is the number of years that the particular treatment can continue before there will be a loss of the ion in question that will prevent tree growth. If the figure is over 10,000, there is little reason to be concerned. If it is under 1,000 years, there may be need to reduce or eliminate that treatment. These figures are arbitrary and are included only as general guidelines.

As knowledge of weathering rates increases, the method should become refined. The quality of precipitation has been measured all over the world. Total soil chemical analyses are difficult, but some data exist in many areas. It takes only one water year to get water quality for treated vs. untreated ground and one to five years to measure how long accelerated loss will occur below the root zone.

[5]The formula that is most useful in predicting the losses of ions from harvest is included below for one element at a time:

$$Q_i = \sum_{j=1}^{n} C_j - \sum_{k=1}^{m} R_k$$

where Q_i = total quantity of ion of concern in a system; C_j = compartments (n) of the system that contain the ion of concern; R_k = compartments (m) in the system that contain the ion of concern that might be removed; and j = year of estimation.

If it is desired to keep Q_i constant over time, then it should be shown that Q_i is non-negative. This can be affected by regulating the R_k (harvest losses). Q_i is composed of the ion concentration as meq/g times the weight of that material in g/ha of: wood (by size classes, 0-0.6, 0.6-2.54, 2.54-7.6, > 7.6 centimeters sound, > 7.6 centimeters rotten); bark; roots; foliage; litter; humus; herbs; and shrubs. Biologically essential ions: available and accessible in soil (weak acid extract .002 NH_2SO_4); about 1/5 of available root zone ion content; precipitation/year: dust fall/year, pollen fall/ year; mycorrhizae (see Fogel and Hunt, 1978, for estimates if data are not available); and other fungi, sclerotia, bacteria, soil animals, above- and below-ground mammals (probably not essential for calculations). The last four items are difficult to measure and are often omitted. R_k can be any of the items in Q_i but usually would be wood, bark, or foliage. Added to R_k is the annual loss of ions below the root zone (RS_i) in excess of losses in the control or untreated area (same soil) as meq/ha/year, with each year added to the former years until the time that treatment loss equals control loss.

$$RZ_i = \sum_{j=1}^{n} L_j$$

where RZ_i = the loss of the ith ion below the root zone following treatment until recovery; L_j = the loss in the jth year; and n = the number of years for recovery.

'The following key is helpful in deciding whether to use one of the tests.

A_1 Soil young, thin (< 1-2 feet deep), potentially erosive, or relatively low productivity for forests (i.e., under 75 percent of maximum growth) . . . test for deficiency hazard. If harvest is anticipated, test for nutrient shock.

A_2 Soils are not young, thin, or of low productivity as described in A_1 above . . . B_1

B_1 Soils are old (> 50,000 years), highly weathered, with deterioration of clays, high rainfall, low total ion content compared to younger soils . . . test for deficiency or depletion of biological life, or nutrient shock.

B_2 Soil not as above . . . C_1

C_1 Soil thin (< 1 meter deep) or highly permeable, > 25 centimeters/hour, or containing clay lenses, or heavy textured (permeability < 2.54 centimeters/hour) . . . analyze for nutrient screening power; anticipate problems with septic systems.

C_2 Soil not as above: IMPACS not needed.

It is important to realize that the criteria and critical data used in the key above are preliminary and were developed for primarily Montana and coniferous forests. Criteria for nonforested land or forested land in other areas may be different.

8. Land-Capability Analysis As a Planning and Regulatory Tool

James J. Jordan

OVERVIEW

Improving the quality and utility of scientific and technical information in the Environmental Impact Statement (EIS) process involves a number of critical elements. Among these are: the process must initially provide for the collection of sound scientific and technical information; there must be a means for incorporating this information within an overall planning framework; the information must be employed in the assessment of environmental impacts of either a plan or a project proposal or both; and, finally and most important, the information must be used in and have some bearing on decisions as they are rendered. Without incorporation of these elements, there is little or no guarantee that either the quality or, more relevant, the utility of information contained in an EIS can be enhanced.

Land-capability analysis, which has attributes that satisfy these critical elements, is a planning and regulatory tool that has been applied to environmental assessment in the Lake Tahoe basin. It has helped promote better environmental decision making by proving to be a technically sound method for collecting data and assessing the environmental impacts of plans and projects. In addition, public decision makers have found that land-capability analysis provides them with an easily applied, straightforward means for evaluating the environmental consequences of proposals. While use of land-capability analysis as a planning and regulatory tool has been challenged, its validity has been upheld by both the scientific community and the courts.

BACKGROUND

The Lake Tahoe basin is astride the California/Nevada state line in the Sierra Nevada. The basin encompasses an area of about 500 square miles, of which 192 square miles, or approximately 40 percent, is the lake's surface. The lake, which is located at an elevation of 6,229 feet, is the largest freshwater alpine lake in North America. It is internationally famous for its clarity. A Secchi disk, which is a white plate that measures 7.78 inches in diameter, can be seen at a depth of 120 feet in the water. The lake is surrounded by tall mountains generally covered with dense stands of conifers. The mountains, which reach to over 10,000 feet and are snow-capped much of the year, provide the area with great scenic splendor.

The Lake Tahoe basin has had a history of fairly strong development in the period of less than 150 years since Kit Carson and Captain John C. Fremont first visited the area. Between the 1860s and later 1890s, the substantial pine and fir forests of the basin were heavily logged to provide lumber for the nearby Nevada silver mining areas. While this activity originally resulted in a serious loss of vegetative cover and an acceleration of erosion into the lake and many of the streams that feed it, substantial reforestation has occurred. Following the subsidence of demand for lumber for the mines, the area was subject to moderate summer use primarily for grazing and recreation until the leisure boom that followed World War II. Beginning in the 1950s, intensive subdivision took place in the area for permanent residences as well as seasonal second-home developments. This was coupled with construction and, more important, maintenance of a network of a year-round road system for access to and movement within the basin. Extensive commercial development also occurred along the road network.

Resorts, ski areas, and other recreation facilities, in addition to large hotel/casinos adjacent to the state line of Nevada, presently attract over 15 million visitors annually (Western Federal Regional Council, 1978). The current population of the area is approximately 80,000 year-round residents; however, because of the resort character of the basin, on a peak weekend use of the area can swell to almost a quarter of a million people (Western Federal Regional Council Interagency Task Force, 1979).

The rapid growth of population in the basin since the 1950s is responsible for many improper land uses as well as environmentally disruptive development procedures. These include removal of vegetation, encroachment into environmentally sensitive areas, disruption of natural drainage patterns, failure to recognize topographic limitations, and accelerated rates of runoff and significant increases in erosion (Bailey, 1974). In certain respects, what has resulted is a startling juxtaposition of unplanned-for development in one of the most magnificent areas of the world.

However, what was occurring in the 1950s and 1960s did not go unnoticed. The lay public, experts, and some elected officials began to recognize that sedimentation resulting from development posed a serious threat to the environmental quality of the basin. In addition, land uses superimposed on, rather than blended with, the landscape and an automobile-dependent transportation system were seriously degrading the quality of the Tahoe experience.

Concern for water quality, air quality, and, ultimately, "Tahoe quality" spurred numerous governmental, as well as nongovernmental, efforts to wrestle with the issue of balancing human uses with the natural and qualitative constraints of the basin.' While these efforts produced some laudable results, they were unable to deal adequately with the most important issue at hand at that time--that of developing and implementing a politically acceptable regional plan to protect the basin.

Probably the most complicating factor related to the protection of Lake Tahoe is the fact that the state line between California and Nevada runs right down the middle of the lake. In addition to the two state governments, there are six local political jurisdictions, three in each state, which have power within the basin. This has caused serious problems in trying to come up with a coordinated management program for the basin. A further complicating factor is that some 70 percent of the basin is federally owned and under management by the U.S. Forest Service.

As noted earlier, because of the evident development ills--especially the degradation of the near-shore waters in the lake due to increasing erosion rates and sedimentation and resultant algae growth--there was quite a popular and political clamor for something to be done to halt the adverse impacts of development in the Tahoe basin. This pressure reached a plateau in 1969 when Congress passed Public Law 91-148 (83 Stat. 360), the Tahoe Regional Planning Compact. The compact called for the formation of the Tahoe Regional Planning Agency (TRPA) to develop and implement a plan for orderly development and environmental quality within the basin.

The proponents of a regional plan for the Tahoe basin recognized that it must be scientifically sound and based upon a systematic process that could withstand a full public airing and, ultimately, the test of the courts. To this end, the U.S. Forest Service, acting as agent for the Secretary of Agriculture as required in the compact, was charged with assisting the TRPA in developing the technical background for the required regional plan. In conjunction with the U.S. Soil Conservation Service and a broad range of other federal and state agencies as well as the TRPA, it undertook a rigorous and extensive resource analysis of all the different physical and cultural factors found in the Tahoe basin. This work resulted in numerous publications covering everything from hydrology to vegetation and fish and wildlife (TRPA and Forest Service, 1971a, 1971b, 1971c). The field analysis and scientific verification that led to these publications form the very underpinnings of the land-capability classification system that was subsequently developed for the Tahoe basin under the direction of the U.S. Forest Service's Dr. Robert G. Bailey.

THE LAND-CAPABILITY CLASSIFICATION SYSTEM

The work of Bailey (1974) and his many contributors
recognized that the systematic classification of land for
various purposes was not new. However, at the time the
system was developed and implemented in a regional
planning context, it was certainly the cutting edge of
what is now a fairly well-accepted practice.

Bailey used numerous factors in arriving at the land-
capability classification system. Particularly important
in this respect were those factors affecting the
hydrologic functioning of the land, primarily soil type
and geomorphic setting.

In examining soil type, the system's authors
considered erosion hazard, hydrologic soil groupings, soil
drainage, and rockiness and stoniness. As noted earlier,
erosion and its subsequent adverse impact on the lake's
water quality and clarity posed one of the Tahoe basin's
most serious environmental threats. Bailey found that
only 30 percent of the basin could be classified as having
only a slight erosion hazard (Table 8.1).

TABLE 8.1
Lake Tahoe basin land area classified
by inherent erosion hazard

Erosion Hazard Class	Area	
	Acres	Percentage
Slight	61,880	30.6%
Moderate	52,310	25.9
High	87,840	43.5
Total	202,030	100.0

Source: Robert G. Bailey (1974).

In relationship to geomorphic setting, the system
classified the basin lands into six distinct units with
numerous subclasses (Table 8.2) that were then grouped
into one of three hazard ratings: high, moderate, and
low.

Following the detailed analysis of soil types and
segregating and depicting geomorphic units according to
their hazard potential, this information was combined to
provide a single hazard rating of the basin.

Unusable units of uniform and widespread instability,
as shown by the prevalence of hazardous conditions
(i.e., high hazard lands), were designated directly

TABLE 8.2
Geomorphic units, Lake Tahoe basin

A. Glaciated granitic uplands

B. Glaciated volcanic flowlands
    B_1 Glaciated volcanic flowlands undifferentiated
    B_2 Rocky ridge lands

C. Streamcut granitic mountain slopes
    C_1 Granitic foothills
    C_2 Strongly dissected lands
    C_3 Steep strongly dissected lands
    C_4 Moderately dissected weakly glaciated lands
    C_5 Subalpine rim lands

D. Streamcut volcanic flowlands
    D_1 Toe slope lands
    D_2 Headlands

E. Depositional lands
    E_1 Moraine land undifferentiated
    D_2 Outwash, till, and lake deposits
    E_3 Alluvial lands

F. Oversteepened slopes
    F_1 Canyon lands
    F_2 Escarpment lands

Source: Robert G. Bailey (1974)

    as class 1. Lands in the remaining units (where
hazardous conditions are variable or otherwise not of
overriding significance) were assigned to a range of
capability classes from 1 to 7 based on combined soil
characteristics . . . . The most restrictive class
(class 1) is divided into subclasses according to
kind of limitation. (Bailey, 1974)

Tables 8.3 and 8.4 provide a summary of this
classification exercise.
    As a final step, one of seven capability classes
along with an allowable percentage of impervious coverage
was assigned to each of the different soils found in the
basin (Table 8.5). Lands in classes 1 and 2 were
determined to be those that should remain in their natural
condition; those in classes 3 and 4 were determined to be
permissible for certain uses but not for others; those in
classes 5, 6, and 7 were determined to be most tolerant to
urban-type uses.
    The most significant aspect of the land-capability
classification system from an environmental planning and

TABLE 8.3
Basis of capability classification for Lake Tahoe basin lands

Capability Levels	Tolerance for Use	Slope Percent[1]	Relative Erosion Potential	Runoff Potential[2]	Disturbance Hazards
7	Most	0-5	Slight	Low to moderately low	
6		0-16	Slight	Low to moderately low	Low hazard lands
5		0-16	Slight	Moderately high to high	
4		9-30	Moderate	Low to moderately low	Moderate hazard lands
3		9-30	Moderate	Moderately high to high	
2		30-50	High	Low to moderately low	
1a	Least	30+	High	Moderately high to high	High hazard lands
1b			Poor natural drainage		
1c			Fragile flora and fauna[3]		

[1]Most slopes occur within this range. There may be, however, small areas that fall outside the range given.
[2]Low to moderately low--hydrologic soil groups A and B; moderately high to high-- hydrologic soil groups C and D.
[3]Areas dominated by rock and stony land.

Source: Robert G. Bailey (1974).

TABLE 8.4
Lake Tahoe basin land area classified by capability

Land-capability Class	Total Area		Combined Rating
	Acres	Percentage	
7	3,030	2%	
6	8,800	4	14% low hazard lands in the basin
5	16,730	8	
4	7,050	4	
3	12,900	6	10% moderate hazard lands in the basin
2	4,770	2	
1	148,750	74	76% high hazard lands in the basin
Total	202,030	100	

Source: adapted from Robert G. Bailey (1974).

regulatory aspect was to translate all of the scientifically based information concerning disturbance hazard, erosion potential, runoff potential, and so forth into a single numerical index for allowable impervious coverage. Subsequent to the effort to develop the system, detailed maps at the scale of 1":400' were developed showing the limits of each soil type and their associated allowable coverage. The system recommended that, if environmental balance were to be maintained in the Tahoe basin, the following limits should be employed:

Land-capability Class	Allowed Percentage of Impervious Coverage
7	30%
6	30
5	25
4	20
3	5
2	1
1	1

The overall thrust of the land-capability classification system was to recognize that

all resource uses and activities must be compatible with a scientifically sound evaluation of the hydrologic limits of land use. Beyond these limits, productivity declines . . . . The capacity of the

TABLE 8.5
Example of capability ranking by soil type

May Symbol	Soil Name	Capability Class	Allowable % of Impervious Cover
Be	Beaches	1b	1%
Cad	Cagwin-Rock outcrop complex, 5-15% slope	4	20
CaE	Cagwin-Rock outcrop complex, 15-30% slope	2	1
CaF	Cagwin-Rock outcrop complex, 30-50% slope	1a	1
Co	Celio gravelly loamy coarse sand	1b	1
EbC	Elmira gravelly loamy coarse sand, 0-9% slope	6	30
EbE	Elmira gravelly loamy coarse sand, 9-30% slope	4	20
EcE	Elmira stony loamy coarse sand, 9-30% slope	4	20
EfB	Elmira-Defo loamy coarse sand, 0-5% slope	7	30
Ev	Elmira loamy coarse sand, wet variant	1b	1

Source: Tahoe Regional Planning Agency (1977).

land to tolerate disturbance in the form of use . . .
and still maintain the normal stability of the soil
. . . is determined by physical and biological
phenomena. (Bailey, 1974)

The author recommended that

once the hazard is recognized, high hazard areas can
be eliminated from development plans. If they must
be included, then development can proceed with use of
appropriate structures and construction techniques to
minimize the impact of development.

Finally, Bailey (1974) concluded that

control of impervious surface alone does not solve
all environmental problems. It is deemed, however,

to be the most critical element in the land
disturbance that has created the basic environmental
problems facing the Lake Tahoe basin--water quality
degradation, flooding, and soil erosion. It is also
considered the most accurately measurable and
constant expression of development impact.

USING LAND CAPABILITY IN DEVELOPING A REGIONAL PLAN

The limits to allowable coverage and the restrictions
to use of high hazard lands recommended by the land-
capability classification system became the underlying
foundation to the regional plan adopted by the TRPA in
1971. The 1":400' mapping of the basin referred to
earlier was developed and the land-capability districts
were overlaid on the maps. Land-use districts were also
developed that allowed for the following types of uses:

General forest
Recreation
Rural estates
Low-density residential
Medium-density residential
High-density residential
Tourist commercial
General commercial
Public service
Conservation reserve
Medium tourist-residential

For each use district, specific purposes, permitted uses,
and limitations to coverage based upon the underlying
capability of the land were identified (TRPA, 1972).
The result of the planning process was that
previously undeveloped land was zoned primarily on the
basis of a strict application of the land-capability
classification system. However, land on which subdivision
had occurred and development had previously taken place
was zoned to allow the existing uses and to try to promote
a harmonious land-use pattern while recognizing the
underlying capability of the land. The limitations of the
land-capability classification system were not strictly
applied in the developed areas of the basin because
overrides to the coverage limits, variances, and
provisions relating to nonconforming uses, structures, and
alterations were allowed under the plan (TRPA, 1972).
The plan that was finally adopted was a compromise
between many competing forces. Throughout the public
review and decision-making processes, all parties--
including the technical staff and the decision makers--
turned time and again to the land-capability
classification system as being the basis for their
recommendations and their subsequent actions. When it was
adopted, the plan presented a comprehensive zoning of all

of the lands within the basin that allowed for approximately 300,000 people to use the area, reducing this capacity from the 800,000-1,000,000 limit that had been proposed prior to the plan's inception.

Needless to say, producing an environmentally influenced plan for a place as sensitive as Lake Tahoe, a plan that significantly reduced the intensity and types of uses, and doing it in 1970 and 1971 produced a number of challenges to the plan and to the underlying land-capability classification system. To date, there have been over $300 million in inverse condemnation lawsuits filed against the TRPA because of what many landowners consider to be downzoning based upon the land-capability classification system. Through the years, the plan has been upheld in the appeals courts and other levels of the judiciary. In 1978, in the first case to reach the United States Supreme Court (Lake Country Estates vs. Tahoe Regional Planning Agency), the court upheld the agency's position.

Over the years, other plan elements, such as a recreation and open-space plan, a transportation plan, a shore zone plan, and a water quality management plan, as well as subregional plan elements, have been incorporated into the original regional plan. These have all drawn extensively upon the land-capability classification system.

USING LAND CAPABILITY IN IMPLEMENTING A REGIONAL PLAN

The TRPA regional plan has largely been implemented through a number of ordinances, including a land-use ordinance, a subdivision ordinance, a shore zone ordinance, and a grading ordinance. In one form or another, all of TRPA's ordinances are based upon the coverage limitations set forth in the land-capability classification system. All commercial developments of three or more acres and residential proposals of five or more units and a host of related projects of similar scale or potentially significant environmental consequences require the development of detailed environmental information reports and must be reviewed by the TRPA to establish their conformance with the regional plan, the agency's zoning, and the land capability of the area in question (TRPA, 1972). Smaller project proposals, or ones of lesser environmental consequence, are required to be reviewed by the six local governments, following the same procedures and using the same criteria. The purpose of this review procedure, which has evolved over the years into a fairly rigorous, if somewhat limited, process, is to serve as an environmental assessment of the various types of development proposals. The TRPA's governing board deliberates monthly whether to approve projects or planned developments based on a de novo hearing process and the recommendations made by the public, an advisory

planning commission, and a professional staff.
        During the years that the agency has been reviewing
projects and plan amendments, the utility and integrity of
the land-capability classification system as a planning
and regulatory tool has been well proven. While many
claim, and rightly so, that coverage is a limited
environmental test, it is one that has significant
scientific merit and is easily understood and applied.
Both the public and decision makers have found that it is
relatively easy to relate coverage limitations to the
soils on a particular site proposed for development and to
establish if the project falls within or exceeds the
coverage limits. Likewise, developers who initially
fought the concept of the land-capability classification
system have now come to live with its constraints,
recognizing that to do so puts their project in a more
favorable position with public decision makers. In
addition, project proponents and technical review staff
members have found that the land-capability classification
system is an inexpensive tool to apply while producing
results that are almost universally replicable.
        Another way that the land-capability classification
system has proven to be valuable is in field enforcement.
The numerous agencies responsible for enforcing conditions
on projects in the Tahoe basin use the system to find out
if the projects, as well as their associated development,
are carried out in the way the they were originally
permitted. In this regard, the system is straightforward
because field enforcement personnel can go out and
actually measure the amount of coverage that is being put
onto a piece of property and, if they find that the
coverage is over the amount allowed, appropriate
enforcement action can be initiated.

PROBLEMS SURROUNDING THE USE OF LAND-CAPABILITY ANALYSIS

        . During the years since it was first applied in the
Tahoe basin, certain problems have arisen concerning the
use of the land-capability classification system. What is
important to note is that none of these problems is due to
weakness in the system itself. Rather, they stem from
misapplication or misrepresentation of the system.
        Underlying the problems associated with applying the
land-capability classification system are the inherent
weaknesses in the structure of the TRPA as set forth in
the compact. The TRPA governing body has five
representatives from California and five from Nevada, with
the eleventh member being a nonvoting appointee of the
president. Of the five members from each state, three
represent the local government jurisdictions and the
remaining two, statewide interests. While many members
consider Lake Tahoe to be of national as well as state
importance, the membership structure has provided a
distinctly local dominance. In addition, the governing

body has been plagued by a strange voting procedure that requires a dual majority in order to take an affirmative action. This flaw led to the agency's granting a "deemed-approved" status to four large gaming casinos in 1973 and 1974. These projects, viewed in terms of their cumulative impact on the Tahoe basin, constituted a serious environmental threat and prompted the state of California to establish a separate California Tahoe Regional Planning Agency and to withdraw much of its support from the TRPA. The compact constituting TRPA has other limitations that have been recognized since the agency's inception (U.S. Environmental Protection Agency, 1975). All of the shortcomings of the compact have led the legislatures of both California and Nevada to propose numerous amendments in recent years, but, as yet, they have been unable to arrive at mutually agreed-upon changes.[2]

In the land use ordinance, which is the principal vehicle for implementing the regional plan, the TRPA governing body allowed for a system of overrides that has resulted in excess coverage where the land-capability classification system would dictate more stringent controls. The initial relaxation of the system constraints served as a bellwether for the difficult time that the governing body of the TRPA was going to have holding steadfast on issues related to the environmental quality of the Tahoe basin.

Another problem is that challenges to the system have been allowed. While the practical application of any tool such as the land-capability classification system must, out of reality, remain somewhat flexible, opening it up to challenges has produced some magical results. Most notable are two conditions that occur on a routine basis. First, project proponents have hired soil scientists and other soil specialists to perform more detailed surveys of a piece of property to try to identify inclusions of different soil types of a higher capability as a means for locating more extensive projects in those areas. Second, slope challenges have been allowed that, for example, have moved an area from a 15-20 percent slope category with 1 percent allowable coverage into a 5 to 15 percent slope category with a commensurate increase to 20 percent allowable coverage.

The land-capability classification system recognized that the Stream Environment Zones (SEZ) and the oversteepened portions of the basin were high hazard lands. The Lake Tahoe basin water quality management plan prepared by TRPA in 1977 provided further evidence of the sensitivity of these high hazard areas and their importance to water quality. The oversteepened portions of the basin have the highest erosion potential and are the most susceptible to the ills of development. Encroachments into the SEZ disturb not only their habitat potential but also their natural stormwater conveyance and treatment capability as well (Morris et al., 1979; TRPA,

1977). As Bailey (1974) recognized,

High hazard lands (class 1 and 2) are characterized by steep slopes and a fragile environmental balance, with unique plants and animals. They also have scenic value as backdrops and foregrounds for surrounding areas. These should remain generally in their natural condition.

This has not been the case; the areas have been allowed the more intense uses associated with development, which have resulted in a further degradation to the Tahoe environment.

Another misapplication of the system recently surfaced when particular interests tried to change the system to recognize areas that have been modified by human activity such as areas where wetlands have been filled to provide land for housing development. As proposed, these areas were to be given a higher capability level and percentage of impervious coverage rather than that dictated by their underlying soil type and geomorphic setting.

NEEDED IMPROVEMENTS

While the land-capability system has proven its scientific integrity, its application has had some glaring weaknesses. In addition, while the system and the 1971 TRPA regional plan that was based upon it were a significant step forward at the time, they are both limited in scope and are unable to deal effectively with all of the environmental problems facing the Tahoe basin at the present time. The problem today, as noted in the Lake Tahoe study conducted by the U.S. Environmental Protection Agency (1975), can be summarized as follows:

The planning and regulation of land use, water quality, and air quality in the Tahoe basin take the traditional form of managing the individual resources of land, water, and air to conform to desirable "end-states." For example, the Tahoe Regional Plan defines, by means of maps and policies, the "ultimate" pattern of land use consistent with the capability of the land to withstand development. The Water Quality Standards define, by means of static indicators, the "ultimate" physical, chemical, and biological condition of the waters consistent with maintaining its purity and clarity. The National Ambient Air Quality Standards define, again by static indicators, the "ultimate" composition of the air consistent with public health criteria.

By focusing on the end condition not-to-be-exceeded, we lose sight of the dynamics of change associated with individual decisions made over time.

Each land use development approved, while perhaps consistent with the planned "end-state," contributes to an increment of cumulative and synergistic ecological change--each square foot of impervious surface changes the hydrology; each pound of sediment and nutrients changes the productivity of the waters; each pound of air pollutants changes the atmospheric quality. It is quite possible that the sum of the individual decisions and ecological changes could result in (1) an "end-state" being exceeded, (2) an "end-state" being reached "prematurely," or (3) the "end-state" for one media being satisfied at the expense of violating the "end-state" of another media.

The "end-state" concept, while theoretically useful for individual media as a planning target, may be irrelevant to guiding the complex growth processes to meet the objective of "preserving the fragile ecology of Lake Tahoe." The threshold concept would assess synergistic rate of ecological change, compare the rates of change to threshold values beyond which ecological damage occurs, and provide feedback and warning signals to guide decision makers in managing the growth process. Finally, the thresholds would provide the linkage between a cumulative set of land development decisions and the federal/state environmental quality standards which may not be exceeded.

As a means for following up on the concepts and recommendations contained in The Lake Tahoe Study, the Western Federal Regional Council (WFRC) produced a federal policy for the Lake Tahoe basin that not only endorsed the concept of thresholds and carrying capacity but also called for the federal government to gain a "fair share" in the use of the land and the resources of Tahoe. This call for a fair share was based on WFRC's evaluation that federally supported programs such as for sewage, transportation, and recreation were paying a disproportional share compared to local interests in relation to the public benefit that was being received. This, in turn, resulted in a subsidy to the local interests at the expense of the more general public interests. Following upon the policies and recommendations contained in the document, the WFRC conducted a review of the Tahoe basin and, in December of 1979, released the Lake Tahoe Environmental Assessment (WFRC Interagency Task Force, 1979). This environmental assessment had seven primary objectives:

1. To organize and present existing data on the Lake Tahoe basin in a consistent and functional framework;
2. To obtain interagency agreement on the data and

identify specific data about which there is
disagreement;
3. To identify data gaps and inadequacies that
require further study to correct or complete;
4. To integrate and summarize the data toward an
understanding of the factors that contribute to
the environmental deterioration of the Lake Tahoe
basin;
5. To document changes that have occurred over time
with a focus on the past ten years;
6. To identify cause-effect relationships with a
focus on federal actions; and
7. To provide the information and framework
necessary for establishing environmental
thresholds.

Of these objectives, the work undertaken to achieve
the last two is of significance in relation to moving
toward what was called for in The Lake Tahoe Study. The
Lake Tahoe Environmental Assessment has helped promote an
understanding, through an extensive analysis of cause-
effect relationships, that actions initiated in one area--
such as building a new casino/hotel--have myriad economic,
social, and environmental consequences or impacts.
Unfortunately, when these cause-effect relationships are
not examined systematically, many serious impacts go
unidentified until it is too late. The Lake Tahoe
Environmental Assessment provided a systems model for the
basin as a whole.
The land-capability classification system was
recognized as the most effective means for establishing a
"land-use end state" that could function as an
environmental threshold in the Tahoe basin. This land-use
end state would have to be aggregated with the other end
states or thresholds for water quality, air quality, and
visual resources as a basis for arriving at an overall
carrying capacity for the basin. However, when this is
accomplished, a more refined and inclusive tool for
evaluating environmental impacts will result. Obviously,
to make the concept of carrying capacity operational, a
new plan that recognizes thresholds and the fact that the
area has finite capacities will also have to be developed
for the basin. If and when this effort is fully
operational, the concept of land-capability analysis will
probably play a major role in both the scientific/
technical and public/political components of arriving at a
carrying capacity and implementing the steps necessary to
remain within that capacity.

APPLICABILITY IN OTHER AREAS

Because it is based on existing soils and geomorphic
data, a land-capability classification system similar to
the one employed in the Tahoe basin could be easily and

economically developed for most areas. Project sponsors and all levels of government would benefit from the types of data about land coverage/land use that result from using the system. Through its application, information is gained about the land area in question, its appropriateness for development, the intensity of development suited for the site, particular soils-land form problems (i.e., rock outcrops, stream zones, and steep hillsides) that will be encountered, and the extent to which development will need to be accompanied by mitigation measures. This type of information is needed in all EISs that have a land-use component.

Land-capability analysis also is a valuable tool when conducting the scoping of an EIS. It provides a timely and effective means for assessing the suitability of a proposed action without necessitating extensive data collection. In addition, use of such a classification system helps to organize information contained in an EIS; promotes document brevity by reducing the often voluminous presentations of geomorphic, geologic, and soils data; and has proven to be an effective aid in synthesizing data and promoting their understanding by both the public and decision makers.

CONCLUSIONS

The land-capability classification system at Tahoe has been applied for over ten years. It has proven to be a scientifically sound tool for measuring certain environmental impacts. While it is limited in its scope, it is easily understood, applied, and accepted in the decision-making process. It has been tested in the courts and upheld. However, it has some serious flaws and weaknesses directly due to the way that it has been applied. While a more extensive and comprehensive model-- one that also incorporates air quality, water quality, visual resources, and land quality--to arrive at a set of coordinated and interrelated environmental thresholds and an overall limit on carrying capacity is needed to deal with the complex problems facing Lake Tahoe, it is likely that land-capability analysis will continue to play a major role. Others should strongly consider the use of land-capability analysis as one means for evaluating many of the consequences of the actions being evaluated in EISs. Even with its limitations, land-capability analysis is a potentially valuable aid for all involved in the EIS process.

REFERENCES

Bailey, R. G. (1974), Land-capability Classification of the Lake Tahoe Basin, California-Nevada: A Guide for Planning. Prepared in cooperation with the Tahoe

Regional Planning Agency and the U.S. Forest Service,
U.S. Department of Agriculture.
Morris, F. A., Morris, M. K., Michard, T. S., and
Williams, L. R. (1979), Meadowland Natural Treatment
Processes in the Lake Tahoe Basin: A Field
Investigation. Las Vegas, Nevada: U.S. Environmental
Protection Agency, Environmental Monitoring and
Support Laboratory.
Public Law 91-148, Tahoe Regional Planning Compact (83
Stat.360), Article III(g).
Tahoe Regional Planning Agency (1972), Land-Use Ordinance
(Ordinance No. 4, as amended, February 1972).
Tahoe Regional Planning Agency (1977), Stream Environment
Zones and Related Hydrologic Areas of the Lake Tahoe
Basin. South Lake Tahoe, Cal.
Tahoe Regional Planning Agency and U.S. Forest Service
(1971a), U.S. Department of Agriculture Planning
Guide Report: Hydrology and Water Resources of the
Lake Tahoe Region.
Tahoe Regional Planning Agency and U.S. Forest Service
(1971b), U.S. Department of Agriculture Planning
Guide Report: Vegetation of the Lake Tahoe Region.
Tahoe Regional Planning Agency and U.S. Forest Service
(1971c), U.S. Department of Agriculture Planning
Guide Report: Soils of the Lake Tahoe Region.
U.S. Environmental Protection Agency (1975), The Lake
Tahoe Study. San Francisco, Cal.
Western Federal Regional Council (1978), Federal Policy
for the Lake Tahoe Basin. U.S. Government Printing
Office.
Western Federal Regional Council Interagency Task Force
(1979), Lake Tahoe Environmental Assessment. San
Francisco, Cal.

NOTES

[1]Early attempts to find solutions to the evident
problems involved such groups as the Lake Tahoe Water
Conference Committee (1947), the Continuing Committee on
Lake Tahoe Problems (1950), the California-Nevada
Interstate Water Compact Commission (1955), the Tahoe
Improvement and Conservation Association (1956), the
Nevada-California Lake Tahoe Association (1957), the Lake
Tahoe Area Council (1958), the Tri-Bi County Planning
Commission (1960), the California-Nevada Joint Tahoe Study
Committee (1960), the California Tahoe Regional Planning
Agency (1967), and the Nevada Tahoe Regional Planning
Agency (1968).

[2]After preparation and presentation of this paper,
the two states finally agreed to a new compact that was
ratified by Congress and signed by the president in
December 1980. This new compact corrected most of the
problems inherent in the previous compact addressed in

this paragraph. However, other problems inherent in the differences between the two states and the local governments continue to plague the Tahoe Regional Planning Agency and its effectiveness in managing the Tahoe basin.

9. The Application of Image-Based Information Systems for Environmental Assessment[1]

Ronald G. McLeod

The issues that land management planners must address arise from the fundamental conflicts that occur when an increasingly expanding and mobile population makes demands on a finite natural resource base. The intricacy and complexities of human activities often place severe pressures on the environment and its delicate ecosystems. It is now required by law to assess the possible environmental impacts that might result from a given activity's competition for resources. In order to adequately perform environmental analysis, modelling, and forecasting, it is frequently necessary to compile a baseline resource inventory. This procedure can be expensive and time consuming, but it is of paramount importance to the development of sound environmental practices.

Several sources of valuable but inexpensive environmental, socioeconomic, and physical data exist through federally funded programs carried out by federal and state agencies. To name only two sources, the Census Bureau makes available the information concerning the demographics of the United States, and the United States Geological Survey provides basic map coverage and information regarding natural resources. Much of these data are available on computer tapes for integration into information-processing systems. This aspect of the data is attractive because, as environmental assessment becomes more detailed and complex, the amount of data integration necessary becomes increasingly cumbersome, increasing exponentially with increasing study-area size. This chapter will illustrate how, with the aid of an image-based information system, environmental assessment is possible using computer-based technology and nonconventional data types and sources.

The efforts of land management planners are focused in the direction of data analysis and modelling in order to help solve the difficult environmental problems facing us today. This direction is clear, since it can provide alternatives and possible solutions to problems. However, analysis and manipulation of large amounts of data are

often hampered by a plethora of problems. The ways and
methods in which information about the environment is
gathered vary considerably and may be driven by
convention, administrative policy, or time and budget
constraints. Several data items may be obtained for a
particular purpose and can represent many data types
(i.e., spatial data such as maps as opposed to tabular
socioeconomic data describing the distribution of
population). More often than not, data describing the
attributes of the landscape and socioeconomic conditions
vary in quality and quantity, posing basic problems in
information integration. Also, the types of data gathered
are dependent upon their intended application. Problems
arise when data from different sources are represented on
different reference systems. Problems of these sorts can
be solved with the aid of a geographic information system.

GEOGRAPHIC INFORMATION SYSTEM

   "The function of an information system is to provide
information to users for decision making in research,
planning, and management. Its inputs are data; its output
is information" (Steiner et al., 1975). Interest here
lies in how information systems of a technical nature can
serve to facilitate the management and integration of
environmental information for environmental assessment.
Here we are concerned with what is termed a "geographic
information system" (GIS). A geographic information
system is a system that provides information referenced on
location. How that GIS is referenced is termed its
"base;" it is usually in relation to a specified point or
area. An example of a base is a standard United States
Geological Survey 7 1/2' quadrangle map sheet where points
are spatially distributed over a Cartesian grid of
latitude and longitude. An image-based information system
is similar to a GIS if the image base or reference is
corrected to conform to a standard map base.
   The bits of data that are gathered for information
systems are obtained in a variety of ways. Collection can
take place through field work, library research,
questionnaire, experimentation, or remote sensing.
"Remote sensing" is a term currently used by scientists
for the study of remote objects (e.g., Earth, moon, and
stars) from great distances (National Academy of Sciences,
1970). Products of remote-sensing technology are aerial
photographs, infrared photographs, and digital images
gathered from high-flying aircraft and satellite
platforms. Images from satellites such as the NASA
Landsat can provide information that can be helpful in
determining the composition and extent of ground cover.
These images can be manually or automatically interpreted
for information on urbanization, range land productivity,
crop productivity, and water quality. Remote sensing can
be a valuable and key tool in data acquisition and

inventory.

Information obtained from remote sensing is generally stored by some information system, either manual or computer based. A GIS differs from a conventional information system in that remotely sensed data are integrated directly into the system; this has a distinct advantage in that other types of nonspatial data can be input to build up the information set. Another plus is that not only can tabular listings and tables displaying reduced data be printed but also maps depicting the spatial distribution of features of interest can be shown.

Getting data into advanced computer information and modelling systems has been a notorious bottleneck in terms of human effort, time, cost, and accuracy (Zobrist and Bryant, 1978). Figure 9.1 shows a land-use planning and management system that illustrates the complexities of integration and inputting several data types into a GIS. Beginning with data capture on the left-hand portion of the figure, which includes the first three categories, the incoming information is structured into a common reference in order to permit comparison of information for analysis, modelling, and forecasting. This sequence leads up to management policy formulation and implementation. Such a system provides the opportunities of feedback loops to modify results. The key box in the figure is the structured data base. Through this portal all data must pass and, with the processes involved here, all data are referenced to a common grid and reduced to its smallest common denominator.

The difficulties of this step are best illustrated in the digitizing process. For example, if in the final stages of a project information must be summed by land ownership, a digital file must be prepared depicting land ownership. What this involves is essentially redrawing the map, not on a drafting table but with a coordinate digitizer in order to get the information through this bottleneck. Many times, only half of the effort is expended in the digitizing process whereas the other half involves editing the errors committed in the digitizing process.

> Inventory procedures in use today by planning and management agencies have usually been developed pragmatically around the types of data routinely available: on soils, geology, vegetation, population, etc. Yet substantial improvement in our understanding of ecological systems . . . makes it possible to specify data/variables/parameters (relevant to management decisions) that have not been directly collected or conveniently available in the past. (Shelton and Estes, 1979)

Collection of surrogate data is possible in many ways, but the method of primary interest here is with the use of

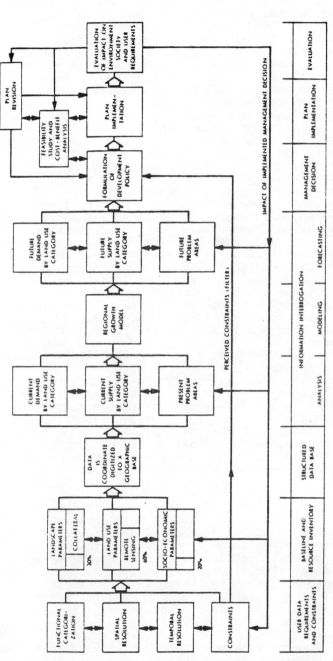

Figure 9.1 Land-use planning and management information system. Data capture includes the first three categories of the information system: (1) user data requirements and constraints, (2) baseline and resource inventory, and (3) structured data base. All data must go through the third category, coordinate digitizing.

remote-sensing technology. With multispectral imagery, techniques of automatic spectral pattern recognition can be applied to reduce the information and produce thematic maps representative of certain aspects of the landscape, including urbanization, soils, vegetation, mineral deposits, and water quality. One such source is Landsat digital imagery.

Landsat imagery is an attractive data source because it is available at a nominal cost and is in a computer-compatible form. Landsat data is based upon the image raster, the ultra-fine mesh equivalent to a grid cell dataset. The image raster with its accompanying data elements is simply a matrix of numbers and is termed a digital image. This data type can be accessed and manipulated with the software (tools) developed for digital image processing.

IMAGE PROCESSING

The discipline of computer image processing is approximately 15 years old. Image processing at the California Institute of Technology's Jet Propulsion Laboratory (JPL) began about two decades ago with imagery returned from the Ranger and Surveyor spacecraft and has continued in support of the National Aeronautics and Space Administration's planetary exploration program. In addition to planetary application of image processing, JPL's Image Processing Laboratory (IPL) has pursued applications based on remotely sensed imagery of the Earth's surface and more recently has concentrated on the registration, correlation, and integration of remotely sensed imagery with nonimaged data bases (Green et al., 1980). Innovative techniques are being developed to facilitate data compilation and integration through the use of the Video Image Communication and Retrieval System (VICAR) and its subset, the Imaged Based Information System (IBIS). VICAR/IBIS is a software system that simplifies execution of image-processing programs. It contains a series of applications programs that includes a whole host of image-processing capabilities, and a series of modular subroutines used by applications programmers for data input/output, program parameter input, and other functions (Seidman and Smith, 1979). The source code and limited system documentation are available through the COSMIC computer program distribution center sponsored by NASA.[2]

In response to the desire to integrate several data types, IPL has pursued applications that developed the ability to reference geocoded datasets and information management systems with thematic maps and remotely sensed imagery. The basic premise is that geocoded datasets can be referenced to the raster scan and that images taken from thematic maps and remote-sensing platforms can be converted to the raster scan. Such a system permits the rapid incorporation and comparison of datasets and adaptation to variable scales. Editing and updating are easily accomplished with this format as opposed to the polygon geocoded format. Thus, VICAR/IBIS has the ability to complement present systems by interfacing graphic and tabular data outputs with the format of the raster scan.

The cases presented in this paper illustrate the capability of a geobased/image-based information system to compile, integrate, and reduce environmental, socioeconomic, and remotely sensed imagery. In the first case, Landsat imagery for the California Desert Conservation Area (CDCA), 25 million acres, was mosaicked and thematically classified into classes of vegetation information and soils information. Estimates of biomass and forage production for vegetation classes were derived with the integration of conventional field data and aggregated by leased-grazing allotment in order to determine the range-carrying capacity for grazing livestock and feral animals. The second case illustrates the integration of remotely sensed Landsat imagery and digital map files (precipitation, drainage basin boundaries, elevation, slope gradient, and slope aspect) for modelling and assessment of environmental water quality in the Lake Tahoe region. The third case presents a study performed to measure the health impacts of air pollutants in Portland, Oregon, by means of remotely sensed data integrated and cross-tabulated with socioeconomic data and a modelled pollution-dispersion plume.

CALIFORNIA DESERT CASE

The Bureau of Land Management (BLM) in the state of California was mandated by Congress to prepare an Environmental Impact Statement and comprehensive, multiple-use management plan for the California Desert Conservation Area (CDCA) by October 1, 1980.[3] The CDCA encompasses an area of approximately 25 million acres, or one-fourth the state of California. The resource information for this sparsely populated portion of the state is incomplete or, in some cases, nonexistent, which poses basic data collection difficulties. In order to complete the EIS and management plan in the approximately three-year time frame, the BLM used Landsat, in addition to conventional mapping and inventorying techniques, to obtain much of the needed resource data. The budget for the task was $8 million and required gathering basic information on vegetation, recreation, geology, energy, minerals, cultural resources, soil, air, water, wildlife, and wilderness. With this information, the BLM was to address the following major issues: (1) protection of archaeological and historical artifacts, (2) Native American values, (3) recreation, (4) wilderness designation, (5) motorized vehicle access, (6) energy

production and plant siting, (7) utility corridors,
(8) mineral exploration and development, (9) domestic
livestock grazing, (10) wild horses and burros,
(11) protection of the natural environment, and (12) land
tenure adjustment.[4]

JPL was contracted to develop and implement remote-
sensing techniques to be used in conjunction with the
Image Based Information System to provide basic inventory
data on the vegetation and soils portion of the project.
One percent of the total budget allocated for inventory
and analysis was committed towards remote-sensing
technology. In the end, BLM wanted estimates and measures
of total biomass available (forageable and nonforageable)
in the CDCA. The need for these figures stems from the
fact that the BLM currently leases 4.5 million acres in 54
grazing allotments to local ranchers for domestic
livestock, both sheep and cattle. Biomass estimates would
give the BLM and ranchers a good approximation of the
carrying capacity of the leased allotments, thus allowing
more efficient management of the range lands. Information
was also required on basic soil types and the fragility/
erodability of soils.

To this end, JPL compiled a digital mosaic of Landsat
data of the CDCA at an 80-meter resolution element (see
Figure 9.2). Using four wavelengths of the
electromagnetic spectrum from green to near-infrared
radiation, multispectral classification was performed to
reduce the large amount of information in the four-band
mosaic to 100 basic information classes on resources
(McLeod and Johnson, 1980). With the aid of the
registered digital terrain information (elevation), the
100 basic information classes on resources were combined
and stratified based on elevation criteria into 28 basic
information classes on vegetation and 15 basic information
classes on soils (see Figure 9.3). Actual biomass values
and coefficients for soil fragility/erodability for the
basic information classes were obtained by low-level
aerial photography transects. The low-level aerial
transects were located in the Landsat mosaic, and the
biomass and soils information manually interpreted from
the low-level aerial transects was correlated with the
classified Landsat data and extrapolated for areas
surrounding each transect.

The biomass and soils estimates were now available
for the entire CDCA; however, the BLM required aggregation
of these estimates not only by leased grazing allotments
but also by land ownership and three slope categories.
Conventional map information for land ownership and
grazing allotments were digitized and converted to a
computer-compatible format for comparison and analysis.
Measures of slope gradient were derived from previously
registered digital terrain information and the task
remained to integrate and reduce all data for use by the
BLM staff. Using the IBIS system discussed in the

Figure 9.2   California Desert digital mosaic. One segment
of the four light wavelengths (near-infrared)
of the Landsat digital mosaic is shown here.
This image represents 7,400 by 7,500
individual samples of data. The imaged data
base was segmented into 1° of latitude by 1°
of longitude images to simplify data storage
and cataloguing, as well as conforming to
standard mapping conventions.

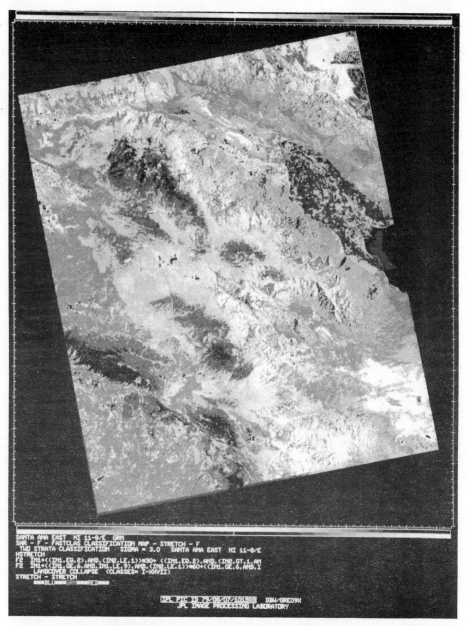

Figure 9.3   The Santa Ana East 1° x 1° image.   The
multispectral information in the mosaic has
been reduced via multispectral classification
into 28 basic information classes.
Integrating this image with ground-collected
data on plant production and grazing practices
yields estimates of range-carrying capacity.

introductory remarks of this chapter, these types of image
raster data (biomass image, land-ownership image, grazing-
allotment image, and slope-category image) were quickly
aggregated and reported in a summary tabulation. To
estimate total usable forage in grazing allotments, it was
important to include three measures of slope gradient
(0-25 percent, 26-50 percent, and above 50 percent)
because, as the slope increases, the forage available to
livestock decreases. It was also important to the BLM
that all areas be stratified by land ownership (pubic vs.
private). Summary tabulations of metric tons of biomass
and forage production for selected grazing allotments are
shown in Figure 9.4. The information generated from this
project was used as basic data input to the California
Desert Master Plan and Environmental Impact Statement. As
to the utility of the data, the EIS stated,

> For the purposes of consistency and simplicity, the
> values obtained from the recent multi-stage sampling
> and remote-sensing survey are presented . . . as the
> most current estimate of carrying capacity. The
> reliability of these estimates is considered to be
> satisfactory when reviewed in comparison with earlier
> survey results from the common areas.[5]

The entire budget for all sections of the plan was on the
order of $8 million, with approximately $160,000 devoted
to Landsat-based technology developed at JPL. The per
unit cost factors out to 0.6 cents per acre.

LAKE TAHOE WATER QUALITY MONITORING DEMONSTRATION[6]

In order to demonstrate the utility of the VICAR/IBIS
system for monitoring water quality, IPL compiled an
integrated and workable data base derived from
conventional and remotely sensed sources[e] for the Lake
Tahoe region. The purpose of the data base was to
integrate water quality-related data from various sources
into a fairly comprehensive system capable of combining
and cross-tabulating information from conventional maps,
in situ measurements, and the Landsat raster data type.
This system permits a regional environmental planner and
manager the ability to visualize and quantify the
integration of disparate data elements in a fraction of
the time that it would take to do it manually. This
system can also apply modelling techniques for input
prediction, enhancing the actualization of the look-
before-you-leap aspect of regional planning.
The data types used as principal input to the
information base on regional water quality are as follows:

1. *Landsat-2 multispectral scanner data.* Since
   Landsat data are received in the image raster
   format and are easily operated on by the VICAR/

BUREAU OF LAND MANAGEMENT
CALIFORNIA DESERT CONSERVATION AREA

- -

STANDING BIOMASS AND RENEWABLE FORAGE
PRODUCTION BY LAND OWNERSHIP
METRIC TONS PER GRAZING ALLOTMENT

GRAZING ALLOTMENT	PUBLIC STANDING BIOMASS	PRIVATE STANDING BIOMASS	TOTAL STANDING BIOMASS	PUBLIC RENEWABLE FORAGE PRODUCTION	PRIVATE RENEWABLE FORAGE PRODUCTION	COMBINED RENEWABLE FORAGE PRODUCTION	TOTAL PIXELS
1	573.43	0.0	573.43	13.49	0.0	13.49	206
2	21842.43	550.86	22393.28	549.51	12.72	612.22	8608
3	68366.00	7194.39	75560.37	1955.37	184.23	2139.60	27095
4	141637.75	4849.91	146487.62	3490.77	146.66	3637.42	56707
5	33470.54	4695.17	38165.71	833.38	112.47	921.85	15311
6	22196.81	1505.92	23701.92	593.48	40.64	634.13	8745
7	11296.34	1665.53	12961.87	344.33	52.25	396.58	5334
8	139427.94	0.0	139427.94	3323.06	0.0	3323.06	38142
9	314165.19	25231.98	339397.06	8476.55	573.11	9049.66	13571
10	19509.17	3438.52	22947.70	520.31	87.37	607.68	9023
11	56630.12	2442.11	59072.22	1359.12	54.01	1373.13	23156
12	7041.93	465.41	7507.39	79.66	4.50	84.16	2002
13	7231.32	1413.39	8644.71	144.09	27.45	171.55	4131
14	500826.56	387787.69	888813.56	7816.42	6845.37	14661.80	387870
15	22378.24	32479.74	54857.96	463.68	669.81	1133.49	27028
16	3010.14	656.75	3666.89	8.46	2.60	11.04	241
17	652944.62	465476.56	1118423.00	4447.50	1819.20	6266.70	136732
18	901.88	99.76	1001.64	13.33	1.43	14.75	269
19	432873.44	22079.96	454953.44	2348.64	207.47	2556.11	61197
20	58174.70	2036.44	60211.12	1002.19	27.52	1029.70	32161
21	311833.94	373846.00	685680.12	952.24	974.11	1926.35	53176
22	5839.24	4806.54	10645.79	121.75	49.02	220.77	5287
23	30181.32	10677.65	40858.97	622.04	221.52	843.55	20439
24	12276.98	1360.91	13637.89	189.13	22.40	211.52	7060
25	16345.71	450.46	16796.18	160.05	3.61	163.47	3537
26	80726.37	79305.50	160031.87	1576.94	1561.15	3138.08	78288
27	6678.58	1713.64	8392.22	138.62	35.30	173.92	7057
28	30041.36	0.0	30041.36	349.34	0.0	349.34	10702
29	62561.74	1477.66	64045.37	1087.37	26.08	1113.45	27943
30	22510.35	9718.66	42228.99	556.60	169.86	756.54	19704
31	77149.69	1275.94	78425.56	1391.06	24.19	1415.24	40656
32	211109.50	69559.69	280669.12	3675.34	1242.76	4918.30	136994
33	205180.75	88035.44	293215.69	3659.83	1563.19	5223.02	144672
34	449.92	5.95	455.88	8.11	0.12	8.22	225
35	43849.18	9625.40	53474.59	539.71	122.50	662.21	23087
36	79676.75	15420.87	95097.62	495.46	52.30	547.76	14661
37	258320.75	33829.37	292150.50	201.51	258.65	1760.21	22731
38	86641.12	31552.20	118193.50	1249.35	470.86	1760.21	71562
39	95094.87	5760.78	100855.62	1316.41	80.12	1396.53	43844
40	214672.31	67114.81	281787.12	3378.36	1099.03	4477.39	125965
41	65707.19	2502.88	68210.06	1076.81	41.92	1118.73	21053
42	51492.22	14042.72	65534.94	646.14	200.17	886.31	44491
43	326987.75	63623.74	390641.37	5248.66	1002.89	6251.55	159674
44	51885.25	5821.68	57706.96	728.26	95.89	826.15	11762
45	211070.50	11355.71	222426.25	2735.20	133.79	2868.99	74886
46	367052.50	25894.94	392947.69	5952.80	512.28	6465.07	158421
47	582347.25	19643.69	601990.94	10028.17	3738.23	13766.41	286210
48	47954.75	5104.79	53059.52	675.99	77.37	753.36	23048
49	1888.57	0.0	1888.57	31.29	0.0	31.29	422
50	377574.37	22397.44	399971.56	5709.79	350.49	6060.28	192224
51	338445.81	17272.24	355718.12	4386.19	228.20	4614.39	154221
52	13587.26	1791.88	15379.15	160.25	19.10	179.35	12355
53	14448.06	0.0	14448.06	181.24	0.0	181.24	7523
109	424994.00	15300.44	440294.12	11313.63	457.66	11771.29	134064
111	22050.55	723.26	22773.91	632.04	14.95	647.56	8809
120	82658.62	0.0	82658.62	1288.07	0.0	1288.07	34597
139	14798.37	1436.55	16234.92	188.98	17.58	206.90	8769
146	32937.52	2136.58	35074.06	663.68	45.45	706.03	13126
200	336593.37	682.56	337275.87	8324.46	8.91	8333.37	214519
202	2325040.00	572.30	2325612.00	65177.15	15.08	65192.44	1202333
204	1459711.00	348.88	1460000.00	52049.59	6.67	22045.48	651984
205	261293.37	83147.69	344440.81	5249.59	1612.54	6862.13	18251
206	9223.51	702.88	9926.39	117.80	13.49	131.29	3208
207	1133.35	50.47	1183.52	8.18	0.24	8.42	1036
210	0.0	1056.43	1056.43	0.0	4.31	4.31	873
220	1569.93	298.43	1868.37	30.33	5.37	35.70	348009
221	906498.50	4264.30	910762.75	12805.93	58.10	12864.03	348009
222	588128.25	3886.41	592014.31	8042.64	50.12	8092.75	368124
223	217.99	4303.91	4521.90	2.27	57.23	59.50	1325
224	13039.25	304520.44	343410.94	976.61	1851.89	2828.70	354402
225	397890.25	7935.29	405825.50	1760.34	32.12	1792.66	287720
226	312.80	0.0	312.80	1.58	0.0	1.58	277
254	11264749.0	8282591.00	19547392.0	159006.12	83460.12	242546.81	9095850

IBIS system, it is used as the base or starting point to which subsequent data planes are added. Land-cover information can be extracted from the Landsat data and used as modelling parameters in stream loading analysis as a function of density and type of cover.

2. *Digital terrain data.* Obtained at a nominal cost from the National Cartographic Information Center, these data provide elevation and topographic information. Derived from the elevation image are measures of slope gradient and slope aspect.

3. *Precipitation data.* A conventional map of annual precipitation of the Lake Tahoe region was digitalized into a computer-compatible format and readied for use with the other data types.

4. *Drainage basin outlines.* A conventional map of drainage basin outlines determined by the Tahoe Regional Planning Agency was digitized for computer integration (see Figure 9.5).

Once these data types are converted to the common grid, cross-tabulations between datasets are easily done. Examples of the kind of cross-tabulations that can be performed are shown in Figure 9.6. The image data have been reduced to tabular format for analysis and depict physical attributes for the drainage basins, as defined by the digital terrain data, for the entire region. A similar procedure could be exercised by constructing a continuous surface image of the precipitation isohyets and cross-tabulating the drainage basin map to obtain figures for rainfall for each drainage basin. Incorporating the terrain data and Landsat cover data could produce estimates of runoff for each basin and, when summed, would produce estimates for the Tahoe basin.

This type of data base has the capability to work well on a regional level. The resolution of the data base is approximately 80 meters, or the dimension of the Landsat resolution element. In the overall view of application of this information in general water quality studies, the lakes and surrounding watersheds of the test site must be of such dimension to accommodate the resolution of the Landsat sensor. Just as discussed earlier in the BLM case, it is necessary to deal with regional areas when a Landsat image-based information system is used.

PORTLAND, OREGON, POLLUTION IMPACT DATA BASE[7]

As a result of the Clean Air Act Amendments of 1977, the Environmental Protection Agency published guidelines and procedures for quantifying population exposures to adverse air quality. The guidelines call for interfacing air quality and demographics data on a grid network

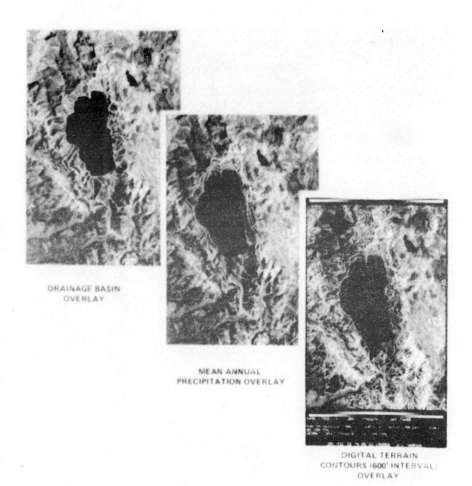

DRAINAGE BASIN
OVERLAY

MEAN ANNUAL
PRECIPITATION OVERLAY

DIGITAL TERRAIN
CONTOURS (600' INTERVAL)
OVERLAY

Figure 9.5   Four data planes used in the Lake Tahoe data
base.   Three data items are registered and
overlaid on Landsat digital data: drainage
basin outlines, mean annual precipitation, and
digital terrain information (contoured here
for easy visualization).

LAKE TAHOE DRAINAGE BASINS

AZIMUTH (ASPECT) AND SLOPE — MAGNITUDE
STATISTICAL SUMMARY REPORT

BASIN NUMBER	DRAINAGE BASIN NAME	AREA (ACRES)	MODAL ASPECT				MODAL SLOPE			
			AVERAGE ASPECT	AZIMUTH (DEG.)	ACREAGE	PCT. TOTAL	AVERAGE SLOPE	SLOPE (DEG.)	ACREAGE	PCT. TOTAL
1	TAHOE STATE PARK	952	26.8	90.4	185.3	19.47	5.5	4.9	154.2	16.64
2	BURTON CREEK	3390	33.9	90.4	357.9	10.56	9.1	4.9	310.3	9.15
3	BARTON CREEK	616	38.5	189.7	196.3	31.88	6.8	3.6	145.7	23.65
4	LAKE FOREST CREEK	592	34.0	135.5	229.6	38.77	7.1	4.6	194.8	32.89
5	DOLLAR CREEK	1100	27.7	90.4	166.3	15.11	7.2	4.9	120.1	10.94
6	CEDAR FLATS	1178	24.5	90.4	422.8	35.89	7.7	6.7	202.7	17.20
7	WATSON	1542	28.6	90.4	186.8	12.11	9.1	10.6	107.7	6.98
8	CARNELIAN BAY CREEK	789	24.1	90.4	161.5	20.48	7.7	8.7	109.3	13.86
9	CARNELIAN CANYON	2644	30.3	135.5	278.7	10.54	8.3	7.6	219.9	8.20
10	TAHOE VISTA	2655	36.5	180.7	446.5	16.84	8.3	7.6	259.7	10.44
11	GRIFF CREEK	3376	47.0	180.7	650.8	19.48	10.4	4.4	253.3	7.50
12	KINGS BEACH	725	55.8	225.9	185.3	25.55	9.0	4.9	110.8	15.26
13	EAST STATELINE POINT	825	33.7	90.4	80.8	9.79	15.2	16.0	91.8	7.69
14	FIRST CREEK	1094	35.3	135.5	79.2	7.24	16.0	18.0	52.3	4.78
15	SECOND CREEK	1116	40.4	189.7	155.2	13.90	14.2	16.4	58.7	5.25
16	HUNT CEDAR CREEK	535	41.6	180.7	156.8	29.29	8.5	8.7	89.1	16.62
17	WOOD CREEK	1384	38.2	180.7	142.5	10.30	13.7	4.9	114.5	8.24
18	THIRD CREEK	4101	38.6	183.7	471.9	11.51	11.5	4.9	260.7	6.33
19	INCLINE CREEK	4172	50.1	225.9	427.5	10.25	12.2	10.6	220.1	5.28
20	MILL CREEK	1344	55.3	271.1	123.5	9.19	16.6	3.6	66.5	4.95
21	TUNNEL CREEK	983	56.0	271.1	82.3	8.37	16.6	6.7	44.2	4.51
22	UNNAMED	560	67.4	271.1	76.0	14.08	16.2	14.8	36.4	6.74
23	SAND HARBOR	1336	60.4	271.1	109.3	8.18	20.7	8.7	69.7	5.21
24	MARLETTE CREEK	3064	48.0	0.5	494.0	16.13	11.4	9.6	434.6	14.29
25	SECRET HARBOR CREEK	2008	55.5	271.1	275.5	13.86	6.6	16.8	113.6	5.63
26	BLISS CREEK	608	69.4	316.2	109.3	17.97	10.8	10.9	45.9	7.55
27	DEADMAN POINT	654	56.5	0.0	63.3	9.69	9.2	16.9	55.4	8.47
28	SLAUGHTER HOUSE	3118	55.1	0.0	552.6	17.72	9.7	0.0	463.4	14.87
29	GLENBROOK CREEK	3347	55.1	0.0	296.1	8.85	11.5	4.9	166.3	4.97
30	NORTH LOGAN HOUSE CREEK	1013	61.1	0.0	80.8	7.97	11.0	8.1	63.5	6.25
31	LOGAN HOUSE CREEK	1349	60.9	271.1	111.0	12.68	11.4	10.6	90.3	6.69
32	CAVE ROCK	1029	62.8	271.1	137.8	13.38	15.7	10.9	47.5	4.62
33	LINCOLN CREEK	1588	54.1	0.0	148.8	9.49	9.2	7.8	139.3	6.97
34	SKYLAND	508	60.9	271.1	99.8	19.63	9.2	4.9	35.4	10.90
35	NORTH ZEPHYR CREEK	1599	56.4	271.1	232.8	14.55	9.8	8.7	107.7	6.71
36	ZEPHYR CREEK	845	52.3	271.1	110.8	13.11	9.7	2.1	62.3	7.49
37	SOUTH ZEPHYR CREEK	225	58.8	271.1	60.2	26.76	9.4	4.4	28.5	12.68
38	MCFAUL CREEK	2481	54.1	271.1	305.6	12.32	9.3	4.4	183.7	7.40
39	BURKE CREEK	3308	45.3	225.9	554.2	16.75	7.4	0.0	435.9	13.18
40	EDGEWOOD CREEK	3683	58.7	271.1	481.4	13.07	11.8	0.0	330.9	8.99
41	BIJOU PARK	2771	56.7	271.1	590.6	21.31	8.5	0.0	544.7	19.66
42	BIJOU CREEK	2044	33.0	0.2	1021.3	49.46	4.5	0.0	950.0	46.48
43	TROUT CREEK	26728	33.7	0.2	3964.7	14.81	13.0	0.0	3883.4	13.79
44	UPPER TRUCKEE RIVER	34845	32.1	0.0	8803.8	25.27	10.4	0.0	7114.3	20.42

Figure 9.6 Summary cross-tabulation report of Lake Tahoe data items. Attributes for drainage basins for Lake Tahoe include: area in acres, average slope aspects, modal slope aspect, area of modal slope aspect, percentage of total area modal slope aspect comprises, average slope gradient, and percentage of total area modal slope gradient comprises.

located in major urban areas. The grid network nodes with their accompanying air quality values would be located in the geographic center of census tracts from which a host of demographic information is derived. A standard procedure of cross-tabulation could be implemented to obtain estimates of health impacts. Such a system, automated or not, could provide federal agencies with periodic comparable data nationwide for major urban areas.

It was thought that the use of an image-based information system with Landsat data could complement the implementation of the EPA guidelines and procedures. In a cooperative effort with NASA/Ames Research Center, EROS Data Center in Sioux Falls, South Dakota, and the Oregon Department of Environmental Quality, JPL was charged with the task of developing the procedures necessary to integrate and cross-tabulate several data types to display the relative health impact on population by air quality. In order to complete this task, all data types had to be converted to the image grid. Three data items were used in the Portland, Oregon, data base:

1. *Landsat-1 multispectral scanner data.* These data, acquired in April 1973, were reduced via multispectral classification to emphasize residential areas. The EPA guidelines assume an even population density throughout a census tract. Since the assumption of uniform distribution is not totally valid, any distribution estimate based upon a satellite residential land-use data map that is better than 50 percent accurate assures a better allocation of population.
2. *Population data.* Census tract boundaries in computer-compatible format were obtained from the U.S. Census Bureau, converted to raster format, and spatially registered to the Landsat multispectrally classified data. Each census tract was uniquely encoded to distinguish one from the other. A 1973 update was available from the Census Bureau for the demographic data for each census tract (see Figure 9.7).
3. *Air quality data.* A model to estimate total suspended particulates from 1973 data on air quality was implemented and values aggregated by the 2-kilometer^2 grid cells used by the Oregon Department of Environmental Quality for the Portland metropolitan area. These grids were spatially registered to the Landsat data and census tract data.

In order to obtain a measure of population for the 2-km^2 grid cells used by the Oregon Department of Environmental Quality, a cross-tabulation operation was performed. The computer program read the number of

204

Figure 9.7 Census tracts registered to Landsat image. Information on census tracts was obtained from the U.S. Census Bureau, encoded, and spatially registered to the Landsat raster grid.

residential pixels as defined by Landsat in each grid cell
belonging to different census tracts. The program then
calculated the percentage of population each tract
contributed to each cell. The percentages were converted
to population counts, summed, and a final population count
for each grid cell was produced. Since the air quality in
each grid cell was known, a further cross-tabulation
operation was performed to obtain a measure of the
magnitude of undesirable combinations of adverse air
quality and population density, as shown in Figure 9.8.
    These techniques could be used in further studies to
predict impacts from the sitings of power plants,
freeways, and factories. A model, such as those suggested
and demonstrated by Hussey and Blackwell (1981),
predicting emissions from a hypothetical power plant could
be implemented.

SUMMARY

    Analysis, modelling, and forecasting of difficult
environmental situations require the integration of data
from various sources. To digest large amounts of
information efficiently and quickly, it is frequently
necessary to convert all data types to be examined to a
common ground, thus avoiding the problem of comparing
apples and oranges. This common ground as demonstrated in
the preceding case applications is the raster scan. Once
all data types are in the image raster, image-processing
techniques for cross-tabulation can be performed to reduce
the data to information that is usable by environmental
planners and decision makers.
    A limiting factor in the utility of these data types
is the resolution. Small projects require fine resolution
whereas regional-scale projects can be completed with the
resolution limits established by the Landsat data. It is
possible to utilize the advantages of image processing and
the raster independent of Landsat data. Very large scale
maps can be digitized to compile a series of data planes
for computer cross-tabulation. This is analogous to the
mylar-overlay procedure so frequently used now. The
computer file is easily updated and queried; all that is
required is that the map used to update the file be
digitized. Such a system may be practical for a long-term
analysis of an area that requires frequent inspection and
analysis for environmental monitoring. At present, the
practicality of such a system is best suited to regional
applications; but as the cost of hardware and software
lowers, local-scale applications can be expected.

REFERENCES

Bureau of Land Management, U.S. Department of Interior
    (1980a), The California Desert Conservation Area--

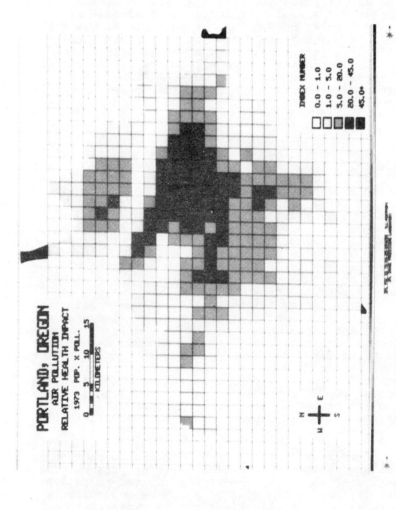

Figure 9.8 Portland, Oregon, air pollution relative health impact by 2-km² grid cells. The darker the grid cell, the greater the magnitude of undesirable combination of poor air quality and population.

Plan Alternatives and Environmental Impact Statement, draft.

Bureau of Land Management, U.S. Department of Interior (1980b), Final Environmental Impact Statement and Plan--the California Desert Conservation Area.

Green, W. B., et al. (1980), "Analysis of Multiple Imagery at Jet Propulsion Laboratory's Image Processing Laboratory." Optical Engineering, March-April, 168-179.

Hussey, K. J., and Blackwell, R. (1981), "Manipulation and Display of Air Quality Data Using Image Processing Techniques." Paper presented at the International Symposium on Energy and Ecological Modelling, Louisville, Kentucky, April 20-23.

McLeod, R. G., and Johnson, H. B. (1980), "Resource Inventory Techniques Used in the California Desert Conservation Area." In Proceedings of Arid Lands Resources Inventories Workshop, La Paz, Mexico, November 30-December 6. U.S. Department of Agriculture Forest Service General Technical Report WO-28.

National Academy of Sciences (1970), Remote Sensing: With Emphasis on Agriculture and Forestry. Washington, D.C.

Seidman, J. B., and Smith, A. Y. (1979), VICAR Image Processing System--Guide to System Use. JPL Publication 77-37. Pasadena: Jet Propulsion Laboratory, California Institute of Technology.

Shelton, R. L., and Estes, J. (1979), "Integration of Remote Sensing and Geographic Information Systems." In Proceedings of the 13th International Symposium of Remote Sensing of Environment, Ann Arbor, Michigan, April 23-27.

Smith, A. Y., and Blackwell, R. J. (1979), The Development of Digital Image Processing Techniques and Information Systems for Watershed Monitoring of Lake Tahoe. Pasadena: California Institute of Technology, Jet Propulsion Laboratory, internal document.

Steiner, D., et al. (1975), "Remote Sensing Data Systems, Processing, and Management." In G. Reeves (Ed.), Manual of Remote Sensing. Falls Church, Va.: American Society of Photogrammetry.

Todd, W. J., George, A. J., and Bryant, N. A. (1973), "Satellite-aided Evaluation of Population Exposure to Air Pollution." Environmental Science: Technology, 3, 970-974.

Zobrist, A. L., and Bryant, N. A. (1978), "Elements of an Image-based Information System." Policy Analysis and Information Systems, 1(2), 71-90.

NOTES

'Acknowledgments: This paper presents one phase of

research conducted at the Jet Propulsion Laboratory, California Institute of Technology, under NAS-7-100, sponsored by the National Aeronautics and Space Administration. The author is grateful to the many persons who worked on the application cases presented. Thanks are given to Tom Logan for contribution of his effort in the Portland case, Andre Smith and Dick Blackwell for their help in the Lake Tahoe case, and Nevin Bryant and Al Zobrist for their efforts in the BLM California Desert case.

[2]The address and phone number follow: COSMIC, Computer Center, 112 Barrow Hall, University of Georgia, Athens, Georgia, 30601. Telephone: (404) 541-3265.

[3]This was mandated by the Federal Land Policy and Management Act, Section 601, Public Law 94-579, the 94th U.S. Congress, 1976.

[4]These issues were identified in the February 1980 draft of The California Desert Conservation Area--Plan Alternatives and Environmental Impact Statement by the Bureau of Land Management, U.S. Department of Interior.

[5]See the September 1980 Final Environmental Impact Statement and Plan--the California Desert Conservation Area, Bureau of Land Management, U.S. Department of Interior. Also, see Appendix, Volume E: Vegetation and Soils and Volume F: Livestock Grazing.

[6]This case was first reported in A. Y. Smith and R. J. Blackwell (1979), The Development of Digital Image Processing Techniques and Information Systems for Watershed Monitoring of Lake Tahoe. Pasadena: JPL/Caltech internal document.

[7]A more detailed description of this case can be found in Todd, George, and Bryant (1973).

10. Toward a Participant Value Method for the Presentation of Environmental Impact Data[1]

Eric L. Hyman, David H. Moreau,
and Bruce Stiftel

The aggregation of discrete measures of environmental impact into a useful decision-facilitating analysis has been the weak link in environmental impact assessment. While methods for identifying and quantifying physical, chemical, and ecological effects of development projects have grown steadily in sophistication and accuracy, analysts have found it difficult both to relate the depth of the products to clients and to draw (or help clients draw) conclusions on appropriate actions. Most existing aggregation methods rely on small groups of experts to make evaluations of alternative environmental values. Few have addressed themselves to the search for theoretically valid ways of eliciting and incorporating environmental values of the broad community into the decision-making process. We have developed a method for environmental impact assessment, SAGE, based upon existing techniques for impact measurement, goal evaluation, and citizen participation. The method is designed to facilitate the aggregation of impact measurements using broadly acquired environmental values. This article presents the SAGE method; detail concerning its conceptual underpinnings may be found in Moreau et al. (1981) and in Stiftel and Hyman (1980).

INADEQUACIES IN CURRENT METHODS FOR ENVIRONMENTAL ASSESSMENT

Environmental impact assessment is a complex process composed of four distinct subprocesses (Figure 10.1): (1) the prediction of the physical outcomes of human actions (for example, the amount of organic material discharged into a river by a factory); (2) the estimation of effects on physical, chemical, and biological systems (e.g., an increase in biochemical oxygen demand, a decrease in dissolved oxygen content of the water, an increase in number of fish killed, an increase in algal blooms, and the acceleration of eutrophication); (3) the scaling of impacts (in other words, a comparison of the polluting effect of a unit of biochemical oxygen demand vs. a unit of phosphate); and (4) the application of value weights to the impacts (such as economic losses in dollars and importance ratings for aesthetic losses).

Many methods for the analysis of environmental impacts do not recognize that the scientific analysis is not absolute. Potential pollutants become actual pollutants only when natural systems are damaged. The causal links between human actions and damages are nondeterministic and the state of nature is uncertain. The analysis should consider cumulative and interactive effects. The amount of eutrophication associated with a unit of organic waste varies with the current health of the ecosystem as well as natural conditions such as rainfall, temperature, river velocity, and level of nutrients in the stream. Therefore, an environmental assessment should discuss the probabilities that impacts of a certain magnitude will occur. Margins of safety should be added when cause-effect relationships are sketchy. The range of uncertainty and confidence limits on the analysis should be identified because the risk assessment is inherently subjective. In order to permit sensitivity analysis, the magnitude of possible loss should be separated from risk probability (Nichols and Hyman, 1982).

Another critical flaw in the present generation of environmental impact assessment methods is the failure to note that both facts and values enter into the analysis. Only the factual determination is "objective." An impact assessment will be irrelevant if it ignores differences in the types of values held by various individuals or by the same individuals under different circumstances. The values of different people may be weighted unequally. Facts and values should be delineated when possible, although they are sometimes difficult to separate. When values are explicit, sensitivity analysis of alternative values is facilitated.

The question of whose values matter is very important because the ultimate aim of the assessment is to select alternatives, devise policies, or suggest mitigation measures that maximize social welfare, and individuals are often the best judges of their own welfare. Also, the principles of democratic government require representation of a broad set of values. Nonetheless, government also has a responsibility toward future generations and to maintain social equity. In some cases, particularly those in which there are major public health and safety questions, serious irreversible or persistent impacts on environmental quality, or highly uncertain and complex scientific issues, expert opinions are most appropriate in setting values, but not exclusively so. Experts have their own special interests and their values may not correspond with norms of social acceptability. In most cases, the participation of publics as well as experts is

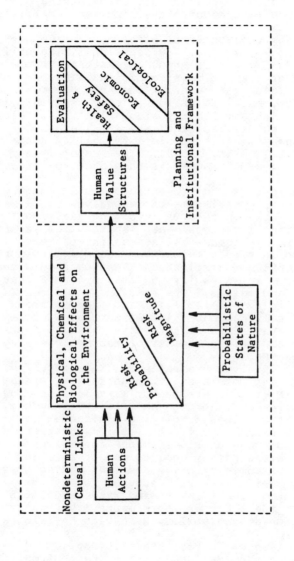

Figure 10.1 Environmental impact assessment.

important in order to obtain a complete representation of value structures, increase available information, improve accountability, reduce conflict in decision making, and smooth implementation. An open, participatory process is also desirable to reduce possible abuses of power within the government, foster ideals of social belonging and self-determination, and educate the populace (McAllister, 1980).

Finally, many environmental assessments have been doomed to oblivion because of low decision-making utility. Data collection and analysis should be matched to the level and needs of the analysis; additional information has an expected value for benefits that can be compared to the costs. Additional information is only desirable if it affects decision making; lengthy discussions of irrelevant information can confuse decision makers. The goal of environmental assessment is to simplify reality rather than duplicate it (Holling, 1978). The temporal and spatial resolution of the analysis should be specific to the case.

Poor communication and presentation is a common cause of the failure to use environmental assessments. Communication can be improved by involving decision makers, environmental professionals, and publics as early as possible in the environmental assessment process. A method should be carried out in a way that is parsimonious and manageable, but not simplistic. Results should be summarized clearly in an easily understood format that tabulates facts and values. The results should be examined for validity, reliability, and freedom from systematic biases (Hyman, 1981a). Assumptions and key variables can be varied in sensitivity analyses so that decision makers can choose the set of assumptions they feel is most reasonable.

Environmental values are reflected in the policy process at different points and through several means. Legislative deliberations are the primary location for broad policy issues and, through the electoral system, are designed to reflect values, including environmental values, in a representative manner. But many specific policy choices that are of significance themselves or that constrain later broad policy choices cannot be made by legislatures. The administrative agencies making these specific policy choices are not designed to be representative; yet some form of democratic accountability is necessary for their proper performance. Various approaches to such accountability have been envisioned and implemented.

Recently, advances in accountability of administrative decision making in the context of multiple-objective analysis have been suggested by Haimes, Hall, and Freedman (1975) and by Keeney and Raiffa (1976). They are distinguished from other methods by at least two characteristics. First, they are careful to group the effects of alternative projects or programs into several accounts where the effects within each account are commensurable but effects in different accounts are incommensurable. Second, they provide formal mechanisms by which decision makers can assign relative values to each account to derive a ranking function that leads to a preferential ordering of alternatives. However, both of these methods have been largely restricted in their applications to participation by experts or by experts and a small group of key decision makers.

The method that is described here is believed to be superior to and easier to apply than either the Haimes, Hall, and Freedman approach or that of Keeney and Raiffa. It can be thought of as an inverse of those methods that attempt to construct an actual or proxy utility function and use that function to deduce a preferential ordering of alternatives. Here a reverse strategy is followed, one synthesized from the concepts of social judgment capturing and the goals achievement matrix (Hill, 1968). The method is called SAGE. Participants are given identical descriptions of a series of alternatives that contain estimates of the contributions of each alternative to each objective. Each participant is then asked to rank the alternatives preferentially; relative weights are then inferred through an analysis of those rankings. Because relatively little time is required of participants in the process, the elicitation of values across societal groups is feasible. SAGE also includes a measure of internal consistency for each participant's assignment of values to alternatives. It does not provide a direct method for aggregating the values of groups into unique social values; it does provide a wealth of information about the degree to which that may be possible in specific circumstances.

SAGE must be understood within an overall framework for assessing the relative social worth of alternative designs. The general framework is that of the rational planning model. It consists of two phases--a design phase and an analytical phase. The design phase includes those steps of identifying objectives, establishing planning guides and criteria, and searching for and synthesizing alternative designs. In the analytical phase, the tasks are: (1) identifying and predicting the consequences of pursuing each alternative; (2) translating those consequences into measures of beneficial and adverse effects on each objective; and (3) eliciting relative values that affected individuals or groups attach to the contributions to each objective when they rank alternatives preferentially. A sketch of the analytical phase including those tasks is shown in Figure 10.2.

This division of the rational planning model is convenient for purposes of this discussion because SAGE is concerned primarily with its analytical phase. However, current versions of the rational model emphasize feedback

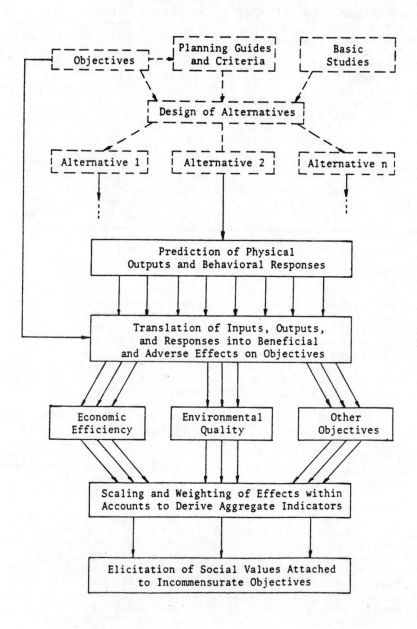

Figure 10.2 Analytical phase of water resource planning.

and the iterative nature of planning. Thus, design and analysis are not completely independent. Design may establish the context for analysis, but results of analysis may provide signals indicating both the direction and magnitude of modifications to alternative designs.

THE SAGE METHOD DESCRIBED

The method consists of four tasks: (1) predicting the physical outputs and behavioral responses to different projects; (2) translating these responses into beneficial and adverse effects on objectives; (3) eliciting weights to be applied to the incommensurable effects; and (4) combining weights and effects in a form useful to the decision-making process.

The first task of SAGE, that of predicting the physical outputs and behavioral responses to alternative projects, is primarily scientific and must be adapted to particular problem settings. For a relatively simple water project such as a single-purpose public water supply system, the basic outputs may be relatively few in number--safe yield, water quality, minimum downstream releases, land uses and terrestrial habitats displaced or destroyed, effects on fisheries and cultural, historical, and scenic sites, etc. Behavioral responses include changes in land uses in the vicinity of the project, rates of water consumption, and recreational use of the reservoir. For more complex projects involving multiple facilities, multiple purposes, and complex ecological, hydrological, or geological systems, the list of output measures may be quite lengthy, and behavioral responses may involve complex effects upon an entire regional economy.

It is impossible to produce a detailed tabulation of all significant outputs of various kinds of projects without considering specific projects at specific sites. At best, one can discuss general scientific principles and methods for predicting these effects. Holling (1978) offers some guidance for the development of efficient and effective fact-finding processes. Two principles are emphasized: (1) the interdependence between the search for data and the objectives and criteria for decision making and (2) the need for a preliminary analysis to define the bounds of the problem and to identify the information that is necessary for making decisions.

Regulations of the Council on Environmental Quality have formalized the preliminary analysis process for those projects requiring environmental impact statements (see 43 FR 55990, November 29, 1978). Those regulations outline a scoping process that invites a broad array of governmental agencies and the public to an early meeting that will lead to:

1. Determination of the scope and significant issues

to be analyzed in depth;
2. Identification and elimination of insignificant issues or issues that have been covered in prior studies;
3. Assignment of responsibilities for technical studies to participating agencies; and
4. Identification of related studies and issues.

Technical studies may be designed as sequential inquiries where successively higher levels of detail and greater precision are pursued only if they are necessary to make good decisions. At each stage of analysis, a decision could be made either to stop and make a decision with available information or to invest in additional technical studies. Checklists such as those developed by Leopold et al. (1971) and Burchell and Listokin (1975) can be useful guides to initiate those studies, but their utility is limited primarily to initial steps in the process.

The second basic task in SAGE is the translation of resource inputs, physical outputs, and behavioral responses into beneficial and adverse effects on the objectives. It is basically a data-reducing task, one of grouping similar kinds of outputs into a few accounts. The multiple-objective evaluation framework recognizes that all effects are not commensurable under a single objective, but it retains the principle that effects should be grouped under as few objectives as possible. Principles for translating energy production, food damage reduction, recreational uses, navigation, irrigation, and other outputs into beneficial effects on the economic development objective are well known. Similarly, many resource inputs can be measured by their opportunity costs and shown as adverse effects on the same objective.

The classification of other kinds of effects into like categories, and the scaling and weighting of those effects within accounts, may require the use of less well-developed methods and measures. For example, an analyst may have to compare, within an environmental quality (EQ) account, such diverse effects as the loss of 300 acres of bottomland wildlife habitat, an improved sports fishery, and enhancement of downstream aquatic life resulting from a proposed reservoir. That problem differs in degree, if not in kind, from the problem of comparing EQ effects with economic effects of the same project. It is also difficult to develop descriptors for aggregate EQ effects that are meaningful for making interaccount comparisons for a given alternative or for comparing similar effects for two different alternatives.

Some techniques for weighting similar kinds of environmental effects have gained widespread acceptance, such as the Wildlife Habitat Procedure used by the U.S. Fish and Wildlife Service. That particular method uses expert judgment to determine acreage equivalents of different kinds of habitats. Other methods have been proposed but not widely applied for comparing different kinds of environmental effects. One such approach is that used by Solomon et al. (1977) in the Water Resource Assessment Methodology. In this approach, the effects of each factor contributing to the EQ account are measured on a scale from 0 to 1, and the relative importance coefficient (RIC) of each factor is calculated using a scoring procedure involving pairwise rankings of all two-factor combinations. An aggregate index of the EQ effects of an alternative is obtained by taking a linear combination of the scaled effects of the factors where each factor is weighted by its RIC.

That method has some limitations. For example, the largest RIC that can be assigned to any factor is (2/n), where n is the number of factors. Also, the selection of a particular scale for each factor may be arbitrary, and the entire process relies heavily upon expert judgment. Nonetheless, when accompanied by an explanatory text and a full description of the actual effects, the method can be useful for summarizing and comparing effects. It does have the desirable characteristic of making the basis explicit. Furthermore, the method for combining those judgments into an overall index is subject to full disclosure.

Whenever such scaling and weighting procedures are used, several conditions should be satisfied. It must be clearly understood that those weights and scales are matters of expert opinion. To be comprehensible to others, particularly to nonexperts, the effects must be described in plain language. It must be understood that those weights and scales have meaning only in specific problem settings. Previously determined weights and scales established either in other problem settings or in the abstract should be avoided.

The third and most essential task in SAGE is that of eliciting the relative values of weights that affected individuals or groups assign to contributions to the several incommensurable objectives. The method used here is based on social judgment theory (Steward and Gelberd, 1975) that incorporates the "lens" model of decision making (Brunswik, 1952). In this method, one uncovers the relative values (weights) by inferring them from prospective decisions made by the interviewees, who are presented with a set of alternative projects and with the associated set of multiple-objective evaluation accounts. Interviewees are asked to rank the alternatives in order of preference on some scale. Then one can readily infer the weights using standard statistical methods.

The social judgment approach resembles procedures for estimating hedonic prices in the analysis of economic decisions (Hyman, 1981b). However, the hedonic approach is used to infer prices from decisions after they have been made (ex post) while social judgment techniques focus on prospective or hypothetical decisions (ex ante). The

social judgment approach is simpler for participants than
are approaches that attempt to construct utility functions
because people are asked to rank alternatives instead of
making explicit trade-offs among the several evaluation
accounts.

Results of a social judgment technique can be
analyzed by hypothesizing that the ranking of an
alternative on an interval scale by each participant is
linearly related to its contributions to each of the
objectives. An error term is included to account for
inconsistencies in a participant's application of the
model and for failures of the model to replicate a
participant's actual weighting process. The model can be
written in mathematical form as follows:

$$y_i = a + b_1 x_{1i} + b_2 x_{2i} + e_i$$

where x_{1i} and x_{2i} are the contributions of the ith
alternative to the first and second objectives,
respectively; y_i is the grade assigned to the ith
alternative; a is a constant; and e_i is the error term.
Then, given a set of n alternatives and data on x_{1i}, x_{2i},
and y_i, i = 1, 2, . . . n for each participant, standard
methods of regression analysis can be used to infer the
weights b_1 and b_2 and to perform an analysis of variance.

An example may be helpful in describing the approach.
Suppose two participants, A and B, are asked to rank nine
alternative designs for a water resource project in terms
of their preferences. Furthermore, suppose each
alternative is adequately described by its contributions
to each of two incommensurable objectives. Specifically,
suppose the nine designs have been formulated to represent
all possible combinations of contributions to the first
objective at the levels 3.0, 6.0, and 9.0 and to the
second object at the levels of 25.0, 40.0, and 70.0. The
nine alternatives are described in Table 10.1. Now,
suppose that the participants use a scale from 0 to 100 to
rank the alternatives. Rankings for each are shown in
Table 10.2 with the preferred orderings shown in
parentheses. In this example, regression analysis of A's
rankings of the alternatives would lead to the following
estimates:

1. The weights are b_1 = 4.8 and b_2 = 0.5. This
   implies that each unit increase in X_1 is valued
   at 4.8 points on the preference scale while a
   similar change in X_2 would be valued at 0.5
   points and that the relative effect of X_1 and X_2
   on the grade is (4.8/0.5), or 9.6.
2. Variations in contributions to the first
   objective explain 56 percent of the variance in
   ranks assigned by A while variations under the
   second objective explain 37 percent. The
   combined explanatory power of these two variables

TABLE 10.1
Alternative descriptions

	Alternatives								
	1	2	3	4	5	6	7	8	9
Contribution to first objective	3.0	3.0	3.0	6.0	6.0	6.0	9.0	9.0	9.0
Contribution to second objective	25	40	70	25	40	70	25	40	70

TABLE 10.2
Alternative rankings

Participants	Alternatives								
	1	2	3	4	5	6	7	8	9
A	38 (1)	54 (2)	63 (4)	56 (3)	68 (5)	82 (8)	77 (7)	70 (6)	95 (9)
B	25 (1)	49 (3)	44 (2)	64 (5)	51 (4)	85 (7)	69 (6)	95 (9)	90 (8)

is 92 percent of the variance in the rankings; the remaining 8 percent can be accounted for by inconsistencies and failures of the linear model to explain the choices.

One note of caution should be observed in interpreting the relative weights estimated by this process. The fact that b_1 is nearly ten times that of b_2 does not imply that the first objective is considered by A to be ten times as important as the second. It does imply that a change in one unit of contributions to the first is nearly ten times as important as a change in one unit of contributions to the second, but it must be remembered that the two objectives are likely to have different units of their underlying scales prior to normalization.

To complete the example, estimates of the coefficients based on B's rankings imply:

1. $b_1 = 7.6$ and $b_2 = 0.4$ and

220

2. Seventy percent of the variance is explained by
    the first objective and 13 percent by the second.

Thus, in the example, participant B places much greater
weight on the first objective than does A, an inference
that is supported both by the relative magnitudes of the
coefficients estimated in the models for the two
participants and by the percentages of the variances of
scores that are attributable to each of the two
objectives.

In the example, persons A and B are not described as
being representative of any particular group. The implied
weights they assign to the objectives are simply those of
two individuals. However, in practice, it may be
desirable to select participants as representative of
either identifiable socioeconomic or political groups
within the affected community. The allocation of planning
resources may dictate that weights be elicited from a
small number of politically representative participants
such as a policy advisory group or, if resources permit,
it may be possible to select statistically representative
participants.

Weights implied by participants can be aggregated by
socioeconomic groups or an ex post analysis of weights can
be applied to identify judgment types, i.e., groupings of
participants who have similar mixes of weights. A
classification of judgment types and their weights may be
useful to decision makers in the formulation of issues,
resolution of conflicts, and building of consensus.

A practical difficulty arises if one restricts the
calculation of SAGE only to real alternatives. In many
water and related land resource projects, the number of
objectives may be approximately equal to or even greater
than the number of alternatives under serious
consideration. When that is the case, regression analysis
cannot be applied because there must be at least (m + 2)
observations to obtain the least-squares estimate of
parameters in a linear model containing independent
variables.

To overcome this difficulty, hypothetical sets of
multiple-objective evaluation accounts can be generated
having entries similar to those for the real alternatives
being evaluated. In fact, a convenient way to construct
the hypothetical accounts is from selected combinations of
entries in accounts for the real alternatives.
Participants then are asked to rank the hypothetical
alternatives. Weights implied by those rankings could
then be used to infer preferential rankings for the real
alternatives.

PRELIMINARY FIELD TEST OF THE SAGE METHOD

A team composed of planners from the Triangle J
Council of Governments in North Carolina and students from

the Department of City and Regional Planning, University
of North Carolina at Chapel Hill, began a field test of
the SAGE method in the Winter of 1980. The method was
applied to the problem of urban development in the Falls
of the Neuse watershed in Piedmont, North Carolina. The
field test is still underway, but we can discuss its
design.

The Army Corps of Engineers will begin construction
of an earthen and concrete dam on the Neuse River in 1982.
This dam will flood approximately 12,000 acres of farms
and woodland and will drain a watershed of 5,700 square
miles. Currently, the population of the watershed area is
120,000. Local governments predict a 60 percent increase
in population over the next 20 years. Local governments
fear that an influx of 70,000 people would increase
nonpoint loadings of phosphorous, sediment, lead, and
toxic pollutants, threatening the ability to use the lake
for water supply and recreation purposes (Triangle J
Council of Governments, 1979a, 1979b).

One of the purposes of the field test is to determine
whether the threat to water quality is real. In addition,
it will assess whether public actions could alter land use
development patterns to maintain the water quality of
Falls Lake in spite of the population growth. The SAGE
method serves as the basic analytical process to answer
these questions.

The study team consists of an ecologist, a planner,
six graduate students in planning, five graduate students
in environmental science, and one law student. The study
is being conducted with the assistance of the Triangle J
Council of Governments (TJCOG), which represents the
political interests of local governments on issues
relating to the Falls watershed.

There are four principal components of the field
test. The first set the groundwork for the study by
identifying the basic alternatives to be considered. In
the second part, the study team established the set of
variables to be used in the assessment and collected data
to help predict future levels of environmental quality
under each of the alternatives. In other words, the scope
of the problem was limited to fit the needs of actually
making public policy decisions regarding urban
development. The third part will evaluate the social
welfare implications of each alternative. In doing so, we
will rely on the value weights of the TJCOG decision
makers and advisory councils. In the fourth part, the
project team will display the evaluations according to
"judgment types."

The project team developed two alternative growth
scenarios for the Falls of the Neuse watershed after
reviewing TJCOG's stated problems and goals (Watershed
Planning Policy Advisory Group, 1980) and discussing the
political feasibility of various land use guidance tools
with local planners. The first alternative, "current

practices," projects future land uses according to existing government policies and procedures. Under this alternative, most new residential growth would be in single-family dwellings on large lots scattered widely throughout the southern portions of the watershed. The second alternative, "advanced practices," projects future land uses based on government policies designed to reduce the total amount of developed land and concentrates the development pattern more compactly. Under the advanced practice alternative, most of the new growth would occur on small lots or in multi-family structures within or close to existing urban areas. In both alternatives, industrial and commercial land uses do not represent a significant portion of growth in the watershed.

The most time-consuming aspect of the field test is the determination of the social welfare implications of development alternatives. First, the study team constructed a list of all factors substantially affected by differences between the alternatives. Then, the impacts were categorized in terms similar to the four accounts of Principles and Standards (U.S. Water Resources Council, 1973) and a separate factor, degree of governmental regulation. In place of the regional economic account, we have substituted regional fiscal impact (Table 10.3).

Each factor was assigned to a member of the study team responsible for projecting impact levels. The projection was based on previous TJCOG studies, general scientific literature, and professional judgment. Then, these results were combined into preliminary impact assessments of the alternatives. Several factors were eliminated on the grounds that there were no substantial differences between the alternatives; these included amount of development in natural hazard areas, ambient air pollution, sediment runoff into Falls Lake and its tributaries, and loss of unique, historical, or archeological resources. For the other factors, the advanced practices scenario generally showed more favorable impacts, but this was not so for all of the factors.

PROSPECTUS

The evaluation of the social welfare implications of each alternative and the display of evaluations according to judgment types remain to be done. As these compose the aspects of environmental assessment newly introduced in the SAGE method, these future tasks will test the viability of SAGE.

While it is impossible to reach firm conclusions about SAGE at this point, preliminary observations can be reported. First, given the physical, chemical, and ecological impacts of proposed actions, a multiple-objective format for informing decision makers need not

TABLE 10.3
Aspects of social welfare considered in the analysis

National Economic Development Account

Agricultural employment
Construction employment
Energy consumption for space heating
Energy consumption for personal, commercial, and
  industrial transportation

Regional Fiscal Impact Account

Road construction and maintenance
Water and sewer line construction
Water supply treatment
Service transportation

Environmental Quality Account

Level of toxic substances in Falls Lake and tributaries
Development in natural hazards areas
Ambient levels of HC, NO_x, and CO in the air
Eutrophication levels in Falls Lake
Sediment runoff into Falls Lake and tributaries
Development in unique natural areas or habitats
Changes in vegetative cover

Social Well-being Account

Size of the population that could be served by mass
transit
Proximity of population to recreation areas
Loss of prime farm lands to development
Loss of unique historical or archeological resources

---

depend on the specification of a social welfare function.
The views of judgment types or socioeconomic groups
limited to the range of variation likely to result from
the proposed actions could serve instead of such a
specification. Second, systematic impact assessment
methods need not be reserved for detailed analytic
investigations. While using less than a person-year of
effort, we have compiled impact data that seem at this
point suitable for use in producing meaningful advice to
decision makers. The final results can be obtained from
the authors.

REFERENCES

Brunswik, E. (1952), "The Conceptual Framework of Psychology." In International Encyclopedia of Unified Science, Vol. 10. Chicago: University of Chicago Press.

Burchell, R., and Listokin, D. (1975), The Environmental Impact Handbook. New Brunswick, N.J.: Rutgers University, Center for Urban Policy Research.

Haimes, Y., Hall, W., and Freedman, H. T. (1975), Multi-objective Optimization in Water Resource Systems: The Surrogate Worth Trade-off Method. New York: Elsevier Scientific Publishing Corporation.

Hill, M. (1968), "A Goals Achievement Matrix for Evaluating Alternative Plans." Journal of the American Institute of Planners, 34, 19-28.

Holling, C. S. (Ed.) (1978), Adaptive Environmental Assessment and Management. New York: Wiley-Interscience.

Hyman, E. L. (1981a), "The Uses, Validity, and Reliability of Perceived Environmental Quality Indicators." Social Indicators Research, 9, 85-110.

Hyman, E. L. (1981b), "The Valuation of Extramarket Benefits and Costs in Environmental Impact Assessment." Environmental Impact Assessment Review, 2, 227-258.

Keeney, R., and Raiffa, H. (1976), Decisions with Multiple Objectives. New York: John Wiley and Sons.

Leopold, L., et al. (1971), A Procedure for Evaluating Environmental Impact. NTIS N71-36757. Washington, D.C.: U.S. Geological Survey.

McAllister, D. (1980), Evaluation in Environmental Planning: Assessing Environmental, Social, Economic, and Political Trade-offs. Cambridge, Mass.: MIT Press.

Moreau, D. H., et al. (1981), Elicitation of Environmental Values in Multiple Objective Water Resource Decision Making. Report prepared for U.S. Department of the Interior, Office of Water Research and Technology. Chapel Hill, N.C.: University of North Carolina, Department of City and Regional Planning.

Nichols, R., and Hyman, E. L. (1982), "An Evaluation of Environmental Assessment Methods." Journal of the Water Resources Planning and Management Division, American Society of Civil Engineers, 108(WR1), 87-105.

Solomon, R. C., et al. (1977), Water Resources Assessment Methodology (WRAM): Impact Assessment and Alternative Evaluation. Report Y-77-1. NTIS AD-AO 36 677. Vicksburg, Miss.: U.S. Army Engineer Waterways Experiment Station.

Steward, T., and Gelberd, L. (1976), "Analysis of Judgment Policy: A New Approach for Citizen Participation in Planning." Journal of the American Institute of

Planners, 42, 33-41.
Stiftel, B., and Hyman, E. L. (1980), "Assessment of Environmental Quality in a Democratic State." The Environmental Professional, 2, 306-314.
Triangle J Council of Governments (1979a), A General Inventory of the Falls of the Neuse Reservoir Watershed. Research Triangle Park, N.C.: Triangle J Council of Governments.
Triangle J Council of Governments (1979b), Proposed Work Program: Comprehensive Planning for the Watersheds. Research Triangle Park, N.C.: Triangle J Council of Governments.
U.S. Water Resources Council (1973), "Water and Related Land Resources: Establishment of Principles and Standards for Planning." Federal Register, September 10, 38, 24778-24869.
Watershed Planning Policy Group (1980), Statement of Problems and Goals. Research Triangle Park, N.C.: Triangle J Council of Governments.

NOTES

[1] The research upon which this article is based was supported in part by funds provided by the U.S. Department of the Interior, Office of Water Research and Technology (Project No. 14-34-001-8408), as authorized by the Water Research and Development Act of 1978. Additional support was provided by the Triangle J Council of Governments, Research Triangle, North Carolina.

11. Comparisons of Methods for Evaluating Multiattributed Alternatives in Environmental Assessments: Results of the BNL-NRC Siting Methods Project[1]

Benjamin F. Hobbs, Michael D. Rowe,
Barbara L. Pierce, and Peter M. Meier

OVERVIEW

The 1971 Calvert Cliffs decision declared that the National Environmental Policy Act "mandates a rather finely tuned and 'systematic' balancing analysis." This spurred the development of a wide range of analytic methods for systematically "balancing apples and oranges" in environmental impact analysis. Many recent power plant impact statements explicitly weigh environmental, technical, economic, and safety factors in choosing a site. Some of the multi-objective methods used are theoretically rigorous; others are less so. Brookhaven National Laboratory has completed a two-year project in which results and theoretical validity of a large number of methods for choosing weights and combining such considerations were compared. Panels of siting experts applied the methods to siting problems in Long Island, Maryland, and the western United States. Three common decision rules—weighting summation, the power law, and exclusionary screening—often chose strikingly different locations. Simple, commonly applied methods for weight selection chose weights consistently differing from the results of techniques that, when applied correctly, yield valid weights. "Valid weights" accurately represent trade-offs decision makers are willing to make. Choice of decision rule and weight-selection technique can make an important difference in siting decisions, as well as in other decisions involving multiple objectives. Users of such methods in environmental impact assessment should take considerable care in choosing and applying them.

INTRODUCTION

An Environmental Impact Statement must do more than describe a proposal's impacts. The National Environmental Policy Act of 1969 requires that "alternatives to the proposed action be considered." Further, the Calvert

Cliffs decision stated that alternatives must be compared using "a rather finely tuned and 'systematic' balancing analysis." Figure 11.1 summarizes the general environmental assessment process. After the problem is defined and alternatives specified, potential impacts are identified. Quantifiable effects are then measured, while less tangible impacts are described. This information can be displayed in a series of accounts so that trade-offs among alternatives are clearly shown. Some of the data are used to determine if alternatives satisfy standards and regulations. In many assessments, the information in remaining accounts is combined to produce a numerical index for total environmental impact or project worth. Sensitivity analyses are then performed to find critical impacts and uncertainties. Finally, if all considerations have not been combined into a single index, trade-offs are made and an alternative chosen. This trading off is not necessarily numerical and is often the result of a subjective weighing of considerations such as cost, environmental impact, and political feasibility.

An example of such a process is stage 3 of the New York Power Pool Statewide Site Selection Survey (New York Power Pool, 1977). Its purpose is to identify preferred power plant sites from a set of approximately 300 candidate sites. Each site is described in terms of environmental impacts (e.g., air quality, water quality, aquatic ecology, land use, terrestrial ecology, and socioeconomics) and costs (e.g., fuel transport, site geology, water supply, transmission, and labor rates). Each of those attributes is measured on a scale of 0 to 4, with higher numbers indicating greater suitability for a power plant. The next step is to calculate a single "Environmental Evaluation Factor" (EEF) value for each site by:

1. Multiplying each environmental attribute by a weight representing its importance. Weights are to be taken as the average of weights chosen by each of several decision makers and
2. Summing those weighted values for each site.

The better a site's EEF is, the less severe the environmental impact of a plant placed there is anticipated to be. An economic factor is developed in a similar manner using the cost attributes. The preferred sites are those that represent a reasonable balance of cost and environmental compatibility.

Prediction of specific impacts is the most difficult and time-consuming part of the environmental assessment process. Yet the other steps can also be troublesome. This paper is concerned with the evaluation of "balancing" stages of the analysis. The following characteristics make impact evaluation difficult:

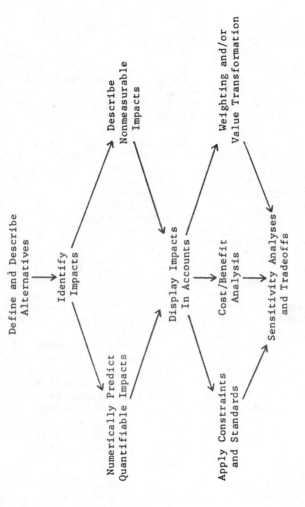

Figure 11.1 Generalized environmental impact assessment process (adapted from Bennington, Lubore, and Pfeffer, 1974).

1. There are many impacts of different types, and
   rarely is one alternative superior in terms of
   all impacts. Thus, in order to make choices,
   trade-offs have to be made. Psychological
   studies show that the use of subjective judgment
   is unreliable and inconsistent in making trade-
   offs among more than a handful of factors at a
   time. The important contributions of remaining
   considerations are ignored, and decision makers
   often do not realize the extent to which they
   restrict themselves (Shepard, 1964). Siting
   decisions are particularly complex. For example,
   Northern States Power Company considered 95 sites
   in its Tyrone Energy Park environmental report
   (Northern States Power Company, 1974). Six
   alternatives were described in terms of 22
   environmental categories in the final stage of
   the analysis;
2. Impact projects are uncertain. Further, decision
   makers often make inconsistent and unreliable
   decisions when risk is present (Tversky and
   Kahneman, 1981); and
3. Several parties are concerned with the decision,
   each having different beliefs about which types
   of impacts are most important. Each alternative
   will benefit some interests, frequently at the
   expense of others.

Each of these complications presents difficult theoretical
and practical problems; no consensus exists on how best to
handle them. This paper focuses on methods for handling
the multiple-criteria aspects of environmental assessment.
The ability of such techniques to include uncertainty and
multiple perspectives will also be discussed.

Environmental Impact Statements have dealt with
trade-offs, uncertainties, and conflicting points of views
in a variety of ways. At one extreme, they can be treated
subjectively or even ignored. In the majority of 48
nuclear power plant environmental reports reviewed for
this research, a subjective, nonquantified judgment is
made about the relative worth of, for example, economics
vs. environmental effects in recommending a site choice
(Pierce and Rowe, 1979). Risk is rarely quantified, and
perspectives of different groups are almost never
discussed.

Other statements, however, used one or more
quantitative analytical approaches to evaluate alternative
sites. Such techniques have the following advantages:

1. Underlying assumptions can be stated explicitly
   and easily documented;
2. Analytical approaches can handle more data more
   consistently than the human mind alone;
3. Opinions and values of a large number of people

can be systematically included in a decision;
4. Consistent and rational techniques for handling risk can be used; and
5. Analytical techniques pinpoint which considerations and trade-offs affect the decision the most. They can help decision makers to think hard and clearly about trade-offs, data needs, and values.

But analytical decision methods also have several disadvantages:

1. Intangibles, such as aesthetics and political considerations, will be given short shrift in any purely numerical procedure.
2. If not used carefully, analytical methods can distort decision makers' values and obscure rather than illuminate a decision's basis. This is a particular danger with complex methodologies whose assumptions and workings are little understood by decision makers.

Nevertheless, analytical methods are at the heart of many environmental impact assessment procedures now in use. Some methods are relatively sophisticated, e.g., decision analysis. Others are simpler. In essence, these techniques are procedures for explicitly incorporating value judgments in decisions. Subjective values are crystalized in the form of "attribute value functions," "weights," and "decision rules" (to be defined below). The resulting evaluations can be no better than the value judgments going into them. Indeed, they can be much worse, if the techniques used for translating judgments into numbers are simplistic, too complex, sloppily applied, misunderstood, or otherwise inappropriate. Sadly, multi-objective techniques are too often abused in siting studies and other environmental impact analyses. Concerned about this problem, the U.S. Nuclear Regulatory Commission sponsored a two-year study by Brookhaven National Laboratory to examine the use of multi-objective methods in siting (Rowe et al., 1979). This paper summarizes portions of that research.
    There is a wide variety of analytical methods for handling conflicting criteria, uncertainty, and multiple decision makers. In the environmental assessment literature (Bennington, Lubore, and Pfeffer, 1974; Jain, Urban, and Stacey, 1977; MacFarlane et al., 1975; Warner and Preston, 1974; Whitlatch, 1976), some of these are known as "checklist," "matrix," and "pollution-indicator" techniques. "Multi-objective decision techniques" is a more general descriptor of these methodologies. Some, if used carefully and if their assumptions are correct, can accurately represent the values of decision makers. Simpler procedures, having less theoretical rigor, are

easier to use. But the numbers they produce might have
little to do with decision makers' values because the
questions such methods ask are often ambiguous or
misleading. Therefore, there is a trade-off between ease
of use and theoretical validity. This makes choosing a
multi-objective method a multi-objective problem in
itself. The first section of this paper presents a number
of widely used multi-objective decision-making techniques.
The second section criticizes their use in environmental
reports on nuclear power plants.

Theoretical rigor matters little if sophisticated and
simple methods yield similar evaluations. If that is so,
the easier approach should be used. But if theoretically
superior techniques result in different choices, then they
might be preferred. The third section presents the
results of experiments, where experts in siting and impact
analysis evaluated sites using different multi-objective
procedures. It is shown that the choice of technique for
"balancing apples and oranges" often made a striking
difference in evaluations of site alternatives. Hence,
care should be taken in choosing and applying a method;
recent applications have generally been too slipshod.
Finally, conclusions are presented.

A SURVEY OF MULTI-OBJECTIVE DECISION METHODS

Most multi-objective environmental assessment
techniques follow these steps:

1. Choose the impacts and characteristics
   ("attributes") that are relevant to the analysis;
   quantify them if possible. This is the most
   difficult and time-consuming part of
   environmental assessment;
2. For each attribute, develop an attribute "value
   function" that translates the attribute to a
   measure of worth or suitability. The Battelle
   Environmental Evaluation System, for example,
   uses a nonlinear transformation to convert
   dissolved oxygen concentration (ppm) into
   "environmental quality units" (Dee et al., 1972).
   This step is usually accomplished by experts in
   relevant disciplines. It is presumed here that
   higher levels of attribute value functions are
   more desirable;
3. Choose a "weight" for each attribute that is
   proportional to its "importance" or
   "significance." This is often done by groups,
   including nontechnically trained representatives
   of environmental and consumer organizations, the
   business community, labor unions, government
   agencies, and other interested parties; and
4. Apply a "decision rule" that weights each
   attribute value function and then calculates a

single indicator of worth or suitability. The
alternative(s) maximizing this indicator is(are)
then chosen.

Methods for choosing attributes and for accomplishing
steps 2, 3, and 4 are exhaustively reviewed in a survey of
multi-objective methods performed by Brookhaven National
Laboratory (Hobbs, 1979, summarized in Hobbs, 1980a,
1980b). The paper emphasizes techniques used in the last
two steps. This is not to say that the first two are
unimportant, for, indeed, they are critical, but the
importance of weighting and choice of decision rule is too
often underestimated. Four decision rules are presented
below, followed by several techniques for choosing
weights. Examples of use in siting or other environmental
impact analyses are given.

DECISION RULES

     Decision rules are the means by which the many
dimensions of an alternative are reduced to a scalar index
of "environmental impact" or "suitability." If an
alternative must pass all of several criteria, with no
trade-offs allowed, then exclusionary screening is the
appropriate rule. If trade-offs are permitted, then one
of the other rules should be applied. Whereas subjective
judgment can only consider trade-offs among a few
attributes simultaneously, these rules can balance a great
number systematically and consistently. Decision makers
state what trade-offs they are willing to make when they
choose weights for these rules. Weighting summation is
the simplest of the three rules. It can be an accurate
representation of a decision maker's values when the rate
at which he/she is willing to trade off any given pair of
attributes does not depend on levels of those or other
attributes. But risk neutrality or absence of uncertainty
is presumed; if risk is present and important, then the
decision analysis multiplicative rule may, in theory, be
more appropriate. It is a difficult method to apply,
however, and is probably impractical when panels of
nontechnically schooled people are to pick weights. The
final decision rule considered is the power law, which
multiplies attributes rather than summing them. It makes
assumptions about decision makers' values that are
difficult to understand and verify. Each of these
decision rules is described in more detail below.

Exclusionary Screening

     This simple method excludes alternatives that are
unacceptable in any attribute. Each attribute's value
function is created by labeling each level of the
attribute as either acceptable or unacceptable. No
weights are assigned. This technique is commonly used to

screen out large portions of a region early in a siting study so that attention can be focused on areas that are most likely to contain suitable sites (Northern States Power Company, 1974; San Diego Gas and Electric Company, 1977).

The critical assumption here is that the attributes are truly exclusionary. Failure to be acceptable in one attribute cannot be compensated for by high suitability in other attributes. Legal requirements, such as population density, proximity to active faults, and endangered species habitat, are of this type. Discretionary attributes, not by nature exclusionary, are frequently treated as such, however. Examples include distance to water supply, transmission distance, wildlife habitat and unique vegetation areas, and access-related costs. Sites found unacceptable by this decision rule because of a poor value in only one attribute might be deemed best under other decision rules that allow trade-offs among attributes.

Weighting Summation

This decision rule chooses the site(s) maximizing the sum of weighted attribute value functions. In symbolic terms:

$$\text{Suitability} = \sum_{i=1}^{n} W_i V_i (X_i)$$

where $\sum$ = the summation sign; $V_i(X_i)$ = value function for attribute X_i; and W_i = the weight of X_i.

Many environmental impact assessment methods are based on this decision rule. An example is the Battelle Environmental Evaluation System (Dee et al., 1972), where total environmental quality equals the sum of 66 attributes that have been translated into "environmental quality units" via value functions. This rule also finds frequent use in siting studies, particularly at the stage where one or a few preferred locations are to be picked from a larger set (New York Power Pool, 1977; Omaha Public Power District, 1975; Pennsylvania Power and Light Company, 1972; Philadelphia Electric Company, 1973; Puget Sound Power and Light Company, 1974). For example, an environmental analysis system based on the weighting summation rule was used in the Tyrone Energy Park environmental report (Northern States Power Company, 1974) to assess the suitability of alternate sites.

Several important assumptions inherent in weighting summation are commonly unrecognized and often violated by users. They include presumptions about attribute value functions, weights, and attribute independence. If violated, the resulting evaluations are distortions of decision makers' preferences.

Attribute value functions must be on an interval

level of measurement with respect to value or suitability. That is, differences between numbers must be meaningful: 0.8 minus 0.6 should mean the same as 0.6 minus 0.4. Unfortunately, siting studies often weight and sum ordinal value functions, which is a violation of measurement theory (e.g., Philadelphia Electric Company, 1973).

Weighting should be done so that, if the decision maker is indifferent between two sites, their numerical suitability is equal. This means that weights should represent the relative value of a unit change in each attribute value function. That is, if W_1 = 2 and W_2 = 1, a change of 0.5 in $V_1(X_1)$ must be just as desirable as a change of 1 in $V_2(X_2)$. This implies that weights must be on a ratio level of measurement. For instance, W_1 = 2 and W_2 = 1 implies that attribute X_1 is twice as important as X_2. This definition of weights differs from definitions often used in siting studies. For instance, siters often choose weights before they choose attributes and/or before their value functions are defined. How can one estimate the relative importance of unit changes without knowing what the units are? For example, one study states a priori that economic and noneconomic considerations should be weighted equally (Detroit Edison Company, 1974). Such a statement is meaningless unless one knows which attributes and value functions are being weighted.

Another important assumption is additive independence. It implies a number of stringent conditions. For one, each attribute's value function must not depend on levels of other attributes (value independence). Also, trade-offs one is willing to make among attributes' value functions must not depend on levels of any of the attributes (preference independence). For instance, the amount decision makers are willing to spend on mitigation of socioeconomic effects should not depend on the level of either of those two attributes or that of environmental impact. Additive independence also implies that decision makers are neutral towards risk or that no risk or uncertainty is present, which, given the state of the art of impact assessment, is unlikely. "Neutrality towards risk" is defined below.

Decision Analysis Multiplicative Form

This decision rule is one of many possible utility functions used by decision analysis. Decision analysis is a general methodology for decision making under risk; consult Keeney and Raiffa (1976) for a detailed exposition of the theory and practice of decision analysis.

The decision analysis methodology allows decision makers' attitudes towards risk to be explicitly considered. "Attitude towards risk" can be explained by the following example. There are two sites with two attributes whose levels are described by probability distributions. In site 1, there is a 50 percent chance of getting both attributes at their best levels, and a similar chance of obtaining their worst values simultaneously. In site 2, there is a 50 percent chance of realizing the best value of X_1 and the worst of X_2 together, and a 50 percent probability of getting the reverse case. A decision maker who is indifferent between the two sites is "risk neutral." One who prefers the first site is "risk seeking," while one who chooses the second is "risk averse." Decision analysis can be used to capture these risk attitudes.

The methodology has been used in environmental assessments. An evaluation of the environmental impacts of solid waste disposal methods (Collins and Glysson, 1980) developed an Environmental Quality Index based on the multiplicative form given below. In that study, several experts helped create attribute utility functions and weights via a Delphi group method (Delbecq, Van de Ven, and Gustafson, 1975). The possible effects of power plants upon Columbia River salmonid populations has been analyzed using decision analysis (Keeney and Robilliard, 1977). There are also several applications in power plant siting (Keeney, 1979; Keeney and Nair, 1977; Sarin, 1980).

The most commonly applied decision analysis rule, the multiplicative form, calculates suitability as follows:

$$\text{Suitability} = \{ \prod_{i=1}^{n} (1 - kW_1V_1(X_1)) - 1\}/k$$

where $\prod$ = the product sign and k = scaling constant, so that suitability ranges from 0 to 1. The $V_i()$ must have the same range.

The alternative with the highest expected suitability is chosen. The $V_i()$ and W_i should be chosen by decision analysis methods that incorporate decision makers' attitudes towards risk. In that case, value functions are referred to as "utility functions."

This decision rule results from the assumptions that all attributes are value (or, more precisely, utility) and preference independent and that decision makers are not risk neutral. Under risk neutrality, this decision rule reduces to the weighting summation form because k falls to 0. Weights should also have the characteristics required by weighting summation.

The Power Law

This rule takes the following form:

$$\text{Suitability} = \prod_{i=1}^{n} V_i(X_i)^{W_i}$$

That is, suitability is equal to the product of each attribute value function raised to the W_i power. If the

W_i sum to 1, then percentage changes in suitability are
weighted averages of percentage changes in attribute value
functions. Site ranks are preserved, however, if weights
sum to any other number. The power law has been used in
nuclear plant environmental reports (Houston Light and
Power Company, 1973; Washington Public Power Supply
System, 1974).

Value independence is assumed, as is preference
independence among logarithms of attribute value
functions. Attribute value functions must be on a ratio
level of measurement, not an interval level. This follows
from the fact that suitability falls to 0 when just one
$V_i(X_i)$ is 0.

This method also presumes that decision makers
perceive value in a logarithmic, rather than linear,
fashion. A decision maker might choose attribute weights
1, 2, and 3 when he actually means e^1, e^2, and e^3.
Researchers in "psychophysics" believe that physical
phenomena are often perceived in this manner (Stevens,
1966) and some management scientists believe this is also
true for value (Gum, Roefs, and Kimball, 1976).

These four decision rules differ in the assumptions
they make regarding decision makers' values. But such
theoretical considerations are unimportant if different
rules result in the choice of the same alternatives.
Later in this paper, evidence is presented that choice of
decision rule can make an important difference.

WEIGHT SELECTION TECHNIQUES

Three of the four decision rules presented above
apply weights to attribute value functions. Weights are
how values of decision makers concerning trade-offs among
attributes are incorporated. The first four weighting
methods ask decision makers to choose weights directly
that represent the "importance" of attributes. Since
"importance" is ambiguously defined, such weights may not
be proportional to the relative value of unit changes in
their attribute value functions. Evidence that this is so
is presented later. This characteristic is required by
the weighting summation and decision analysis
multiplicative decision rules. For the power law, it is
the worth of changes in the logarithm of value functions
that is important.

In contrast, the indifference trade-off and decision
analysis weighting techniques, if applied correctly, yield
weights that accurately represent trade-offs decision
makers are willing to make; however, they are more
difficult to use. The final technique presented here,
multiple regression, is an entirely different approach.

The first technique, *categorization*, asks decision
makers to sort attributes into categories such as "high
importance," "average importance," and "low importance"
(with weights 3, 2, and 1, respectively). Weights from

this method are probably only on an ordinal level of measurement, as ratios of weights are arbitrarily fixed. That is, only the order of the numbers, not their magnitude, is meaningful. There is evidence that categorization tends to understate ratios of weights relative to other weighting methods (Hobbs and Rowe, 1979).

Rating, the most commonly used weighting method in siting, asks decision makers to rate, say on a scale of 0 to 10, the "importance" of each attribute.

Ratio questioning asks questions of the type, "What is the ratio of 'importance' of attributes X_1 and X_2?" At least (n - 1) such questions, with all n attributes involved at least once, must be asked to establish a weight set. Extra questions act as checks.

Metfessel allocation requests decision makers to allocate 100 points among the attributes in proportion to their "importance."

The *indifference trade-off* technique, unlike the above methods, guarantees theoretically valid weights, if applied correctly. It asks questions of the type, "How much $\Delta V_1(X_1)$ of $V_1(X_1)$ would you give up to obtain $\Delta V_2(X_2)$?" For example, "How many acres of prime farmland are you willing to give up to lower the number of salmonids killed by the 100,000 each year?" The purpose is to obtain the rate at which decision makers will trade one attribute for another. The weights for X_1 and X_2 are related by the equation: $W_1/W_2 = \Delta V_2(X_2)/\Delta V_1(X_1)$, which follows from the definition of weighting summation. As in ratio questioning, enough questions are asked to solve for a unique (up to a scaling constant) set of weights. Consistency checks are especially important here, as decision makers will probably be very inconsistent on the first try. Such checks will cause them to think harder about their values and the trade-offs involved.

Decision analysis weighting chooses theoretically valid weights that reflect attitudes toward risk. This method is usually applied in conjunction with the decision analysis multiplicative form. Weights can be chosen in a number of ways. One common variation asks,

At what probability, p, are you indifferent between:
1. A site with attribute X_i at its best value and all other attributes at their worst and
2. A lottery where there is
   a. chance p of obtaining all attributes at their best levels and
   b. chance (1 - p) of getting all attributes at their worst levels?

If all value functions are scaled from 0 (worst) to 1 (best), then the weight of X_i is precisely p. If decision analysis weights sum to 1.0, the decision maker is risk neutral; a greater sum indicates risk averseness, while a

lesser sum implies risk-seeking behavior.
Since decision analysis and indifference trade-off
weight sets are, in theory, both valid, one should be able
to derive a set of decision analysis weights in the
following manner. First, determine one attribute's weight
by the above procedure. Then multiply a set of
indifference trade-off weights by the ratio of that
attribute's decision analysis and indifference trade-off
weights. This is the procedure most frequently used to
obtain decision analysis weights.
If the sum of decision analysis weights is 1.0, then
the decision maker is risk neutral and weighting summation
is appropriate (given value and preference independence).
Otherwise, the multiplicative form should be used.
In *multiple regression* weighting, decision makers
need only assign ranks or overall ratings of suitability
to a number of multi-attributed alternatives. Attribute
weights are generated by multiple regression, which
minimizes the sum of squared deviations of predicted ranks
or ratings from the ones actually made. A fundamental
philosophical difference exists between this approach and
that of other weighting methods. This technique attempts
to imitate subjective evaluations, while other procedures
try to improve them. There is also a practical
difference. Regression weights tend to be more clustered
on a few attributes than do weights chosen by other
techniques. Regression weights can even take the wrong
sign. Psychologists suggest that the reason for this is
that decision makers cannot cope with complexity and,
thus, treat important attributes unevenly while ignoring
less important attributes altogether when making holistic
judgments (Shepard, 1964).
Each of the above weighting techniques can be applied
by groups. A common procedure is to average rating
weights given by experts and representatives of interest
groups. For example, three groups weighted 31 attributes
in calculating an overall impact index for highway
corridor alternatives in Utah (Crawford, 1973). The
Delphi and nominal group procedures have been developed in
an effort to maximize group effectiveness in such
exercises (Delbecq, Van de Ven, and Gustafson, 1975).
They find use in several siting studies (New York Power
Pool, 1977; Pennsylvania Power and Light Company, 1977;
Voelker, 1977). The four simpler weighting techniques are
easier to apply in group settings, but the resulting
weights may or may not accurately represent trade-offs
that individual members or the group as a whole are
willing to make. Decision analysis (Gros, 1975) and
regression (Burnham, Nealey, and Maynard, 1975) have been
used to determine the preferences of each of several
interest groups regarding power plant site
characteristics. Differences and similarities of opinion
can be explored in this manner.
Other weighting methods are available (Hobbs, 1979)

but will not be discussed here. As with decision rules, theoretical considerations are irrelevant if similar results follow from different methods. Evidence is presented below that shows that the results of invalid techniques can differ from the outcomes of methods that, in theory, yield valid weights.

CURRENT PRACTICES

When electric utilities apply for a nuclear power plant construction permit, they submit an environmental report to the U.S. Nuclear Regulatory Commission (NRC). The report becomes the basis of the NRC's Environmental Impact Statement.

The site selection chapters of 48 environmental reports submitted since February 1973 were reviewed to determine what multi-objective methods were used and whether they were correctly applied (Pierce and Rowe, 1979). The process of site selection generally has three stages: candidate area selection, candidate site selection, and final or proposed site selection. Each stage can and often does use a different method. Of the studies reviewed, 13 applied weighting summation. These include 9 at the final site selection stage, 5 at the candidate site choice stage, and 3 at the candidate area selection stage. The power law was also used in 2 of those 13 studies. Eight of the 48 statements applied exclusionary screening at the candidate area or site levels.

The most striking characteristic of the 48 studies is the lack of specific information about the site selection process. Many studies contain elaborate descriptions of alternatives, but few present a clear picture of the methodologies used or the trade-offs made in selecting a proposed site. In addition, attributes used to evaluate alternatives are not concisely defined and methods of choosing weights, where used, are not specified. It is difficult, therefore, to determine whether or not the fundamental assumptions of decision rules are met. In general, from the information presented, it is only possible to confirm that an acceptable site was chosen, not that a sound and comprehensive site selection methodology was used.

The most common violation of methodological assumptions is algebraic manipulation of ordinal numbers, usually through use of categorization attribute value functions in weighting summation. Ordinal weights, also chosen by categorization, were often applied. None of the studies reviewed acknowledge the existence of theoretical requirements necessary for the valid application of the decision rule used. Most appear to violate one or more basic assumptions. Most of the 13 studies using weighting summation appear to violate the level of measurement requirements and the assumption of attribute independence.

Nevertheless, conclusions about the significance of these errors to study results are necessarily nondefinite since, in most cases, descriptions of methodologies lack sufficient detail to determine how they were applied. Many siting studies other than those for nuclear power plants surveyed above have used analytical multi-objective methods. They appear in other impact statements and in the literature and have been surveyed elsewhere (Hobbs, 1979).

EMPIRICAL COMPARISONS OF DECISION RULES AND WEIGHTING METHODS

As stated above, theoretical considerations mean little unless different methods choose different alternatives. If they do, then analysis should carefully consider which decision rules and weighting methods are most appropriate. This portion of the research had panels of experts on siting and environmental impacts of power plants apply different methods to the same sets of alternatives (Hobbs and Rowe, 1979; Rowe and Pierce, 1979). From the results, several conclusions were drawn about what theoretical considerations are most important in choosing among methods.

Several hypothetical siting problems were presented to different groups of experts. In the Maryland Analysis I (Hobbs and Rowe, 1979), five persons from the Maryland Power Plant Siting Program, a university, and Oak Ridge National Laboratory separately chose weights by several different methods. One of the Maryland participants also chose exclusionary screening areas. Eighteen attributes were weighted, including indicators of population, endangered species, water availability, aquifer recharge, and engineering feasibility, among others. They described each of the 18,500 91-acre cells comprising the study area (the five western-most counties of Maryland). The weight sets were used to generate candidate areas for a pair of nuclear power plants with evaporative cooling towers. Adjacent groups of four or more cells scoring in the top 8 percent were designated as candidate areas. This is about the same fraction of the study area chosen for candidate areas in an actual siting study of eastern Maryland. Examples of candidate areas generated are shown in Figure 11.2. County boundaries are omitted to disguise exact locations of cells. The top 2 percent cells are white, outlined in black. The remaining candidate areas are shown in black.

In the Maryland analysis II (Hobbs and Rowe, 1979), a smaller number of attributes (nine) was used for the study area. Fourteen siting experts from utilities, consulting groups, government, academia, and the League of Women Voters each chose weights by several of the simpler methods and provided cutoffs for exclusionary screening runs. The same panel also selected weights and cutoffs

a. Weighting Summation (Rating Weights) Candidate Areas

b. Weighting Summation (Indifference Tradeoff Weights) Candidate Areas

Figure 11.2 Examples of candidate areas generated: (a) weighting summation (rating weights) candidate areas and (b) weighting summation (indifference trade-off weights) candidate areas.

for the western United States analysis (Hobbs and Rowe, 1979) in which hypothetical candidate areas were chosen for six GW(e) nuclear energy centers in the 11 western states. Seven attributes covering population, seismic, land use, slope, and cost concerns were used.

The 14-member panel also chose weights by simpler, less valid weighting techniques for the Long Island analysis II (Rowe and Pierce, 1979), which evaluated 11 nuclear power plant sites in eastern Long Island, New York. Sites were described by the following attributes: site cost, land use, transmission distance, water quality and aquatic ecosystems, terrestrial ecosystems, population, and aesthetics. A panel of Brookhaven environmental scientists and a League of Women Voters representative weighted the same attributes in the Long Island analysis I (Rowe and Pierce, 1979). In addition to the simpler weighting methods, they also applied the indifference trade-off, decision analysis, and multiple regression techniques. In each of the above studies, attribute value functions were created by persons familiar with siting and the particular study area.

First, the results of the different decision rules are contrasted, then followed by comparisons of weights and site evaluations made by different weighting methods. There have been several other studies, which are surveyed elsewhere (Hobbs, 1979), that also compare the results of different multi-objective methods.

COMPARISONS OF DECISION RULES

Exclusionary Screening vs. Weighting Summation

As often as not, these two decision rules yielded strikingly different candidate areas. In the Maryland analysis I, only one person chose areas by both rules. Only one-third of the cells picked by one method were chosen by the other.

Differences were less prominent in the Maryland analysis II, probably because fewer attributes (9, as opposed to 18) were used. Nevertheless, large differences sometimes arose. The group using mean rating weights and median exclusionary criteria, for example, chose areas that overlapped less than 50 percent. In the western United States analysis, six persons' exclusionary screening candidate areas were compared to their weighting summation areas. For three of the persons, the decision rules disagreed more than they agreed, i.e., the overlap was less than 50 percent.

Decision Analysis Multiplicative Form vs. Weighting Summation

Only in the Maryland analysis I were candidate areas generated by decision analysis. A wide range of risk

attitudes was simulated by altering the sum of weights in
the multiplicative rule. Candidate areas reflecting risk-
averse attitudes were almost identical to those reflecting
risk-neutral or risk-seeking preferences. Thus, risk
attitudes are a minor influence, and the simpler weighting
summation rule can be used since it represents complete
risk neutrality. The same conclusion was made in the Long
Island analysis I. Rarely did rankings of sites change
significantly when the multiplicative rule was used
instead of weighting summation.

Power Law vs. Weighting Summation

Power law candidate areas were generated by each of
the ten rating and indifference trade-off weight sets
chosen in the Maryland analysis I. The differences
between the rules' candidate areas for a given set of
weights were large; on the average, areas overlapped less
than 40 percent. This is roughly equivalent to the
overlap found between weighting summation and exclusionary
screening in the same study. These differences can be
contrasted to the average overlap of weighting summation
(rating weights) areas chosen by different persons, taken
a pair at a time. The mean "between-persons" overlap was
higher, about 60 percent. Thus, choice of decision rule
between weighting summation and the power law appears more
important, on the average, than does who selects the
weights.

The differences in candidate areas caused by changes
in weights are much diminished when the power law is
applied. This is because of its multiplicative nature: it
tends to choose sites that are moderately good in all
attributes no matter what weights were used. In contrast,
weighting summation can and will often pick locations that
are extremely good in highly weighted attributes but bad
in others. Weights matter much more in the latter case.

In the Long Island analysis II, however, there were
few important differences in site ranks. For almost every
set of weights, the sites ranked 1 and 2 by one rule were
ranked the same by the other. Other ranks were
reshuffled, however. Fewer attributes were used in that
analysis, and two sites were best in most of the
attributes compared to the remaining nine sites.

COMPARISONS OF WEIGHTING METHODS

As done above in the case of decision rules,
candidate areas and site ranks are being compared below.
In addition, the weights themselves were contrasted, using
correlations (Pearson's r). A correlation of 1 indicates
that one set of weights is simply a linear transformation
(with a positive slope) of the other. A zero correlation
indicates that the weights are not at all linearly
related. Correlations give indications of differences in

weights that are not confounded by the peculiarities of
the locations being evaluated. Differences due to choice
of method are measured using correlations between pairs of
weight sets chosen by different methods by the same
person. Correlations between methods can be compared to
correlations between weight sets chosen by different
persons. This gives an indication of the importance of
"choice of method" vs. "choice of person." In one study,
each person applied rating twice. The correlations
between each person's rating weight sets give an
indication of method reliability, which can be contrasted
to differences due to choice of weighting method.

Categorization, Rating, Ratio
Questioning, and Metfessel Allocation

    All these methods ask for direct assessments of
attribute importance, where "importance" is usually
ambiguously defined. Hence, they do not assure that
weights represent trade-offs decision makers are willing
to make. In general, differences among these methods are
less than differences among persons. In the Maryland
analysis II, the median correlation among each person's
categorization, rating, and Metfessel allocation weight
sets was 0.88, compared to a median "between-persons"
(rating weights) of 0.31. The "between-persons"
correlations were taken between every possible pair of
rating weight sets. Similarly, differences in candidate
areas due to choice of method were much smaller than
differences due to choice of person. The same weighting
techniques were used in the western United States analysis
and the Long Island analysis II; in both cases, the same
conclusions were made.
    In the Long Island analysis I, correlations among
categorization, rating, ratio questioning, and Metfessel
allocation were uniformly higher than "between-persons"
correlations. Further, they were similar in magnitude to
correlations of rating weight sets chosen by the same
person at different times. Hence, differences in weights
among those methods are, on the average, no greater than
what might be expected from method unreliability alone.
Nevertheless, differences between ratio questioning
(weighting summation) and rating (weighting summation)
site ranks are greater than those between power law and
weighting summation ranks. Half of the time, the top-
ranked site chosen by ratio questioning differed from the
one picked by rating.

Rating vs. Indifference Trade-off

    This is a comparison of a method that asks for a
direct assessment of "importance" (rating) to a technique
that derives weights from trade-offs made by decision
makers (indifference trade-off). In theory, the latter is

much more likely than the former to yield valid weights.

In the Maryland analysis I, there were large differences between each person's rating and indifference trade-off weights. The average "between-methods" correlation of weights was only 0.306; this is close to the mean "between-persons" (rating weights) correlation of 0.176. The weighting summation candidate areas also differed greatly. One person's rating and indifference trade-off areas are shown in Figure 11.2, where the overlap is only 40 percent. The mean overlap of each participant's rating and indifference trade-off (weighting summation) candidate area is 52 percent, less than the average "between-persons" (rating weights, weighting summation) overlap (62 percent).

In the Long Island analysis I, differences were not quite as pronounced but still significant. The median correlation between indifference trade-off and each person's first set of rating weights was 0.44, just less than the median "between-persons" (rating) correlation of 0.48. These are less than the median correlation between each person's pair of test/retest rating weight sets, 0.65. However, site ranks produced by the two methods were similar.

Indifference Trade-off vs. Decision Analysis Weighting

In theory, both of these methods choose theoretically valid weights. This implies that one set should be proportional to the other. But this was not the case in the Maryland analysis I. Instead of being constant, ratios of weights varied by a factor of 10 or more for one of the two persons who chose decision analysis weights and by a factor of 1.6 for the other. This means that the participants had inconsistent risk attitudes. It appears that the participants had difficulty dealing with hypothetical probabilities used by the decision analysis method. This points out the importance of consistency checks in the more difficult weighting techniques.

Multiple Regression vs. Other Weighting Methods

Multiple regression chooses the weights that best imitate subjective overall evaluations, while the other techniques attempt to improve those judgments. Regression weights were derived in the Long Island analysis I by having each person rate each of the 11 sites on a scale of 0 to 10. The attribute value function values for these sites were then regressed against those overall ratings to obtain a set of regression weights for each person. The site ranks differed strikingly from rankings made using any other weight set and decision rule. Participants were unable to evaluate all attributes simultaneously and consistently; many attributes were disregarded or given uneven consideration. Not surprisingly, the calculated regression weights bore little resemblance to weights picked by any other weighting technique. In fact, almost half of the regression weights were negative.

CONCLUSIONS

Environmental Impact Statements are often used to compare alternatives having a bewildering variety of environmental, social, and economic effects. Trade-offs, uncertainty, and multiple decision makers make evaluation difficult. Increasingly, multi-objective decision methods are used to incorporate subjective values into such decisions in a consistent and logical manner. Some are simple to apply, while others can represent values of decision makers more accurately. The theoretically more rigorous techniques can lead to distorted results, however, if decision makers misunderstand or distrust them or are careless in using them. No technique can guarantee a "good" choice; a method can be no better than the data on attributes and decision-maker values that go into it.

Each decision rule makes particular assumptions about a decision maker's value structure. A rule that is appropriate in one context may not be so in another. It has been demonstrated that choice of decision rule (from among exclusionary screening, weighting summation, and the power law) can make an important difference in site decisions. Whether or not a difference is made depends on the number and complexity of trade-offs. Choice of decision rule has proven to be generally as important as choice of persons to select weights. Hence, analysts should take considerable care in choosing a rule and in checking whether its assumptions are valid. Few differences were found to arise, however, between weighting summation and the decision analysis multiplicative form. Thus, in such cases, one may as well use the simpler model.

Weights are needed by most multi-objective techniques to make trade-offs among attributes. In weighting summation and the decision analysis multiplicative form, weights should be proportional to the relative value of unit changes in their attribute value functions. Weights are often chosen in a slipshod manner by methods that ask only for direct assessment of the ambiguously defined "importance" of each attribute. The results of such exercises can have nothing to do with the trade-offs decision makers are willing to make. Practical methods for choosing valid weights are available, but they are more difficult to apply. In general, valid methods choose significantly different weights and sites than invalid weighting techniques. Those differences are comparable to differences in weights and sites chosen by different persons. Therefore, there is strong justification for the extra time needed for applying valid techniques; indifference trade-off is the easiest of these. Because decision makers have difficulty evaluating complex alternatives, multiple regression weighting is inappropriate when there are more than four or five attributes.

Most multi-objective techniques ask decision makers to be more precise in their value judgments than they like to be or can be. Methods are being developed that allow decision makers to be imprecise with weights and attribute levels (Sarin, 1977a, 1977b). Instead of point values, ranges can be specified. If the ranges are not "tight" enough to eliminate all but one alternative, decision makers are asked to restrict them further. Only as much precision is required as is necessary to make the decision. This type of method helps decision makers learn about their values and the problem. More experience in environmental assessment and siting is needed with these techniques.

REFERENCES

Bennington, G., Lubore, S., and Pfeffer, J. (1974), Resource and Land Investigations Program: Methodologies for Environmental Analysis, Vol. 1: Environmental Assessment. MTR-6740. McLean, Va.: MITRE Corporation.

Burnham, J. B., Nealey, S. M., and Maynard, W. S. (1975), "A Method for Integrating Societal and Technical Judgments in Environmental Decision Making." Nuclear Technology, 25(4), 675-681.

Collins, J. P., and Glysson, E. A. (1980), "Multi-attribute Utility Theory and Environmental Decisions." Proceedings of the American Society of Civil Engineers, Journal of the Environmental Engineering Division, 106(EE4), 815-830.

Crawford, A. (1973), "Impact Analysis Using Differentially Weighted Criteria." In J. L. Cochrane and M. Zeleny (Eds.), Multiple Criteria Decision Making. Columbia: University of South Carolina Press.

Dee, N., et al. (1972), "An Environmental Evaluation System for Water Resources Planning." Water Resources Research, 3, 523-535.

Delbecq, A. L., Van de Ven, A. H., and Gustafson, D. H. (1975), Group Techniques: Nominal Group and Delphi Processes. Glenville, Ill.: Scott Foresman.

Detroit Edison Company (1974), Environmental Report, Greenwood Energy Center, Units 2 and 3, Construction Permit Review, Vol. 3. U.S. Nuclear Regulatory Commission Docket No. 50-452/353.

Gros, J. (1975), "Power Plant Siting: A Paretian Environmental Approach." Nuclear Engineering and Design, 34, 281-292.

Gum, R. L., Roefs, R. G., and Kimball, D. B. (1976), "Quantifying Social Goals: Development of a

Weighting Methodology." Water Resources Research, 12(4), 617-622.
Hobbs, B. F. (1979), Analytical Multi-objective Decision Methods for Power Plant Siting: A Review of Theory and Applications. BNL-NUREG-51204, NUREG/CR-1687. Upton, N.Y.: Brookhaven National Laboratory, Division of Regional Studies.
Hobbs, B. F. (1980a), "A Comparison of Weighting Methods in Power Plant Siting." Decision Sciences, 11(4), 725-737.
Hobbs, B. F. (1980b), "Multi-objective Power Plant Siting Methods." Proceedings of the American Society of Civil Engineers, Journal of the Energy Division, 106(EY2), 187-200.
Hobbs, B. F., and Rowe, M. D. (1979), A Comparison of Regional Screening Methodologies. BNL-NUREG-51205. Upton, N.Y.: Brookhaven National Laboratory, Division of Regional Studies.
Houston Light and Power Company (1973), Environmental Report, Allens Creek 1 and 2, Construction Permit Review. U.S. Nuclear Regulatory Commission Docket No. 50-466/467.
Jain, R. K., Urban, L. V., and Stacey, G. S. (1977), Environmental Impact Analysis: A New Dimension in Decision Making. New York: Van Nostrand Reinhold Co.
Keeney, R. L. (1979), "Evaluation of Proposed Storage Sites." Operations Research, 27(1), 48-64.
Keeney, R. L., and Nair, K. (1977), "Nuclear Siting Using Decision Analysis." Energy Policy, 5(3), 223-231.
Keeney, R. L., and Raiffa, H. (1976), Decisions with Multiple Objectives: Preferences and Value Trade-offs. New York: Wiley.
Keeney, R. L., and Robilliard, G. (1977), "Assessing and Evaluating Environmental Impacts at Proposed Nuclear Power Plant Sites." Journal of Environmental Economics and Management, 4, 153-166.
MacFarlane, D., et al. (1975), Power Facility Siting in the State of Illinois, Part II: Environmental Impacts of Large Energy Conversion Facilities. Environmental Technology Assessment prepared for the Illinois Institute on Environmental Quality. Oakbrook, Ill.
New York Power Pool (1977), Statewide Site Selection Survey. Prepared by United Engineers and Constructors, Boston, Mass. New York: New York Power Pool.
Northern States Power Company (1974), Environmental Report, Tyrone Energy Park 1 and 2, Construction Permit Review. U.S. Nuclear Regulatory Commission Docket No. 50-484/485.
Omaha Public Power District (1975), Environmental Report, Fort Calhoun 2, Construction Permit Review. U.S. Nuclear Regulatory Commission Docket No. 50-548.
Pennsylvania Power and Light Company (1972), Environmental

Report, Susquehanna 1 and 2, Construction Permit
Review. U.S. Nuclear Regulatory Commission Docket
No. 50-387/388.

Pennsylvania Power and Light Company (1972), Delphi
Assessment. Allentown, Penn.: Pennsylvania Power and
Light Company.

Philadelphia Electric Company (1973), Environmental
Report, Fulton, Construction Permit Review. U.S.
Nuclear Regulatory Commission Docket No. 50-463.

Pierce, B. L., and Rowe, M. D. (1979), Quantitative
Nuclear Power Plant Siting Methods: A Review of
Current Practice. BNL-NUREG-28115. Upton, N.Y.:
Brookhaven National Laboratory, Division of Regional
Studies.

Puget Sound Power and Light Company (1974), Environmental
Report, Skagit 1 and 2, Construction Permit Review.
U.S. Nuclear Regulatory Commission Docket
No. 50-522/523.

Rowe, M. D., Hobbs, B. F., Pierce, B. L., and Meier, P. M.
(1979), Evaluation of Nuclear Power Plant Siting
Methodologies. BNL-NUREG-51206. Upton, N.Y.:
Brookhaven National Laboratory, Division of Regional
Studies.

Rowe, M. D., and Pierce, B. L. (1979), A Comparison of
Site Evaluation Methodologies. BNL-NUREG-51203.
Upton, N.Y.: Brookhaven National Laboratory, Division
of Regional Studies.

San Diego Gas and Electric Company (1977), Environmental
Report, Sundesert 1 and 2, Construction Permit
Review. U.S. Nuclear Regulatory Commission Docket
No. 50-582/583, Vol. 14, Appendix S.

Sarin, R. K. (1977a), "Interactive Evaluation and Bound
Procedure for Selecting Multi-attributed
Alternatives." In M. Starr and M. Zeleny (Eds.),
Multiple Criteria Decision Making. TIMS Studies in
Management Sciences, 6. Amsterdam: North Holland
Publishing Co.

Sarin, R. K. (1977b), "Screening of Multi-attribute
Alternatives." OMEGA, 5(4), 481-489.

Sarin, R. K. (1980), "Ranking of Multi-attribute
Alternatives with an Application to Coal Power Plant
Siting." In Multiple Criteria Decision Making,
Theory and Application. Berlin: Springer-Verlag.

Shepard, R. (1964), "On Subjectively Optimal Selections
among Multi-attribute Alternatives." In M. Shelley
and G. Bryan (Eds.), Human Judgments and Optimality.
New York: Wiley.

Stevens, S. S. (1966), "On the Operation Known as
Judgment." American Scientist, 54(4), 385-401.

Tversky, A., and Kahneman, D. (1981), "The Framing of
Decisions and the Psychology of Choice." Science,
211, 453-458.

Voelker, A. H. (1977), Facility Siting: An Application of
the Nominal Group Process. ORNL-NUREG-TM-81. Oak

Ridge, Tenn.: Oak Ridge National Laboratory.

Warner, M., and Preston, E. (1974), A Review of Environmental Impact Methodologies. Prepared by Battelle-Columbus Laboratories, Columbus, Ohio. Sponsored by U.S. Environmental Protection Agency, Socioeconomic Environmental Studies Series, EPA-600/5-74-002, Washington, D.C.

Washington Public Power Supply System (1974), Environmental Report, Units 3 and 5, Construction Permit Review. U.S. Nuclear Regulatory Commission Docket No. 50-508/509.

Whitlatch, E. E. (1976), "Systematic Approaches to Environmental Impact Assessment: An Evaluation." Water Resources Bulletin, 12(1), 123-137.

NOTES

'Acknowledgment: The research supporting this paper was sponsored by the U.S. Nuclear Regulatory Commission and the Maryland Power Plant Siting Program. Responsibility for accuracy rests with the authors; the opinions expressed are exclusively those of the authors.

12. The Scoping Concept and Citizen Involvement: An Opportunity for Rejuvenating NEPA

James R. Pease and Richard C. Smardon

INTRODUCTION

The National Environmental Policy Act of 1969 (NEPA) set into motion a series of changes in our national consciousness and institutions seldom attained by an act of Congress. The changes are still unfolding, affecting every aspect of our social, political, and economic systems, as well as that evasive concept of quality of life. Like it or not, the Environmental Impact Statement (EIS), a key provision of NEPA, is now part of federal administrative procedure.

Therein lies the problem. What began as an exciting planning tool to balance environmental protection with development needs has been transformed into a cumbersome and costly procedure, incomprehensible to most people. While the purpose of the EIS is to provide information for better decisions, agencies have often used the process to produce documents justifying a decision already made. Environmental groups, on the other hand, have found that NEPA procedural requirements provide ready-made legal tools for challenging projects connected to federal actions. However, such litigation is increasingly expensive in time, money, and energy for all concerned.

Planning is a process of rational compromise to avoid polarization; in order for NEPA to be truly a planning tool, it must be able to accommodate differing values and vested interests. The concept of "scoping," or identifying key issues and problems before research is begun on an impact statement, provides a mechanism for building sensitive adjustment into the preparation of an impact statement.

Recognizing that impact statements were not fulfilling their original purpose, the Council on Environmental Quality (CEQ) initiated a process for revising the NEPA guidelines in 1977. The revisions have gone through several stages and were published as final regulations in the Federal Register on November 29, 1978. In accordance with CEQ regulations, federal agencies must adopt criteria for determining which projects

categorically require impact statements and which projects
do not. For those projects that do not clearly fall into
one of these categories, an environmental assessment is to
be done. The assessment is intended to be brief, running
several pages in length, and provide the basis for
determining whether or not to prepare an impact statement.

When an impact statement is to be prepared, agencies
are required to use a scoping process (Sec. 1501.7) to
identify the range of actions, alternatives, and impacts
to be considered in depth in the impact statement and to
identify and eliminate from detailed study the issues that
are not significant or have been covered in other impact
reviews. The guidelines direct agencies to include other
actions that are closely related, interdependent, and/or
cumulative in nature in the scoping process. The study of
alternatives shall include mitigation measures. In
identifying significant impacts, indirect and cumulative
impacts as well as direct impacts shall be included in the
scoping report.

The scoping process shall also identify the
relationship between the timing of the EIS and the
agency's decision-making schedule. This provision is
intended to make more explicit how the agency will use
environmental analysis in its planning program. The
scoping requirements establish another set of
administrative procedures in an already cumbersome
process. Most agencies had established an internal
procedure to focus, at least in a general way, the scope
of the EIS analysis. If agency implementation of the
scoping requirements does not go beyond codifying into
administrative procedures its internal and informal method
of organizing impact analysis, then not much will have
been gained.

However, the scoping concept does have potential for
contributing to several of the objectives outlined in the
regulations, including making impact statements more
understandable, linking the environmental analysis closer
to agency planning processes, and reducing the likelihood
of legal challenge by improving the focus and quality of
the impact statement. The key to whether scoping is
effective in these ways, it seems to us, lies in the
extent to which interests and expertise outside the agency
are made part of the process. There are two aspects to
this outside participation: broad public participation
and the use of a mediator not affiliated with the agency.
While public participation is essential, the use of a
mediator will depend on a number of factors discussed
later in this chapter.

Several sections of the regulations address agency
responsibility to involve the public in its planning and
impact analysis programs. The scoping phase would provide
an excellent mechanism for involving the public before
agency planning becomes committed to a course of action.
By providing opportunities to participate at this stage,

various public and private interests, such as environmental organizations, business groups, local and state officials, technical experts, and affected citizens, could identify their key concerns. The agency takes a risk of higher exposure and increased controversy over its project but, in return, reduces the probability of communication breakdown and resultant legal challenge at later stages of impact statement preparation and review.

Several questions arise in attempting to formulate an effective scoping process. What techniques and procedures are more effective? How are participants selected? How can the process be organized in an efficient way to maintain the participants' interest and produce a useful report? These questions will be addressed in the following section.

ENVIRONMENTAL IMPACT ASSESSMENT PROJECT

In 1975, the Oregon State University Extension Service received funding from the U.S. Department of Agriculture (USDA) for a project to develop a scoping process with emphasis on citizen involvement. The project was organized into four major phases: (1) preparation of technical materials to be used by citizen groups; (2) formulation of a citizen involvement (scoping) process; (3) testing the technical materials and scoping process in three demonstration projects involving actual impact statements (the projects were a U.S. Forest Service timber management plan, an Oregon Department of Transportation highway project, and a Soil Conservation Service small watershed impoundment); and (4) an evaluation of the scoping process and the technical materials based on the experience gained from the three demonstration projects.

From our experiences with the demonstration projects and the follow-up evaluations, we concluded that scoping procedures should include the following elements:

1. A systematic approach with a set of assessment materials that cover the range of probable impacts and are easily used by scoping participants;
2. An independent scoping coordinator (or mediator) who is not affiliated with the sponsoring agency and an impact specialist employed by the sponsoring agency who can work closely with the independent coordinator and the public involvement committee;
3. A carefully organized program of public involvement to include a committee broadly representative of various interest groups; and
4. A budget and time schedule appropriate for the project under study that allows for meshing with normal agency procedures.

Each of these elements will be discussed in light of our experiences with the demonstration projects and literature in the field.

ASSESSMENT MATERIALS

In order to use time most efficiently, resolve conflicts, and organize diverse perspectives and information, a set of well-organized assessment materials is indispensable. The materials provide a focus for all aspects of the scoping process, aid in facilitating group discussions, and lead to specific products. In our project, the assessment materials included an assessment form and manual. The manual provides step-by-step instructions for filling out the form and a set of reference checklists (Smardon, Pease, and Donheffner, 1976). A reference handbook (Smardon, Pease, Furuseth, and Donheffner, 1976) was also developed. The handbook, manual, and assessment form are all keyed to 13 impact topics that, in turn, are broken down into subtopics. The assessment form includes questions for the source and type of data used as well as direct and indirect impacts. It also establishes a procedure for ordering, in terms of priority, the major issues and problems to be analyzed in the draft impact statement. This sifting of issues into priority levels is contained in the language of the CEQ regulations (Sec. 1500.4). An educational program (Furuseth, Pease, and Smardon, 1977) on NEPA and impact statements, including a slide-tape program, was developed as an educational tool for use with citizen groups and public involvement committees.

Even with a set of structured assessment materials, citizen-involvement group discussions can easily wander without strong leadership by the coordinator. While some tangential discussion is necessary, the interest of individuals within the group will wane if the group's activities are not kept moving toward a specific product. Given the limits of time and the complexities of most projects requiring impact statements, the group should be frequently reminded that its task is to identify issues and problems, not to study or resolve them.

ROLE OF INDEPENDENT SCOPING COORDINATOR

An important component in the effectiveness of the citizen group deliberations was the guidance provided by the independent environmental impact coordinator. Use of a third party in mediation and interagency sessions is supported by literature in conflict resolution (Burt et al., 1978). O'Riordan (1976) also commented that the group coordinator is critical to the effectiveness of the group.

In performing this role, the coordinator must be able to organize and moderate small to large groups; this

requires a knowledge of group dynamics. The coordinator
must be technically proficient in environmental impact
assessment as well as planning methodologies and policies
used by different agencies. For example, the coordinator
working with our three demonstration projects had to
familiarize himself with the Forest Service EIS process
and timber management planning, highway impact assessment
and transportation planning, and the Soil Conservation
Service's procedures for environmental impact assessment
and water resource planning under the U.S. Water Resources
Council's principles and standards for planning. The
coordinator also must be relatively uncommitted to the
merits or problems of a project or at least be able to set
aside his or her own proclivities while performing the
role of educator and facilitator.
     The effectiveness of the coordinator can be
organizationally enhanced in two ways. First, use of
local county agencies such as cooperative extension agents
can facilitate formation of citizen groups because of the
agent's intimate knowledge of local, social, and political
situations. Second, a designated impact specialist within
the sponsoring agency aids the process by providing his or
her knowledge of project or activity characteristics and
internal agency procedures.
     In our project, a faculty member of the Oregon State
University Extension Service performed the role of
coordinator. While this arrangement worked reasonably
well with our project, it was apparent that there are
problems that may work against this role in other states.
As a public educational agency, the Cooperative Extension
Service is sensitive to controversy and interest-group
pressure since its budget for various programs is
dependent upon political support at the local, state, and
federal government levels. Also, the success of all its
programs depends on its positive public image and broad-
based public support. Any involvement in EIS procedures,
even an educational role, can be interpreted by some as
taking sides on a public issue.
     Alternatives to having the Cooperative Extension
Service provide scoping leadership might include the
following: a special institute established at a
university, a nonprofit organization outside of university
administration but located near a university, a state
agency with existing expertise, or private consultants.
Consultants may or may not suffer similar credibility
problems depending on their own reputations and support
sources for other consulting contracts.
     Finally, the agency may wish to perform the role of
impact coordinator itself. This approach will work better
in some agencies than in others because of internal
organization. That is, it may be possible to buffer the
impact assessment unit from pressures within the agency by
internal structuring. However, even in the best
situation, the agency is susceptible to challenges of its

objectivity.

Good rapport between an independent coordinator and the lead agency is essential to the success of a scoping process. The best procedure would be to have the coordinator meet with agency staff at an early stage to plan the scoping activities in detail. The coordinator needs to know what the agency will be able to do or, more important, what it will not be able to do in the way of support and/or cooperation. Early discussions may resolve possible issues of conflict that could emerge later.

PUBLIC INVOLVEMENT PROGRAM

Given the requirements for public involvement in the CEQ regulations, one may ask what has been done in the way of documentation of citizen participation that would provide specific guidance on citizen-participation approaches in conjunction with scoping procedures. Although there is some general literature on citizen participation (Sewell and Coppock, 1976) and specific literature on citizen participation in relation to water resource planning (Bishop, 1979; Ertel and Koch, 1976; Warner, 1971), energy planning (Burt et al., 1978), urban planning (Arnstein, 1969; Burke, 1968; Cole, 1974), and wildlife planning (Erickson and Davis, 1976; Wagar and Folkman, 1974), there is little literature available specifically for citizen-participation approaches structured for environmental impact assessment. However, Runyan's (1977) work reviewed a number of approaches and provided some criteria for judging the usefulness of the approaches reviewed. Erickson and Davis (1976) also provided a valuable service in compiling some general principles to use with public involvement activities. These general principles and judgment criteria will be discussed in this section of the chapter.

An important point to note is that most agencies involved with public participation have invested their efforts in either massive-scale techniques (e.g., public hearings, soliciting written input, mass media, and agency reports) or individuals (i.e., key contacts). Very few agencies have invested effort in small-group techniques, such as workshops, ad hoc committees, or advisory groups or boards. The approach that we will outline is of the small-group variety, but it also has the capability of starting with key contacts or individuals and escalating to the massive scale.

Another point we wish to make is that many analytical methods have been proposed in the impact assessment literature with claims of "objectifying" aspects of environmental impact analysis. The dominant mode is often that of "professional expertise" that supposedly objectifies what would otherwise be subjective judgments in environmental impact analysis. Mathews (1975) has well illustrated the fallacy of objectivity in environmental impact assessment and pointed out that each step, from identifying major activities to determining trade-offs among activities and impacts, is characterized by essentially subjective value judgment. To progress beyond "professional art," it is necessary to adopt a "value framework" (Mathews, 1975). A value framework involves identifying points in the assessment process where specific value decisions occur. We propose applying public-participation techniques to identify values and perceptions of different publics affected by the proposed project or activity during the scoping stage.

The following organizing principles can be summarized from our experience with the scoping groups for the the three demonstration projects.

Broad and Balanced Representation

The coordinator was responsible for selecting the participants of the scoping group. The group was organized to include several types of participants. First, we sought to involve effective spokespersons for different interest groups and organizations who would be expected to have an interest in or be affected by the proposed project. Selection of effective spokespersons is important to create a "dynamic balance" so that one interest group does not dominate others. In this way, no interest group will be masked and maximum interaction and discussion will occur. Second, the group included local officials, such as planning commission members, and local citizens knowledgeable about the area of proposed activity. Technical experts on various subject fields were also invited to participate. Most of these people were employees of public agencies, such as a state fish and wildlife department, or university faculty.

Publicity about the scoping project in local newspapers invited participation of others. However, not many participants were added in this way. The total group of participants numbered 30-40. Not all attended each session. The groups met once a week for 10 weeks. An agenda was sent out to all group members, and only those interested in the particular topics scheduled for the scheduled session participated. An invitation to participate was sent to each individual, signed by the lead agency and the coordinator. Follow-up telephone calls were necessary to ensure participation of key people.

Discussion Focused on a Few Issues

Once initial introductions, orientation, and discussions are completed, it is wise to set an agenda as soon as possible. The scoping group can discuss a few concrete issues or questions at a time, utilizing the assessment materials mentioned earlier as guidance.

Experience with our own demonstration projects and the conflict resolution literature (Burt et al., 1978) supports the thesis that no more than two to four separate major discussion items should be dealt with at each session.

Efficiency of Individual Time Involvement

Since the scoping meetings are demanding of time and attention, it is important to minimize group time expenditures and maximize efficiency, albeit in a fairly informal manner. Initially, it was conceived that appropriate state and federal agency personnel should be included throughout all demonstration project meetings. However, it quickly became apparent that this was unreasonable due to time constraints of agency personnel. The solution to this problem was to involve technical agency personnel only when a subject area was covered on which they had particular expertise. Subsequently, each group meeting was organized around specific topics, using the 13 topical areas of the assessment materials and involving agency personnel as technical consultants at appropriate points.

Extending the principle of time efficiency further, it would be better to develop a three-step scoping process for complex projects. The first step would involve technical peer reviews of proposed alternatives and available planning data and methodology. The second step would include multimedia presentations by agency staff for use with the citizen groups followed by the structured discussions utilizing the technical assessment materials. Third, the multimedia presentations could be used for general public meetings and/or television broadcasting. Comments from the general public could then be incorporated into the deliberations of the citizen advisory group. In retrospect, this approach probably should have been used in the Siuslaw timber management demonstration project in order to cover a broader audience and reduce expensive use of technicians' time to educate very few members of the citizen group. It is obvious that participants will avoid situations in which they must commit large amounts of time to subject areas not directly pertinent to their interests. Thus, if we can "package" presentation materials and establish levels of technical review without misrepresentation or oversimplification, we will reduce time requirements and increase interest levels.

Magnitude of Citizen Involvement

As previously mentioned, review of the literature (Runyan, 1977) indicates that most agencies preparing EISs use massive-scale or intimate-scale techniques for public involvement. Relatively few agencies use small groups.

Our results and a few other citizen-participation programs (Ostheimer, 1977; Reinke and Reinke, 1973; Wagar and Folkman, 1974) indicate that the small-group scale is the best mode of involvement if feedback and interaction are the desired goals of the involvement process. In some cases, a sequential approach may be desirable; for example, start with a few key contacts to assemble the citizen advisory group, meet with the citizen group to scope potential issues and impact, and, finally, organize a massive-scale public-involvement program to make further "soundings" about the citizen group's insights.

Contextual Decisions about Specific Techniques

Ideally, the process of impact assessment should be custom fitted to the individual project. In other words, to be most effective, the citizen-participation process should be scaled to project type and size. The need for variation in the assessment process was made clear with the experiences gained from the demonstration projects. In the Thomas Creek Watershed project, the necessary information and issue identification could have been accomplished in half as many meetings using fairly sophisticated techniques. Conversely, the Siuslaw timber management plan needed more meeting time than was available because of the activity's complexity and the broad geographic area affected. Also, the three-step process of citizen involvement described above would have improved scoping for this project.

Decisions as to representation, intensity, efficiency, magnitude, and specific techniques of public involvement will depend on the situation at hand. One problem is that it is often difficult to get key people to participate. However, the aforementioned organizing principles, the use of assessment materials, and clear and concise graphic presentation of technical material should yield good results for the effort expended.

MESHING: BUREAUCRATIC FIT AND TIMING

Some of the most difficult problems encountered in our demonstration projects concerned "bureaucratic fit" and timing. The bureaucratic-fit problem occurred because specific administrative procedures had become institutionalized in certain agencies and our proposed scoping was perceived as "not fitting" or "at odds" with the standardized procedures. We found that some of these procedures were:

1. Unbalanced in substantive area focus, i.e., procedures over- or under-emphasized physical and social environmental concerns;
2. Too simplistic or complex in determining whether an EIS was needed;

3. Too loose in scoping the breadth and depth of EIS or environmental assessment content, for example, a casual in-house approach was often used; and
4. In general, heavily biased by supposedly "objective professional judgments" on what were the appropriate issues to be addressed in an EIS or environmental assessment.

In all three demonstration projects, fairly open and cordial working relationships were enjoyed between the independent coordinator and the participating agencies. However, even with the best working relationships, there are bound to be coordination and communication problems and political pressure. In two of the projects, sensitive political issues created difficulties in carrying out the intent of the demonstration project. In one case, a politically strong interest group felt that this kind of Cooperative Extension Service involvement would raise questions not to its benefit. The interest group made serious efforts to disrupt the process by putting political pressure on the Extension Service. When this strategy did not work, its members agreed to participate on the citizen advisory group to protect their own interests, then eventually contributed substantially to the effort.

In the other case, local political attitudes on the proposed project's alternatives had already formed, and strategies had been planned to follow through with promoting the desired alternative. The demonstration project was perceived as "stirring up the waters" and creating undesirable conflicts.

It is likely that these political sensitivities are the rule rather than the exception with major projects. They may work against an open and balanced process to determine significant impacts and certainly will inhibit the way the process is carried out. Some of the key people may choose not to cooperate because of these sensitivities. To be effective, the scoping process must recognize these sensitivities and develop ways to accommodate them.

Timing of citizen involvement processes seems to be a universal problem (Ertel and Koch, 1976; Ingram and Ullery, 1976) in all planning activities. The scoping process and use of accompanying tools is a "front-end" process. That is, it is designed to be used before or during the initial preparation of the Environmental Impact Statement. Timing is critical. Initiating the process too far in advance of impact statement preparation could create extensive lag time, with a resultant decrease in citizen-group interest and lack of continuity for both planning professionals and citizens. With regard to this issue, the Corvallis bypass demonstration project was probably too early, as there was an extended period until preparation of the draft EIS was started.

On the other hand, the application of the assessment process on a project for which EIS preparation has already been initiated may make it difficult to refocus the planning approach. In the case of the Siuslaw National Forest timber management plan, we were probably too late for maximum effectiveness, as much of the inventory and analysis had been completed for physical environmental issues. However the citizen group did explore many social and economic issues that previously had not been considered.

At the time of our project, scoping was not part of the EIS procedure, at least not in any systematic way. The problem of timing would not be as difficult if the scoping process were institutionalized and made part of an agency's standard procedures. However, such institutionalization may make the scoping process susceptible to internal political pressure, as discussed earlier.

EVALUATION OF THE ASSESSMENT WORKING MATERIALS

The assessment materials prepared in the project included an assessment form and manual, a resource handbook, and an educational package. They were developed for use by local governments, agency personnel, educational institutions, and others involved in environmental impact assessment. They should be used with the guidance of an impact specialist. We did have all of these tools evaluated by peer professionals in the field as to their present and potential usefulness to impact assessment work (Pease and Smardon, 1977). The results of the reviews of the Environmental Assessment Resource Handbook are most interesting in this regard.

For instance, one section of the handbook that included generic checklists of potential impacts from 18 different types of projects and activities was useful to agencies, consultants, environmental groups, and others. It illustrated the need for practical tools of this kind. A technological advancement beyond the printed hierarchical cause-effect checklist in the handbook is the computerized IMPACT system (Thor, Elsner, Travis, and O'Loughlin, 1978; Thor, Smardon, and Adams, 1979) evolving through the final development stages by the U.S. Forest Service. This is a computerized cause-effect network of multitudes of impacts caused or precipitated by wildland-related management activities (e.g., surface mining, forestry practices, and recreational and range development). The system is highly interactive and can be used by someone using a portable keyboard terminal with a phone connection to the main computer.

Other parts of the handbook of particular usefulness to reviewers were the legal/policy overview of major federal acts, memoranda, and court cases affecting the implementation of NEPA and the compilation of agency objectives, standards, goals, and specifications that could be used to review Environmental Impact Statements. While reviewers felt these types of sections were valuable, they rapidly become outdated as agency procedures change.

It is only logical, then, that this type of legal and administrative information should be computerized in a readily updatable format. This information has to some extent been computerized by the Construction Engineering Research Laboratories, Department of the Army, in Champaign-Urbana, Illinois. This system, called CELDS, contains up-to-date (within six months), capsulated state legislation from all 50 states pertaining to environmental quality. However, the legal material was collected under the criterion of effect on military installations and may not include environmental regulations and laws that affect other kinds of activities. Other legal information systems exist, such as LITE and JURIS, but both have utility problems for nonlawyers according to Jain, Urban, and Stacey (1977).

MONITORING AND EVALUATING CITIZEN-INVOLVEMENT STRATEGIES

Many of the operational difficulties we encountered in the demonstration projects could be smoothed out with experience, particularly those problems of timing, agency relationships, and effective adjustment of technique. As experience with the process and knowledge of information sources are gained, more guidance can be provided for appropriate use of the organizing principles.

Citizen-involvement goals or objectives need to be clearly stated or agreed upon. In some cases, this may be unrealistic as certain agencies will not want to have these goals and objectives clearly stated if their intent is to co-opt the citizen-involvement process. Nevertheless, we maintain that the identification of issues and impacts may be perceived as nonthreatening and even helpful early in the planning stages. However, as decision points draw nearer, such as the evaluation of alternatives, the political sensitivity of the scoping process increases.

More important is the fact that there is little previous research work that attempts to monitor and evaluate citizen-involvement work in relation to environmental assessment. More work is needed such as that of Ertel and Koch (1976), which evaluated citizen-participation programs, and that of Twight (1977), which used statistical techniques to analyze key assumptions in citizen-participation strategy. Finding fruitful citizen-involvement strategies is critical to its meaningful incorporation into the environmental planning process. We cannot hope to find optimum or even adequate citizen-involvement strategies unless we monitor and evaluate these efforts in different planning contexts.

Scoping is a technique that can substantially improve
the content and usefulness of impact statements.
Incorporating citizen involvement into the scoping process
provides a means of rejuvenating NEPA by making the impact
statement the planning tool it was originally intended to
be.

REFERENCES

Arnstein, S. R. (1969), "A Ladder of Citizen
    Participation." American Institute of Planners
    Journal, 35(4), 216-224.
Bishop, A. B. (1979), Public Participation in Water
    Resources Planning. Report No. 70-7. Alexandria,
    Va.: U.S. Army Institute of Water Resources.
Burke, E. M. (1968), "Citizen Participation Strategies."
    American Institute of Planners Journal, 24(5),
    287-294.
Burt, R. S., Fischer M., Corbett, T., Garrett, K., and
    Lundgren, M. (1978), Resolving Community Conflict in
    the Nuclear Power Issue: A Report and Annotated
    Bibliography. Report prepared for Union Carbide
    Corporation, Nuclear Power Division for
    U.S. Department of Energy, Y/OWI/SUB-78/22336.
    Berkeley: University of California, Department of
    Sociology.
Cole, R. L. (1974), Citizen Participation and the Urban
    Policy Process. Lexington, Mass.: Lexington Books,
    D. C. Heath and Co.
Council of Environmental Quality (1978), Draft National
    Environmental Policy Act Regulations. FR
    43(112):25239-25247, Part II.
Erickson, D. L., and Davis, A. C. (1976), "Public
    Involvement in Recreation Resources Decision Making."
    Proceedings of the Southern States Recreation
    Research. Ashville, N.C.: Southeastern Forest
    Experiment Station, Forestry Service, USDA.
Ertel, M. O., and Koch, S. G. (1976), Citizen
    Participation in Comprehensive Water Resources
    Planning. Publication No. 77. Amherst, Mass.:
    University of Massachusetts, Institute for Man and
    Environment and Water Resources Research Center.
Furuseth, O. J., Pease, J. R., and Smardon, R. C. (1977),
    "The Role of Impact Statements in Public Decisions."
    Slide-tape program in Environmental Impact Education
    Program, leaders' materials. Corvallis, Ore.: Oregon
    State University Extension Service.
Ingram, H. M., and Ullery, S. J. (1976), "Public
    Participation in Environmental Decision Making:
    Substance or Illusion?" In W. R. D. Sewell and U. T.
    Coppock (Eds.), Public Participation in Planning.
    New York: John Wiley and Sons.
Jain, R. K., Urban, L. V., and Stacey, G. S. (1977),

266

Environmental Impact Analysis: A New Dimension in Decision Making. New York: Van Nostrand Reinhold Co.

Mathews, W. H. (1975), "Objective and Subjective Judgments in Environmental Impact Analysis." Environmental Conservation, 2(2), 121-130.

O'Riordan, T. (1976), "Citizen Participation in Practice: Some Dilemmas and Possible Solutions." In W. R. D. Sewell and J. T. Coppock (Eds.), Public Participation in Planning. New York: John Wiley and Sons.

Ostheimer, J. M. (1977), "The Forest Service Meets the Public: Decision Making and Public Involvement on the Coconino National Forest." Eisenhower Consortium Bulletin 5, Rocky Mountain Forest and Range Experiment Station, Fort Collins, Col.

Pease, J. R., and Smardon, R. C. (1977), Analysis and Evaluation. Special Report 481. Corvallis, Ore.: Oregon State University Extension Service.

Reinke, K. B., and Reinke, B. (1973), "Public Involvement in Resource Decisions: A National Forest Seeks Public Input for Recreation Development." Journal of Forestry, 71, 656-658.

Runyan, D. (1977), "Tools for Community-managed Impact Assessment." American Institute of Planners Journal, 43(2), 125-135.

Sewell, W. R. D., and Coppock, J. T. (Eds.) (1976), Public Participation in Planning. New York: John Wiley and Sons.

Smardon, R. C., Pease, J. R., and Donheffner, P. (1976), Environmental Assessment Form Manual. Special Report 465. Corvallis, Ore.: Oregon State University Extension Service.

Smardon, R. C., Pease, J. R., Furuseth, O. J., and Donheffner, P. (1976), Environmental Assessment Resource Handbook. Corvallis, Ore.: Oregon State University Extension Service.

Thor, E. C., Elsner, G. H., Travis, M. R., and O'Loughlin, K. M. (1978), "Forest Environmental Impact Analysis: A New Approach." Journal of Forestry, 76(11), 723-725.

Thor, E. C., Smardon, R. C., and Adams, R. (1979), "IMPACT in California and Colorado: Applications of a Computer System before It Was Complete." Research Note PSW-336. Berkeley, Cal.: Pacific Southwest Forest and Range Experiment Station, Forest Service, USDA.

Twight, B. W. (1977), "Confidence or More Controversy: Whither Public Involvement?" Journal of Forestry, February, 93-94.

Wagar, J. A., and Folkman, W. S. (1974), "The Case for Small Groups: Public Participation in Forest Management Decisions." Journal of Forestry, 72(7), 405-407.

Warner, K. P. (1971), A State-of-the-arts Study of Public Participation in the Water Resources Planning

Process. NTIS Report PB 204 245. Springfield, Va.

PART 3

Keying Analysis
to Decision Makers

INTRODUCTION

Whereas Part 1 conveyed a sense of the redefined scope of environmental impact assessment and Part 2 presented examples of techniques for data gathering and analysis of elements and groupings of elements required by the redefined scope, this part offers guidance on making information useful to and used by decision makers. Selina Bendix stresses the fact that even the right information cannot be used by decision makers if that information is not presented clearly and comprehensively in a style that is understandable and an amount that is manageable. Bendix provides Environmental Impact Statement (EIS) practitioners with methodical guidance on how to write a socially useful EIS.

What approaches enable decision makers to understand and use the information presented in a well-written EIS? Ruth-Ellen Miller suggests techniques that can permit decision makers to examine assessment results from different perspectives and social, economic, institutional, and political context that might occur in the future when the impacts projected will occur. Miller's suggestions for closing the gap between the EIS and decision makers precede Robert E. Henshaw's paper, 'The Impact Judgment: A Technical Impasse?" Henshaw points out that the sensitization of decision makers to the significance of scientifically derived information must be accompanied by a reciprocal sensitization of scientific and technical practitioners to the political implications of their research and analyses.

How to integrate and manage the differences in perspectives of the EIS practitioners and decision makers is a question of organization requiring a careful examination of the relationship of scientific and political precepts and processes. Shelby J. Smith-Sanclare concludes this chapter with an examination of the evolution of this relationship in two federal entities in "Organizational Environmental Management: The Los Alamos National Laboratory and Tennessee Valley Authority Experience."

13. How to Write a Socially Useful EIS

Selina Bendix

The intent of the National Environment Policy Act (NEPA) is to improve the governmental decision-making process by providing a broad and relevant information base as input to decision makers. This information is to be presented in the format of an Environmental Impact Statement, or EIS. An EIS can be the basis for a good decision, which does not solve a present problem only to create a more difficult future problem, or it can be a futile exercise in paper shuffling. Most EISs fall between these good and bad extremes. The purpose of this paper is to discuss how to write an EIS that is useful both to the decision maker and to the concerned citizen. The suggestions can also be used as a guide to the review of EISs.

In writing an EIS, as in writing anything, it is important to consider your audience and what you want them to do with the information you give. The greater your expertise in your field, the more important it is for you to break out of your own mental framework and don the hat of your reader. It does not matter how "right" you are; if the information is not communicated to your audience, what you write is useless.

Dealing with a controversial issue can be nerve-wracking for all concerned. Do not let this paralyze your thinking: the more controversial an issue, the more important it is that all parties have accurate information. A good EIS helps people to cut through emotions and rhetoric to form opinions and make decisions based on fact. I shall attempt to give guidelines that can be used to create a cogent, concise EIS presented in a manner conducive to use, rather than to the collection of dust on a shelf.

Many of the examples in this paper are derived from my six and a half years of experience as San Francisco Environmental Review Officer. In the year since I left that position to become a private consultant, I have continued to find it useful to follow my own advice.

Who is your audience? Your are a biologist who has surveyed the biota on the site of a proposed power plant. You know that the California Department of biologists at

Fish and Game are going to read your report carefully, so
you write your section of the EIS as one professional to
another, right? Wrong.

In the process of proving to the Fish and Game
biologists that you are a competent biologist worthy of
their trust, you have written something appropriate for a
professional journal, but you have become unintelligible
to the members of the community activist group opposing
the power plant, the city council members who would like
to be able to have an informed opinion and to be able to
decide whether to approve the plant. None of these people
are biologists. Not only do they not understand the
biologists' technical terminology, they do not even know
the biology that biologists take for granted when talking
to each other. You have to give the reader enough
information to allow him or her to judge the validity of
the biologist's conclusions.

Some of your readers do not trust you; they suspect
that you have been bought out by one side or the other.
Other readers think that biologists are all a little nutty
and do not have their priorities set up with the real
world in mind. You have to convince all the doubting
Thomases that there was a good reason to do a biological
survey of the site, that this survey was undertaken in a
rational and efficient fashion, and that your conclusions
are reasonable. In other words, you have to give the
reader some insight into the logic of your specialty.
Interestingly enough, you will not lose Fish and Game in
the process; they will like this type of a presentation,
too, even though it would not be appropriate for a
professional journal.

I commented on behalf of the City and County of San
Francisco on a U.S. Bureau of Land Management (BLM) 1974
EIS:

> In the section on the use of coal, it says
> "recoverable reserves of coal include at least 28
> billion tons of 1 percent or less sulfur content"
> (page 365). There is no explanation of what the
> significance of this level of sulfur content is. I
> presume, therefore, that the assumption is that the
> reader knows whether this represents a high, low, or
> a medium sulfur content, and what the significance of
> varying sulfur content of coal is for the
> environment. There is certainly no information in
> the document to enable the reader to understand the
> significance of this statement.

> The general public does not have a technical
> education. Many portions of this document I doubt
> could be comprehended by a person without a technical
> education. Terms such as "purse seining"--page 13,
> "gill netting" and "surface jugs"--page 16, "urban
> impacted area"--page 28, "safe profiles"--page 174,

273

"industrial groundfish"--page 269, "sour crude"--page 369, "heat wheels" and "heat pipe"--page 383, and many others are found throughout this document without any definitions.

Consider the following sample sentence from page 193: "In this paper Sanders concluded that species density patterns for polychaetes, gastropods, bivalves, and ampeliscid amphipods which are residents of the subtidal benthos, exhibit stress patterns dependent on distance from the spill and time of exposure of organisms to the fuel oil." I wonder how many readers of this document are going to be willing to go to a dictionary to look up the number of terms in that one sentence they are unfamiliar with?

An EIS is not supposed to be written as a statement from one technical expert to another. It is supposed to be an explanation of technical issues to nontechnical people who must be involved in the decision-making process. If the technical language is not translated into lay language, then this objective of the EIS is not attained. (Bendix, 1975)

Think of your audience as ignorant of your field but vitally interested--they are, if they have an opinion about the project. Assume that they have never been exposed to anything more than junior high school science, even if they are professionals in their own right. Do not write as if you think your audience is stupid. The reader badly wants your information (at least some of the readers do); you just have to give it in a form that will be useful. If you want to get a good sense of whether you are writing for the right audience, ask your secretary to read ten pages and point out every passage that is obscure. Or ask a teenager to read it. One of the reasons that I always have student interns in my office is that they are good test subjects for EIS language. If an intern does not understand a passage, I rewrite it.

All technical terms do not have to be left out; when used, they do have to be explained. The same is true of acronyms. If acronyms are to be used frequently, it helps to put a list at the front of the EIS. A list like this is also a help in telling you when there are too many acronyms. In one case, I found a "helpful" list of two full, single-spaced pages of acronyms at the beginning of a preliminary draft Environmental Impact Report for a sewage treatment plant. (Environmental Impact Report, or EIR, is the equivalent of an EIS under California's little NEPA law, the California Environmental Quality Act, CEQA.) It was obvious that this was acronym overkill, and I asked the consultant to cut the list.

Particularly watch out for similar or identical acronyms for two organizations. I known when ACS means

American Chemical Society and when it means American
Cancer Society; I find that my audiences do not. I think
of AIA as American Institute of Architects; to my husband
it is the American Insurance Association.
   A similar problem can arise with the term "master
plan." In San Francisco we have the Comprehensive Plan
for the City and County of San Francisco, usually known as
"the master plan" to all engineers and administrators
dealing with it. We also have numerous "master plans" for
hospitals and educational institutions as required by our
institutional master plan ordinance. They are all known
as "the master plan" to the staff of any particular
institution. We had total chaos in environmental
documents until I established a rule that only the
Comprehensive Plan for the City and County of San
Francisco could be referred to as "the master plan." All
of a sudden, passages about compliance of something like
the wastewater master plan with the city's master plan
became intelligible.
   Environmental Impact Reports for San Francisco's
wastewater master plan (11 certified, 3 in progress) have
provided an ongoing challenge of explanation of sewage
treatment to a nonengineer audience. These are some
examples of how this has been handled:

   After pretreatment and flow measurement, the influent
   would flow to primary sedimentation tanks, which
   retain the wastewater long enough to allow for about
   60 percent of the suspended solids to settle by
   gravity to the bottom of the tanks. These settled
   solids (sludge) would be slowly scraped along the
   bottom of the tanks to a collection trough, or sludge
   gallery, from which sludge would be pumped to a
   storage area. . . .

   The proposed secondary treatment method would use
   rotating biological contactors . . . . The facility
   would consist of banks of 12-foot diameter plastic
   disks, the contactors, which slowly rotate, half-
   immersed in tanks of wastewater. Microorganisms
   (bacteria, algae, protozoa, fungi, etc.) would attach
   themselves to the plastic disks and consume the
   organic matter in the wastewater. Aeration of the
   wastewater and direct exposure to the air as the
   disks revolve would provide oxygen for the organisms
   on the disks. . . .

   It is feasible to control wastewater treatment plant
   odor emissions, as actual applications of such
   technology at the main plant in Sacramento and at a
   plant in Honolulu have shown. Even with such
   control, the potential would still exist for
   malodorous gases and aerosols to be emitted from the
   Southwest Water Pollution Control Plant site. Such

emissions could occur either through accidental spillage of sewage or grit screenings, failure of the secondary treatment units (due to illegal or accidental introduction of toxic material into the sewer system), failure of the odor control system to adequately remove malodorous gases, or total upset of the odor control systems (e.g., through electrical failure). (City and County of San Francisco, 1979)

A variety of specialized experts in fields such as archaeology, botany, chemistry, economics, invertebrate zoology, meteorology, sanitary engineering, urban planning, and so forth may contribute to an EIS. Every EIS team needs someone who can edit all of this specialized input into a text that reads as if written by one author. This editor is just as important to the team as the sanitary engineer, maybe more important. If the information in the EIS is not usable, the engineer's expertise is irrelevant.

Reflect controversy in document organization. A good way to annoy the antagonistic citizen or the legislator whose office has been besieged by phone calls is to bury the impact that is of most public concern after one hundred pages of impacts over which there has been no evidence of public interest (even if you think there should have been concern). If people are up in arms over the architectural merits of a building proposed to be torn down to make way for something else, the reader's mental temperature simply goes up if pages of materials on the geology and air quality of the site must be plowed through before reaching the discussion of the architectural merits of the building and the reasons that the building is not being retained.

Standard outlines are cherished by some agencies as a means for quick review of documents and by some consultants as a fast way to write EISs, but they are not a good means of implementing the intent of NEPA. The nature of the project and the significance and controversiality of impacts determine the format best designed to lay out the facts about each particular case. If an impact seems important to you as an agency person and the public has not recognized the importance of this impact, give the reader the information about the controversy that got him or her interested in reading the EIS. Then, when you have convinced the reader that the document is a reliable source of information, educate him or her to understand the other important impacts.

The table of contents is the place where the reader starts forming a reaction to an EIS. I can tell a lot about an EIS by reading the table of contents. I look for what I predict to be the most controversial impacts; if they are after page 100, the EIS is probably windy or trying to bury important information. For example, in a radar installation EIS, I looked first for an analysis of the controversial question of the biological effects of microwave radiation. So did the U.S. Department of Health, Education, and Welfare, Center for Disease Control, which commented on the Crossman Peak Radar proposal in Arizona:

> The potential occupational and public hazards associated with the proposed facility should be addressed in more detail. While the proposal's electromagnetic radiation hazards are discussed in Appendix 2, it may be desirable to include a short discussion of the potential radiation hazards in the body of the EIS with a better depiction of the immediate areas around the antenna that are exposed to the radar beam. The probability of equipment malfunction and exposure of maintenance personnel at the facility to excessive radiation should be discussed. (U.S. Bureau of Land Management, 1980)

Unfortunately, the agency response was:

> The scoping process did not identify radiation hazards as a significant issue, and FAA engineers indicated that such hazards would be reduced to a low level through safety checks designed into the system. We thus did not deem necessary further discussion in the EIS.

Needless to say, this constitutes a misinterpretation of the intent of the President's Council on Environmental Quality (CEQ) regulations. Impact significance is not a function of the ability to recognize the impact at the time of scoping. The scoping process cannot be perfect because something unforeseen may always turn up as a proposal is investigated; but scoping is a good way of preventing overkill with extensive, trivial information masking the important facts. It is a good weapon against the syndrome of "I put it in because I had the information."

It is frustrating for an agency to receive comments on a draft EIS that say, "This project is going to have disastrous environmental impacts that you have not adequately considered, period." What can one say in response? If you give enough information about issues that are controversial in the affected community and present it well, you will turn the vague, unfocused EIS comments into more specific comments on the analysis of specific impacts—these are much easier to answer and constructively add to the dialogue about the project.

In urban project EISs, I look for the sections on transportation, air quality, and noise impacts because traffic produces most of the post-construction air and noise impacts. If they are separated by other unrelated sections or if noise comes before the traffic that produces it, then I decide to watch carefully for logical faults in the analysis. It pays to be kind to your reader; you get fewer nasty comments.

A recent California final EIR (Department of Mineral Services, 1980) lacked: page numbers in the table of contents for the subheadings (noise, traffic, socioeconomics, etc.) in a 40-page impacts chapter; the address and telephone number of the lead agency; and page numbers and titles for several of the more important tables. The EIR actually contained much useful information that the casual reader would find only by chance and that a decision maker might never find. The difficulty of finding things in this document was so annoying that it became a game to find all the things the authors had done wrongly. This, of course, resulted in extensive comments. The agency involved would have been better off if the staff time that went into responding to voluminous comments had been spent on putting out a better draft EIS.

The whole is greater than the sum of the parts. According to Webster (1957), "piecemeal" means "(1) piece by piece . . . (2) into pieces or parts." My name for the practice of breaking up a single project into sections with separate EISs, without a program EIS for the whole project, is "piecemealing." Piecemealing at best results in losing sight of the forest in preoccupation with individual trees; at its worst, it is a device to avoid in-depth environmental review. There are many temptations in piecemealing because the smaller the scope of the EIS, the easier it is to be sure you have thought of everything, the smaller the probable number of concerned public groups affected, and the less expensive and time-consuming the environmental review process.

These advantages may be illusionary, as the current Hartford, Connecticut, to Providence, Rhode Island, Interstate 84 situation demonstrates. The U.S. Department of Transportation (DoT) planned three EISs and one or more supplemental EISs for this highway. They apparently thought that piecemealing would allow them to approve and design one part of the highway while another part was still undergoing NEPA review. On December 13, 1979, the U.S. Environmental Protection Agency (EPA) formally referred this matter to CEQ.

According to a CEQ legal memorandum (Liebeman and Yost, 1980), EPA's principal concern was that construction of I-84 on the conditionally approved alignment would increase traffic over the Scituate Reservoir and through its watershed, which would increase the risk of hazardous spills and degradation of the watershed. This reservoir is the sole source of drinking water for approximately half of Rhode Island. Alternate routes are available.

EPA has recommended that CEQ request DOT to rescind approval of the final EISs for the Connecticut segments and prohibit any design work until DOT has completed the new EIS for the Rhode Island segment on alternative corridors and a single EIS on the entire highway from Hartford to Providence. (Liebeman and Yost, 1980)

On April 30, 1980, CEQ replied to the EPA referral, stating,

The Department's "conditional" approval of two Connecticut segments of I-84 poses two serious issues. Either the approval is indeed so open and contingent on the completion of the EIS process that the Department is willing to waste $16 million in design work and forego $54 million in expected savings without prejudice to the final decision or the decision is made for all practical purposes, and the remaining EIS process in Rhode Island and Connecticut is badly compromised. In our view, the former situation is not credible, and the latter is not legal. (Speth, 1980)

Beware of setting a singular study perimeter. To keep from confusing people you should have a single study area for all impacts investigated, right? Wrong. If you set a single study area, you will inevitably have unnecessary information about some study perimeters and you may have insufficient information about others. For example, the transportation and air pollution impacts of a freeway may be regional, while the noise impacts are confined to a narrow corridor along the roadway.

Problems in defining the study area have occurred in several recent San Francisco EIRs for downtown high-rise buildings. San Francisco has prevailing off-shore winds from the northwest. When these winds sweep across an area with relatively low buildings and little relief and then hit a tall building, the air swirls down the front of the tall building to form high-speed eddies at the base of the building that are unpleasant to pedestrians. In order to prevent this from happening, San Francisco requires wind tunnel modelling and design mitigation if necessary, a practice I recommend to other urban areas.

The consultant handling the wind tunnel modelling had a rule of thumb for the size of the area around the building in which impacts could be expected and set up the study perimeter accordingly. When the completed reports on several projects came to me, I discovered that wind speeds were still statistically significantly above background at spots on the perimeter of the study area. This left me not knowing how far from the site the impact would be felt. Of course, I had to request that additional studies be done, at a cost considerably above the cost of getting those measurements initially.

When the details of a project are still fluid, solve

the indeterminacy problem with a worst-case analysis. For example, pick the noisiest element of the project, such as pile driving for foundations of tall buildings, and determine the perimeter of the area in which this noise level would be audible above background, paying particular attention to sensitive receptors such as hospitals, schools, broadcast studios, and residences. It is often helpful to map the area where the noise will be audible. People want to know what is going to happen to them; each reader will look at the map and find out if the impact will be perceptible at the reader's home or place of work. An informative map prevents many phone calls from people who want to know if they will hear the construction noise. Information about noise increases imperceptible to the human ear or lost in the general ambient noise background is useless and unnecessary.

You might think that the scoping process should take care of setting reasonable study perimeter limits, but often it cannot set physical limits because data developed in the process of analysis of impacts will determine the logical location of the study perimeter. What can be done in the scoping process is to delineate what measure of significance will be used to determine the study perimeter, for example, the area of greater than 10 percent change for traffic. In some cases, of course, perimeters can be established in advance--for example, on the basis of known habitat preference of a plant.

Respond to concerns of the ignorant. The ignorant vote, too! Just because you (or your geologist or structural engineer) know that a slope is stable, and cannot slide if something is built on it, does not mean that the home owner next door knows this. Just because you know that an off-shore earthquake fault just waiting to let go is one of a type that cannot produce tidal waves does not mean that the concerned citizens along the shore know it. If you do not explain the nonexistent problems that people are worried about, they will not listen to your explanations about the real problems.

In San Francisco we had a case in which the attention of the decision makers was captured by public concerns about the effects of a major earthquake along the San Andreas Fault on a proposed project. These concerns were presented by an eloquent medical doctor who was reasoning from false assumptions that none of the decision makers knew enough to recognize. Before attention could be focused on the real merits of the case, it was necessary (1) to explain surveying bench marks and explain why all measurements to be added and subtracted must be made with respect to the same bench mark to have any meaning, thus explaining why the unlikely event of a tidal wave would not inundate the west side of the city, and (2) to draw a diagram to explain that, if the surface of the water table cracks as the result of an earthquake, groundwater will go into the sewer rather than sewage flowing out of the crack. The civil engineers were aghast that any intelligent adult could not know such things. The decision makers were intelligent; they simply had never had need to think of such things until a controversial sewer proposal was before them. After they understood why the nonexistent problems were nonexistent, they were ready to proceed to the real problems.

It is particularly important to document carefully issues about which people may have formed definite opinions without realizing how little they knew. In such situations, it may be very difficult to change people's minds, no matter how wrong they are. This problem has been extensively studied by Slovic and Fischoff (1979), who have stated,

> The psychological basis of . . . unwarranted certainty seems to be people's insensitivity to the tenuousness of the assumptions upon which their judgments are based . . . . The danger from such overconfidence is that we may not realize how little we know and how much additional information is needed about various problems and risks we face.
>
> Overconfidence manifests itself in other ways as well. For example, a typical task in estimating failure rates or other uncertain quantities is to set upper and lower bounds such that there is a 98 percent chance that the true value lies between them. Experiments with diverse groups of people making many different kinds of judgments have shown that, rather than 2 percent of true values falling outside the 98 percent confidence bounds, 20-50 percent do so (Lichtenstein, Fischoff, and Phillips, 1977). Thus people think that they can specify such quantities with much greater precision than is actually the case . . . . One way to reduce the anxiety generated by uncertainty is to deny the uncertainty.

It may not, in fact, be possible to change the minds of some people who have formed opinions on the basis of inadequate or misunderstood information. The only chance you have is if you present a good argument logically and understandably. Remember that each member of your audience thinks that he or she is just as logical as you are. If you think of your audience as reasonable, intelligent people who will do the right thing, you have a much better chance of convincing them than if you think of them as unreasonable opponents. People sense what you think of them in the way you write. Do not try to write when you have just finished a telephone conversation with someone who was very angry and did not want to be confused with facts. Your hostility will show. Wait until you have recovered to the point of seeing the situation as humorous and challenging; what you write will then be more constructive.

One of the challenges to EIS writers is capturing readers' attention when most people are convinced that the only alternatives are to build or not to build a particular alternative. This is easier to handle orally than in writing. Strategies that can be used to focus attention on the development of real alternatives include the following: (1) tell the project sponsor that with so much (agency) (public) opposition it is a good idea to have a fall-back position; (2) tell opponents that if they are right, that the project sponsor never seriously considered alternatives, then surely these opponents can define alternatives for consideration for inclusion in the EIS and tell the sponsor that, if all the alternatives are ridiculous, a fair analysis will demonstrate this and make clear why the proposed alternative was selected; or (3) tell project opponents that it may be politically impossible to turn the project down and, therefore, they should concentrate on what could be done to the project to minimize its impacts. The basic idea is to try to get everyone to work with you to develop the best possible information base, mitigation measures, and so on. When you make an effort, you can redirect a lot of real or potential antagonism into constructive cooperation.

Do not present mitigation measures as a wish list. "Coulds" and "mights" use up a lot of space and leave the reader in limbo. The mitigation portions of EISs are often the most unsatisfactory because the reader cannot tell which measures are, in fact, to be implemented. Every mitigation measure should indicate one of the following: (1) the measure has been incorporated into the proposed project; (2) the measure is under consideration and a decision will be made at a stated time on the basis of stated criteria; or (3) the measure must be implemented by another governmental agency that will or will not be requested to look into the matter. Now the reader knows what will and will not be done and can consider the necessity of requests for further mitigation as a condition of approval. The sponsor's reasons for not adopting a mitigation measure can be evaluated for validity, and the necessity for additional information in order to judge whether certain mitigation measures should be imposed as a condition of approval can be assessed.

Decision makers do not have a lot of time to consider each case. Mitigation measures and alternatives are often the crux of the decisions that must be made. If you as staff think that the reasons for rejecting a mitigation measure are not valid, lay out the facts that brought you to this conclusion. If you feel this way because of valid reasons, not just because the sponsor was unpleasant to deal with and you would like to see him or her suffer for it, the facts should convince the decision maker that you are right. Do not be afraid when the sponsor sees the facts differently from the way you do. Give the facts

according to the sponsor; then get an independent review
and give the conclusions of your construction consultant
on the costs of implementation, or other similar action.
Stating both sides is fair to the reader and allows the
reader to decide which side is right.

Specify the degree of statistical validity. (How
good is your crystal ball?) The writer of an EIS must
often make predictions using a relatively small
information base. However, what is "relatively small" to
the professional who wants to make a statistically valid
prediction may be a surfeit to the decision maker.
According to Robilliard (1977), "many will be overwhelmed
by the amount of available knowledge but surprised at the
lack of firm conclusions, and consequently may ignore the
whole ecological issue as much as possible."

Much excess EIS length arises from a subconscious
fear of making decisions about what to include and what to
leave out. In the end there will not be enough room for
every potentially relevant piece of information; so it is
much better to confront these fears sooner rather than
later. Be courageous and eschew the verbal "squid effect"
in which the real issues are beclouded by an excess of
verbiage.

I was once chided by a consultant for editing his
submission to make it, in his view, "incomplete." He
assured me that I was running the risk of legal challenge
for incomplete coverage because in an EIR for a high-rise
office building in the middle of the San Francisco
financial district I would not allow discussion of the
question of the existence of economically interesting
mineral resources under the street. Even if there had
been any, two levels of subway would have been in the way
of recovery. Short of diamonds, I doubt that the site
would have been considered a potential mine--and even with
diamonds I still have my doubts. It was a waste of space
for him to have included the issue.

Transportation planners would like to know a great
deal of detail about where the cars attracted by a major
project will go. Determining this requires the use of
many assumptions. Traffic projections start out with a 10
percent probable error of traffic counts and accumulate
uncertainty as assumptions are made. There is not much
point in pursuing such calculations when differences of
2-5 percent are showing up and you know that the probable
error is in excess of 10 percent. The perimeter for such
calculations should be the area where a difference of more
than 10 percent in vehicle trips could occur. If the
traffic impacts are of great concern, then worst-case
assumptions that are carefully spelled out should be made.
In this way, it is possible to say the impact could not be
greater than so-and-so much, and probably would be less.

It is necessary to indicate the mathematical limits
of prediction methodology. There is too little use of
statistical analysis in EISs. This is indispensable in

explaining what is a significant predicted increase in pollution and what is not. It is difficult for the decision makers to understand that statistically insignificant increases in air pollution due to each of a series of unrelated projects may result in a cumulatively significant effect on air pollution, but this is something they have to grapple with if they are going to make good decisions.

On the other hand, do not let people push you into making predictions that you know are meaningless. It would be simpler for the decision makers if staff and/or consultants had a good crystal ball to read the future so that decisions would not have to be made in the presence of uncertainty; however, life is just not that simple.

A common problem is presented by small-scale impacts that are not subject to statistical behavior even if base-line data are obtainable. In San Francisco, for years we had requests for prediction of the socioeconomic effects of the construction of single, small apartment houses (four to ten units) in predominantly single-family and duplex neighborhoods where impacts over a two- or three-block radius from the proposed project site were of concern. We finally convinced people that there was no statistically valid means of prediction from such a small information base and that any such predictions would simply be misleading.

Another facet of the problem of statistical reliability arises from the handy, small calculator. There is an abundance of information in EISs now given to four to eight significant figures--whatever the calculator happened to be set to read out. That looks very nice and reassuring until one realizes that these results were calculated from input data having only two significant figures. Not only are results with more significant figures than the input data had to start out with mathematically meaningless; they mislead the reader into thinking that much more is known than is actually the case and give a false illusion of security to the decision maker who does not realize the degree of uncertainty of the data. They also irritate the mathematically alert reader, who may then be inclined to distrust the rest of the document.

Do not ask the reader to accept your statements on faith alone. "The change in noise level would be minor;" "the amount of sewage produced would be insignificant"--why should the reader believe unsupported assertions? Remember that the accident at Three Mile Island has confirmed distrust of experts in many minds. Whenever you can, give people enough information to come to the correct conclusion on their own. "There would be a 3 dBA increase in ambient noise level 100 feet from the project; the threshold for human perception of noise difference is 3 dBA" or "the proposed project would cause a 0.01 percent increase in the flows to be treated by the sewage

treatment plant that serves this area" are preferable.
The reader can come to the correct conclusion without
worrying about the reliability of the expert and you avoid
arguments over opinions of magnitude of importance. For
example, is elimination of parking a positive or negative
impact? If you want to park in the area, it is a negative
impact. The label for the impact depends on your
framework of reference. Nothing in NEPA says that you
have to label an impact "positive" or "negative" until you
reach the "unavoidable adverse impacts" section. A good
strategy is not to use positive and negative designations
on impacts until this section. At this point, the reader
can match independent conclusions with the agency's and
decide if the two are in acceptable agreement.

An EIR prepared by the California Department of
General Services (1980) contains an "environmental matrix"
that labels all impacts as "beneficial," "none," "minor
adverse," or "major adverse." Under "labor force" I found
"major adverse" checked. In the chapter on environmental
impacts and mitigation measures, the only reference to
labor force that I could find was the following paragraph:

> Employment: The Western Addition Project Area
> Committee (WAPAC) has expressed concern about whether
> or not local workers will be employed by the State's
> contractor during construction of the State Building.
> The Committee has asked the State to enter into an
> agreement in compliance with the Redevelopment
> Agency's 50 percent low-income area residency hiring
> goal, whereby the construction contractor would
> employ 50 percent of his workers (on a craft-by-craft
> basis) from low-income residents of the Western
> Addition area. The State has agreed to do so.

I am still wondering what the major adverse impact is.
A U.S. Bureau of Reclamation (1977) EIS for an
electrical transmission line listed herbicides that would
be used for vegetation control in the right-of-way; they
included aminotriazole, maleic hydrazide, and simazine,
which are all carcinogenic in mice and rats. The entire
evaluation of impact was one sentence: "these herbicides
will be applied in minimal amounts so that they will not
leach into the ground water, which averages 50 to 100 feet
below the surface." These herbicides are described as
"plant specific." This turned out not to mean what I
would call "specific." Chloroflurecol "retards many
grasses and controls broadleaf weeds and vines."
Glyphosate "for control of many annual and perennial
grasses and broadleaf weeds plus many tree and woody brush
species . . . is nonselective" (Meister, 1980). If this
is "specific," then I wonder what "minimal amounts" are?

How big is large? The previously mentioned
California Department of General Services (1980) EIR
contains the statement, "large trees, shrubs, and ground

cover are planned in the courtyard and on the outside grounds as well." The sentence is ambiguous because "large" could apply only to "trees" or to "trees, shrubs, and ground cover." As the latter is improbable, let us assume that "large" applied only to "trees." How big is a large tree? In California we have redwoods over a hundred feet tall. Is large 100 feet? Twenty-foot trees are large in most landscaping terms, but expensive. In the current taxation climate of California, will they have the money to put in 20-foot trees? Or will they be lucky to have any money for landscaping at all? All these musings on my part could have been eliminated by indicating the height and species of the trees planned. In most cases, words such as "large," "small," "big," "little," "significant" or "insignificant," and "positive" or "negative" can either be replaced by quantitative facts or deleted.

In one case I was suspicious that adequate field work had not been done for an EIS. When I found references to a "recent field inspection," I promptly commented, "When was the 'recent field inspection' conducted?" (Bendix, 1976). In a previous (1975) EIS, "recently enacted legislation" turned out to be California's McAteer Petris Act, which was passed in 1965.

A U.S. Department of Housing and Urban Development (HUD) (1976) EIS stated that bus service to the project area was "adequate." If the author had given the statistics instead of making a value judgment and not bothering to put in the figures, he would have been better off. I happened to know how area residents felt and commented, "Residents have already complained about the lack of service of public transport to the area. The implied assumption that it is adequate needs documentation" (Bendix, 1976). My comments on this document also suggested that the number of days the area experienced concentrations of pollutants in excess of standards be described by something more specific than a "small number of days" and I also asked, "What is a 'normally acceptable' noise level?"

The adverse impacts of bad graphics. How many people know that architects have conventions about shadows that have nothing to do with the physical possibility of shadows being cast by the sun? I did not know this until I started reading EIRs and EISs. In one EIR, in order for the shadows shown and the north arrow both to be correct, San Francisco would have to be in the southern hemisphere. No architect would be bothered by this, I suppose, but it bothers me. I am sure that most readers of the EIR assumed that at some time of day and year, shadows such as those shown would actually occur. The few people who realized that this was impossible probably thought that the stupid bureaucrats had goofed again. Eliminate excess detail. Much of what appears on architects' drawings is meaningless and distracting to someone unfamiliar with such drawings. Similarly, you do not need the detail of navigational maps for land-based coastal projects.

The City and County of San Francisco (1978) EIR for the notorious Dow project in California had lovely color photographs of the region with no indication of the location of the site, the direction from which the view was seen, or the height of the proposed project compared to the relief shown. The graphics were beautiful, but they did not belong in an EIR.

You cannot quantify aesthetics. As concerns about historic buildings and energy-conserving advantages of building reuse compared to demolition and construction increase, there are more and more arguments about the merits of older buildings. Aesthetics is a matter of opinion and a very touchy area for government to set foot in. Government has no business legislating what is beautiful, but planners must have a hand in project design in order to fulfill their role as guardians of a community's character. Controversy over architectural merit extends beyond old buildings to new ones. The architect thinks that he has created a masterpiece that relates sensitively to the site; some members of the public see the design as an abomination. How should such issues be dealt with in an EIR or EIS?

The following examples of the handling of aesthetic issues are taken from the EIRs for two controversial projects proposed for the same portion of San Francisco's Union Square. Each of these passages was the result of debate between proponents, opponents, and city staff, much of it concerning the use of architectural and planning terminology. The project was partially described in a direct quote from the architects:

> After several attempts, it was determined that the (existing) building simply could not function as a new Neiman-Marcus store. We, therefore, proceeded to design a new store which would function properly and preserve the most significant architectural feature of the old building, the rotunda dome. The new design places the rotunda on the corner of Geary and Stockton Streets facing Union Square, enclosed in glass making it visible from the Square. (City and County of San Francisco, 1978a)

This was followed by a statement of the City Planning Department Design Guidelines for the site and a discussion of the ways in which the proposed building did and did not comply with the design guidelines. This analysis ultimately led to recommendations for design changes to bring the design into closer compliance with the design guidelines that become conditions for project approval. This type of analysis was also used for the second case, where the appropriate design guideline was stated at the beginning of each paragraph:

The facade of the upper floors should present a scale
and texture similar to the office buildings and hotel
facades on the square, rather than most typical
contemporary department store facades. The
articulation of the facade of the proposed building
would be less ornamental than the Renaissance style
of the St. Francis, and more detailed in line and
contrast than the simplicity of the Quantas Building.
The recessed windows on the second and top floors of
the proposed building would repeat the recessed
window treatment found on the second and top floors
of the Quantas Building. The modular structure of
the facade of the proposed building's 50-foot wide
granite elements separated by the recessed glass
elements would give a similar effect to that of
modular structure of the St. Francis Hotel's three
vertical elements of approximately similar widths
separated by dark recesses. (City and County of San
Francisco, 1978b)

CONCLUSION

The common thread through all the examples presented
in this paper is concern for the question, "Who is the
audience?" An EIS must state as neutrally as possible the
key facts that the reader needs to develop an informed
opinion about a project. I have tried to describe some of
the means of achieving this aim.
Time taken to consider the applicability of these
points to a particular case can often avert later time
expenditures for reorganization, revision, and cutting. A
logically organized, well-written EIS can do more to clear
the way for approval of a good project than any advocacy
document can. The facts speak for themselves: if there
is only one reasonable alternative, this will become
apparent.
After using all the guidelines above, before you
publish a draft EIS, sit down with the document and
pretend that you are the most vociferous and feared
project opponent—politician, community leader, whoever it
may be. What parts of the EIS will that person read
first? Read them. What will be the reaction? If you do
this regularly, you can learn to spot the unnecessary red
flags that cause unnecessary problems. Edit so that what
has to be said is said in a way that informs the critical
reader and defuses controversy. If you do it right, you
will have a socially useful EIS.

REFERENCES

Bendix. S. (1975), Comments on behalf of the City and
County of San Francisco on the Bureau of Land

288

Management's (1974) DEIS Proposed Increase in Acreage
to Be Offered for Oil and Gas Leasing on the Outer
Continental Shelf. February 21.
Bendix, S. (1976), Comments on behalf of the City and
County of San Francisco on DEIS, Phases II and III of
the Residential Development of the Hunters Point
Redevelopment Area in San Francisco, California.
HUD-R09-EIS-76-20, May 2.
Bureau of Land Management, U.S. Department of the Interior
(1974), DEIS Proposed Increase in Acreage to Be
Offered to Oil and Gas Leasing on the Outer
Continental Shelf. DES 74-190.
Bureau of Land Management, U.S. Department of the Interior
(1980), FEIS Crossman Peak Radar Proposal. January.
Bureau of Reclamation, U.S. Department of the Interior
(1977), DEIS New Melones 230 kv Electrical
Transmission Line, Central Valley Project. DES
77-33.
City and County of San Francisco (1978a), FEIR, Neiman-
Marcus Department Store, Vol. 1. EE 77.257,
December.
City and County of San Francisco (1978b), FEIR, Saks Fifth
Avenue Union Square Project. EE 74.285, March 16.
City and County of San Francisco (1979), Final
Environmental Impact Report, Southeast Water
Pollution Control Plant. August.
Department of General Services, California Agriculture and
Services Agency (1980), FEIR for the San Francisco
State Building.
Liebeman, L., and Yost, N. (1980), Legal opinion--referral
under 40 C.F.R. Part 1504 of Interstate 84, proposed
between Hartford, Connecticut, and Providence, Rhode
Island. April 30.
Meister, R. T. (1980), 1980 Farm Chemicals Handbook.
Willoughby, Ohio: Meister.
Robilliard, G. A. (1977), "Carrying Capacity of Ecologists
in the Environmental Consulting Niche." Bulletin of
the Ecological Society of America, 58, 4.
Slovic, P., and Fischoff, B. (1970), Preliminary draft of
a chapter in the forthcoming book by L. Gould and
C. A. Walker (Eds.), Too Hot to Handle: Social and
Policy Issues in the Management of Radioactive
Wastes. New Haven: Yale University Press.
Speth, G. (1980), personal communication to Hon. Neil
Goldschmidt, April 30.
U.S. Department of Housing and Urban Development (1976),
DEIS, Phases II and III of the Residential
Development of the Hunters Point Redevelopment Area
in San Francisco, California. HUD-R09-EIS-76-20.

14. The EIS and the Decision Maker: Closing the Gap

Ruth-Ellen Miller

INTRODUCTION

Environmental impact assessment has evolved over recent years in response to a nationally felt need for decision makers to consider their actions in terms of possible long-term effects. In general terms, the purpose for performing an assessment is threefold:

1. To gather together relevant data concerning the innovation and its impacts;
2. To convert that data into meaningful information on the nature and scope of those impacts; and
3. To communicate that information in such a way that it becomes a part of the knowledge base of those who are to make decisions concerning the innovation.

Over the last decade, this process has been undertaken numerous times with varying degrees of success at each stage. Often the necessary data has not been available, or an effective methodological approach has not been worked out, or there just was not time or money enough to think out and put together a top-notch report. Errors of the first and second kinds (commission and omission) can sometimes result in significant reductions in utility. Such reductions may also result from what Ian Mitroff (1977) termed an "error of the third kind:" finding the right solution to the wrong problem.

Any or all of these problems may in themselves reduce the effectiveness of an Environmental Impact Statement (EIS), but they are compounded, in many cases, by a very subtle fourth error: the assumption that the audience is operating from the same perspective as that of the author. Because of this assumption, most EISs are written in technical language using the logic of optimization. Because of the invalidity of this assumption, most EISs are lost in agency archives.

What, then, can the author of the EIS do to ensure his or her efforts are not wasted? How can these errors be avoided? What alternatives are there?

THE EIS PROCESS

Roles and Expectations

In order to address these questions, it is necessary to examine the perceived roles of the participants in the social impact assessment (SIA) process and the expectations associated with those roles. Three major roles in the process sometimes overlap but are nonetheless quite distinct. They are:

1. The analyst--performing the assessment;
2. The client--funding the assessment; and
3. The user--making decisions based on the assessment.

Each of these roles involves a specific set of perspectives and expectations. The analyst is concerned with the quality of the data and their analysis. The usefulness of the final report is, to him or her, reflected in an acceptable presentation of the relevant data and in good quality analytical methodology. The results he or she seeks tend to be based on optimization--the greatest benefit for the least cost. Certain standard approaches and procedures, as well as some concern about retaining a client (or job), may affect results, but usually only within the logical framework of analysis.

The second major role, that of client, functions within a somewhat different set of perspectives and expectations. As a funding agency or organization, the client has standard operating procedures and policies, deadlines, and long-range plans based on incremental changes and hierarchical chains of command, each of which contributes to his or her selective perception and (stated or unstated) expectations for a given EIS. In addition, the individual monitoring the project will, him or herself, have certain preconceptions, values, hopes, and fears that will be reflected in the way he or she directs or responds to the project's progress--although these will often be couched in the terminology of the analyst.

The user, as well, works within an organizational framework. He or she also has individual expectations and perceptual limitations that define the way the SIA will be used in the decision-making process. This is often multiplied as a variety of planners, executives, citizen groups, and later writers are included as users of a given SIA.

In his work on technology assessment, Harold Linstone (1980) suggested a potentially useful schema for dealing with these variable sets of expectations. Drawing on the work of Graham Allison (1971), Linstone suggested that people come to a problem with overlapping perspectives (see Figure 14.1).

Within this framework, three major perspectives are

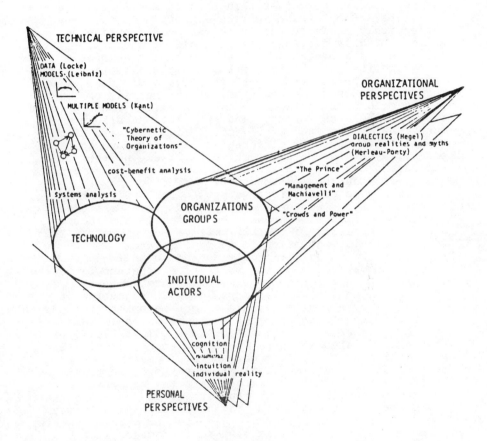

Figure 14.1   Linstone's multiple perspectives on decision
making (1981).

292

defined--the technical (T), the organizational process
(O), and the individual (P)--which define the way the
system under study is viewed, the kinds of questions asked
about it, and the kinds of information perceived. As
Figure 14.1 illustrates, an individual operating primarily
from the T perspective will rely heavily on data, formal
models, and analytical methods such as cost-benefit
analysis. He or she will apply these to an understanding
of the technology in question and, to some extent, any
organizations associated with the technology. By
contrast, someone operating mainly from an organizational
(O) perspective perceives things in terms of group-defined
realities and myths and applies a process (e.g.,
dialectical) model to the organization's functioning.
While virtually disregarding the role of the tools that
may affect the organization, this perspective does
recognize the possibility of individuals affecting it,
which the T perspective does not. The individual
perspective, on the other hand, relies heavily on
intuition and the personal view of reality, tending to see
tools, techniques, groups, and institutions all as
functions of the individual actors involved with them.
     Because of these differences, a person operating
primarily within one perspective is likely neither to
understand nor even to accept the validity of insights
gained from another perspective. Moreover, he or she is
less likely to deal effectively with the different bodies
of evidence that emerge in social and policy research
(e.g., the personal awareness of racial tension among
staff members against the affirmative action report that
says the racial situation is in good balance).
     Further, these perspectives tend to shift in
importance depending on the role which a person is taking
in approaching the problem. For instance, when a
researcher (analyst) takes a position in a government
agency (becomes a client), his or her perspective tends to
shift from the technical to the organizational framework;
thus his or her actions and decisions will reflect the
values associated with that role (Linstone, 1980). So
also will his or her information requirements. Where
before quality data and analysis were most important, now
he or she may be more concerned with the responses of
other organizations to the innovation, and the role that
his or her own organization may have to play. Finally,
the shift into the agency may have led to a shift in his
or her own personal values or perceived needs such that
formerly useful information that does not conform to the
new framework is now not even perceived, or is simply
dismissed as irrelevant.
     Linstone suggests, therefore, that information should
be provided from all three perspectives so that each can
function as a basis for understanding the others. To that
end, he suggests interviews with key actors and
representatives of key agencies and organizations as a

major source of information for the assessment process, as
well as a shift away from the technical report as the
primary mode of communication of results (Linstone, 1980).

Restating the Problem

The practical effect of such a suggestion is to
require that the analyst expand his or her problem
definition. The problem is no longer, "What are the
likely short- and long-term impacts on a society or
community of such-and-such an innovation?" but, rather,
something more like, "What are the agencies, actors, and
systems that will most strongly affect or be affected by
this innovation and how can the key actors be led to
understand--ultimately to be able to act on the
understanding of--the situation?"

This kind of a problem statement requires specific
information--much of it nonquantifiable--gathered and
analyzed within a framework established for a specific
assessment, and leading to a presentation of results that
may be highly nontechnical in its format and language.'
It requires that the assessment team include not only
those who are methodologically expert but also those who
know the community surrounding the innovation well enough
to be able to point out the real key actors. Finally, it
requires an understanding of those key actors as the
audience for the assessment and, as with all
presentations, it requires that the results be formulated
in a way that communicates directly to them--maximizing
the clarity of the message while maintaining the noise.

To some extent this new problem statement requires,
therefore, a shift away from more quantitative analytical
techniques toward an investigative reporting approach.
Interviewing becomes as important as measurements of
traffic flow; networking as useful as cost-benefit
analysis; and understanding the power structure as
relevant as delineating land-use change patterns.

Gathering the Data

Within this expanded definition, new kinds of data
become important. In addition to the standard literature
search, site measurements, etc., data are needed
concerning the specific people involved, their roles,
their abilities, their perceptions of the process, and
their expectations for outcomes. Key actors and decision
makers need to be identified and queried at every stage of
the innovation's development and use. Agencies that might
affect or be affected by the innovation are also
important, along with the degree to which they can modify
the expected course of events. Sources of technical
support and beneficiaries from technological advantage are
other factors to be noted. In addition, affected social
institutions and processes are absolutely essential

elements of data in assessing any human innovation.

Another form of data required by this approach is the goings-on around related issues. Often, a particular impact assessment is undertaken in an environment in which a number of changes are being made: a new shopping center as part of a plan to upgrade an area; a new technology as a replacement for one that is dependent on increasingly rare resources; and so on. Such related issues can provide insights into the nature of the one under study.

Locating this kind of data involves a thorough knowledge of the community in which the innovation is likely to take place. Often, for instance, the apparent power holder (e.g., a commission chairperson) may act simply as an advisor to the real actor (e.g, the commission's executive secretary or the old man in the old house on the hill). Or it may be that a similar innovation was attempted--or accomplished--before, and people remember how disastrously--or marvelously--it worked. These things are rarely found in the literature, but they come out easily in the interviewing process.

Analysis: Converting Data into Information

There are many analytical tools for dealing with numerical or statistical data. They can be very useful for establishing scales of impacts and for identifying certain kinds of relationships.

There are few tools, however, for analyzing qualitative data and, as yet, few models to follow. Ethnographers, those who describe the way in which a culture functions, provide what may be the most useful model for social impact analysis (see Mead's Growing Up in New Guinea and later follow-up studies as a classic example). Political scientists and social philosophers are another potentially useful source (e.g., Whitehead's work on interaction events). Each of these disciplines operates from a fairly well-defined theoretical framework that permits the investigator to perceive elements and relationships and to attribute causation in system observations. Experience and resulting intuitive understandings become very important in such qualitative analyses, providing guidelines for eliminating irrelevant data and recognizing patterns.

It is these patterns that, when synthesized, become the analysts's model of the community or social system. At first this will be a mental model, an image of the people, institutions, events, and their connections. Usually holistic in nature, this model is experienced as a sense of the _gestalt_ of the system. As the analyst tries to verify or communicate this model, it is once more broken down into elements, attributes, relationships, and events--either in the form of a verbal description or of a diagram of some sort. Building such verbal and structural models can be a very effective tool for clarifying one's

perception of the *gestalt* and for communicating aspects of
the perceived pattern (although models never seem to
communicate the whole quite as the original viewer sees
it).

Communicating Results

As the focus shifts away from data gathering and
analysis and moves toward information sharing, the reason
that so many EISs are sitting on archive shelves rather
than acting as useful resources becomes obvious. By far,
the greatest majority of impact assessments are written
from the technical perspective to others operating within
the technical perspective; they ignore the other
dimensions of decision making completely. Such
assessments focus on the quantitative analysis of
numerical measures and the rational arguments that depend
on them.

Yet, in order to reach the client or user who is
operating within the organizational perspective, it is
necessary to provide information about the impacts on the
organizations involved and the responses available to them
within the framework of their standard operating
procedures and policies. In order to satisfy a key
actor's personal concerns, hope, and fears, it becomes
necessary to provide more than just rational arguments.
If the assessor is to make complex interactions and
control loops real to the user, then he or she must
provide a way for the user to experience them at a "gut
level."

A number of impact assessment teams and futures
researchers have attempted alternative approaches to the
standard reports in an attempt to have their clients and
users make better use of their results. Some of these are
documented by Lipinsky (1978) in his article,
"Communicating the Future." Working at the Institute for
the Future, he and his team were completing a study of the
potential effects of electronic funds-transfer systems for
a large banking corporation. There was some difficulty
communicating; so the team wrote a report that was in the
form of a novel, circulated it informally, and then held
the formal briefing as planned. The method was declared
effective when the executives arrived at the briefing
prepared to ask specific questions--for the first time in
the history of the project. This experiment inspired the
Institute to consider other alternative media for
presenting study results--including Bell Canada's
multimedia shows--with an emphasis on those that engage
the intuitive and aesthetic as well as the rational
faculties of the mind.

In another, very different kind of study, researchers
at Stanford Research Institute (SRI) International's
Center for the Study of Social Policy developed a series
of anecdotal sidebars to go along with formal scenarios in

the final report. These integrated the societal future
being described with appropriate transportation futures by
describing "a day in the life" of individuals in those
societies as they moved from place to place using the
modes of transport available to them there and then (SRI,
1977).
   To achieve the necessary synthesis, to ensure that
the user has a sense of the possible realities, these
researchers have found that rational data are not enough;
nor is logical argument. A multichanneled approach,
combining the rational, analytic, aesthetic, and
intuitive, is required for new information to become a
part of the audience's knowledge base.

Multichanneled Communication

   This last concern, the need for a broader-ranged
communications medium, is so fundamental to any attempt to
"close the gap" between analyst and decision maker that it
will be the focus for the rest of this paper. However,
understanding its implications requires a look at
communication as a process involved with images: their
sharing, formation, and use. Stories related, games
played, and discussions participated in, along with other
experiences with their responses, all provide inputs to
the individual's image and are absorbed and fitted into
place, to modify the goal for the individual--operating as
such through another system of communication within the
mind and central nervous system of the individual.
   In interpersonal communication, one individual (the
sender) translates elements of his or her image into the
symbols of a common language (words, facial expressions,
body language, tone of voice, and direct use of or
reference to familiar objects that have been assigned
meaning in the culture) that another individual (the
recipient) perceives, translates, and filters through his
or her own image. He or she then makes notes of his or
her own emotional response to the message and absorbs the
message and the response. (The recipient may or may not
then translate appropriate elements of the newly modified
image into symbols that can then become a responding
message to the original sender.) The modification that
has taken place in this process may be major or
insignificant, conscious or unconscious, depending on the
individuals involved, their culture(s), the novelty
included in the original message, and the skill with which
the message was sent--the effectiveness of the
communication.
   The effective communicator is one who chooses to send
a message using that combination of elements from the
common symbol set that the recipient can absorb and
respond to with a minimum of filtering or translating.
This requires that the effective sender be familiar with
both the symbols in the common set and with the filtering

and absorbing process. The former requires extensive
examination of other effective communicators and the
latter extensive observation of the sender's own images.
Given these, the sender can expect that most of his or her
message is perceived as it was sent--most of the time.
Moreover, effective communicators whose messages are
received by a fairly large audience may find that their
translated image becomes, in fact, part of the common
symbol set and even of the shared cultural image.[2]
    In this way literature, particularly the classic
stories, novels, plays, and poems, clearly acts as a means
whereby individual images are shared and formed. They
create in the reader's (or hearer's) mind images that are
the equivalent of physical experience in terms of the
reader's emotional response and the filtering and
absorbing process. These images are built up from
sequences of words heard or read--sequences the writer
composes as an attempt to describe the images in his or
her own mind, using whatever comparison or similitude he
or she can to represent what he himself is "seeing."
    The novel, story, and play are concerned with the
consequences of action. They portray a specific set of
circumstances, and the action that evolves within them, in
such a way that the audience may experience, albeit
vicariously, the need for and the consequences of that
action. To the extent that they succeed in this, they may
be considered substitutes for the action itself, or "mind
experiences."
    The writer, therefore, is creating a human experience
through the medium of words on paper. Using this limited
symbol set, extended through references to other symbols,
he or she attempts to communicate "effectively," to reach
the audience through multiple channels, directly and with
a minimum of filtering and a maximum of intuitive and
emotional response. He or she does this by building word-
images to describe his or her own mental images. He or
she succeeds insofar as he or she has thoroughly explored
the mental images and carefully chosen the language, form,
and symbols used to present them.

A Potential Model for Communicating Impacts

    In an essay contemplating why some authors concerned
with the human effects of technologies and policies
"didn't write an essay, a documentary, a philosophical or
sociological or psychological study," Ursula LeGuin (1979)
says,

> They write science fiction, I imagine, because what
> they have to say is best said using the tools of
> science fiction, and the craftsman knows his tools.
> . . . using the great range of imagery available to
> science fiction they say what it is they have to say
> through a character.

Such authors, imagining the not-yet-real, choose a form
that can convey a sense of reality, which has demonstrated
itself, according to critic Mark Rose (1976), as "an
excellent medium for the exploration of the taste, the
feel, the human meaning of scientific discoveries."

Unlike other forms of fiction, this speculative--or
social science--fiction (SF) deals with images of things
that have not yet come to pass but might. As such, it is
peculiarly appropriate for the communication of impact
assessment results. Like the investigator, the SF writer
must bring a degree of technical training to the process
and research the material sufficiently to be credible.
Like the investigator, the writer's images and training
provide the foundation for both the questions asked and
the answers sought. Those whose training is heavily
weighted to the technical or "hard" sciences tend to focus
on "gadgets" and their workings. (Robert Heinlein is an
excellent example.) Those whose background is in the
social sciences emphasize the institutions and cultural
patterns. (Ursula LeGuin typifies this group.)

Perhaps the most obvious aspect of SF that suggests
it appropriateness to such a use, though, is the fact that
the focus is at least as much on the field of interaction
as it is on the characters' interaction. In fact, for
most of SF the character exists primarily as a means to
portray the field. In practice, this means that when we
finish reading award-winning SF works such as Dreamsnake
or Rendezvous with Rama[3] we haven't any real notion about
who the characters have become as a result of their
experiences, but we are very excited about the potential
implications of the social and technical "what-if's" that
have been presented. We may even find them penetrating
our other thoughts and dreams for a time after putting the
book down--exploring ways we might have done things or
considering what might happen next. The mental images
form and reform, shaping the ideas of the story into our
own personal mental image of reality. The vehicle of the
fiction creates a temporary reality for the images so that
they can speak to our unconscious and become part of our
knowing.

GUIDELINES FOR SYNTHESIS

The Council on Environmental Quality's recommended
format for EISs (1980) includes three sections that are
particularly amenable to a user-oriented approach, and to
the use of fiction. These are: the summary, the
description of alternatives, and the description of
environmental consequences. Dickert and Jorgensen (1974)
have suggested a summary table to which the user can refer
and which the assessor can use as a checklist device.
Markley (1977) has offered another sort of table, focusing
on the organizational concerns, as illustrated in Table
14.1. Such tables can simplify both the summarizing

TABLE 14.1
Sample "organizational process" summary (focusing on generating employment)

Brief History, Relevant Studies Underway or Recently Completed and Key Informants	Alternative Strategies and/or Programs Being Proposed	Knowledgeables and "Influentials" (Institutional Groups and Persons)	Key Uncertainties and Emergent Issues
Employment Act of 1946 -Joint Economic Committee of Congress -Council of Economic Advisors -Annual manpower reports	Laissez faire -Eliminate minimum wage -Reduce corporation tax -Reduce regulatory influences	National Commission on Manpower Policy (Robert Hall) Joint Economic Committee (Lucy Falconi)	Capital availability Full employment vs. inflation (Phillips curve trade-off) "Right" to employment
MDTA, CETA, EEA, etc.	Full employment in planned economy -Humphrey-Hawkins Bill	Department of Labor (Melvin Hans)	Environmental preservation vs. jobs availability
Phillips curve; policy implications	-Humphrey-Javits Bill -Public service employment	Work in America Institute (Jerry Rosso)	Capability of work force
Report of National Commission on Manpower Policy	Pragmatic evolutionary -Job sharing -Career education -California Jobs Creation Act	Employment Development Department (Carl Poirot)	Minimum wage laws (especially for youth) Family income vs. individual work

Table 14.1 (cont.)

Brief History, Relevant Studies Underway or Recently Completed and Key Informants	Alternative Strategies and/or Programs Being Proposed	Knowledgeables and "Influentials" (Institutional Groups and Persons)	Key Uncertainties and Emergent Issues
Surveys showing California attitudes against income maintenance	"Radical left" -Reduce substitution of technology for labor -Worker participation in management -Public ownership	George Washington University (Sar Levitan) National Manpower Institute (Willard Wirtz) California State Assembly (Assemblyman Lockyer) Center for Needs (Leo Barnes)	Capital Effect of welfare and unemployment insurance policies on work incentive Changing family structure Equity pushed to the point of ethnic quotas

Source: Developed under the author's guidance as part of the project described in Markley (1977).

process and the user's search for relevant information--
especially if headings in the table of contents and index
conform to those on the summary table. Combined with a
brief story depicting the choices and their effects, such
a summary could be a very effective reporting device.

Moreover, the story is more than an effective
communications medium: writing the SF story becomes a
vehicle for exploring the interactions and impacts that
result from an innovation. Just as the assessors, in
constructing their analysis, inevitably discover some
overlooked inconsistency in the process, the writer, as he
immerses himself in the story--becoming a character living
in that society--achieves whole new insights and
understandings about that societal system. This is
particularly true when some elements that logically go
together (e.g., corporate dominance and highly regimented,
bureaucratic power structures) just cannot work on a day-
to-day, getting-things-done basis (i.e., informal power
nets become essential).

If, then, the purpose of a given EIS is, in the
largest sense, to lead the key actors to understand the
effects of their actions, it makes very good sense for the
analyst and the client to consider seriously the use of
either existing or specially composed SF stories as part
of their presentation.

The descriptions of alternatives and environmental
consequences are also sections that could be improved by
the use of speculative stories--either in the form of
existing works or through the creation of new ones. The
systematic use of existing works would lead to studies
that reflect the basic hopes and fears of a community, as
well as provide an alternative perspective on the study's
subject or on the society forecasted. There are, however,
some limitations and potential problems with this method--
most significantly the present lack of topical
bibliographies. Table 14.2 offers an initial list of
works by topic, including a few anthologies and critical
discussion that are topic-oriented. Other sources of
information concerning relevant works include the numerous
fans and collectors, many of whom are associated with
engineering firms and "think tanks"--book storekeepers,
librarians, and information specialists who are familiar
with the genre and who, in many cases, will be delighted
to search for archival and out-of-print material. By
using them as part of the initial literature search for
the assessment, these people can be incorporated into the
process early on and provide materials as the research
progresses.

In general, those studies focusing on projects
involving lasting human issues--e.g., urban renewal in a
long-established ethnic neighborhood, dam building or
mining on wild or Indian lands, the boomtown effects of
mining operations, or the potential for mass disasters due
to poor building design (a la Towering Inferno)--are far

TABLE 14.2
Potentially relevant works of speculative fiction

Topic/Title[1]	Author	Hypothesis
TRANSPORTATION		
Automated Roadways		
"THE ROADS MUST ROLL"	Robert Heinlein	Conveyor-type passenger strips are developed and become "Road Cities" extending between major metropolitan areas and managed by a paramilitary service corps.
"Repent, Harlequin! Said the Ticktockman"	Harlan Ellison	Conveyor-type passenger strips are the main form of transportation and are essential to the economic system.
Matter Transmitters		
"IT'S SUCH A BEAUTIFUL DAY"	Isaac Asimov	Matter Transmitters are the only form of transportation in some communities, leading to significant value changes.
ONE STEP FROM EARTH	Harry Harrison	Matter Transmitters permit the settling of the Solar System, the Galaxy, and finally the Universe.

Topic/Title[1]	Author	Hypothesis
CRYOGENICS		
Door into Summer	Robert Heinlein	The "Long Sleep" permits a man to see his work as others will see it.
"THE GRAVEYARD HEART"	Roger Zelazny	An elite group of wealthy people live their lives attending seasonal festivals and being maintained in suspended animation between parties.
SPACE COLONIZATION		
"THE MARTIAN WAY"	Isaac Asimov	Colonists on Mars come to terms with their position in the Solar System as significantly different from Earth's.
"THE SEEDLING STARS"	James Blish	Space colonies provide the jumping off point for outer space travel.
THE MOON IS A HARSH MISTRESS	Robert Heinlein	The Moon as a penal colony.
FARMER IN THE SKY	Robert Heinlein	Jupiter's moons can be "terra-formed."
THE GREEN HILLS OF EARTH	Robert Heinlein	A collection of stories exploring the possibilities of lunar and planetary colonies, including asteroid mining.
MENACE FROM EARTH	Robert Heinlein	Viewed from the colonists' point of view, Earth may not be all good.

Table 14.2 (cont.)

Topic/Title[1]	Author	Hypothesis
Floating Worlds	Cecelia Holland	Colony culture may be so different as to be incompatible with Earth's.
MAN PLUS	Frederick Pohl	It may be necessary to create new life forms to colonize other planets.
The Ophiuchi Hotline	John Varley	A modified Western culture will dominate life across the solar system.
DESTINIES	(journal)	Articles and short stories describing and promoting colonization of inner space.
ARTIFICIAL INTELLIGENCE		
"EVIDENCE"	Isaac Asimov	An android can be a successful politician.
WHEN HARLEY WAS DONE	Donald Gerrold	Sufficient electronic complexity leads to creative intelligence surpassing that of humans.
The Moon Is a Harsh Mistress	Robert Heinlein	Sufficient complexity and attention leads to self-awareness.
THE GENESIS MACHINE	James Hogan	Man-machine symbiosis is possible.
2001	Arthur C. Clarke	Machine self-awareness can be dangerous.

Topic/Title[1]	Author	Hypothesis
EXTENDED LONGEVITY		
"METHUSELEH'S CHILDREN"	Robert Heinlein	Genetic manipulation through careful breeding can extend lifespan significantly.
TIME ENOUGH FOR LOVE	Robert Heinlein	Combined with cloning to replace body parts, it can extend life indefinitely.
THE BLUE CHAIR	Joyce Thompson	To give birth is to give up immortality.
"ETERNITY LOST"	Clifford Simak	The possibility of immortality is corrupting.
"TOMORROW AND TOMORROW AND TOMORROW"	Kurt Vonnegut	Immortality without youth can be hell.
The Pigeon Affair	Irving Wallace	The discoverer of life-extenders is in a hazardous position.
GENETIC ENGINEERING		
THE OPHIUCHI HOTLINE	John Varley	Recombining DNA permits whole new food stuffs and human clones.

[1]All capitals in the title indicates that the hypothesis provides the dominant theme in the story. Mixed capitals and lower case indicates a secondary theme. Quotation marks indicates a short story.

more amenable to fictional treatment than those focusing
on such mundane projects as street paving, building a
motel along a frontage road, or moving a power line
underground. The more lasting and basic the concern, the
greater the likelihood of finding one or more pieces of
fiction to be included in this type of synthesis.

In those situations where it is not possible to find
stories about the innovation itself, there are a number of
works that provide excellent societal forecasts for
specific periods in time. These typically span a variety
of social, political, and environmental changes and may be
appropriately used as descriptions of context in which the
project can be embedded to see its possible effects.
Examples of these include Orwell's 1984 (adjusted for
another year, perhaps), Brunner's The Sheep Look Up and
Stand on Zanzibar, and Heinlein's The Past through
Tomorrow, Beyond This Horizon, or The Moon Is a Harsh
Mistress.

To make use of such works as part of the impact
assessment, a project team may choose one or more of
several alternatives. They may:

1. Read selected novels and short stories as part of
    the "scoping" process early on in the study;
2. Include one or more works in or alongside the
    report;
3. Include passages as relevant in a report; and
4. Refer the reader to relevant works as a way to
    "flesh out" a scenario or exemplify a set of
    impacts.

Which of these is selected will depend on the subject of
the study, the intended audience for the report, any
regulations or contractual obligations limiting the
contents of the report, and the availability of suitable
works of fiction.

In the case where existing works are unavailable, but
the fictional approach seems appropriate for depicting the
impacts in a way that the user can relate to, it may be
most appropriate to develop one or more new works. This
method has the advantage of ensuring a coherent final
product in which the fiction is obviously and directly
tied to the analysis. It, too, however, is limited by the
capacity of the subject to capture the writer's
imagination and lead to a work that is more than a series
of anecdotes, such as those presented in the SRI (1977)
study described above. For this process, the project team
should include a professional SF writer, or a technical
writer with leanings and training' in that direction.
The product could be a summary piece, presenting the
options and the possibilities and problems associated with
each of them. It could also be a series of alternative
"solutions" to the problem presented, demonstrating the
impacts associated with each. This could be put together

by a series of professional writers in a workshop setting or using the anthology process, or it could be the product of one writer's efforts or of the various team members, polished up by a professional.

CONCLUSION

Over the past decade, environmental impact assessment has begun to take form as a discipline. Yet significant criticisms have been levied at both the process and the contents of the statements. To a considerable extent, these criticisms result from a communications problem--one that evolves out of a misperception about the nature of the audience to which the statements are addressed and out of a misunderstanding of what effective communication is or can be.

By taking into consideration the roles and expectations of the various actors in the assessment process, it becomes possible to address some of the problems associated with both the process and the product. These include different approaches to data gathering, analysis, and communication of results, with the greatest emphasis on the last.

Communication has been defined by some theorists as the process of forming and sharing mental images; to the degree that a report reflects the writer's images and suggests similar ones to the reader, it may be said to be communicating effectively. The implication is that fiction--those narratives that rely on and emphasize the development of mental images--may be the most appropriate form for communicating certain kinds of information. Specifically, it would be appropriate for developing the kinds of understandings required for decision makers to use EISs.

One form of fiction, called "speculative" (or "social science") fiction, has been developed as a medium for exploring and sharing the possible consequences of technological developments. Combined with more traditional reporting techniques, such fictions can provide the kind of imagistic communication needed for EISs to be most effective. They can be used by the team as part of their own research process, included in reports, or simply referred to as appropriate to the subject. Their use can, however, also increase the complexity of the assessment process. There is, at the least, additional literature to search and, possibly, a whole new stage in the process--researching and writing one or more stories to be included in or alongside the report. Nonetheless, regardless of the way in which the assessment team uses them, works of fiction can provide useful insights into the problems and possibilities of an innovation, in a form that engages the reader's interest-- as only a good story can.

REFERENCES

Allison, G. (1971), Essence of Decision: The Cuban Missile Crisis. Boston, Mass.: Little-Brown.

Block, L. (1979), Writing the Novel: From Plot to Print. New York: Writer's Digest Books.

Boulding, K. (1977), The Image (11th ed.). Ann Arbor, Mich.: Ann Arbor Press.

Bradley, M. Z. (1977), "My Trip through Science Fiction." Algol, Winter, 11-20.

Bragg, D. P. (1980), personal communication, April.

Brunner, J. (1973), Stand on Zanzibar. New York: Ballantine.

Brunner, J. (1979), The Sheep Look Up. New York: Ballantine.

Campbell, J. (1960), Prologue to Analog. New York: Doubleday.

Ciriacy-Wantrup, S. V. (1971), "The Economics of Environmental Planning." Land Economics, February, 42.

Clarke, A. C. (1973), Rendezvous with Rama. New York: Del Rey.

Council on Environmental Quality (1979), Regulations for Implementing the Procedural Provisions of the National Environmental Policy Act. Washington, D.C.: Government Printing Office.

Davenport, B. (1969), The Science Fiction Novel. Chicago: Advent.

Dickert, T. G., and Sorensen, J. (1974), "Some Suggestions on the Content and Organization of Environmental Impact Statements." In T. G. Dickert and K. R. Domeny (Eds.), Environmental Impact Assessment: Guidelines and Commentary. Berkeley, Cal.: University Extension Press.

Duncan, H. D. (1968), Symbols in Society. London: Oxford University Press.

Elgin, D., et al. (1975), Alternative Futures for Environmental Planning. Report to the Environmental Protection Agency. Menlo Park, Cal.: SRI International.

Elkins, C. (1979), "Science Fiction vs. Futurology." Science Fiction Studies, 6.

Ernst, D., et al. (1975), An Assessment of Electronic Funds Transfer Systems. Report to the National Science Foundation. Washington, D.C.: Arthur D. Little.

Fensterbusch, K., and Wolf, C. P. (1977), Methodology for Social Impact Assessment. Stroudsburg, Penn.: Dowden, Hutchinson, and Ross.

Hall, A. D., and Fagen, W. (1973), "The Definition of System." In W. Buckley (Ed.), Systems Research for the Behavioral Scientist. New York: Brazillier.

Heinlein, R. (1948), Beyond This Horizon. New York: Signet.

Heinlein, R. (1966), The Moon Is a Harsh Mistress. New
     York: Berkley.
Heinlein, R. (1977), The Past through Tomorrow. New York:
     Berkley.
Hesse, M. B. (1966), Models and Analogies in Science.
     South Bend, Ind.: University of Notre Dame Press.
Jung, C. G. (1968), Man and His Symbols. New York: Dell.
LeGuin, U. (1967), The Left Hand of Darkness. New York:
     Ballantine.
LeGuin, U. (1974), The Language of the Night. (Collected
     essays, edited and with an introduction by S. Wood.)
     New York: Ballantine.
Lem, S. (1976), "The Structure of Science Fiction." In
     M. Rose (Ed.), Science Fiction. Englewood Heights,
     N.J.: Prentice-Hall.
Linstone, H. (1980), The Role of Alternative Decision-
     making Models in Technology Assessment. Report to
     the National Science Foundation. Portland, Ore.:
     Portland State University.
Linstone, H., and Simmonds, W. C. (1977), Futures
     Research: New Directions. Reading, Mass.: Addison-
     Wesley.
Linstone, H., et al. (1981), The Multiple Perspectives
     Concept with Applications to Technology Assessment
     and Other Decision Areas. Final report to the
     National Science Foundation. Portland, Ore.:
     Portland State University.
Lipinsky, G. (1978), "Communicating the Future." Futures,
     February.
Markley, O. W. (1977), "A Trends Assessment Program for
     Social Forecasting and Policy Analysis." Research
     Memorandum No. 29, EPRC. Menlo Park, Cal.: SRI
     International.
McIntyre, V. (1979), Dreamsnake. New York: Berkley.
Mead, M. (1954), Growing Up in New Guinea. New York:
     Mentor.
Mitchell, A., et al. (1975), Handbook of Forecasting
     Techniques. Prepared for the Institute on Water
     Resources, Army Corps of Engineers. Menlo Park,
     Cal.: SRI International.
Mitroff, I. (1977), "On the Error of the Third Kind." In
     H. Linstone and W. C. Simmonds (Eds.), Futures
     Research: New Directions. Reading, Mass.: Addison-
     Wesley.
Myers, G. E. (1973), The Dynamics of Human Communication.
     New York: McGraw-Hill.
O'Connor, F. (1974), "The Nature and Aim of Fiction." In
     J. Hersey (Ed.), The Writer's Craft. New York:
     Alfred Knopf.
Orwell, G. (1961 ed.), 1984. New York: Harcourt, Brace,
     Jovanovitch.
Pierce, J. R. (1961), Symbols, Signals, and Noise. New
     York: Harper and Row.
Rose, M. (1976), Science Fiction. Englewood Heights,

310

N.J.: Prentice-Hall.

Shaw, B. (1976), "Escape to Infinity." Foundation, June, 10.

SRI International (1977), Transportation in America's Future: Potentials for the Next Half Century, Part 1: Societal Context. Report prepared for the U.S. Department of Transportation. Menlo Park, Cal.: SRI International.

Suvin, D. (1979), Metamorphoses of Science Fiction. New Haven, Conn.: Yale University Press.

Trask, G., and Burkhardt, C. (Eds.) (1963), Storytellers and Their Art. New York: Doubleday.

Varley, J. (1978), The Ophiuchi Hotline. New York: Bantam.

Vaughn, F. (1979), Awakening Intuition. New York: Anchor Press.

von Bertalanffy, L. (1968), General Systems Theory. New York: Brazillier.

von Bertalanffy, L. (1980), A Systems View of Man. Boulder, Col.: Praeger.

Waddington, C. H. (1977), Tools for Thought. New York: Basic Books.

Watzlawick, P., et al. (1967), Pragmatics of Human Communication. New York: W. W. Norton.

Wiener, N. (1954), The Human Use of Human Beings. New York: Anchor Press.

Wrightsman, L. S. (1972), Social Psychology in the '70s. Monterey, Cal.: Brooks/Cole.

NOTES

[1] This suggestion is seconded by workers in community development such as D. P. Bragg of Texas A and M University, whose work has led to the "most dog-eared reports in the county" and to special briefings that have gone so far as to suggest the firing of a city manager to achieve the community's objectives (Bragg, 1980).

[2] Thus we have the words "Romeo," "odyssey," and "utopia" as meaningful terms in our language, although they were created as part of stories to fit far distant times and places.

[3] These two works, by McIntyre (1978) and Clark (1977), respectively, were chosen because of the very different story and character types they represent. Yet the central notion for both is the same: the possibility of life-forms who do everything in threes rather than twos. As a result, they provide a set of alternative perspectives on the same notion--as is often the case over the history of this genre.

[4] Many technical writers also enjoy writing fiction. For these there are workshops held around the country, often called "clarion workshops," by local SF writers in conjunction with colleges and science fiction

associations. In addition, a good technical writer can,
by reading several works of SF, begin to pick up the
structure and style associated with this kind of fiction.

15. The Impact Judgment: A Technical Impasse?

Robert E. Henshaw

The Environmental Impact Statement (EIS) has been criticized as inadequate to its task because, with rare exceptions, EISs fail to differentiate critical impacts from trivial ones. Most EISs are descriptive and nonanalytical and tend to provide little more than tables of effluents or "laundry lists of species" and similar synoptic data (Odum, 1977). Although the function of the EIS is to facilitate decision making, descriptive EISs cannot provide the basis for enlightened decisions. This impasse between the presentation of descriptive data and the final use of those data, however, can be overcome. Furthermore, since the decision of acceptability or unacceptability of the proposed action represents a social policy decision, overcoming this impasse requires a coupling of the descriptive data with the social importance of those data.

In the following discussion, I will demonstrate that evaluative judgments and decisions can be deduced logically from questions appropriately constructed to include both fundamental facts and social values. Using my own discipline of terrestrial ecology to illustrate, I suggest that the use of only seven "biosocial" criteria can provide the basis for an informed decision. By extension, similar sets of carefully chosen "geosocial," "chemosocial," etc. criteria could be devised coupling technical facts to social questions in other disciplines.

The problem of low analytic value to EISs derives largely from two sources: the lack of clear unifying concepts and inadequately trained environmental analysts.

AN ORIENTED UNIFYING CONCEPT

The concept of impact is usually defined as any change in the environment caused by an activity or a factor (e.g., Ward, 1978). This, of course, provides neither the analyst nor the reviewer with orientation on critical issues. Congress, in creating the concept of the EIS in the National Environmental Policy Act of 1970 (NEPA), certainly did not intend such an encompassing and deficient definition of impact. NEPA does not require an

"Environmental Change Statement" or an "Environmental
Modification Statement;" rather, the act captures the
thrust of the dictionary definition--"a striking together;
violent contact; collision" (Webster's New World
Dictionary, 2nd College Edition). Thus, the intended work
of the EIS is to differentiate the significant and
functionally degrading or improving impacts and not to
report, as one EIS actually did, that the impact would be
"38 meadow mice bladed out." To achieve the necessary
focus, both writers and reviewers of EISs must track the
same issues for the same reasons.

IMPROPERLY TRAINED ENVIRONMENTAL ANALYSTS

Environmental analysts must learn to ask questions
and discuss topics as do the critical lay public and the
social planners and political leaders who must act on the
basis of the EIS. However, most environmental analysts in
all disciplines are not trained to interpret so broadly.
NEPA created a new niche and marketing opportunities
for environmental "experts" and environmental consulting
firms sprang up like mushrooms during the 1970s. Field
personnel and team leaders frequently were hired with no
more experience than undergraduate or master's level
laboratory courses. Project managers often held a
doctorate in a traditional discipline, e.g., ornithology
or trophic ecology, which by the nature of much advanced
training most often qualified them as a specialist in one
subdiscipline but provided them with no ease in seeking
broad social interpretations of environmental actions.
Utilities and other major developers also hired in-house
master's degree-level environmentalists and then defined
each as an expert in all disciplines for which the company
was held accountable. Similar hiring practices were used
by federal and state regulatory agencies as they prepared
for the deluge of EISs. By the end of the "environmental
decade," more than 100,000 professionals had found
employment in the environmental impact field
(Cheremisinoff and Morresi, 1977).
In many respects, this could be considered a case of
the blind leading the blind. Inadequately trained,
descriptively oriented, specifically disciplined "experts"
with environmental consulting firms scoped studies for the
applicant or responded to naive requests for proposals as
instructed. Environmental regulations overspecified data
requirements and failed to direct concern to significant
issues. Environmental lawyers for agencies docketed
applications and approved EISs if the raw data specified
in the regulations were present, but they did not reject
EISs when comprehensive analyses were substantially
lacking.
In the absence of a viable concept of impact, no
mechanism has been available to facilitate social judgment
of technical information. Like the proverbial old

Scotsman who, when asked the way to a distant town, replied, "You can't get there from here," published EIS methodologies have generally failed to provide the necessary linkage between basic descriptive data and cost-benefit analyses. The result has been that proponents read the EIS as demonstrating no significant impact, and the intervenors read the same data as demonstrating the opposite. While reasonable differences in value systems can account for some disagreement, greater concurrence would be obtained if questions were appropriately phrased.

To illustrate this impasse, consider the following six recommended steps proposed in one text on environmental analysis of terrestrial ecosystems (Canter, 1977). Note that there is no apparent way to deduce steps 5 and 6 from steps 1 through 4.

1. Describe the flora and fauna, the community types, and their distribution.
2. Identify rare and endangered species.
3. Discuss past and current management practices.
4. Discuss natural succession of ecological communities.
5. Predict the impacts of alternatives quantitatively or qualitatively.
6. Summarize the critical impacts to the ecosystem.

APPROACHES TO PREDICTIVELY USEFUL EISs:
STRUCTURAL AND FUNCTIONAL COMPONENTS

Environmental scientists began to recognize the deficiencies in the EIS process and the need to structure the EIS into a functional specific analysis of expected impacts (e.g., Sharma et al., 1976). Because impacts affect the dynamic processes of the ecosystem (Cooper, 1976), the analyst should report on some descriptive characters, e.g., dominant and key species, but emphasize the functional characteristics of the community, e.g., food relationships and productivity, as well as time dimensions (Ward, 1978). Odum (1977) emphasized this point further, stating, "One can increase the useful information content many-fold by assessing more functional and integrative properties [of the ecosystem]." He suggested that if the EIS process were to move "from component analysis to more holistic approaches incorporating interactive, integrative, and emergent [biological] properties [it would provide] a far better basis for impact assessment." It is clear that such analyses would provide better estimates of biologically important impacts to ecosystems, but it is doubtful that they would facilitate identification of socially important impacts to biological systems.

Gradually there emerged the concept of ecosystem tolerance of impact. Cairns (1976), for instance, proposed ecological "persistence" that incorporated the concepts of "inertia" (how long will an ecosystem tolerate a perturbation and recover?), "elasticity" (can the ecosystem snap back after impact?), and "resiliency" (how many times can an ecosystem recover from a repeated impact?). These latter properties are valuable and certainly enhance predictive capabilities. Ward (1978) also called for the use of systems analysis and mathematical models to impacts. While such techniques may provide a formal approach to data, equations are not necessarily better than human judgment for defining and assessing socially significant impacts.

THE USE OF INDICES

Indices have been proposed to facilitate quantification and objectivity of both quantitative and qualitative assessments (Inhaber, 1976). Indices may be convenient when applied to objective data on discharges, water quality, and so forth where data can be quantified and compared to a standard value specified by law. Inhaber himself, however, acknowledged the near impossibility of developing biological, erosion, and, especially, aesthetic indices. Indicator species that are characteristic of certain conditions or are differentially sensitive to specific perturbations are valuable and commonly used when appropriate. However, as Mellanby (1978) states, "Biological indicators are really only of much use if we already know what the most important pollutant is likely to be." Clearly, simply providing functional biological descriptions, whether or not using indices or indicator species, does not facilitate definition and evaluation of the impacts considered important by the tax-paying public and other interested parties.

THE DEVELOPMENT AND USE OF "BIOSOCIAL" CRITERIA

The following seven criteria are emergent properties of the terrestrial ecosystem. They incorporate descriptive data as well as a social question or measure of those data. They do not, however, provide the final answer on the degree of acceptability of a proposed action. Rather, they provide the basis for reasoning the decision. That decision will vary with locale, political unit, social choices among the defined biological outcomes, etc.

1. Is the ecosystem unusual?
2. How biological fit is the ecosystem?
3. How productive is the ecosystem?
4. How much biological persistence would the ecosystem have?
5. How long would it take to replace the ecosystem if destroyed?

6. Are there "bioadministrative" issues?
7. Are there "bioaesthetic" issues?

1. Unusual Character of the Ecosystem

This might be less precisely called "biological uniqueness." This would acknowledge special areas such as sensitive bogs, erodable alpine tundra, and scenic deep forest; functionally important areas such as forest edges (ecotones) and communities along a river; or economically important areas such as habitats of hunted animals and merchantable timber forests. Any biological characteristic that elevates the need for protection in the ecosystem should be noted. However, no automatic conclusion is provided that the ecological area should or should not be impacted. Rather, the decision maker can weigh biological losses against societal gains if the area were to be impacted.

Biologically unusual or unique areas and characteristics confer a special significance. Such character does not in itself indicate whether added value is attributed by society. For instance, a patch of virgin forest in an otherwise cut-over region may be interpreted as highly valuable, while a patch of second growth forest in the same location or a patch of abandoned farmland in an otherwise densely forested region may not be. Biologists often think species or ecosystems are most interesting at the edges of their geographic range; society may not. Noting unique factors that might escape the untrained eye is an obligation of the EIS. Proposing the decision whether or not to impact is not. Society still may opt for protecting the unusual or enhancing the ordinary. In either case, the readers have more information on which to found their decisions on the impact's acceptability.

2. Biological Fitness

One should note the presence or potential of any existing retarding forces that reduce the health and vigor of the ecosystem. Presence of such factors as severe insect infestations, forest or animal diseases, or erosion can reduce the biological significance of a site even if it is otherwise valuable. A major fire could reduce fitness in a fire intolerant community. The EIS must assess the severity and permanence of the factor reducing fitness even though that factor is not causally related to the proposed action. A site may be so debilitated that the proposed impact is considered desirable. To the extent that diversity of ecological components conveys a degree of stability or fitness, measures of species diversity and evenness should be reported and interpreted. Ecosystems of lower fitness may be less valuable to protect from permanent loss. They also might recover more

slowly from a temporary impact such as a construction lay-
down area.

3. Ecosystem Productivity

Ecosystems function at rates determined in part by
soil fertility, what species are present, and related
factors. The rate of growth or function can be scaled in
a variety of ways, e.g., grams of carbon fixed, exchanged,
and stored, or in terms of production of quantities of
plants or animals. If the products of the community are
harvested, productivity may be scaled as deer taken,
hunter hours spent, tourist dollars spent, board feet,
pounds of milk, tons of grain, etc. Quality of products
should also be quantified as appropriate. Productive
areas are most costly to lose permanently to a proposed
development, but they may also respond more vigorously
after a temporary impact.

4. Biological Persistence

If a site is not to be obliterated, but must sustain
a repeated or presumably sublethal impact, then its
expected inertia, elasticity, and resiliency should be
described. Incorporating components of productivity and
fitness, the relative capacity to thrive under impact
should guide choices among alternative locations for
development and choices of acceptable forms and
intensities of impacts.

5. Biological Replacement Time

Ecosystems change by succession of community types,
for instance, from grassland through several stages to
climax forest. Thus, each stage has a replacement time
through natural succession that includes, at a minimum,
the length of time each preceding stage must persist
precursorily to the growth time for that stage. In the
northeastern United States, one might expect the following
replacement times: grassland, 1-5 years; shrub community,
10-20 years; evergreen forest, 40-100 years; and climax
hardwood, 100-400 years, assuming no intermediate stages
are skipped. Aquatic ecosystems proceed through similar
successional stages. If an area is to be cleared for a
temporary or low-value purpose, early ecological stages
would likely be chosen. A later successional stage might
be more easily justified for a permanent installation than
for a temporary disruptive use. Decision makers may
differ in the value they assign to each ecological stage
depending on the prevalence of each community type in
their region, but such information still can guide their
decision. It should be noted that through a variety of
management techniques resource managers can accelerate,
stop, or reverse ecological succession. Decisions on

mitigation of impact may take advantage of such managerial control.

6. "Bioadministrative" Issues

Society may choose to place special value on certain areas, e.g., wilderness areas; wildlife or forest refuges; cultural, historical, or aesthetic sites; agricultural districts; wetlands; or the breeding and feeding habitats of certain species. For instance, it may say, "We like to have song birds present" or "We wish to afford extra protection to redwood forests" or "Shorelines shall be developed for public use rather than for private interests." These are different sorts of statements, but all assign disproportionate importance to an ecosystem or ecosystem component for their considered social value rather than for biological value (in contrast to criterion 1 above). Zoning laws, public park designations, and endangered species laws are examples in which biological entities are assigned a value by administrative means. Thus, the citizens through their legal system give prior and, to varying extents, overriding protection to such designated units. Such societal designations, made in advance of a given application, must be accorded great, but not necessarily overriding, weight. EISs, then, must review all existing bioadministratively designated areas or components.

Certain species of plants and animals that are threatened with extinction due to loss of habitat or to the precariously low number of remaining individuals are accorded special protection through endangered species laws promulgated by the federal government and many states. Society made a critical distinction in assigning special value to these certain species and this must be respected to slow the rate of man-caused extinctions. Decision makers must weigh the relative values (to society) of the proposed action and the impact of that action on the vulnerable species. The EIS must provide reasoned discussion so that the species' value is not inferred simply by its presence on the endangered species list.

Most guidelines for preparing an EIS place endangered species at the top of the priority list for required sections (e.g., Canter, 1977). However, endangered species can be overemphasized. True, extinction is permanent; and, equally true, value of a proposed action is comparatively temporary. But endangered species have an assumed importance because they are designated species. Some listed species are of greater biological significance than others; some of greater social significance than others. An obscure subspecies of a common species (e.g., the Block Island meadow mouse) may be of less biological importance than a prominent unique species (e.g., the peregrine falcon). One has only to consider the misuse of

the snail darter by critics of the Tellico Dam as a
surrogate focal issue to stop construction when cost and
feasibility were the major and more arguable issues.
Endangered species are designated by society--that is,
they are accorded a bioadministrative distinction.
Currently, the California condor, the eastern bluebird,
and the gray wolf are being accorded greater weight in
decision making.

There are no firm rules or guidelines to establish
levels of justifiable weighting to be assigned to each
bioadministrative unit. Indeed, none should be devised.
Each case is arguable and should be reviewed in the
context of local and regional value systems. In general,
any biological entity to which society has given prior
distinction is a potential bioadministrative issue and
should be accorded a different sort of analysis in the EIS
than that applied in the preceding criteria.

7. "Bioaesthetics"

Society derives pleasure from scenic beauty, forest
majesty, historical significance of an old tree,
occasional sightings of a colorful bird, and so on. While
not trained to analyze why society has certain tastes, the
biologist may be able to determine to what organism(s) and
to what extent aesthetic values are assigned. The
function of the biologist preparing an EIS is not to
assign aesthetic value to environmental components but to
determine from others what factors are valued and to what
extent and, then, to place these into the contexts of the
wider region and a long time frame. These contexts will
determine the degree of emphasis aesthetic issues will be
given in the EIS.

As noted above, resource managers today can control
ecological succession. Thus, if society determines it
desires certain ecosystems, it is possible to varying
degrees for the managers to provide them. The EIS writer
should discuss habitat modifications, mitigation, and
necessary rehabilitation programs.

DISCUSSION

"Comprehension of an EIS should be accessible to the
general public" (Cheremisinoff and Morresi, 1977). Since
this is the case, the responsibilities of the writer are
great. Level and content of the EIS cannot be reduced,
but they can be made comprehensible by clear, well-
grounded reasoning, and sound evaluation of alternative
actions. Furthermore, public opinion helps dictate what
functions are considered compatible with the environment.
This means the professional scientist who contributes to
the EIS is responsible not only for scientific rigor in
description of the site but also wisdom in evaluating the
acceptability of the proposed action. For this reason,

Edington and Edington (1977) argue that the scientist, in furnishing such evaluations, is practicing outside his or her area of competence and such statements should be considered "public opinion" rather than "scientific opinion." Indeed, without a sound basis for reasoning about predicted impacts, the environmental specialist would, in fact, be little more than an informed layperson. Odum (1977) states, "There is much to be said for a procedure that combines a few carefully selected systems-level properties that monitor the performance of the whole . . . thus providing a far better basis for impact assessment." I propose that coupling selected integrative functional properties of the ecosystem with social questions involving those properties provides a vehicle to aid the environmental analyst to reason out the degree of acceptability of proposed actions.

In my work as an environmental analyst and a reviewer of EISs, I have found these criteria can provide the basis for a rigorous and well-reasoned decision on the proposed action because they are synoptic of both important biological factors and critical social issues. Beginning graduate students in environmental analysis classes have found that these criteria provided them immediately with a surprising level of sophistication and focus in analysis of illustrative ecosystems.

Similar sets of criteria in aquatic ecology have attempted to integrate biological and social issues. For instance, Truchan and Basch (1976) indicate they attempt to answer four questions:

1. Are there rare and/or endangered species affected?
2. Does the loss of organisms comprise a significant portion of the sport and/or commercial fish catch?
3. What is the ecological significance of such loss?
4. Will the population in the water body be affected?

While these questions do not fully achieve the breadth and predictive value of the above terrestrial "biosocial" criteria, it is immediately apparent how to apply the concepts of the "biosocial" criteria to achieve a more complete list of aquatic ecological criteria. Consider, for example, that pollution discharge engineers look upon the receiving water body as an integrator of effects; therefore, their attitudes about the discharge level of a pollutant are adjusted based on the characteristics of the receiving water body.

The biosocial criteria may be neither exhaustive nor free of complexity. However, they do provide a manageable framework for integrating scientific and social factors into comprehensive issues understandable to experts, the public, and the decision maker.

REFERENCES

Cairns, J., Jr. (1976), "Estimating the Assimilative
    Capacity of Water Ecosystems." In R. K. Sharma,
    J. D. Buffington, and J. T. McFadden (Eds.), The
    Biological Significance of Environmental Impacts.
    NR-CONF-002 (proceedings of the conference).
    Washington, D.C.: U.S. Nuclear Regulatory Commission.
Canter, L. W. (1977), "Prediction and Assessment of
    Impacts on the Biological Environment." In
    Environmental Impact Assessment. New York: McGraw-
    Hill.
Cheremisinoff, P. N., and Morresi, A. C. (1977),
    Environmental Assessment and Impact Statement
    Handbook. Ann Arbor, Mich.: Ann Arbor Science
    Publishers.
Cooper, W. E. (1976), "Ecological Effects." In R. K.
    Sharma, J. D. Buffington, and J. T. McFadden (Eds.),
    The Biological Significance of Environmental Impacts.
    NR-CONF-002 (proceedings of the conference).
    Washington, D.C.: U.S. Nuclear Regulatory Commission.
Edington, J. M., and Edington, M. A. (1977), Ecology and
    Environmental Planning. London: Chapman and Hall.
Inhaber, H. (1976), Environmental Indices. New York:
    Wiley Interscience.
Mellanby, K. (1978), "Biological Methods of Environmental
    Monitoring." In J. Lenihan and W. W. Fletcher
    (Eds.), Measuring and Monitoring the Environment,
    Vol. 7. Glasgow: Blackie Press, Environment and Man
    Series.
National Environmental Policy Act (1970), Public Law
    91-190.
Odum, E. P. (1977), "The Emergence of Ecology as a New
    Integrative Discipline." Science, 195(4284),
    1289-1293.
Risser, P. G. (1976), "Identification and Evaluation of
    Significant Environmental Impact on Terrestrial
    Ecosystems." In R. K. Sharma, J. D. Buffington, and
    J. T. McFadden (Eds.), The Biological Significance of
    Environmental Impacts. NR-CONF-002 (proceedings of
    the conference). Washington, D.C.: U.S. Nuclear
    Regulatory Commission.
Sharma, R. K., Buffington, J. D., and McFadden, J. T.
    (Eds.) (1976), The Biological Significance of
    Environmental Impacts. NR-CONF-002 (proceedings of
    the conference). Washington, D.C.: U.S. Nuclear
    Regulatory Commission.
Truchan, J. G., and Basch, R. E. (1976), "Michigan
    Regulatory Position on Impingement and Entrainment
    Effects and Their Determination." In L. D. Jensen
    (Ed.), Third National Workshop on Entrainment and
    Impingement. Section 316(b)--Research and Compliance
    Proceedings. New York: Ecological Analysts.
Ward, D. V. (1978), Biological Environmental Impact

Studies: Theory and Methods. New York: Academic
Press.

16. Organizational Environmental Management: The Los Alamos National Laboratory and Tennessee Valley Authority Experience

Shelby Smith-Sanclare

OVERVIEW

This paper provides a brief look at two environmental organizations. Using the Environmental Impact Statement (EIS) procedures, the paper compares the agencies' responses to critical areas within the procedure. It then discusses change from the EIS procedure to a broader environmental process and suggests that environmental quality is both a conceptual and managerial process.

Los Alamos National Laboratory (Los Alamos), the Tennessee Valley Authority (TVA), and other national laboratories and agencies have different organizational approaches for meeting environmental requirements. I will identify the agency structures in which the environmental roles function and describe the EIS procedure, locating the key concerns for Los Alamos and TVA. Finally, I will suggest changes in the process focus and a direction for the environmental process of the eighties.

Before continuing, however, there is one distinction I would like to make. A procedure leads to a specific product, an EIS or other environmental document, while a process is a continuing series of events (and perhaps products) that leads to environmental decision making. The procedures for environmentally related documents are formalized through regulations, while the process may be as varied as the organization instituting it.

LOS ALAMOS AND TVA ORGANIZATIONAL STRUCTURES

Los Alamos has environmental responsibility for about 27,000 acres of remote, high-altitude plateau that consists of a series of relatively narrow mesas separated by deep, steep-sided canyons. The six major vegetative complexes, from sub-alpine grassland through conifers to juniper grasslands, are fragile lands. They do not recover easily, if ever, from insult and require careful consideration when an action is proposed. These lands are bounded by national forest, park lands, and several Indian reservations, each with its own environmental requirements and multiple regulations and restrictions. Los Alamos has 6,800 employees, principally scientists and technicians, who conduct energy- and weapons-related research funded by

the Department of Energy (DOE). In any actions,
therefore, a potential exists for conflict between
national interests and regional impacts.
    Prior to 1979, Los Alamos was organized as a
traditional hierarchy. The bulk of the activity and
responsibility for environmental concerns resided in the
Health Division, specifically H-8 (Environmental
Surveillance Group), where traditional monitoring, data
gathering and interpretation, and response to governmental
regulations resided. DOE required Los Alamos to develop
an EIS for the laboratory's operations; H-8 began the
effort. A Laboratory Environmental Review Committee
(LERC) was formed by the director's office and consisted
of representatives from the division level: financial
management office, engineering, public relations, legal
liaison, and the associate director of research. Because
of the EIS responsibility, a representative from the
Health Division also sat on LERC.
    In addition to the EIS work, Los Alamos management
recognized the need for a more consistent and structured
approach to all environmental documents (environmental
reviews, assessments, etc.) that closely aligned with
other health and safety documents such as quality
assurance, air and water quality regulations, the
Occupational Safety and Health Administration (OSHA), the
National Institute of Occupational Safety and Health
(NIOSH), and so forth. A permanent position, the
Environmental Evaluations Coordinator (EEC), was created
within H-8. While reporting to the section and division
leaders in a traditional sense, the EEC also had the role
of acting as an at-large member of LERC, working closely
with the head of the committee, who represented the
director's office, and the various program offices and
divisions to coordinate environmental document development
and assure timely review through LERC. The EEC provided
early warning of changing trends, worked to set and
evaluate criteria, and coordinated the measures for
environmental performances. Not being aligned to a
program interest meant the EEC could reflect laboratory/
DOE policy and act as an impartial reviewer of a program
interest's potential environmental impact. No technical
staff was assigned to the EEC; nor was a budget.
Principal duties were staff coordinating, advising,
interpreting, and technical responsibility.
    In 1979, the management of Los Alamos changed to a
matrix structure; further integration of environmental
reporting was developed; and throughout the laboratory
procedures began that incorporated the various
environmental requirements. With the matrix-type
organization, an EEC and one or two assistants orchestrate
all the environmental requirements and activities. It
requires strong technical support services, competent
program response, and cooperation on all levels. Not
recognizing that particular actions trigger an

environmental requirement or refusing to include the EEC
in the early stages of program development creates the
opportunity for later conflict. The approach is strongly
personality dependent, requiring solid organization,
cooperation, and development skills. Traditional line
authority is not built into the position; the ideal of
total organizational commitment to environmental quality
is mandatory.

TVA has environmental responsibility for about
360,000 acres of reservoir land, a 170,000-acre
demonstration area (Land between the Lakes), and 40,000
acres of power properties, a total of 570,000 acres of
noninundated property. TVA recognizes that, as a unique
federal agency and the country's largest utility, its
influence extends to the seven-state, 41,000-square-mile
region and beyond. Its 50,800 employees span a range of
trades and labor and professional responsibilities that
has few, if any, counterparts in either industry or other
federal agencies. An agency reorganization in 1979
resulted in a six-office traditional structure that
reports to a general manager and a three-member,
presidentially appointed board of directors.

The concept for an Environmental Quality Staff (EQS)
developed in the Spring of 1979 and was implemented that
Fall. EQS was a policy-oriented, regulatory-familiar
group acting as TVA's environmental conscience. It
provided guidance for the National Environmental Policy
Act (NEPA) procedures, assisted with regulatory
requirements, made recommendations on existing or new
policy, and developed new initiatives, coordinating with
various program and project efforts.

EQS resides administratively within the Office of
Natural Resources (ONR) for many of the same reasons that
the EEC resides in the H-Division at Los Alamos. Data
gathering and interpretation, monitoring, and guidance for
regulations and permit applications exist as functions
within ONR. Until April 1981, EQS also had the same
across-office responsibility and reporting avenues to the
general manager's office that EEC did to LERC: a dual
tracking system through ONR to the general manager. Major
reorganizations within TVA have affected EQS. Currently,
the Director of Environmental Quality reports to the
Office of Natural Resources and Economic Development
(ONRED). The dual reporting line is lessened and
essentially remains a staff function. One important
difference now exists between TVA and Los Alamos
structures: ONRED administers programs through various
divisions. At Los Alamos, H-Group essentially provides a
direct service function. It is possible in TVA for other
offices, and also other divisions within ONRED, not to
distinguish the EQ role as a corporatewide, service
function comparable to law or planning and budget.
Without this understanding, "turf protecting" may occur,
resulting in lack of cooperation and openness. This fear

of lost program control discourages rather than welcomes a specialized staff service to help with complex and confusing rules and regulations. Also lost is EQ's creative problem-solving approach to potential or existing environmental conflicts. Reticence to seek EQ involvement is being mitigated by the intensive efforts of EQ to talk with each program group and to accumulate a series of examples that assure the programs of EQ's intent. A written NEPA procedure provides official guidance. (This document was approved by the board and transmitted to the Federal Register in July 1980.) TVA's policy and procedure for compliance interface was approved by the general manager in August 1980. Time, however, is required to develop a track record of accomplishments and build a rapport among all the offices and programs. To date, this effort has been reasonably successful.

In April 1980, the board gave additional responsibilities to EQ, primarily in compliance and in research and development. Now fully implemented and staffed, EQ is identified as a focus for environmental affairs in TVA and is recognized as the initial contact for outside agencies and groups. Authority also was given to implement an efficient, effective, and integrated environmental program. This included establishing environmental standards and commitments, determining the level of environmental review and the scope of EISs, review of assessment and compliance budgets, and setting specifications for monitoring and data gathering.

THE ENVIRONMENTAL IMPACT STATEMENT PROCEDURE

Figure 16.1 identifies five basic components of the EIS procedure and suggests a few critical areas for understanding the interactions that occur: beginning the procedure, scoping the requirements, preparing the document, reviewing the document and commitments, and implementing the intent.

BEGINNING THE PROCEDURE

Both Los Alamos and TVA identify the focal point for environmental responsibility (EEC, EQ); yet, in both organizations, the activity that requires the potential assessment or statement resides within the programs. Early involvement provides lead time for proper data development, document preparation, and review. It allows the necessary program adjustments if limiting environmental factors are placed on the activity. Should the environmental document be triggered by an antagonistic group outside the organization, conflicts can get out of proportion. Defensive postures develop. Sometimes conflicting pressures are applied to the program. If the project is approved, considerable cost overruns and time expansion occur and the program is not as successful as

Procedure Beginning	→	Scoping	→	Preparing EA or EIS	→	Reviewing and Commitments	→	Implementing
How was EIS triggered? What triggered EIS? When was EIS triggered?		Internal: Precision Level represented Policy implications External: Adversarial situations Issue identification Conflicts of values		Who Guidance Authority Funding		"Fox guarding the hen house"--who reviews? Commitments Incorporate change		Changes during Compliance monitoring Post-evaluation New projects for old problems

Figure 16.1 Basic components of EIS procedure.

envisioned. Every agency has its own unique examples.
One of the key sections in the EIS document is the
alternatives section. Its development should parallel the
development of the procedure. The alternatives range from
the broadest, "Which of several project alternatives did
you choose to meet your program goals?," to the most
common alternative, "Which of several sites did you select
for implementing the project?" Other alternatives occur
in building and equipment design, construction and
materials, or even the phasing of the project. The
environmental group, providing guidance on how to document
such decisions and giving insight into what environmental
procedures will be required of each alternative, precludes
later scrambling when the actual document is being
prepared for a site-specific action. Criteria for
environmental evaluation can be developed or applied as
the project is thought through, thus providing a framework
for decision making at each level.

In TVA, the procedure usually is triggered when the
program requests assistance or advice from the NEPA
individual in EQ assigned to that program office or when
the NEPA individual reviews the office programs and future
plans and notes the need for an EIS or EA. At Los Alamos,
the project leader contacts the EEC directly or, more
often, the engineering, construction, and design group
contacts the EEC because the project director files a job
request through engineering.

SCOPING THE REQUIREMENTS

Prior to the Council on Environmental Quality (CEQ)
regulations, scoping took place without public
participation, and in TVA often without proper internal
representation. Now, scoping is a mandated part of the
procedure and requires public participation. The first
step is an internal scoping that includes precise
information with experts participating. This initial
scoping determines the level of decision making required,
what policy is needed, and what level of data and
documentation will be necessary. When an organization
presents a project for agency and public participation, it
must be, as Stephen Kaplan suggested earlier in this
volume in his A Process-oriented Approach to Human
Concerns in Environmental Decision Making, at a clear and
nonexpert level of presentation. That can only occur if
the facts are clear and the pros and cons from the
project-advocate side are understood. The public scoping
contains potential for conflict if the project by its very
nature is controversial, the issues are not clearly
identified, or there is a conflict between the information
as it is presented and the information as it is perceived.
If the EEC or EQ is involved early, these areas are
anticipated and the organization is better prepared prior
to scoping meetings. In Los Alamos, the LERC provides a

mechanism for this in-house expertise; in TVA, a combined technical review group of EQ and program representatives serves this function. The public meeting function is carried out with the cooperation of the Citizen Action Office in TVA, while the combined efforts of the DOE regional and local offices and the Public Information Office at Los Alamos provide the forum for public participation.

PREPARING THE DOCUMENT

In both agencies the program or project group prepares the documents. Guidance is given by the EEC at Los Alamos and the NEPA coordinating group within EQ at TVA. Both philosophical and practical reasons exist for this approach. If the project or program group initiating the action has the principal responsibility for creating the environmental document, then they, knowing more precisely their program activity, can insure that the program decisions reflect environmental values and avoid potential environmental conflicts. They are, in fact, assuming environmental responsibility for their actions. Ideally, environmental costs can be attached to the corresponding programmatic actions. This does not always apply. For example, at Los Alamos the H-Division is budgeted to provide most of the data, evaluation, monitoring, and guidance as a service function. If a project requires special monitoring equipment because such data do not presently exist, there can be a conflict about which group provides the funds: the service group (H-Division), because that is its overall responsibility, or the project group, because the data are directly project related and are not immediately needed without the project activity. Another conflict occurs in a large project when the EEC and staff have to spend an unusual amount of time on one project, thus precluding activity on other projects or programs.

Because the budgeting for environmental staff and data services does not relate directly to projects and because neither the EEC nor H-8 has a project or program budget review function, there is not a close link between the allocation of environmental funds for individual projects and the overall service functions. In TVA, a project that spends funds for data acquisition and monitoring services budgets through the program office housing the project. At one time, EQ and PCS reviewed these assessment and compliance budgets to assure adequate environmental studies are budgeted by the program group to meet the information needs prior to document preparation. The groups providing services for programs resisted this three-way response to EQ environmental requirements and program needs, and this function has been omitted.

Budget responsibility, the only significant difference in the approach thus far mentioned, could not

withstand program opposition. This is not to imply that
controlling the purse strings is the only effective way to
assure an appropriate level of accountability for timely
environmental service. Close association among the three
interacting groups, however, could provide a clearer
understanding about the services required, the timeliness
of response expected, and the budget constraints imposed.
A moderating influence on any one group with unrealistic
demands could occur, but it did not withstand the early
testing of this authority.

REVIEWING THE DOCUMENT AND COMMITMENTS

Appropriate review of the EIS is critical. All
agencies are sensitive to charges of the fox guarding the
hen house. If the group that prepares the document
reviews and/or approves it as well, credibility of the
product may be lost and charges of conflict of interest
occur. Many argue, and it is tempting, that a one-step
group provides a more efficient and expedient way to
fulfill the environmental commitment. When budgets and
time are critical, it is difficult to argue effectively
against such an approach. Accountability is focused. The
EEC and EQ are subject to this pressure, too; but
isolation of the environmental function, loss of a sense
of environmental responsibility by the project group,
redundancy in hiring, and creation of paper mills are
compelling counterarguments.

The EEC guides preparation and recommends approval to
LERC after technical review is completed by the H-Division
groups and other operating divisions as needed. LERC
makes final approval before sending the document to the
director for signature and forwarding to DOE, which has
ultimate responsibility. In TVA, the EQ technical group
reviews the document before it is released with NEPA group
approval to the general manager's office for ultimate
board approval.

Document review is the time when commitments made for
environmental actions and mitigations are formally
identified and the continuing responsibility for
compliance is assigned. The compliance function in Los
Alamos remains in H-8, but persons other than the EEC,
specifically the quality assurance and safety analysis
people, assume responsibility. Likewise in EQ, the
compliance staff takes that responsibility. TVA's
procedure is formalized by the compliance interface
document, while at Los Alamos the procedure continues
informally, with the quality assurance and safety analysis
review staff using the notes prepared by the EEC as well
as the same files.

IMPLEMENTING THE INTENT

TVA has a reasonable degree of project review. A

procedure is in place to allow change in a project and
assure it remains faithful to environmental commitments.
A number of staff continue to track the project and work
with the design and construction changes as they occur to
ensure this success. In Los Alamos this potential exists
through the quality assurance and safety analysis review
programs. The environmental document is incorporated into
their subsequent documents; however, the number of staff
for this activity is limited.

Funding new actions necessary to deal with
unanticipated environmental problems created by a past
project is an area that only now is coming into focus. To
date, little post-project evaluation occurs in any agency.
With funds continuing to be restricted, new initiatives on
old projects remain low in priority. Los Alamos has
limited environmental staff, and the mechanism for such
activity is not yet in place. EQ has the potential for
such a program through their initiatives area. EQ can
identify an area for potential research and study using
its own research staff. Compliance staff may target
actions that need to be incorporated into a specific
program process. These two avenues are still in the
infant stage of development but are proceeding well.

This comparison of Los Alamos and TVA reveals
initially two fundamental differences: the staff size
dedicated to environmental activities and the budget
review authority. More important, however, is the
similarity of the two staffs. Both, armed with delegated
authority, still must rely on the program or project
office for early cooperation. (They are staff rather than
line functions.) Both require rigorous internal scoping
and provide guidance for document development. Document
preparation, review, and approval are separately housed
functions. Both Los Alamos and TVA are developing project
evaluation and future environmental initiatives for past
and future projects, but the realities of restricted
budgets limit these aspirations.

TOWARD THE EIGHTIES

During the early seventies, procedures were developed
that mandated the approach to NEPA requirements. Thinking
and documents quickly incorporated legally defensible
positions with reams of data and technical back-ups.
Along with that approach, a mitigation strategy for
projected adverse environmental effects was developed.
The organizational responses reported here represent this
focus. Better decisions certainly are possible with
better documentation. New and evolving approaches can be
developed only if sound, validated documentation can
indicate the rationale behind the proposed changes. Our
environmental awareness is rising. More people believe
environmental quality is a value to be incorporated in the
decision process. No one questions the value of clean

334

air, clean water, or a stable soil base. The questions
are more focused on such issues as real economic trade-
offs, degrees of harm and benefit, and willingness to
accept the levels of required risk. Such questions as who
benefits and who pays are heard.

Arbitration as an approach to environmental
requirements is beginning to receive attention. It was
first used by labor negotiators and later by environmental
groups seeking common grounds of agreement. Organizers of
the 1980 American Law Institute-American Bar Association
course on environmental law incorporated several speakers
experienced in applying arbitration techniques. Donald
Straus of the American Arbitration Association spoke, as
did William Futrell, on mediation alternatives. (See also
the August 1980 issue of Planning for an article on
RESOLVE, the Center for Conflict Resolution founded in
1977.) Scoping requirements in the CEQ regulations
present a greater opportunity for arbitration.
Arbitration becomes the strategy of first choice at the
time of scoping. Mitigation becomes a contingency
strategy dependent on the results of that arbitration.
More attention will be paid to this area in the future,
and organizations will incorporate this role with the
other environmental activities. More emphasis, too, is
being placed on the alternatives considered. A wider
range of options than the action or no action or site
selection alternative is being stressed. Questions are
being raised. How does this project alternative fit in
relation to the total corporate program effort? How does
the product of this project meet organizational goals?
How, if this project is successful, will it not only
affect the environment of this corporate domain but also
influence the environment of the state, region, or nation?
Decision making affects the specific project and the
program development for the corporation. These issues
need debate and policy decision at the uppermost
management level. Currently, technical staff review the
issues and debate the consequences of specific project or
program actions, but they do not perform the management
and policy roles I speak about.

THE CORPORATE ENVIRONMENTAL ROLE

The symposium for which this paper was prepared was
convened to discuss ways to ensure greater quality and
utility of scientific and technical information in EISs.
Here I have discussed various procedures to do that; but
these are procedures, one step in a larger environmental
process, a process that incorporates environmental
concepts in to decision making. The environmental role
must have a broader scope than a single project or program
effort, more than EA or EIS generation. It must be one of
the principal inputs into corporate management and
decision making. The process provides a conceptual

framework within which corporate and program decisions are developed. Thus, the environmental role must be a process that aids the organization in achieving its corporate or public policy objectives.

I do not advocate environmental efforts becoming the endpoint or target of corporate decision making. Nor do I suggest that environmental concerns be the vehicle through which company- or agency-selected strategic concepts are implemented. To compartmentalize the environment in so neat a package, to create a program whereby the environment becomes a single program vying for its place in the corporate sun, is to compromise its usefulness and effectiveness. Rather, I advocate that environmental concerns take the part of a missile guidance system providing the adjusting, guiding, and feedback roles necessary to assure that the corporate mission achieves targeted objectives within the framework of a quality environment.

In addition to this conceptual role, the environmental process must include another corporate-level function, that of program and project design. If the environmental role becomes a process, the design of projects will incorporate environmental considerations at the beginning rather than forcing an end-of-the-product mitigation to comply with NEPA and other environmental regulations. If arbitration is used during the scoping process now required by CEQ to identify trade-off values and if it replaces mitigation as a primary principle of operation, then objectives can be adjusted in the least costly stage. Areas that cannot be adequately mitigated are also identified early, and potentially infinite costs are weighed against the true need for the project. An organization will not try to place band-aid solutions on cut-artery problems. These are issues, if faced early, that may make a significant change in approach.

Each person working to improve the quality and utility of scientific and technical information is providing information for decision making. This focus is usually a single project. The project requires diverse talents and resources located throughout an organization, usually in several different line-managed areas. The information developed for these purposes translates as a staff function. The most efficient way to handle the requisite environmental products seems to be through this staff function or a matrix management system. Sometimes, an environmentally sensitive manager is selected to meet the demands of environmental issues and oversee the production requirements. But that project and product are only part of the overall environmental impact the organization is creating by its decisions. A quality environment cannot be achieved unless the improved information is used to support strong, upper-level decision making. Thus, environmental quality must be translated from a concept backed by data to a managerial

process backed by philosophy or orientation.
What I am advocating is not simply environmentally
sensitive management. Instead, environmental managers
must assume a more prominent position in the highest
organizational levels. Environmental quality is both a
conceptual and management process. It must be in place
and supported by strong corporate decision making as well
as sound technical and programmatic staffs producing
impact documents and complying with environmental
regulations.
     At Los Alamos, the EEC staff function resides in a
service organization. Constant contact with top
management provides some influence, but the focus is still
product related, not corporate decision related. The
product is provided so the organization may carry out its
proposed mission within legally prescribed boundaries.
That mission is not decided with the help of an
environmental manager who discusses corporate
environmental impacts, costs, etc. The EEC is not part of
the strategic management of the laboratory. The
environmental issues become considerations in response to
decisions already made. Potentially defensive, reactive
postures are created by the relationship established in
the decision-making process. Likewise, EQ, although
staffed with more professionals having policy functions
and budget review, is not a corporate decision maker. The
line function of the environmental manager is from the
natural resources program through the environmental
director to the staff who produce environmental products
as a service function to the agency. The staff-advisory
and line-productive roles are traditional in most
organizations. It is beyond the scope of this
presentation to elaborate on a proposed new method of
environmental management. I suggest, however, that the
traditional staff role for environmental issues is not
appropriate if we desire more effective corporate
environmental responsiveness. We must encourage and
support the acceptance of environmental managers who
function as corporate strategic managers as well as direct
producers of environmental products. The precedent for
this dual role exists in the legal, financial, and
administrative areas of strategic management. Matrix
management and other styles that incorporate a broader
spectrum of decision makers provide the easiest entrance.
The true challenge is to identify the environmental
management role in the most traditional management
structure and provide through that role an effective
corporate response to environmental issues.

PART 4

Analysis and Case Study

INTRODUCTION

This last grouping of papers contains a variety of retrospective analyses and case studies by academic observers, EIS practitioners, and state-level governmental decision makers. Stuart L. Hart, in "The Costs of Environmental Review: Assessment Methods and Trends," traces the relationship between the maturation of the Environmental Impact Statement (EIS) process and its associated costs at the state and federal levels; Hart also documents the relationships between overall project cost and the stage at which an EIS is prepared and mitigative measures adopted. Granville H. Sewell and Susan Korrick trace the improvement of the scientific quality in environmental assessment in "The Fate of EIS Projects: A Retrospective Study." These two overviews document not only changes in the scope of the process and the implications of those changes but also suggest the changed expectations associated with the use of the process.

Lloyd C. Irland offers a case study of spruce budworm control in Maine as a medium for suggesting improvements to the EIS process. Irland's examples of day-to-day realities that frustrate mandated EIS procedures--and vice versa--provide reminders of the need to temper environmental policy objectives with organizational capabilities and ecosystem realities, especially when each operates according to its own, often intractable, schedule.

Three state-level case studies conclude the chapter. Dennis Lundblad describes Washington's experience with "The Interface between Federal and State EIS Requirements: An Overview." Samuel G. Mygatt summarizes the uses of scoping in the Massachusett's EIS experience; Sharon Decker explains how the Massachusetts' experience was used in "Changing the Environmental Review Procedure in Minnesota."

Following this chapter, after a review of recent changes in EIS procedures, the editors present overall conclusions from the many presentations made at the symposium and those reworked for this book. Their observations of the EIS process, current research, and emerging techniques combine to suggest certain future directions for environmental assessment and form a basis for an expression of their preferred future for such assessment.

17. The Costs of Environmental Review: Assessment Methods and Trends

Stuart L. Hart

OVERVIEW

An often cited criticism of environmental programs in general and Environmental Impact Statement (EIS) programs in particular is that such activities encourage excessive government spending and impede economic growth. But while much attention has been given to the assessment of the costs and benefits of pollution-control programs, little effort has been made to analyze or measure the costs of the EIS process. The staff of the Research and Decision Center, therefore, sought to close this gap by examining the costs of the EIS process of the 18 "mini-NEPAs," or state environmental policy acts (SEPAs).

As an aid to understanding the full costs of the EIS process, an EIS Cost-accounting System was developed; the costs are arrayed in a matrix that provides a graphic display of where costs are incurred, what form they take, and how they interrelate. There are, however, many difficulties associated with any attempt to operationalize the system to assess EIS costs: since a major goal of all EIS requirements is to make environmental analysis a routine and integral part of agency operations, it may not be possible to determine exactly the full and separable cost of EIS activities (witness the many other similar environmental requirements that are mandated simultaneously). The effort becomes even more difficult since most agencies do not keep detailed or standardized records of EIS-related costs and have no internal mechanism for evaluating the relative merit of the various types of EIS-related expenditures. Given the many theoretical and practical pitfalls, a comparative case-study approach was chosen as the most appropriate.

Since most states have incurred significant problems in initial program implementation (e.g., project backlog, procedural restructuring, and delay), the costs of environmental review can be usefully expressed in terms of a program "curve"--states appear to experience an initial period of program establishment followed by a transition period of process clarification and backlog processing.

Gradual program "maturation" results in a stabilization of the number of actions requiring EISs at a reduced level relative to the initial and transition periods. Furthermore, fewer EISs are prepared relative to the number of Negative Declarations, suggesting that the trend is toward greater use of the Negative Declaration to achieve mitigation of impacts and away from litigation to achieve delay or injunction.

Two major conclusions are suggested by the analysis of state and federal programs of environmental review: (1) most actions or decisions do not require the preparation of EISs and (2) the costs of environmental review are generally insignificant when compared to other accepted planning, design, and regulatory costs.

Assessing EIS costs contains an implicit "catch-22:" since a major goal of all such programs is to make environmental analysis an integral part of agency operations, the costs associated with such activities become harder to identify as environmental considerations are better integrated into planning and decision making. Thus, a "successful" EIS program is defined, in part, by its inability to be evaluated accurately in terms of economic efficiency. Despite this, both the current emphasis on improving the efficiency of environmental analysis and the trend toward fiscal restraint suggest that a more in-depth analysis of EIS costs might be appropriate. However, given the relatively small magnitude of EIS-related costs indicated by this study, a more rigorous assessment may not be worth the cost. This is a dilemma that all EIS practitioners will have to wrestle with in the near future.

INTRODUCTION

An often cited criticism of environmental programs in general and EIS requirements in particular is that such activities encourage excessive government spending, impede economic growth, and contribute to unemployment. But while much attention has been given to the assessment of the costs and benefits of pollution control programs (e.g., Council on Environmental Quality (CEQ), 1973; Freeman, 1979; Portney, 1977) and the economic impact associated with such programs (e.g., CEQ, 1978; Data Resources, Inc., 1979), little effort has been made to analyze or measure the costs—let alone the benefits—attributable to the EIS process established by NEPA more than a decade ago. Indeed, most research pertaining to EIS programs to date has focused either on the procedural and decision-making aspects (e.g., Anderson, 1973; Andrews, 1976; Jain and Hutchins, 1978; Liroff, 1976) or the methodological aspects of impact assessment (e.g., Holling, 1978; Leopold, 1971; March, 1978; Warner, 1974). Although the CEQ (1975, 1976) attempted to document EIS-related costs within federal agencies, the lack of an

overall evaluation framework resulted in problems of data
comparability due to the diversity of agency accounting
systems; indeed, many agencies had no established method
for determining such costs because the EIS process had
become so intertwined with other planning procedures and
regulatory requirements. Further, the use of individual
agency cost estimates did not provide a structured view of
the relative costs associated with various program
functions (e.g., preparation, administration,
coordination, and review). Work initiated by Enk (1976),
therefore, sought to close this methodological gap; the
published results of this research (Hart and Enk, 1980)
form the basis for the approach, information, and
conclusions presented in this paper. Some closing
observations are also offered regarding the current trends
toward improving the quality and utility of EISs and
achieving greater fiscal responsibility.

Since the signing of NEPA on January 1, 1970,
eighteen states have initiated similar comprehensive,
environmental review programs utilizing EISs as the key
implementing provision. (See Hart and Enk, 1980, for a
description of the actual programs.) Using these state-
level programs as "laboratories" to supplement the
existing analyses of the federal experience, the form,
extent, and evaluational difficulties of EIS-related costs
are examined.

THE NATURE OF THE COSTS OF THE EIS PROCESS

Before embarking on an exploration of environmental
assessment costs, it is important to understand the full
spectrum of costs associated with such efforts in both the
public and private sectors. To this end, an EIS Cost-
accounting System has been developed that provides a
graphic display of where these costs are incurred, what
form they take, and how they interrelate (Table 17.1).
Since a major goal of all EIS requirements is to make
environmental analysis a routine and integral part of
agency operations, however, it is seldom feasible to
determine directly the full cost of EIS activities.
Estimates of the order of magnitude of such costs are,
nonetheless, both possible and desirable.

The matrix approach used in the EIS Cost-accounting
System may be applied to an individual project or on a
program basis at any level of government by simply
choosing the applicable participants in the vertical
column; these include the EIS-responsible agency, project
originating agency, review agency, clearinghouse agency,
private applicant, and citizen/consumer. Definitions of
these participants are provided at the bottom of the
matrix. The spectrum of potential cost areas is arrayed
beneath each participant listing in Table 17.1. Thus, for
example, at the state level there may be separate EIS-
responsible and clearinghouse agencies and several review

TABLE 17.1
EIS cost-accounting system

Function	Cost Element							
	Administration of the Law	EIS Preparation	EIS Review	EIS Distribution and Circulation	Delay			Mitigation
					Inflation	Opportunity	Uncertainty	
EIS Responsible Agency[1]								
Salaries:								
Administration/management[2]	+		+	+				
Review staff			+					
Clerical staff[3]	+		+	+				
Consultants	+		+					
Legal counsel and litigation	+							
Hearings (on rules and regulations)	+							
Staff training	+							
Public information and assistance	+		+	+				
Overhead[4]	+		+	+				
Equipment, materials, and telephone	+		+	+				
Office space[5]	+		+	+				
Travel	+		+	+				
Total Dollar Cost								

| | Cost Element | | | | | | | |
| | Administration of the Law | EIS Preparation | EIS Review | EIS Distribution and Circulation | Delay | | | Mitigation |
Function					Inflation	Opportunity	Uncertainty	
Project Originating Agency⁶								
Salaries:								
Administration/management		+	+			+	+	+
EIS preparation staff		+				+	+	+
Incoming EIS review staff		+	+			+	+	+
Clerical staff		+	+			+	+	+
Consultants		+	+			+	+	+
Legal counsel and litigation		+	+			+	+	+
Hearings (on projects)		+	+			+	+	+
Overhead		+	+	+		+	+	+
Equipment, materials, and telephone		+	+	+		+	+	+
Office space		+	+	+		+	+	+
Travel		+	+			+		
Total Dollar Cost			+					
Review Agency⁷								
Salaries:								
Administration/management			+					+
EIS review staff			+					+
Clerical staff								+

Table 17.1 (cont.)

Function	Cost Element							
	Admini- stration of the Law	EIS Prepa- ration	EIS Review	EIS Distri- bution and Circu- lation	Delay		Uncer- tainty	Miti- gation
					Infla- tion	Oppor- tunity		
Consultants			+					+
Legal counsel and litigation			+					+
Overhead			+					+
Equipment, materials, and telephone			+					+
Office space			+					+
Travel			+					+
Total Dollar Cost								
Clearinghouse Agency*								
Salaries:								
Administration/management				+				+
Staff (EIS collection and distribution)				+				+
Clerical staff				+				+
Overhead				+				+
Equipment, materials, and telephone				+				+
Office space				+				+
Travel				+				+
Total Dollar Cost								

Function	Administration of the Law	EIS Preparation	EIS Review	EIS Distribution and Circulation	Delay			Mitigation
					Inflation	Opportunity	Uncertainty	
Private Applicant' (if any)								
Staff (prepare documents, supply information)		+			+	+	+	+
Clerical staff		+			+	+	+	+
Consultants		+			+	+	+	+
Legal counsel and litigation		+			+	+	+	+
Overhead					+	+	+	+
Equipment, materials, and telephone		+			+	+	+	+
Office space		+			+	+	+	+
Travel		+			+	+	+	+
Total Dollar Cost					+	+	+	+
Citizen/Consumer[10]								
Donated time			+					+
Consultants			+					+
Legal counsel and litigation			+					+
Equipment, materials, and telephone			+					+
Travel			+					+

Cost Element

Table 17.1 (cont.)

Function	Cost Element							
	Administration of the Law[1]	EIS Preparation[2]	EIS Review	EIS Distribution and Circulation[3]	Delay			Mitigation
					Inflation	Opportunity	Uncertainty	
Added cost of goods and services								+/−
Total Dollar Cost			+		+/−	+	+	+
Summary								
Added cost of goods and services (borne by consumer)					+/−	+	+	+/−
Final public project construction cost					+/−	+		+/−
Final private project construction cost					+/−	+	+	+/−

[1] The agency responsible for implementing the SEPA and overseeing other involved agencies. Term is used interchangeably with "coordinating agency."

[2] Managers and supervisors of those staff persons doing the actual EIS preparation, review, and circulation work.

[3] Personnel assigned to record keeping, typing, filing, etc.

[4] Includes both indirect expenses (i.e., heat, lights, etc.) and personnel benefits.

⁵All personnel assigned to EIS work require office space. This is a direct cost attributable to the EIS process and applied to both public and private agencies.

⁶An agency that undertakes projects of the nature that would require an EIS as mandated by the SEPA.

⁷An agency that does not originate statements on projects with significant environmental effect but, rather, reviews EISs that are submitted by other agencies.

⁸The agency responsible for the review of procedures of the SEPA by acting as a collection and distribution center for EISs.

⁹A private developer that needs government approval of some sort for a proposed project and may, therefore, be responsible for an EIS under SEPA.

¹⁰The EIS process frequently involves concerned citizens and citizen groups affected by a proposed project. In participating in the EIS review process, these citizens incur both direct expenses as well as the indirect but real expense represented by their expenditure of time. In addition, the consumer will pay higher prices for goods and services when the EIS process adds to project costs and these costs are passed along in higher prices.

agencies, while at the local level all of these functions might be performed by a single agency.

The matrix arrays the cost elements of environmental review against the public and private bodies involved in the EIS process. Eight elements are displaced at the top of the matrix; the presence or absence of costs as well as their potential for being positive or negative factors is determined by following either a given function across the matrix or a given cost element down the matrix. Thus, for example, inflation may result in either a cost (+) or a savings (-) to a private applicant preparing an EIS, depending upon certain circumstances.

Although eight headings are shown at the top of the matrix, these can be arranged into the following four principal elements of cost:

1. *Document preparation, review, circulation, and administration of the law.* This category (the first four headings on the matrix) includes the preparation cost of EISs, Negative Declarations, and other environmental documents as well as the supporting tasks related to the distribution and review of these documents by appropriate agency personnel and members of the public. Administration of the law pertains to the development of policies and principles for the SEPA statute. This would include, for example, the cost of promulgating rules and regulations, suggesting amendments to the statutes, training of staff, and informing the public as to what the law requires. These costs are incurred by both the private applicant and the public on private projects while public projects entail costs to the public sector only. Estimating these costs involves either obtaining budget and/or cost-accounting data or assessing personnel time commitments (the costs of which often do not appear in any budget). This category of cost constitutes the major focus of the cost analysis conducted in this study.

2. *Delay.* The cost of delay attributable to the EIS process has two components: inflation and opportunity costs.
   - Inflation is the increase in cost due to a time of generally rising prices for goods and factors of production. If construction is delayed during an inflationary period because of the EIS process, the cost of that construction may rise during the delay period. The developer will thus pass along his or her increased costs to the consumer. If the consumer's disposable personal income does not rise as fast as the general price level, then the increased cost of the developer's product

will represent a real added cost to the consumer.
- Opportunity costs are those accruing to an investor whose money might have been used in alternative ways. For both private and public projects, a delay caused by the EIS process may result in foregone net benefits or revenues from a project.

3. *Uncertainty*. The EIS process adds an element of administrative uncertainty to the completion schedule of a proposed project and this uncertainty has consequences in terms of costs. Because the probability of eventual project approval cannot be established quantitatively, the developer often will require a higher rate of return on his or her investment. The cost of abandoned projects or projects never initiated because of uncertainty must also be recovered or amortized, and this applies to public as well as private projects. These added costs must be passed along to the consumer in order to maintain the profitability of the project.

4. *Mitigation*. The EIS process may result in requiring the public or private developer to moderate the impact of the proposed project. The process of achieving mitigation often adds administrative as well as planning, engineering, and architectural expense. However, in order to estimate the net costs associated with such environmental review, one must also consider the monetary benefits associated with the mitigation of impacts. Mitigation (like inflation) may, therefore, increase or decrease the final cost of the project.

Thus, while the costs of delay, uncertainty, and mitigation are real and may be significant, they are exceedingly difficult to calculate and, for this reason, have been largely omitted from this cost analysis. Consequently, the analysis focuses on the costs of program administration and document preparation, circulation, and review. Calculating these costs, however, is no simple task, either, since there are many stumbling blocks associated with such measurement efforts; these measurement difficulties are the topic of the next section.

PROBLEMS IN ASSESSING EIS-RELATED COSTS

Given the complexity of EIS-related costs, it may not be possible to determine the exact costs of environmental review programs. Indeed, assessing EIS costs contains an implicit "catch-22:" since a major goal of all such programs is to make environmental analysis a routine and

integral part of agency operations, the costs associated
with such activities become harder to identify as
environmental considerations are better integrated into
agency decision making. Thus, a "successful" EIS program
is defined, at least in part, by its inability to be
evaluated accurately in terms of economic efficiency.

Any attempt to assess the costs unique to the EIS
process poses several classical analytic difficulties.
These include:

1. *The problem of prior passage.* Many agencies
developed environmental procedures prior to the
passage of EIS laws. For example, the
U.S. Forest Service developed procedures in
accordance with laws passed prior to NEPA; the
EIS requirement simply elaborated upon the older
management system. How does one go about
distinguishing those efforts from similar
requirements mandated by EIS programs?

2. *Separability questions.* All agencies are
responsible for complying with a plethora of
environmental laws requiring specific analyses.
Often the content of specific regulatory laws
overlaps with the broad concerns covered by EIS
procedures. The Federal Water Pollution Control
Act Amendments and the Endangered Species Act are
two good examples of this. Furthermore, multilevel EIS requirements (i.e., NEPA-SEPA) often
blur the responsibilities unique to either of the
two individual mandates.

3. *Accounting anomalies.* Most agencies do not keep
detailed records of EIS-related costs; nor do
they have established mechanisms for evaluating
the merit of various types of EIS-related
expenditures. In the absence of budgetary line
items, the activities of EIS preparation and
review often become so intermixed with other
related activities (e.g., preliminary design,
site review, and permit application) that
determining separable costs may not be possible.
For those agencies that do attempt to calculate
EIS costs, there is little consistency in their
methods; for example, some agencies may include
only the costs of EIS review while others will
include preparation as well as review costs.

In addition to the above analytical difficulties,
there is also a critical operational impediment to
determining EIS costs: few states have appropriated
meaningful sums of money for EIS requirements. Despite
this widespread lack of appropriations, however, the costs
of minimum compliance exist and must be internalized
within existing agency programs. This is usually
accomplished in one of the following three ways:

(1) shifting funds from other program operating budgets;
(2) shifting staff time from other funded programs; or
(3) placing additional responsibilities on existing staff.
Thus, in order to gain an accurate image of the real costs
of environmental review, it is critical to identify and
estimate the amount of staff time and resources "borrowed"
from other sources.

Recognizing and acknowledging all of these problems,
Hart and Enk (1980) attempted to assess certain public-
sector costs of environmental review to serve as an
indicator for the overall program costs. The analytical
approach taken was one of comparative case-study; given
the analytic and operational pitfalls outlined above, a
more survey-oriented approach was deemed inappropriate.
Given the time constraints of the study, the investigation
was limited to the agency in each state responsible for
coordinating the EIS program, and the one or two most
active project-originating agencies. It was not possible
to assess the costs of each EIS prepared, and it was not
considered desirable to estimate overall costs by using an
"average" EIS figure and multiplying by caseload since the
costs of EISs are so highly variable.

THE COST OF ENVIRONMENTAL REVIEW

Of all aspects of environmental review, the costs of
administering and coordinating the program are the easiest
to estimate since they are usually incurred by a central
core of staff. States vary considerably in the amount of
effort invested by the coordinating agency in such
functions as guidelines preparation, program assistance,
and document review. That effort, whether funded by
appropriation of through "borrowed" time, is generally a
good indication of the overall level of program coverage
and implementation.

In Maryland, for example, where the state EIS program
applies only to state-level actions and the coordination
role is filled by the partial and unbudgeted commitment of
one person's time, coordinating costs have averaged only
$7,000-10,000 per year. At the other extreme is New York
State, where coordinating costs may run as high as
$700,000 annually; this does not include the costs to
localities of implementing EIS procedures as required
under the state act.

Unlike program coordination, the costs of document
preparation, circulation, and review are extremely
difficult to assess given the integrative nature of the
EIS process and the decentralized nature of agency and
public review. Since the magnitude of these costs varies
greatly, the only general statement that can be made
concerning preparation and review costs is that, with few
exceptions, states provide little, if any, additional
money for the execution of these very tangible and
sometimes expensive requirements. That is, most agencies

charged with the preparation or review of EISs receive no
additional staff or funding to perform these functions.
Despite the problems inherent in assessing EIS-
related costs, four states--California, Washington,
Wisconsin, and Minnesota--have attempted to determine the
total cost associated with their environmental review
programs. (The EIS Cost-accounting System should again be
consulted for a graphic display of where these costs are
incurred and how they interact.) Since any effort of this
sort requires a number of "leaps of faith" and is
necessarily based on a judgmental sample of the total
rather than on an exhaustive examination of every agency
and every project, the figures should be considered only
good indicators of cost magnitude rather than precise
documentation of actual costs. The following excerpts
provide a comparative capsule of the cost estimates
generated by the statewide studies (see Hart and Enk,
1980, for greater detail):

- In Wisconsin, where the EIS requirement applies
  only to actions directly undertaken, supported, or
  approved by state agencies, the estimated total
  cost of SEPA-related activity was $605,584 for the
  period July 1, 1974 to June 30, 1975. This
  entailed the preparation and review of 1,573
  screening documents and 65 preliminary
  environmental reviews (similar to draft EISs) or
  final EISs.
- In Minnesota, where the EIS requirement applies to
  major actions directly undertaken, supported, or
  approved by state agencies as well as major
  private actions of more than local significance,
  the total for the program from 1974 to December 1,
  1977 was estimated to be $2.5 million
  (approximately $625,000 per year), $300,000 of
  which was incurred by local governments. This
  entailed the preparation and review of 221
  preliminary assessments (75 percent prepared by
  localities) and 60 EISs (13 prepared by
  localities).
- In Washington, where the EIS requirement applies
  to all actions undertaken, sponsored, or approved
  by state and local agencies, approximately 80
  percent of the environmental documentation takes
  place at the local level. (In 1975, 168 EISs were
  prepared by localities as compared to 19 by state
  agencies.) The total estimated cost for this
  program was approximately $4.5 million per year,
  $1-2 million of this being incurred at the local
  level. Thus, while 80 percent of the EISs are
  prepared at the local level, less than one-third
  of the cost is incurred there since state projects
  tend to be much larger in scale.
- In California, where the EIS requirement also

applies to all actions undertaken, sponsored, or
approved by state and local agencies,
approximately 90 percent of the environmental
documentation takes place at the local level. (In
1974, 3,400 EISs were prepared by localities as
compared to only 200 by state agencies.) The
total estimated cost of this program is broken
down as follows:

State agencies	$ 7	million
Local government	$16.8	million
Private applicant	$10	million
Total cost per year	$33.8	million

When allowances for project delay, uncertainty,
and mitigation costs are included, the cost was
estimated to be in the range of $50-75 million per
year. Even including these rather large
allowances for economic conditions, however, this
represents about 0.5 percent of total project
costs, or $2-3 per capita annually.

TRENDS IN COST AND CASELOAD

EIS requirements tacitly assumed the existence of a
highly structured, well-coordinated, comprehensive
decision-making system into which environmental factors
could be incorporated. The lack of such organized
decision pathways in many situations, however, resulted in
project backlogs and necessitated considerable initial
expenditures aimed at reforming governmental practices so
as to foster the coordinated review of environmental
impact. In addition to these costs of initial
"restructuring," there was also the one-time expense of
establishing (often through the courts) an appropriate
policy of retroactive applicability (i.e., which existing
projects should, by virtue of their potential impact, be
required to comply with the EIS law despite the fact that
they were proposed prior to its passage).

Thus, in implementing EIS requirements, states
experienced an initial period of program establishment
followed by a transition period of process clarification
and backlog processing (see Figure 17.1). As states
gained more experience with their EIS programs, they
slowly emerged from the transition period; this maturing
process seemed to be characterized by two trends in
caseload--both of which had the indirect effect of
reducing program costs: (1) the overall number of actions
requiring EISs appeared to stabilize at a lower level than
that experienced during the transition period and
(2) fewer EISs were prepared relative to the number of
Negative Declarations. This cross-over in caseload
occurred during the transition period and generally
stabilized at a level of about 10-20 Negative Declarations

for every EIS prepared.

The former trend--the stabilization of the number of actions requiring EISs after the transition period--was prominent in several states, although it was most apparent in the pioneering SEPA states where limited experience resulted in problems (such as the "grandfathering" issue) that were carefully avoided by later state EIS programs.

At least partly responsible for the latter trend--the dramatic change in the ratio of EISs to Negative Declarations--was the growing emphasis placed on the preparation of programmatic or generic impact statements at both the state and federal levels. Widespread preparation of these program-level analyses greatly reduced the number of individual EISs required. The phenomenon may, however, also be at least partially attributable to the gradual attainment, by agencies and localities, of procedural compliance with the law. That is, by faithfully complying with all the procedural requirements of the law, agencies and project originators have effectively "beat the system" by proceeding with their projects as planned. The Negative Declaration with attached mitigative requirements, therefore, becomes the most practical (but not necessarily the best) means for achieving the substantive end of the law. The trend is thus toward greater use of the Negative Declaration to achieve mitigation of impacts and away from litigation to achieve delay or injunction.

CONCLUSIONS

Ignoring the estimated 80-90 percent of all actions that can be categorically exempted from the EIS process (e.g., maintenance and repair activities, minor new construction, routine permitting, etc.), the vast majority of actions with the potential for adverse environmental effects require only a preliminary environmental assessment to document the nonsignificance of their impact. Furthermore, there are 10-20 Negative Declarations issued for every EIS prepared. Since 80-90 percent of all actions can be categorically exempted from EIS requirements, this means that less than 1 percent of all state agency actions entail the preparation of an EIS. Moreover, evidence suggests that only a small fraction of these actions (at most one-fifth of 1 percent) encounter delay, litigation, or other complications. Thus, even a vast majority of actions on which an EIS is prepared receive routine approval following the review process (Hart and Enk, 1980).

Similar trends have been noted at the federal level where, out of the some 11,000 EISs prepared between 1970 and 1978, 1,052 lawsuits were filed but only 217 cases resulted in injunction (2 percent of all projects requiring EISs). These figures do not include the tens of thousands of projects for which EISs are not required

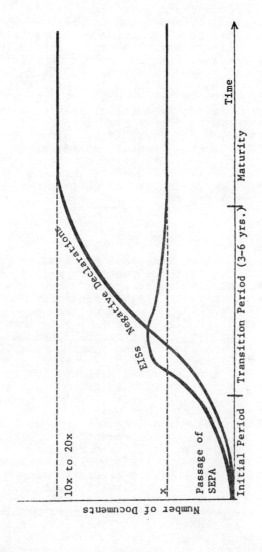

Figure 17.1 Generalized dynamic of caseload.

(CEQ, 1979). Thus, most actions or decisions do not require the preparation of Environmental Impact Statements.

With respect to cost, there is a great deal of variability among state programs; from an estimated $30,000 per year in Indiana to an estimated $30 million in California. However, it has been the experience in the states that, on the average, the EIS process constitutes only about 0.5 percent of project costs. At the federal level, this cost drops to as little as 0.1 percent of project costs, reflecting the larger scale of federal projects (U.S. General Accounting Office, 1977). A small-scale project may, however, incur EIS-related costs in excess of 1 or 2 percent since there is a minimum threshold cost of environmental review regardless of project size; controversy may also drive up the cost of EISs for large-scale projects. In general, though, the costs of environmental review appear to be insignificant when compared to other accepted planning, design, and regulatory costs.

OBSERVATIONS

The Environmental Impact Statement process has grown and evolved significantly over the past ten years since its inception. Now, in its second decade of use, the EIS process has moved from the initial implementation and transition stages of Figure 17.1 to the maturation functions of refinement and fine tuning. Key to this phase is a focus on improving both the quality and utility of the documents and the process. But, just as the overall assessment of EIS-related costs was complicated by many thorny theoretical and practical problems, so too is the assessment of the differential costs of "good" vs. "bad" analysis. Indeed, good scientific and technical information costs money—a fact that many practitioners fail to realize. At the same time, "good" science and "good" policy analysis are not the same thing; the former strives for full understanding, while the latter recognizes that reduction of uncertainty is the best that can be hoped for in making complex public decisions.

Indeed, rigorously conducted scientific analysis is often so costly and time-consuming that it cannot be used to provide policy-relevant input on many social problems. As Lindblom (1979) has stressed, formal analysis is only one method among several (e.g., ordinary knowledge, casual empiricism, and informal experimentation) for effectively gaining information relative to public decisions. A few analysts have begun to develop both the personal approaches (e.g., Schon, 1980) and the institutional apparatus (e.g., Holling, 1978) for melding scientific assessment with public sector administration. The cost implications of such refinements, however, are unclear. For example, since such approaches attempt to model the dynamics and impacts of alternative policies as simply as possible, the cost associated with the traditional lengthy description of existing conditions is greatly reduced. However, such approaches also require the continual reassessment and correction of initial expectations or predictions, thus entailing higher transaction costs for decision maker and scientist alike.

Such ambiguity coupled with the current fiscal situation (with the government calling for tighter evaluation of its activities and more tangible proof of the cost-effectiveness of its programs) would seem to suggest that a more in-depth analysis of EIS costs is appropriate. However, given the relatively small magnitude of EIS-related costs indicated by the foregoing analysis, a more rigorous, comprehensive assessment may not be worth the effort since the costs of such an effort may exceed any possible benefits derived from the added analytical resolution. This dilemma is, no doubt, one that all EIS practitioners will have to wrestle with.

REFERENCES

Anderson, F. (1973), NEPA in the Courts. Baltimore, Md.: The Johns Hopkins University Press.

Andrews, R. (1976), Environmental Policy and Administrative Change. Lexington, Mass.: D. C. Heath.

Council on Environmental Quality (1973), Environmental Quality: Fourth Annual Report of the CEQ. Washington, D.C.: GPO.

Council on Environmental Quality (1975), Environmental Quality: Sixth Annual Report of the CEQ. Washington, D.C.: GPO.

Council on Environmental Quality (1976), Environmental Impact Statements: An Analysis of Six Years' Experience by Seventy Federal Agencies. Washington, D.C.: GPO.

Council on Environmental Quality (1978), Environmental Quality: Ninth Annual Report of the CEQ. Washington, D.C.: GPO.

Data Resources, Inc. (1979), The Macro-economic Impact of Federal Pollution Control Programs: 1978 Assessment. Washington, D.C.: CEQ.

Enk, G. (1976), "The Economics of Environmental Impact Statements." Proposal submitted to the Rockefeller Foundation. Rensselaerville, N.Y.: The Institute on Man and Science. Available from the Research and Decision Center, Medusa, N.Y., 12120.

Freeman, M. (1979), Benefits of Air and Water Pollution Control: A Review and Synthesis of Recent Estimates. Washington, D.C.: GPO.

Hart, S., and Enk, G. (1978), Green Goals and Greenbacks: State-level Environmental Review Programs and Their

358

Associated Costs. Boulder, Col.: Westview Press.
Holling, C. S. (Ed.) (1978), *Adaptive Environmental Assessment and Management.* New York: John Wiley and Sons.
Jain, R., and Hutchins, B. (Eds.) (1978), *Environmental Impact Analysis: Emerging Issues in Planning.* Urbana, Ill.: University of Illinois Press.
Leopold, L., et al. (1971), *A Procedure for Evaluating Environmental Impact.* Geological Survey Circular 645. Washington, D.C.
Lindblom, C., and Cohen, D. (1979), *Usable Knowledge: Social Science and Social Problem Solving.* New Haven, Conn.: Yale University Press.
Liroff, R. (1976), *A National Policy for the Environment.* Bloomington, Ind.: Indiana University Press.
Marsh, W. (1978), *Environmental Analysis for Land Use and Site Planning.* New York: McGraw-Hill.
Portney, P. (Ed.) (1978), *Current Issues in U.S. Environmental Policy.* Baltimore, Md.: The Johns Hopkins University Press.
Schon, D. (1980), *The Reflective Practitioner.* Cambridge, Mass.: MIT, d manuscript.
U.S. General Accounting Office (1977), *The Environmental Impact Statement--It Seldom Causes Long Project Delays but Could Be More Useful if Prepared Earlier.* Washington, D.C.
Warner, M. (1974), *A Review of Environmental Impact Assessment Methodologies.* Washington, D.C.: U.S. EPA.

18. The Fate of EIS Projects: A Retrospective Study

Granville H. Sewell and Susan Korrick

A FUNCTIONAL PERSPECTIVE

This paper explores possible approaches for improving the Environmental Impact Statement (EIS) process by examining a collection of final EISs and the outcomes of the federal actions they advanced. Conversations with informed respondents during the tracing of outcomes also were used to provide insights.

From a procedural viewpoint, the EIS process begins with a series of documented decisions within a governmental agency and then broadens contacts to outside agencies and, eventually, the general public. Initial documentation is governed by agency regulations but steps involving coordination with other agencies and the public are governed by the Council on Environmental Quality (CEQ) Regulations on Implementing National Environmental Policy Act Procedures.[1] The process culminates in the filing with the U.S. Environmental Protection Agency (EPA) of a draft EIS and, after a procedure known as "review and comment" (R&C), a final EIS. The initial guidelines were issued in 1970 and, after several minor modifications, were essentially rewritten as mandatory regulations in 1978, with some changes added during the following year.

From a functional viewpoint, the EIS process represents a logical distribution of costs and benefits. An underlying thesis of this paper is that the different participants in the EIS process invest their time and other resources with a mixture of professionalism and self-interest in mind. Thus, the EIS documentation should be viewed as partially reflecting this mixture of self-interest and professionalism and not simply a mandated effort to satisfy a regulatory requirement. Prospective costs and benefits will vary in each case, however, so the calculus used to justify an effort will also vary.

THE SURVEY

The survey for this paper was conducted from late 1978 to 1980. There were two stages: the characteristics of 100 EISs filed in October 1973 were compared with the outcomes of assessed action and, next, 10 of the actions described in the 1973 EISs were investigated in a field survey during 1979. Selection of these EISs was based on several considerations. October 1973, the month when the primary group of 100 EISs was filed, represented a compromise date. A sufficient period of time, nearly four years, had passed since passage of the National Environmental Policy Act of 1970 (NEPA) for development of procedural regulations within governmental agencies. On the other hand, the passage of more than six years since October 1973 seemed sufficient for the planned action to have been started and, it was hoped, completed in most cases.

In the subsequent collection of data, there were two complications; one was foreseen, the other not. The length of time for completion of some major projects, such as highways, after filing of EISs exceeded five years. This meant that some projects were not completed when field visits were made. Yet some projects may never be completed because work has been suspended. Also, a few projects covered by "grandfather" considerations also fell into the analyzed group. About five projects, primarily major water resource development facilities, had begun construction in the late fifties but a decision was subsequently made that an EIS should be prepared. This EIS was eventually filed during October 1973. Thus, the EIS process could not significantly affect the design of the projects and the EIS preparation was essentially a formality.

PROJECT TYPE

More than a third (35) of the EISs in the sample involved highway or road construction (Table 18.1). Water development projects constituted the next largest category, including construction of dams and related facilities (12), dredging and disposal (5), and flood control (12). Nine projects involved urban construction, five of them associated with the rebuilding of towns in Pennsylvania damaged by hurricane Agnes in June 1972. Fifteen projects involving five national park or national forest areas were management plans or policies for federal lands. Most of these, plus three focusing on the use of chemical pesticides, were not site specific since they analyzed possible actions at locations to be later selected if circumstances dictated their desirability.

AGENCY

As indicated by the type of project, the agency dominating the filing of the 100 EISs in 1973 was the Federal Highway Administration (FHWA) with 35 projects. The U.S. Army Corps of Engineers had the next largest number, 16, while the U.S. Departments of Agriculture and

TABLE 18.1
Number of EISs by project type, 1973

Highway and road construction	35
Urban construction	7
National park, forest, or wilderness designation	5
Dams and related facilities	12
Vegetation and other pest control	3
Power plants and related facilities	5
Management of federal facilities	11
Dredging and disposal	5
Flood control	12
Other	5
Total	100

Interior prepared most of the remainder (Table 18.2).

DELAY FACTOR

A popular concept concerning the EIS is that the process of preparing and filing the document imposes a serious delay factor and is responsible for a significant portion of the extended time required for federally sponsored projects. Telephone interviews suggested that other factors are delaying the projects, and a more in-depth study would probably show that EIS preparation paralleled other planning efforts, imposing little or no significant time penalty.[2] Of the 100 projects, 29 were completed as described in the EIS (Table 18.3). These included, for example, a bridge, several highways or urban streets, several flood control or watershed projects, a fish ladder, and a lease for drilling on the outer continental shelf. Seven others were completed but slightly differently than as envisioned in the EIS. For example, monitoring of lobster beds in Massachusetts showed increased mortality due to fresh water intrusion during construction on the Charles River. The condition was remedied by installation of a salt water pump, which was removed when construction was completed. In one FHWA road project, the pre-construction soil study for the EIS was inadequate, necessitating an additional $500,000 expenditure to correct the resulting problems. Use of various herbicides in vegetation management in three national forests raised several problems: results in some cases were not as effective as expected; some sprays were to be used near streams but were found to be too toxic, necessitating substitution; and post-spraying follow-ups in one case indicated that some vegetation should be

TABLE 18.2
EIS breakdown by agency, 1973

Transportation	
Federal Highway Administration	35
Federal Aviation Administration	2
Interior	
Sport Fish and Wildlife	1
National Park Service	6
Bureau of Reclamation	3
Bureau of Land Management	1
Unspecified	1
Agriculture	
Forest Service	11
Soil Conservation	7
Rural Electrification	1
Defense	
Army Corps of Engineers	16
Labor	1
Energy-AEC/NRC	1
General Services Administration	2
National Capital Planning Commission	1
International Boundary and Water Commission	1
Environmental Protection Agency	1
U.S. Coast Guard	1
U.S. Water Resources Council	1
Housing and Urban Development	5
Total	100

replanted and maintained for deer browsing and small bird cover.

Twelve projects were cancelled before any action was taken. Many of these involved highways, and the comments on these EISs suggested that other agencies and environmental groups had strongly disapproved of the projects being undertaken. In at least two cases, contacts in the lead agency confidentially suggested during interviews that the projects had been favored by local political figures but could not be considered justified by professionals in the agency responsible for undertaking action. In other words, the lead agency stalled until the political winds shifted and the project could be safely dropped.

The largest category of projects was for actions still being undertaken, and these included uncompleted highways, watershed protection projects, timber management plans, and a test operation of a nuclear power plant. Action on three projects was begun but subsequently

TABLE 18.3
Project Status

	Number of Projects
Completed as planned	29
Completed with modification	7
Cancelled before any action	12
Action ongoing	32
Action begun but suspended	3
Postponed but expected	12
Other (no action necessary)	5
Total	100

suspended. One of these projects was the Bayou Bodcau, a
water development project under the U.S. Army Corps of
Engineers in Texas, a project included on President
Carter's "hit list" of water development projects
considered unjustified. In this case, the agency assumes
that action will not be resumed. For S.R. 20, a road
project in Washington State, the proposed bypass that was
the subject of the EIS has been deleted from construction
plans due to lack of funding. A new bridge proposed by
this EIS may eventually be built but alternatives are
again being studied. The proposed Amistad Recreation Area
of the National Park Service has been partially completed,
but the remainder of the project is awaiting future need
and availability of funds.

In 12 cases, actions were indefinitely postponed but
are still expected to occur. In seven instances, the
agency responsible for action had placed priorities
elsewhere, postponing action for "lack of funds." In some
cases, however, the low priority could be related to
public opinion factors as well. An example would be
construction of the Dwight D. Eisenhower Civic Center for
Washington, D.C. Other projects lacking agency funding
priority were reconstruction of highways in Kansas,
Florida, and Nebraska; improvement of a small watershed in
Indiana; and construction of a dam in Texas. In the case
of designating 6,375 acres in the Cumberland Gap National
Historical Park as wilderness and another 3,810 acres as
potential wilderness, the U.S. Congress had not
appropriated funds for relocation of a road. In two other
situations, designation of 7,700 acres for a Colorado
National Monument Wilderness Area and construction of a
8.5 mile expressway near Lansing, Michigan, actions were
delayed because of conflicts among local interests.

In the remaining three cases of delay, projects were
stalled by agency procedures or requirements not related

to the EIS process between the governmental agencies. In
the Southern Tier Expressway project of New York State, a
suit by the Seneca Nation to void a right-of-way proposed
in the EIS was upheld. An agreement was subsequently
reached, which included the transfer of 795 acres of
Allegheny State Park land, but transfer approval from the
Department of the Interior was required. In another
highway construction project, an archeological site was
discovered after submission of the EIS; so a survey and
salvage project is underway. Because of the changed
circumstances, the FHWA Chief Counsel suggested combining
this EIS with one for another road section. This was done
and the final EIS was filed in 1977. In yet another
highway project, a U.S. Coast Guard permit was needed for
channelization, but the Coast Guard refused to act until
disputes over forecasts of environmental effects could be
resolved.

ENVIRONMENTAL EFFECTS

    In 55 percent of the projects, including some
incomplete projects, the forecast of environmental effects
appears to have been accurate (Table 18.4). This
conclusion is based on the lead agency's judgment and, in
most cases, the opinion of observers. When possible, the
study team visited sites to verify conditions, but an
effort was made in every case to verify by an independent
authority that the agency evaluation was correct. A
judgment was also made whether progress on incomplete
projects was sufficient to evaluate the accuracy of the
forecast.

TABLE 18.4
EIS accuracy of description of environmental effects

	Percentage
Forecast believed accurate	55%
Effects less severe than forecast	2
Unanticipated issues/problems raised[1]	19
Action would not cause site-specific effects	7
Other (projects not begun, probably abandoned)	17
Total	100

[1]Includes projects cancelled because impacts were
  eventually regarded as unacceptable.

    In 19 percent of the projects, unanticipated issues
or problems arose. For example, an FHWA road project--
Waldo Boulevard-StH42--was completed as described in the

EIS. However, the EIS did not anticipate the increase in local park usage and number of new shops built, developments directly related to improved access from the new road. The Limerick Nuclear Station, subject of an EIS for issuance of an operating license, was far behind in its construction schedule. During tests, the unit seemed to be less efficient than expected; so it was not known if, when, or how it would be completed. Thus, the issuance of the operating license was a moot issue.

At the Rutherford County Airport, North Carolina, which was completed in October 1975, possible erosion was anticipated in the EIS and letters of comment. Planned controls were nevertheless assumed to be adequate, an inaccurate assumption. Erosion at the airport became a major continuing problem. A land use management plan for the Centennial Mountains, Targhee National Forest, did not anticipate the expanded use of off-road vehicles and subsequent interference with elk habitat. The Upper Castleton River (Vermont) watershed project was never begun. The EIS, however, was widely recognized as scientifically deficient. It made no mention of the local bird and mammal populations; nor did it recognize that wetlands to be unavoidably committed to the project included the state's most extensive inland cattail marsh, which functions as a breeding ground for rare birds.

In 2 percent of the actions, environmental effects were reported as less severe than forecast. In the South Fork watershed project, more emphasis than that described in the EIS has successfully been placed on the development of wildlife habitat as opposed to public use. In the Topock Marsh-Havasu Refuge habitat enhancement project, diking to permit management of water elevations within the marsh was carried out. Marsh habitats for water birds developed more rapidly than expected and wildlife populations responded with rapid growth.

SCIENCE CONTENT

The science content of an EIS is applied or problem-solving science.[3] The purpose is to predict the environmental changes that would result in the environment from a set of actions. In other words, the critical process is to identify the dominant cause-effect relationships and use these to extrapolate empirical observations to a logical conclusion. Four steps are assumed to be involved: (1) the problem must be defined in terms of dominant and critical cause-effect relationships testable by empirical evidence (within this step is the procedure defined as "scoping" in the CEQ regulations); (2) based on the problem and nature of the evidence, suitable theories governing environmental cause and effect must be formulated on the basis of laws developed within the physical sciences; (3) empirical data suitable for the problem and cause-effect theories must be collected; and (4) these must be extrapolated to produce a description of the expected environmental impacts. Thus, the quality of the scientific content of EISs can be evaluated using four criteria: (1) definition of critical problems, (2) suitability of change theories, (3) appropriateness and reliability of empirical data, and (4) adequacy of the analyses used to construct the impact prediction.

To select a subsample for "quality" analysis, summaries of all EISs collected for the study were subjectively graded on the basis of the projects' qualitative and quantitative potential to affect the environment. Nineteen of the 100 were judged to have the potential for significantly affecting the environment, and ten sites were visited during a field survey in North Carolina, Tennessee, and Florida. Quality scores were assigned by a minimum of two readers. The qualitative standard applied was approximately the same as in grading papers within a graduate professional school. The results are summarized in Table 18.5.

In general, the EISs were mediocre by normal academic standards. The language in most cases resembled engineering specification documents. (Both the engineering specifications and the EISs were probably written by the same contract engineers.) Each EIS, however, was distinctive. The Mills Avenue Extension (Florida) EIS ranked highest in quality. It was relatively long, 65 pages, and the major criticism of it was the failure of the document to identify key issues sufficiently early to delete extraneous material. However, the EIS accurately described the project's physical and social context, eventually defined issues, provided original empirical data, documented other information, and displayed sensitivity for a wide range of possible concerns. On key issues, sophisticated analytical techniques were used. For example, the NCHRP 117 Model was used to predict noise impacts, but the application of the model was first validated by applying it to current conditions. A visual inspection of the project in 1979 indicated no unanticipated environmental impacts, which was the situation reported by the Florida Department of Transportation.

A North Carolina project, NC 107, involved construction of a four-lane highway on the fringe of the Great Smokey Mountains National Park, a situation certain to raise serious environmental issues. The main justification for the project, however, was to reduce the isolation of the Western Carolina University, a rapidly growing institution in the town of Cullowhee. Writers of the EIS indicated sensitivity towards criticism being received from the university's science faculty, and they quickly focused on issues that were obviously delicate problems in their university relations. Instead of providing and analyzing data and then predicting impacts,

TABLE 18.5
Evaluation of EIS science content

Project	Problem Definition	Theory Selection	Data Quality	Analytical Adequacy	Remarks
Mills Avenue Extension (Florida)	2	1	1	1	Minor changes in dense urban area
Highway N.C. 107 (North Carolina)	2	2	3	2	Sensitive mountain environment
Highway Tenn. 63 (Tennessee)	3	3	3	3	Effective enhancement of project environment
Cordell Hull Dam (Tennessee)	3	3	3	3	Retrospective EIS
Blue Heron Bridge (Florida)	3	2	3	2	Bridge replacement in dense urban area
Rutherford Airport (North Carolina)	3	3	3	3	Poor design and implementation

Table 18.5 (cont.)

Project	Problem Definition	Theory Selection	Data Quality	Analytical Adequacy	Remarks
Highway I-75 (Florida)	3	3	3	3	Major highway in southern Florida
Red Boiling Springs Watershed (Tennessee)	2	2	1	3	Minor projects with slight impacts
Highway U.S. 11W (Tennessee)	3	3	3	3	Expansion of roadway
Lake Okeechobee (Florida)	2	2	2	2	Water control in Everglades watershed
Average	2.6	2.4	2.5	2.5	

Key: 1 = high quality; 2 = medium quality; 3 = low quality.

however, the EIS primarily contained a description of engineering steps being planned to reduce impacts. Since construction was still occurring in 1979, no assessment of the results could be made. The Tennessee 63 EIS posed a different situation. The EIS could generally be described as a collage of information, some useful but most irrelevant. However, the actual project was an outstanding example of sensitive, imaginative highway engineering. Considerable effort was devoted to preserving environmental features and to creating visual and wildlife amenities whenever opportunities could be found. In other words, a weak EIS cannot be automatically equated with an environmentally damaging action.

The Cordell Hull Dam EIS was a retrospective document written after most of the dam's construction had been completed; the poor quality of the EIS reflected this origin. The body of the EIS consisted of a cursory 16 pages, a small number for probably the most massive Tennessee Valley Authority (TVA) water project constructed during the 1970s. About 32,000 acres were allocated to TVA use, and the reservoir inundated about 10,000 of these acres. Key issues, such as temperature stratification of the impounded water and resulting change in aquatic ecosystems, were ignored. As the Cordell Hull Dam project was insufficiently examined by the EIS process, the Blue Heron Bridge suffered from a figurative overkill, with about 55 pages of information. Essentially, the bridge replaced another older, more intrusive bridge serving downtown Palm Beach. Many reasonable questions were examined competently by the EIS although the available data were limited. The entire analysis, however, was not placed into perspective by early identification of key issues and analytical resources were not used optimally.

The 16-page EIS for the Rutherford Airport described planned engineering details, not the site's environment. Potential issues involving vegetation, soils, fauna, and drainage patterns were not identified. Despite the preoccupation with engineering matters and a warning received in comments on the EIS, severe erosion still occurred. Superficially, the EIS for the Highway I-75, the emerging coastal artery of western Florida as well as the only cross-Florida highway in the lower peninsula, resembled the Rutherford Airport EIS in quality of content even though the format was more sophisticated. However, the environmental issues of the cross-Florida highway had been sufficiently sensitive to prompt the Florida Department of Transportation to appoint a 17-member panel of specialists, including scientists, to study potential environmental impacts. The EIS focused on engineering details but both the careful wording and thrust of the EIS suggested that more comprehensive documents had contributed to its content.

Red Boiling Springs, Tennessee, was a community plagued by floods, culminating in a disastrous flood during 1969. To prevent a recurrence, several small dam structures were being constructed upstream from the community. To serve their purpose, the pools behind the dams had to remain close to empty until flood conditions occurred. One earthen dam was completed and resembled a grassy hillock in a farmer's pasture. The small pond behind the dam was surrounded by a lush pasture with a large herd of grazing cattle. A second structure was still under construction in a narrow, nearly dry creek bed. The EIS only sketchily identified key issues and the strongest aspect was the scope and appropriateness of the data.

Highway U.S. 11W was an unimaginative widening of an older highway from two lanes to four. The EIS stated that

> the major ecosystems in the project area are streams, forest lands, residential land uses, pasture lands, commercial land uses. All of these systems are interrelated with each other and any adverse effect to one may damage one or all of the other systems.

Ecosystems were scarcely mentioned again, the remaining discussion being focused on engineering details. Some concern was expressed for historical structures that could be disturbed by the highway but little attention was focused upon potential secondary development.

Lake Okeechobee in Florida is the main reservoir of fresh water to serve the entire development of southern Florida as well as the delicate ecosystems, such as the Everglades. The proposed action was to raise the lake's level so more water could be impounded for irrigation, industries, and domestic use. As prepared by the U.S. Army Corps of Engineers, the EIS raised issues, offered data, and performed analyses. However, large amounts of extraneous information confused the reader and--as revealed in comments--the issues selected by the Corps did not seem to be the most environmentally or socially significant ones.

INTERPRETATION

This retrospective examination of EISs and resulting projects has to be interpreted cautiously. The sample was small. One hundred EISs represent only about 10 percent of all EISs filed during 1973. The ten that were analyzed in more detail constituted about 1 percent of those filed. About seven years, a significant time in the existence of NEPA, passed between filing and this study. Regulations changed, and the art of preparing an EIS presumably improved. However, two observations on the functions of the EIS appear appropriate.

Quality Control

The EIS process provides a significant degree of
quality control over actions by the federal government.
Draft EISs tend to be advocacy documents because proposals
for action and exposure of decision-making processes
create a situation of vulnerability for the responsible
individuals.‘ Self-interest as well as professionalism
often cause proposed projects to be described in the best
possible light. In the survey, most EISs were for
projects that were intelligently conceived, carefully
developed, and seemingly justified on the basis of social
value. On the other hand, persons preparing the comments
for the R&C had less vulnerability to criticism as well as
different senses of professionalism and self-interest plus
different information sources that enabled them to provide
advocacy from a different orientation. At least one-
quarter of all the project-based EISs involved actions
that were modified after completion of the EIS, often in
response to points raised in the EISs. This lack of
finality is akin to a recent EPA survey of 51 waste water
treatment projects, which found at least one major change
in all but one of the proposed plants occurred because of
the EIS process (CEQ, 1980). When sensible comments are
ignored, as in the case of the Rutherford Airport where
additional precautions against erosion were not taken,
problems ensue.

In the rare cases where projects were critically
flawed in conception, the EIS process in the examples
surveyed could be skillfully used by professionals in the
agencies to facilitate correction or cancellation of the
project. For instance, the Department of Transportation
deliberately used the EIS process to delay a narrowly
based, inadequately justified project. The Soil
Conservation Corps project in Vermont was cancelled when
the EIS revealed a lack of understanding of the
environmental consequences of the action.

Coordination

The EIS has become a critical tool for coordinating
actions by the federal, state, regional, and local
governments when natural resources are affected. In the
cases surveyed, the EIS documentation provided a vehicle
for establishing interpersonal relationships; a vigorous
exchange of information appeared to flow from the
contacts. Every state and territory has established a
clearinghouse that, among other things, assures thorough
distribution of the EIS-type of document.

In numbers and quality, comments provided by
governmental agencies at all levels appeared to provide
the most consistent sources of constructive advice. In
discussing their participation during telephone interviews
for this survey, the authors of comments still registered

a high degree of enthusiasm for the professional exchange even though their comments had been prepared more than five years earlier. Given this positive experience, another tool would presumably have to be invented for providing critical information and opportunities for intergovernmental participation in decision making if the EIS did not exist.

CONCLUSION

NEPA and the EIS requirement have been evolving for over a decade. NEPA's original purpose was to provide the federal agencies with a mandate to weigh environmental impacts of their decisions (Liroff, 1980) and the EIS requirement as the action-forcing mechanism. To a remarkable degree, the purpose was served but, in the process, the EIS has acquired other functions. From one perspective, the EIS can be regarded as encouraging rational resource planning by early inclusion of environmental considerations and identification of alternative actions. From another perspective, the EIS documentation and public participation activities constitute public disclosure that furthers the objectives of the Administrative Policy Act of 1946.

The EIS has already been refined in response to evolving needs. The new regulations encourage brevity by providing page limitations. Scoping enhances a focus on critical issues and diminishes inclusion of excessive descriptions. Formats have become more standardized. The delays have been reduced by automatically triggered deadlines. Professionalism has been encouraged over self-interest by requiring identification of EIS preparers. Summaries and supplements improve the flexibility of documentation.

Multiplying the functions of EISs typically requires the expansion of its content. In turn, this raises the costs of EIS preparation and processing. In the future, however, some adjustments may be possible without significantly increasing costs. A consensus should be reached on the inclusion and editing of comments, which are key elements in quality control and coordination. Now they sometimes appear in the draft EIS or are included only in summarized form.

Private sector actors are generally omitted from the federal EIS requirement until their actions affect a federal decision-making arena. However, improved coordination between city, state, and federal agencies could trigger the EIS requirement at an earlier stage, improving the "piggy-back" concept. Public distribution is still limited to expressions of interest, and the forcing of unsought copies upon the public would obviously not be justified. However, educating the public that the EIS can be a means of information on governmental decision making could enhance its value and, hence, its

availability. In the final analysis, the EIS will
continue to survive only as long as a broad and powerful
constituency believes with sufficient determination that
it should survive.

REFERENCES

Boulding, K. E. (1980), "Science: Our Common Heritage."
    Science, 207(22), 831-836.
Council on Environmental Quality (1980), Environmental
    Quality--1980. The 11th annual report.
Culhane, P. J., and Friesema, H. P. (1977), "Why
    Environmental Assessments Fail." Paper presented at
    the meeting of the American Society for Public
    Administration, Atlanta, Georgia, April 1.
Liroff, R. A. (1980), "NEPA--Where Have We Been and Where
    Are We Going?" APA Journal, April, 155.

NOTES

[1]Council on Environmental Quality, Regulations on
Implementing National Environmental Policy Act Procedures,
40 CFR 1500-1508; 43 FR 55990, November 29, 1978;
corrected by 44 FR 873, January 3, 1979; effective July
30, 1979.
[2]This was also the conclusion of the U.S. General
Accounting Office (1977), The Environmental Impact
Statement--It Seldom Causes Long Project Delays but Could
Be More Useful if Prepared Earlier. CED-77-99.
Washington, D.C.: U.S. Government Printing Office.
[3]A systematically derived prediction could also be
termed a technology of "know-how," not a science, but the
boundaries of definitions are, in Kenneth E. Boulding's
words, "fuzzy." See Boulding (1980).
[4]See Liroff (1980) and Culhane and Friesema (1977)
as cited in the references.

19. Improving the EIS Process: A Case Study of Spruce Budworm Control

Lloyd C. Irland

Battles over pesticide use were a prominent feature of the environmental policy conflicts of the 1970s. Because of its annual recurrence since 1972, Maine's spruce budworm spray program provides a valuable case study of the role of the Environmental Impact Statement (EIS) process under the National Environmental Policy Act (NEPA) in developing policy for the use of insecticides. In this chapter, I shall argue that because of the poor application of the EIS process in the spruce budworm case and because of inherent obstacles to the effective use of EISs in such programs, the process did not fulfill its potential. The EISs were neither useful decision-making tools for policy makers, nor useful information tools for the public, nor aids to administrators and researchers.'

Most of the obstacles to a more effective EIS process can be overcome by "tiering" the statements and using a multi-year programmatic approach. In 1980 and 1981, the U.S. Forest Service adopted a five-year programmatic approach to the problem, but the agency has not yet decided to tier the statements for all forest pesticide uses.

Aerial spraying of chemical insecticides to reduce defoliation of spruce-fir forests by the spruce budworm is a highly controversial and costly management practice. In 1976, about 20 million acres in Quebec, Maine, and New Brunswick were sprayed to control eastern spruce budworm; large projects have been mounted against western budworm and the gypsy moth as well. In Maine, major spray programs against budworm were conducted in every year since 1972 (Table 19.1). Similar ecological and health issues have been raised concerning widespread aerial spray programs against fire ants, rangeland caterpillars, grasshoppers, and mosquitoes.

The EIS process, as actually applied in this program, has had a strikingly limited impact on program planning and on public and professional understanding of the issues. The EISs have been either lengthy technical tomes or brief summaries virtually useless to everyone. Economic, health, and ecological analyses were of highly

TABLE 19.1
Summary of past aerial spraying for
spruce budworm control in Maine

Year	Insecticide	Thousand Acres Treated
1954	DDT	21
1958	DDT	302
1960	DDT	217
1961	DDT	53
1963	DDT	479
1964	DDT	58
1967	DDT	92
1970	Fenitrothion (Accothion)	210
1972	Mexacarbate (Zectran)	500
1973	Mexacarbate (Zectran)	450
1974	Mexacarbate (Zectran)	430
1975	Carbaryl (Sevin 4 Oil)	496
	Fenitrothion (Sumithion)	1,499
	Mexacarbate (Zectran)	238
1976	Carbaryl (Sevin 4 Oil)	3,460
	Trichlorfon (Dylox 4)	40
1977	Carbaryl (Sevin 4 Oil)	808
	Trichlorfon (Dylox 4)	55
	Acephate (Orthene Forest Spray)	58
1978	Carbaryl (Sevin 4 Oil)	967
	Trichlorfon (Dylox 4)	54
	Acephate (Orthene Forest Spray)	96
	Bacillus thuringiensis (Thuricide 16B)	21
1979	Carbaryl (Sevin 4 Oil)	2,543
	Trichlorfon (Dylox 4)	97
	Acephate (Orthene Forest Spray)	110
	Bacillus thuringiensis (Thuricide 16B, 24, 32, 32B)[1]	41
1980	Carbaryl (Sevin 4 Oil)	1,169
	Bacillus thuringiensis	200
1981	Carbaryl (Sevin 4 Oil)	
	Acephate (Orthene Forest Spray)	
	Bacillus thuringiensis	

[1]Thuricide 24, 32, and 32B were applied under
experimental use permits granted by the
U.S. Environmental Protection Agency (EPA).

uneven scope and quality, partly due to inadequate basic
data. In several important respects (notably economics),
misgivings expressed in EISs over the years have had no
impact on policy or on operational, research, and

demonstration programs of responsible agencies.
In this paper, I identify the key obstacles as the complexity of the decision-making system and a series of management problems. I then suggest means for improving the EIS process for insect control and evaluate the Maine experience. My findings validate the view that tiering and programmatic statements will improve the EIS process.
In the final analysis, the EIS process as applied during the 1970s to spruce budworm control did have some benefits. Even a perfect EIS process, however, will not guarantee the "right" decisions. Where decisions are based on poor understanding of consequences and have such a basic ethical content, the EIS process alone can facilitate well-informed decisions, but it cannot determine the "right" answers.

THE COMPLEXITY OF THE DECISION-MAKING PROCESS

The effective use of EISs in the spruce budworm program was hindered by several complexities in the decision-making process. Some of the most difficult problems of NEPA implementation have arisen in such programs, as they have for highway and public housing programs. In the budworm case, the principal actors are especially numerous, as described in Table 19.2.
The complex decision system is partly due to the fact that the federal role arises from its grant of funds to a state program. This means, first, that the federal decision maker (the Area Director, State and Private Forestry) is a decision maker in name only. He does not directly control the scope and methods of the planned program; nor does he make the final political decision on grant awards. In the past, the inclinations of area office staff, and even the Washington office, have been overruled at various political levels.
Second, there has been difficulty in defining precisely the decision context for the EIS. In many grant programs, the federal funds are necessary; without them, the project is not carried out.[2] In the budworm case, it has been clear that, without the federal contribution (about one-third until 1980), the project would still be carried out. So should the federal EIS treat the consequences of a full spray project or only of the part of a spray project that is federally funded? This has not been the approach taken. The early EISs treated the decision as a federal decision to carry out the whole project. More recently, the cost-sharing and strategic assistance roles of the federal government have been emphasized. But the ambiguity remains. In the early 1980s, it is quite clear that the federal EIS is not discussing a spray/no spray decision but a financial assistance question. In short, this ambiguous decision context has made it more difficult to define the role of the EIS in the decision process clearly.

TABLE 19.2
Actors in the Maine spruce budworm program

Congress	Authorizes funding for cooperative forest pest control; state delegation wields influence on federal agencies, especially on funding.
Office of Management and Budget	Oversees U.S. Forest Service budget.
Secretary's office, U.S. Department of Agriculture	Arbitrates disputes over program operation and funding.
U.S. Forest Service Washington HQ Area Office Field Office	Administers cost-sharing programs, technical assistance, and research on forest pest management.
Maine Forest Service	Manages spray program.
Wood-using industry	Consumes wood; sets limits of technical adjustments to changing wood supply.
Landowners	Manage land; determine acceptance of alternatives to spraying.
Environmental groups	Oppose spraying by litigation, advocacy journalism, legislative means.
Courts	Provide an avenue for civil remedies for aggrieved parties; assure compliance with laws and regulations.
Press	Provides public information on issues, problems, and conflicting views.
U.S. Environmental Protection Agency	Registers pesticides; interprets label language; enforces proper application of pesticides.

Third, the use of an annual EIS for the budworm program has rendered it difficult to distinguish clearly

between the impacts of a given year's project and the
implications of a program of spraying stretching over a
period of years. By the late 1970s, impact statements--
and public comments--were emphasizing the impacts of
repeated annual treatments on the environment and
nontarget insects, on economic feasibility, and on long-
term wood supply. Scientific impact assessment remained
hindered by the lack of basic data, as described below.
The EIS strategy adopted for 1981 was chosen to address
this problem; it called for preparing a five-year
programmatic EIS plus an annual assessment of each
individual project.

Fourth, the actual federal decision being made is to
supply funds for a spray operation that could be
undertaken even without federal assistance. The decisions
being made are not environmental in nature. Pesticides
are registered by the EPA; and application standards are
developed by state regulatory bodies, the EPA, and the
Maine Forest Service, in consultation with Forest Service
specialists. Although the EIS discusses alternatives to
pesticide spraying, it cannot be a decision vehicle for
alternatives since those are controlled by private
landowners. The decision on federal funding is ultimately
one of making a policy interpretation of federal
legislation that authorizes pest control cost-sharing on
private land³ and one of resolving a political struggle
over federal money.

In sum, applying the EIS process to the budworm case
has been difficult because of the complex decision
process, to a degree unusual in most federal programs.
First, uncontrollable factors complicate the decisions;
the designated responsible federal official is often
overruled at the political level. Second, there remains
ambiguity in the decision context--if the state will do
the project even without the federal funds, then how can
the decision be described that is faced by the federal
government? Is it even a "major federal action" after
all? The multi-year nature of the decisions is in
conflict with a piecemeal annual funding process. To deal
with this, a programmatic approach has been adopted.
Finally, the dominance of policy and political
considerations, which are only given limited review in the
EIS itself, raises questions about the use of the EIS
process in this particular case. Given that the EIS and
its findings play almost no part in actual decision
making, perhaps it should be viewed as an information tool
only, or discarded entirely.

INHERENT OBSTACLES TO EFFECTIVE USE OF THE EIS PROCESS

In the Maine spruce budworm program, the EIS process
has not been particularly effective in improving the
quality of decisions, in effectively informing the public,
in receiving interagency review, and in changing the

substance of programs. Why has this been so? Four inherent obstacles deserve special mention: schedule conflicts between the EIS process and operational needs, difficulty of predicting outcomes, poor economic evaluation, and lack of credibility of EPA pesticide registrations.[4]

SCHEDULE CONFLICTS

In many federal programs, delayed project implementation is costly and inconvenient and is usually resisted by operating agencies. But in few other situations are the time barriers as absolute as in insect control (Table 19.3). In the budworm case, the insects are vulnerable only during three to four weeks of early Summer.

An annual cycle of EIS preparation, then, conflicts with logistical and decision requirements for conducting spray projects. The result has been that FESs have been issued after the state has written multi-million dollar contracts for supplies and aircraft. At that stage, the proposed project can hardly be characterized as an open question. By that time, severe pressure is placed on the federal decision makers who decide whether federal funds will be granted.

The evaluation of past project success is finished in Summer and Fall, and forecasts of the following Spring tree condition and insect populations are not available until September or October. The drafting of the EIS, then, must begin before a project proposal is complete. During the review of draft EIS and preparation of the final EIS, decisions on insecticides and contracts are made. By early May, insecticide shipments (often totaling 20 to 60 railroad tank cars) begin from the plants. Total state liabilities in the form of cancellation penalties, contract guarantees, and sunk costs can reach millions of dollars several weeks before the spraying begins. At some times, the EIS process has not been completed within the prescribed "comment period" before action can begin. In 1976-78, the final decision on federal funding was not made by the U.S. Office of Management and Budget until the spray project was actually underway.

Actual or threatened litigation is becoming a perennial feature of the aerial spray program.[5] The late completion of annual EISs does not allow for timely judicial review of decisions.

In recent years, regulatory agencies have been actively involved in spray projects. Their licensing and rule-making decisions should take place before the issuance of bids and the FEIS. In 1979, however, a major review of rules was underway by the Maine Board of Pesticides Control during the project itself. While not strictly a part of the EIS process, the untimely formulation of regulations and licensing decisions

TABLE 19.3
Timing constraints in EIS process: spruce budworm spray projects

	Aug.	Sept.	Oct.	Nov.	Dec.	Jan.	Feb.	March	April	May
Planning	Evaluate past project	Prepare project proposal		Refine project			Plan environ. monitoring	Plan field work	Organize project staff	Start spraying
Implementation				Interview bidders-- insecticide and aircraft	Request bids; Choose insecticides	Arrange other supplies; Coordinate with regulatory agencies	Award contracts			
EIS Process	Preliminary proposal for assistance	Prepare DEIS and economics			Issue DEIS	File AD-623[1]; Review period	Prepare and print FEIS	Issue FEIS	30-day action time	
Decisions Required	Need a project				Establish rules federal funds	State funding		Establish rules		
Decisions Received	Need a project			Choose insecticides			State funds		Federal funds LITIGATION	

[1] Application for federal financial assistance.

deprives the user of the FES of significant information on the program, not to mention the planning dislocations that result.

The programmatic EIS strategy offers a way around these schedule conflicts, by allowing the use of a brief environmental assessment that can be prepared early in the planning cycle each year, optimally before Christmas. Such an assessment would at least be available for review before early project planning and contracting decisions have created irreversible commitments.

DIFFICULTY OF PREDICTING OUTCOMES

The general structure of the budworm problem and its control alternatives are well understood. But there is no scientific basis for predicting outcomes that would meet the standards for rigorous impact assessment. It is impossible to predict with precision most of the key magnitudes related to impacts: timber losses with and without spraying; long-term effects of alternatives to spraying; environmental impact of uncontrolled mortality; environmental impact of repeated spraying; acreage and location of future required spraying; future duration of outbreak; and future cost-benefit relationships.

These problems arise because of the difficulty of studying an episodic pest and because of the inherent natural variability of forest pest outbreaks. Given the great degree of uncertainty, a significant role is played by professional judgment. In such a controversial area, there is no convincing way to resolve conflicting opinions. This problem, of course, exists in some measure in all environmental impact assessment problems.[6]

POOR ECONOMIC EVALUATION

Despite repeated efforts to improve it, economic evaluation has been inadequate. Precise benefit-cost analysis faces severe difficulties (Irland, 1977). At times, even the rough analyses that have been made have not been published with the DEIS. The lack of staff for this work at state and federal levels, together with the inability to make credible forecasts of losses with and without control are the major factors responsible. This has made the balancing of environmental against economic and health factors almost impossible. Sound policy evaluation models, based on biological simulations, are available. But they lack the precision necessary for forecasts that could be used in benefit-cost analyses; furthermore, they were not constructed with any such purpose in mind.[7]

LACK OF CREDIBILITY OF EPA PESTICIDE REGISTRATIONS

Users of pesticides face a dramatic conflict in the

EIS process. The normal administrative view has been that EPA registration establishes safety when an insecticide is applied according to the label. The prospect of re-evaluating all the health and environmental data on a major insecticide is not an attractive one to an EIS writer. From a policy viewpoint, there seem to be good arguments for not duplicating the EPA process. In spruce budworm EISs, the approach taken to this problem has varied from extensive review of pesticide data to little or none.

In the herbicide litigation in the Pacific Northwest, however, a court ruled that the EIS cannot rely on EPA determination of safety but must make an independent review.' This ruling produced a massive EIS for the herbicide program on national forest lands in Washington and Oregon. The ruling appears to have had no effect on the budworm EISs, however. Initially, responsible federal field office officials were not even aware of the ruling.

The public and professional credibility of EPA pesticide registration is not high at the moment. It would be tedious to cite the abundant available documentation in official government reports and in professional literature that supports this assertion. Even if one had confidence in the original determinations, new evidence and new problems arise yearly. The state of thought on pesticide safety is never static.

The public has witnessed chemicals declared safe by the government and outside experts later being banned after extensive controversy. We find that we all carry minor body burdens of long-lived toxic materials. We learn that companies have withheld data. We see a major testing lab go bankrupt after revelations that its personnel faked data over many years. The registration process is far behind schedule. Monitoring studies and analyses remain unpublished and circulate in photocopy form for years. Results of major enforcement investigations are leaked to the press and never issued in writing. Ambiguous or contradictory label language receives conflicting and confusing interpretations, leaving users and the public without operating and enforcement guidance.

Under these conditions, user agencies have no choice but to completely repeat health and environmental safety reviews on pesticides. Until recently, they have had to make their own interpretations of vague label language.' Such reviews simply cannot be conducted properly by overworked field staff untrained in pesticide toxicology and the analysis of medical research findings.

This situation means that EIS writers for pesticide uses in forestry must assume the burden of demonstrating that a given pesticide is acceptable in terms of its impact on public health. Although forestry agencies are not capable of making such judgments, it might be argued that forcing them to do so would raise their consciousness of the ambiguities of making judgments about human health effects.

MANAGEMENT PROBLEMS

Over the course of the years, several management problems in the EIS process have been evident. The inability to deliver needed expertise at the field level, the inadequate involvement of attorneys, and inadequate public and interagency review are especially clear in the budworm program. These are problems that, in contrast to the inherent problems reviewed above, are in some degree subject to management control. My suggestions for overcoming these obstacles are summarized in the next section.

CONFLICTS BETWEEN DECENTRALIZATION AND CENTRALIZATION: LACK OF EXPERTISE AT FIELD LEVEL

EISs for Maine budworm projects have been prepared at field level by a small insect and disease management staff at Portsmouth, New Hampshire. These staff people work closely with state personnel on the EIS throughout the process, aided by review and guidance from the regional office and Washington.

This is consistent with general U.S. Forest Service policy favoring planning, management, and EIS preparation at field level "close to the action." In a process demanding such specialized knowledge of health and environmental issues, this creates serious problems. The document is drafted by persons lacking technical training in these fields and burdened with administrative and other duties. The caliber of expertise and availability of technical libraries and outside experts simply cannot be provided in small towns in the field. Finally, the long chain of command increases the likelihood of confusion and misunderstanding between the offices involved and increases the time lags in review and decision making.

INADEQUATE INVOLVEMENT OF ATTORNEYS IN EIS PLANNING AND DRAFTING

The litigation in the Spring of 1979 revealed serious misgivings on the part of attorneys in the Maine attorney general's office, the solicitor's office of the USDA, and the Department of Justice. Their view was that procedures for obtaining legal advice in the early stages of EIS preparation were not adequate. Correcting this situation in the future is more a management problem than one of EIS process per se. Since 1979, more careful attention to preventive, advance consultation with attorneys has been evident.[10]

INADEQUATE PUBLIC AND INTERAGENCY REVIEW

Reviewing the outside comments on past budworm EISs (Table 19.4) reveals several significant weaknesses. Many of these weaknesses cannot be remedied by the issuing forestry agencies themselves. First, the number of comments from the public and public interest groups has been small. Even in the highly controversial 1979 project, only a few members of the general public commented. Obscured by the table is the fact that many of the comments tabulated as "nongovernment" are, in fact, by affected landowners, chemical companies, and their trade associations.

The record suggests that the spruce budworm EIS process has not been especially successful in communicating with and soliciting responses from the affected general public in this case. In the Fall of 1979, in preparation for 1980, a scoping session was held to allow for more general comment by the interested public. A hearing was held in early January.

The record for interagency review on budworm EISs is dismal. Several state agencies submitted more or less detailed comments in various years. But, on the average, the record of review by state and federal agencies is strikingly weak. The expertise available in other agencies in environmental, health, and spray application constraints to be used has simply not been tapped. This is probably due to the overworked conditions in the reviewing agencies. The record for budworm suggests a fruitful area for comparative studies in other programs and for action by the Council on Environmental Quality (CEQ) to strengthen interagency review procedures. The CEQ should carefully review interagency review procedures and issue guidelines to strengthen the process.

Clearly, there have been serious management obstacles to the effective use of the EIS process as a decision-making tool in the budworm case. Many of the obstacles have been outside the control of any single agency and, in most cases, the participants have been well aware of them. Their persistence has been due to overloaded agendas, the rush imposed by the schedule constraints outline above, and mere bureaucratic inertia. The existence of a powerful political decision-making system at the top levels has reduced the incentive for change.

OVERCOMING THE OBSTACLES

The standard prescriptions for improving the EIS process seem especially applicable to the budworm case.[11] Briefly, tiering the EIS process for forest spraying would address several of the problems simultaneously. A nationwide programmatic EIS on the use of insecticides in forest insect control should be prepared. The insecticides, environmental and health data bases, the

TABLE 19.4
Summary of reviews of DEIS, Maine spruce budworm projects, 1975-1981

Year	Date of DEIS	Date of FEIS	Pages of Text, Body of FEIS	Economic Analysis Included in FEIS	Number of Non-government Comments	Number of State and Federal Comments	
						Total	Longer than Two Pages
1974	1/11/74	4/10/74	44	Yes	8	6	2
1975	1/10/75	4/15/75	30	Yes	4	4	1
addendum to 1974							
1976	1/30/76	4/19/76	71	Yes	8	5	3
1977	1/30/77	4/27/77	31[1]	Yes	5	6	4
1978	1/6/78	4/21/78	38[1]	Yes	16	4	2
1979	11/29/78-- amended DEIS 1/9/79[2]	3/28/79	56[1]	No	15	16	3
1980	12/79[3]	4/80[3]	85	Yes	31	17	3
1981	10/80[4]	2/12/81	79	Yes	23	15	3
1981	Environmental assessment	3/81	21	No	n/a	n/a	n/a

[1]Extensive appendices were attached.
[2]In December 1978, the DEIS was withdrawn and replaced with an amended DEIS in January.
[3]Statement not dated.
[4]Draft programmatic EIS.

human and environmental questions, and the value conflicts are the same for all forest pests controlled by aerial spraying. The technical expertise required can be marshalled at the headquarters level. The best available outside expertise can be involved. The needed interagency coordination can be accomplished at the top level. The use of a single national statement would clearly facilitate the involvement of agencies with health expertise. Its preparation at headquarters level would simplify the personal contacts. More important, reviewing agencies would not be "nickeled and dimed" by a stack of EISs on different pest problems but would face a single policy document for all insecticide uses. This would enhance their incentive to participate extensively and would avoid time-wasting duplication.

Another major advantage of preparing a national forest spraying EIS is that it would be the best vehicle for making multi-year policy decisions. The broad guidance on the role of chemical insecticides, acceptable application practice, label interpretations, and federal funding policy can best be developed in a nationwide program EIS.

Since forest pest control efforts cannot be evaluated on a year-to-year basis, a multi-year program EIS approach is required. Some pests may be controlled by a single application of spray but, in most cases, multi-year efforts involving a range of management actions, research, and demonstration are required. We must recognize that senior administrators face strong incentives not to prepare national program EISs. The risk of legal challenge halting an entire national program may appear to outweigh the benefits of the tiering approach.

Times will change; programs will be re-assessed; and insect impact, spray effectiveness, and environmental and human health concepts will change. Therefore, continual updating of the national and individual project EISs will be necessary through the use of addenda and other means.

The individual forest pests of interest here have different insect-forest interactions, present risks to different values, and require different management alternatives. Their management programs must be explained in year-to-year project EISs or environmental assessments that need not address the overall policy issues covered in the national document.

A national, tiered EIS would be the best vehicle for setting out policy on the federal role in cost sharing, technical assessment, and research on pest management. The lack of clearly explained policy has hindered all participants, including U.S. Forest Service management, from achieving their goals.

EVALUATION

We have reviewed a program in which the effective use

of the EIS process faces particularly severe difficulties:
the complex decision system, the difficulty of defining
the federal role, the weak knowledge base, and the
management problems are reviewed above. Where does this
bring us?

EIS PROCEDURAL REFORM

First, my analysis of the EIS process for budworm
supports the validity of the CEQ's view that tiering and
using programmatic EISs will materially upgrade the
usefulness of the process.

COSTS AND BENEFITS OF EIS PROCESS

A good deal of discussion has arisen about the
economic costs of the EIS process in staff, dollar
outlays, and delay. Much effort has been invested to show
that such costs are really inconsequential. But few
analysts have addressed a more subtle category of
opportunity costs.
The Maine Forest Service and U.S. Forest Service
staffs involved spend several professional person-years on
each EIS. This time and money are unavailable for
addressing serious program problems that need urgent
attention. In the budworm case, the EIS process has
exacted extremely heavy opportunity costs in terms of work
that could have improved the program. These staff
resources could have significantly upgraded program
performance in promoting alternatives to spray, better
environmental monitoring, and more precise insecticide
application. The programmatic approach now in use should
economize on staff time significantly.
Despite its shortcomings and despite the variable
content and quality of EISs on Maine spruce budworm
projects, the process has had some major benefits. Its
impact on program substance, while hard to assess, has
probably been marginal.[1][2]
The EIS process has forced program planners to keep
current with new data and has provided a stimulus to
improved environmental and health monitoring. The
statements have informed interested persons to some extent
about the justification for and impacts of the program.
More important, through the review process, the FES has
become a means for groups with divergent viewpoints to
communicate with others and with decision makers in
Washington. The cumulative importance of this
communication process should not be underestimated.

LIMITATIONS OF EIS PROCESS

Inadequate knowledge, deep value conflicts, and tough
policy decisions will characterize the environmental
management decisions of the 1980s. We think that the

lessons learned from the experience with spruce budworm can be useful in meeting these challenges. In particular, the early marshalling of appropriate expertise, clear identification of broad policy decisions, and careful tiering of the process are required. This is important to maintain the legitimacy of the EIS process and to give meaning to the opportunity for judicial review. In the budworm example, up to 1981, the policy decisions were made annually and have been the major source of delay and frustrations for federal and state administrators. Failure to tier the EIS process resulted in the FEIS being issued after serious and irreversible program commitments have been made and in ineffective use of available expertise.

While improvements can be made, we should not ask for too much from the EIS process, either. Better tiering or multi-year decisions cannot make the basic value conflicts go away. Better use of available expertise and better interagency review cannot make the deep uncertainties in knowledge go away. We cannot eliminate congressional and industry political pressures from the decision-making system.

Decisions like those demanded by spruce budworm control require balancing serious and partly unknown risks. The EIS is not the only ingredient in agency decisions. The EIS process cannot determine the "right" answers. But it can provide a more effective vehicle for analysing forest protection programs and putting decision makers on record that they recognize the uncertainties.

REFERENCES

Barney, P. E. (1981), "The Programmatic EIS and the NEPA Regulations." Land and Water Law Review, 16(1), 1-31.

Baskerville, G. L. (1976), Report of Task Force for Evaluation of Budworm Control Alternatives. Report to Cabinet Committee on Economic Development. Fredericton, New Brunswick.

Burke, R. E. (1979), "Effectiveness of Spraying." Augusta: Maine Forest Service (mimeo).

Falk, J. (1979), Harvesting Systems for Silvicultural Control of Spruce Budworm. Misc. Report. No. 221. University of Maine at Orono, Life Sciences and Agricultural Experiment Station.

Field, D. B., and Shottafer, J. E. (1979), Utilizing Spruce Budworm Damaged Timber in Maine. Information Report No. 3. University of Maine at Orono, Cooperative Forest Research University.

Irland, L. C. (1977), "Notes on the Economics of Spruce Budworm Control." Technical Note No. 67. University of Maine, School of Forest Resources.

Irland, L. C. (1980), "Pulpwood, Pesticides, and People:

Controlling Spruce Budworm in Northeastern North
America." Environmental Management, 4(5), 381-389.
Lesser, D. M. (1980), "Putting Bite into NEPA's Bark: New
CEQ Regulations for the Preparation of EISs."
University of Michigan Journal of Law Reform, 13,
367-404.
Lund, Wilk, Scott, and Goodall (1979), Study of
Alternatives to State Management of Spruce Budworm
Spraying. Prepared for the Maine Department of
Conservation. Augusta.
Maine Forest Service (1979a), Environmental Monitoring of
Cooperative Spruce Budworm Control Projects, Maine
1978. Augusta: Maine Forest Service.
Maine Forest Service (1979b), Spruce Budworm Research in
Maine: A User's Guide. Augusta: Maine Forest
Service.
Maine Forest Service (1981a), Forest Insect Manager Report
for 1980. Augusta: Maine Forest Service.
Maine Forest Service (1981b), Environmental Health
Monitoring Report, 1980. Augusta: Maine Forest
Service.
Maine Forest Service (1981c), The Spruce Budworm in
Maine--1980 Cooperative Spruce Budworm Suppression
Project. Augusta: Maine Forest Service.
Oliveri, S. (1979), "A Technical Review of Planning and
Guidance Procedures In Maine's Spruce Budworm Spray
Operation." Augusta: Maine Forest Service (mimeo).
Robinson, G. O. (1975), The Forest Service. Baltimore,
Md.: Johns Hopkins.
Seymour, R. S., Mott, D. G., and Kleinschmidt, S. M.
(1980), "Future Impacts of Spruce Budworm Management:
A Dynamic Simulation of the Maine Forest, 1980-2020."
Orono, Maine: U.S. Forest Service (mimeo).
Smith, A. L. (1979), "The Forest Service, NEPA, and
Clearcutting." Natural Resources Journal, 19,
424-431.
U.S. Forest Service (1977), FES-Western Spruce Budworm
Management Plan. Missoula, Mont.
U.S. Forest Service (1981a), FPES Proposed Cooperative
Five-year (1981-85) Spruce Budworm Management Program
for Maine. Broomall, Penn.
U.S. Forest Service (1981b), Environmental Assessment
Proposed Cooperative Spruce Budworm Integrated Pest
Management Program, Maine 1981. Broomall, Penn.
U.S. Forest Service (annual), FES-Cooperative Spruce
Budworm Suppression Project, Maine. Upper Darby and
Broomall, Penn.

NOTES

'At points in this paper, judgments may seem one-
sided or unduly harsh. I offer them in earnest hope that
the experience may benefit others seeking to improve

environmental management decisions generally. I can
criticize in fairness. For three years, I had senior
administrative responsibility in the Maine Forest Service
for this program; therefore, I am partly responsible for
many of the shortcomings noted here. This paper will not
recount the technical complexities and biological
uncertainties involved in forest insect control by aerial
spraying. Abundant background information may be found in
the annual U.S. Forest Service EISs and in publications of
the Maine Forest Service; both are listed in the
references.

[2]There is some case law on EIS requirements in grant
programs of this nature. See City of Boston v. Volpe, 646
F. 2d 254 (1st Cir., 1972) and Silva v. Dowrey, 474 F. 2d
287 (1st Cir. 1973).

[3]The authorization was made by the Cooperative
Forest Management Act of 1978.

[4]This paper emphasizes the key problems in the Maine
budworm case, with no effort to survey all of the issues
that have arisen with respect to the budworm program. A
comparison of the budworm case with the criteria listed in
the CEQ's Tenth Annual Report, pp. 580-581, is useful.

[5]Fitzgerald et al. v. U.S. Forest Service, et al.
Docket No. 29-57B (D. Me. 1979), bench ruling, affirmed by
Mem. Op. No. 74-1408 (1st Cir., 1979).

[6]For specifics, see papers by Burke, Oliveri, Irland
(1980), Falk (1979), Field and Shottafer (1979), and the
Maine Forest Service (1979a, 1979b, 1981a, 1981b, 1981c)
in the references.

[7]See Baskerville (1976), Irland (1977), and Seymour,
Mott, and Kleinschmidt (1980). Also see the economic
analysis of the program in the 1981 FEIS.

[8]See Citizens against Toxic Sprays v. Bergland, 428
F. Suppl. 908 (D. Ore. 1977).

[9]For example, it has not been explained how to spray
one insecticide and at the same time "protect wildlife."

[10]Robinson (1975, p. 277), in a general review of
U.S. Forest Service policy making, recommended more
extensive involvement of attorneys in the agency's
decision making.

[11]Useful reviews of the subject are Barney (1981),
Lesser (1980), and Smith (1979).

[12]The presence of the federal funding "carrot" has,
by itself, enabled federal officials to force some changes
in the Maine program, but this cannot be attributed to the
NEPA process itself.

20. The Interface Between Federal and State EIS Requirements: An Overview

Dennis Lundblad

In 1980, just having passed Earth Day Ten, we are also marking the eleventh anniversary of the National Environmental Policy Act (NEPA) and the ninth anniversary of the State Environmental Policy Act (SEPA) in Washington State. This paper will briefly outline the legislative history and draw from the working experiences of those 9-10-11 years to share with scholars, public administrators, and business representatives a number of practical formulae for environmental policy implementation.

Since Environmental Impact Statements (EIS) are the most visible and controversial, although least frequent, manifestations of environmental policy laws, the hope of this paper is to improve the utility of EISs.

As legislative background, the passage of NEPA in 1969 by the United States Congress was decisive. Several states also produced their own SEPAs within a few years. In Washington, SEPA was enacted by the legislature in 1971 at the peak of environmental activism and law making. Predictably, SEPA was written parallel to NEPA. Now, through its several years of implementation, SEPA has been amended more frequently than NEPA but, perhaps curiously, still retains the language that has been noted as giving it a much stronger statement of citizens' environmental rights than found in NEPA. An added provision of SEPA applies comprehensively to "all branches of government of this state." This includes cities, counties, special districts, and state agencies.

Because SEPA was a very general policy statement, the satisfactory form and content for complying with the law were uncertain. In turn, this uncertainty led to variations of use, misuse, and nonuse of the statute and EISs. Its uncertainty also drew political attention and the law was amended in 1973, 1974, and 1977 with a goal of increasing its specificity.

A significant 1974 amendment established the Council on Environmental Policy (CEP) for two years with the mission of preparing definitive guidelines for SEPA procedures, EIS timing and content, and the reduction of

394

"wasteful practice and duplication." The guidelines were
adopted by CEP as state regulations in 1976 (197-10 WAC).
The declines that occurred in EIS numbers in 1975, 1976,
and 1977 to below the 1974 level reflect a widespread
better understanding of what was required to satisfy SEPA.
Table 20.1 summarizes this experience. According to the
1974 amendment, the Washington State Department of Ecology
(WDoE) inherited the administrative duties of CEP on June
30, 1976. In 1978, in response to petitions for change,
WDoE revised the guidelines to their present content.

TABLE 20.1
SEPA-NEPA: eight years of environmental reporting
in Washington (based on documents received in the
Department of Ecology), January 1980

		Draft EISs			
Year	Local Agencies	State Agencies (Excluding WDoE)	Washington Department of Ecology	Total SEPA Draft EISs	Federal Agencies (NEPA)
1972	139	5	6	150	25
1973	260	26	6	292	18
1974	317	14	8	339	45
1975	188	15	11	214	36
1976	168	7	12	187	30
1977	233	18	5	256	34
1978	368	23	2	393	44
1979	307	18	7	332	43
Total	1,980	126	57	2,163	275

The overall objective of NEPA and SEPA is to provide
environmental impact information to decision makers prior
to their decisions on proposals. This information is an
adjunct to the social and economic implications that are
assumed to be already provided. The shortfall in
effectively accomplishing this objective under NEPA has
produced obfuscation, trivia, and bulk in EISs. Except
for administrative and legislative re-evaluation, SEPA was
initially often implemented with a similar result.
Moreover, the uncertainty embodied in the broad policies
of NEPA and SEPA resulted in peculiar interpretations.
For example, an environmental "detailed statement" was
variously construed to be a one-page, justifying synopsis
of a proposal or a 500-page glut of trivia. Veracity of
scientific information was often a forgotten ethic.
Public review opportunities for environmental reports
ranged from an excessive three months to a lean fifteen

days and were restricted to certain licensed technical
professionals.

All of these varying interpretations in the meaning
and use of NEPA and SEPA frequently resulted in reports
that were counterproductive to the main objective; the
reports were often so obviously self-serving and shallow
that they were meaningless or they were so voluminous that
they were seldom, if ever, read. In sum, little of the
increased environmental awareness intended for decision
makers was realized. So much for history.

A renaissance and somewhat amplified version of the
objective of SEPA and, it is hoped, NEPA is more
instructive:

> The intent of this process and its reporting is to
> provide environmental impact information to decision
> makers prior to their decisions on proposals and to
> present that information concisely, comprehensibly,
> and credibly.

The discussion and formulation of such a broad instruction
are very stimulating to practitioners but they are often
challenging to accomplish. The translation of this broad
directive into a rational process that will produce useful
results is usually taxing, requires a major effort, and
desperately needs a sense of reasonableness. To capture
the quintessence of a laudable but general policy such as
SEPA and its objectives requires determination in the best
ways to be effective, not to be excessively costly, to
achieve usefulness, to pass the test of reason, and to
avoid seemingly endless procedures.

Given that grand instruction and philosophy, where
can we go from here? The answer lies in experience or, of
course, incredible foresight if we have not faced this
question before now. Fortunately, there is roughly a
decade of experience from which to draw ideas for EIS
improvement to achieve greater environmental awareness.
Experience with SEPA has shown that an EIS can only
achieve usefulness by being read by the people who make
decisions. Additionally, when viewed positively as a
joint exercise in issue identification and problem solving
between government and a project proponent, the
development of an EIS also will become a constructive
process for all parties. Process and substance augmented
by public involvement and a comprehensible reporting style
are adequate ingredients for EIS usefulness. An exemplary
scenario illustrates the application of these combined
ingredients:

> To wit: a major metallic mineral processing
> plant is proposed to be built adjacent to the
> Columbia River and a productive agricultural area.
> The proposal is brought to the attention of the
> Washington State Department of Ecology. A first

estimate of the various needed environmental
approvals is made. WDoE is identified as the state
agency responsible for SEPA compliance. An EIS is
deemed necessary.

Through the medium of SEPA, the proponent,
consultant, local groups, and the agencies with
jurisdiction join early to review the project and to
make an initial estimate of environmental impacts.
The most significant potential impact is in the realm
of air quality, specifically odor.

EIS drafting is started. Initially needed are
the scientific background data on the existing
environment. WDoE and the consultant compile data
from the various jurisdictional sources. WDoE, with
the consultant, reviews probable air emissions and
estimates the relationship with air emission
standards and pollution-control technology. Except
for a concern over holding-pond water evaporation,
other elements of the environment are not expected to
be significantly affected. Community issues involve
economic growth and employment vs. induced
development and loss of the semi-rural character of
the area. Estimates of employment and population
impacts are made by WDoE and confirmed through other
sources.

The draft EIS is issued; a public hearing and
local meetings are held. Concerns over impacts in
air quality remain. Because of the unique
detectability of odor at very low compound
concentrations, precise measurement and widespread
agreement on a standard do not exist. The EIS
explains this situation.

In discussion and comment through the medium of
EIS review, alternative methods are examined for
managing air quality and potential odor problems.
Concern over the impact of sulfur dioxide on orchards
is also expressed. However, measurement and control
of this compound relative to vegetation are more
sophisticated and dependable than they are with odor.

A special consultant is engaged to examine the
project as a whole and to give attention specifically
to air quality. Following completion of the
technical analyses, the final EIS is written to
include people's concerns, government responses, and
the results of technical analyses. Subsequently,
permits are prepared that contain some of the most
stringent conditions ever recommended in Washington.

The SEPA process has involved all parties,
especially the decision makers. Moreover, the draft
and final EISs have actually been read by those same
parties. Solutions and compromises have been found.

A postscript and an evaluation are appropriate at
this point. The postscript provides fine irony: while

the plant represented in the EIS received the conditional environmental permits, it was subsequently built in another state under different conditions.

An overall evaluation of the process, the EIS and its substance, the use of verified technical information, and the public information is positive. The process brought people into communication with each other. The process, together with preparation of the EISs, identified early the most significant issues and probable impacts. EIS focus was directed to provide the greatest coverage to the significant issues. Less space and time were devoted to minor aspects. Finally, the EIS was prepared in a sufficiently clear and concise manner to be understandable and manageable.

The technical/scientific data represented state-of-the-art technology. Verification of the data increased credibility. When verification could not be accomplished for inclusion in the EIS, permit conditions were established by decision makers to ensure later follow-up. Results of technical/scientific analyses were presented concisely and clearly in summary form in the EIS, thus enabling an understanding of the situation by nontechnical individuals.

In terms of management, the entire process was accomplished in a reasonable time and without excessive cost, considering the controversial nature of the proposal. Schedules were set and largely adhered to; the only exceptions were the additional time necessary to conduct verifying technical analyses and that taken to respond to heightened public concerns.

Procedurally, the scoping and consultation concepts now embodied in the NEPA regulations were used effectively. Timing of public meetings/hearings closely coincided with the need to air project information and to hear public concerns. The site of the proposed project was seen firsthand by the involved staff and decision makers. Finally, although federal agencies chose not to participate, an invitation for their early involvement was extended.

In summary, the problems and uncertainty in early implementation of SEPA ranged from a lack of consistency in the process to nonuse of technical information and the EIS itself. Uncertainty attracted political attention and the statute was amended in 1973, 1974, and 1977. The resultant greater specificity in the law and the development of definitive guidelines provided better direction for substance and form both in the overall process and in the EIS. Significant improvements have been realized to the end that the process has become informative and constructive, and verified technical/ scientific information is presented summarily and comprehensibly in the EIS. When clarity, conciseness, and veracity are employed, EISs are actually read and used. An efficient assessment and decision-making process

concerning a controversial industrial proposal in a semi-
rural setting in Washington best illustrated the
usefulness of the SEPA process and EIS document. EIS
utility has been increased, tested, and proven. While
SEPA may change in the future, a sound basic framework has
been established and is working in Washington.

21. The Uses of Scoping: The Massachusetts Experience

Samuel G. Mygatt

BACKGROUND

The structure of an environmental review process can have a significant effect on the quality and utility of the information it generates, because the way the structure apportions responsibility can predetermine the motivation of various participants in the process. For example, a common problem in the making of environmentally sound decisions is that the operational arm of an agency usually has more clout than does the environmental review arm. This is a structural problem, because the structure gives two responsibilities, often conflicting, to the same agency. One solution to the problem is that used by the Tennessee Valley Authority: to centralize the environmental review function within the chairman's office. Another solution is the Massachusetts approach: to entrust oversight of the environmental review process to an autonomous agency.

Between 1973 and 1977, the Massachusetts Environmental Policy Act (MEPA) was modelled after the National Environmental Policy Act (NEPA). In 1977, prompted by a tendency to prolixity, poor quality, and delay in environmental review, a coalition of interest groups representing industry, environmentalists, utilities, labor, and legislators worked together to improve the functioning of MEPA. They came up with a redesigned act, of which a major innovation was a process for scoping Environmental Impact Reports (EIRs). Scoping in Massachusetts has key differences from scoping as it occurs under NEPA. Its specific advantages may make it a useful alternative model for consideration by other states. This paper reports on and assesses those advantages.

THE MASSACHUSETTS PROCESS

In Massachusetts, the scope of the EIR is prepared by the MEPA Unit, a small (six-person) professional staff reporting to the Secretary of Environmental Affairs. The report is prepared by the project applicant, whether that

400

be a private person (needing state permits or funding) or
a state agency. The action, as under NEPA, is by the
agency, after review of the report. For private projects
(the bulk of our filings), the functions of scoping,
reporting, and deciding are thus assigned to three
different entities. For public projects, the reporting
and decision functions are carried out by the same agency,
but the scoping is still the province of the MEPA Unit.
Public or private, the adequacy of the EIR, in terms of
conformity with the scope, is determined by the MEPA Unit
and the Secretary. In contrast, under NEPA, the scope,
the report, and the decision are all prepared by the lead
agency.

The Massachusetts structure has the following
benefits:

1.   Scoping is carried out and the EIR is judged by
     an independent entity in a relentlessly public
     and participatory process. On controversial
     projects, this does much to abate the suspicion
     that naturally arises when the agency that
     determines the complexity and expense of the EIR
     has a vested interest in implementing the project
     without delay or excessive cost.
2.   For a private project, the applicant, not the
     permitting agency, prepares the EIR. This means
     that the entity with the most at stake determines
     how fast and how well the EIR is prepared. This
     contrasts with Massachusetts' previous experience
     under a NEPA-like structure in which an agency
     was responsible for preparing the EIR on a
     private project. The EIRs then generated were
     slow in the making and indifferently prepared.
     Now the process is quicker and more effective.
3.   Making the private proponent responsible for EIR
     preparation enables the project to be reshaped,
     and mitigating measures to be adopted, as the EIR
     work proceeds. Even where coordination is
     excellent between the EIR developer and lead
     agencies, the need for back-and-forth exchange
     during the study's preparation increases delays.
     Under less auspicious circumstances (as in a
     federal coal conversion EIS we reviewed
     recently), the document may identify the best
     mitigating measures, but then shrug them off as
     measures that the lead agency cannot force on the
     proponent. When the proponent prepares the EIR
     and an independent entity evaluates it, this lack
     of accountability does not occur.

Once a well thought-out structure is in place, the
quality of the review hinges upon the ability and
authority of the reviewing agency. Scoping is only as
useful as the questions it asks, and the report is useful

only if it is assured that, first, the answers given are clear and correct and, second, the information it contains is taken into account by the decision maker. The remainder of this paper addresses the ability of the scoping process to ensure that the right questions are asked.

ASKING THE RIGHT QUESTIONS

Perhaps the most important principle of scoping is: get your feet wet. Too often, decisions are made in government offices or hearing rooms, without having done anything more than driving by the site. Whatever the project--housing project, shopping center, sanitary landfill--a sensible scope cannot be issued without a good feel for the land. Proponents have an understandable tendency to minimize environmental problems. Only a careful site visit will identify these problems. Examples are two housing units we reviewed, which had already received site suitability findings from the funding agency. At the time of our site visit, these were under water! (The funding agency had no inkling that there might be issues concerning wetlands.)

A second simple principle is: develop a means for good local input. Town boards, and especially neighbors, know far more about the local environment than do state agencies. Development of a good notification procedure is essential--and a challenge. Our experience is that official notices and newspaper ads are much less effective than contacting town boards by telephone and finding out from them who would be most concerned or have the most to offer.

Although each scope we develop is sui generis, we are learning to use a number of techniques that improve the quality of the report. Having studied vague, amorphous reports, we now often specify which analytic tools and criteria should be used. Air quality models and soil run-off calculation methods (and possibly even coefficients) should be established in advance when possible.

It is important at the time of scoping to consider secondary effects carefully; the people developing the project are not likely to take these into account. For example, a project may be traffic constrained by a problem intersection some distance away; such an intersection should be identified for further study during scoping. Similarly, the coal ash generated by a utility's conversion to coal (clearly a transport, disposal, and financial problem for the utility) can create a significant secondary problem for municipalities by pre-empting scarce landfill capacity. If not searched out during scoping, this kind of secondary issue will not receive the review it deserves.

It is also important in scoping to exclude issues. Some consultants have a financial incentive to inflate the

breadth or depth of the study. Scoping is a useful
mechanism to counteract this tendency. In addition,
during scoping of a controversial project, peripheral
issues will sometimes be injected by the opposition. A
definitive statement in the scope as to why these issues
are not environmentally significant is often all the
treatment such issues warrant. The result is an EIR that
gives more concentrated attention to the real issues.

More often, however, local concerns are real, and
scoping is a valuable way to define, evaluate, and respond
to them. The scoping agency must listen carefully to
local comments, weigh them, and decide whether or not to
reflect them in the scope. If further study is not
required, the scope should explain why. This can enhance
local understanding of an issue; it will also let the
public know that its comments have been heard.

An important prerequisite to useful scoping is a
skilled, dedicated, multidisciplinary staff. In scoping
to cut the fat out of a study but leave the meat and in
making quick administrative decisions that affect by many
thousands of dollars the costs of an environmental review,
mistakes are unacceptable. If important issues are not
recognized in time, the environmental review loses much of
its value. If needless work is done to overstudy
projects, the backlash can weaken the legislative support
that environmental review clearly needs. Thus, the
success of a Massachusetts-style program is somewhat
precarious and heavily dependent on individuals. In our
experience, though, the benefits have outweighed the
risks, and the results have been gratifying.

22. Changing the Environmental Review Procedure in Minnesota[1]

Sharon Decker

BACKGROUND

On April 3, 1980, Governor Al Quie signed a bill that redesigned the environmental review procedures for Minnesota. Although political observers had speculated that no major changes to environmental programs could be made during the 1980 session due to nearly equal representation of the two parties and a lack of clearly established leadership in the legislature, this legislation easily passed through both houses in the final days of the session. The surprising passage of this bill was the result of a carefully drafted proposal and some delicately balanced compromises between business and environmental interests.

Minnesota has had an environmental review process since 1973. The Minnesota Environmental Policy Act (MEPA) and companion legislation created the Minnesota Environmental Quality Board (EQB) and established the environmental review procedure. Minnesota's environmental review procedure was patterned after the National Environmental Policy Act and centered around the Environmental Impact Statement (EIS). The original law specified that an EIS must be ordered for "major actions" that have the "potential for significant environmental effects." The EQB, which is composed of the heads of seven state agencies, four citizen representatives, and a representative from the governor's staff, was given the authority to decide, on a case-by-case basis, which projects were major actions with the potential for significant environmental effects. The board was also given the authority to review and determine the adequacy of completed EISs.

Soon after the process got underway, a major problem became obvious. With all decision making centralized in the EQB, the board was inundated with reports and assessments and requests to review specific projects. Since most board members had their own agencies to run and could devote only a very limited amount of time to the EQB activities, this workload was unmanageable. In an effort to relieve this burden and return some of this decision-

making authority to the local governmental levels, the
rules for the process were amended in 1976.

The 1976 rules provided that the local, county, or
state agency having the most approval authority over a
project ("responsible agency") could decide if an EIS were
warranted. This decision, however, was subject to review
and reversal by the EQB. The 1976 amendments greatly
improved the process by specifying the types of projects
that required preliminary review, providing a standard
format for the preliminary review document, and relieving
the EQB of the majority of the EIS decisions. For a while
it appeared that, with these improvements, the major
problems had been solved and the process would work
smoothly and efficiently. But as more projects were
reviewed, new problems emerged and developed into major
stumbling blocks.

THE EXISTING PROCESS

The 1976 rules specified that actions falling into
any of 31 listed categories must undergo preliminary
environmental review. These categories applied to both
public and privately proposed projects and described
certain types of projects (e.g., "construction of a
pipeline greater than six inches in diameter and 50 miles
in length," 6 MCAR § 3.024 B.1.g.) and certain types of
impacts ("any action that will eliminate or significantly
alter a wetland of Type 3, 4, or 5 . . . of five or more
acres in the seven-county metropolitan area, or of 50 or
more acres outside the metropolitan area," 6 MCAR § 3.024
E.1.4). If a proposed project fell into one or more of
these categories, a preliminary review document called an
Environmental Assessment Worksheet (EAW) had to be
prepared. The worksheet was essentially a 12-page
checklist that required a brief description of the project
and a listing of its anticipated environmental impacts.

On the last pages of the worksheet, the "responsible
agency" indicated whether or not an EIS should be required
for the project. The worksheet containing this decision
was then distributed to various state and regional
agencies and underwent a 30-day review period. During the
30-day review period, the decision by the "responsible
agency" could be challenged by a governmental agency
having jurisdiction over the project, by a member agency
of EQB, or by a petition containing the signatures of 500
or more persons. Such a challenge required the EQB to
review the project and make its own decision on the need
for an EIS.

PROBLEMS

The environmental review process, of course, always
had its critics. But as the process evolved, the critics
became more numerous and more vocal until it seemed as

though the environmental review process was under fire
from all sides. Environmentalists criticized the EQB for
what they considered to be a conservative use of the
environmental review procedures. Primarily, the EQB was
criticized for refusing to order EISs on most of the
projects brought to their attention by agency challenges
or citizen petitions. Out of 52 challenges and petitions
reviewed by the board in three years, only four state EISs
were ordered.

Business interests complained of excessive delays and
uncertainties in the process. Delays seemed particularly
excessive when the EQB was required to decide on the need
for an EIS. Under the 1976 rules, a formal hearing or
informational meeting was usually required before the
board could make its decision on the EIS need. In the
past, it had taken a minimum of four months for a final
decision to be reached. In one notable case, over two
years elapsed from the time the challenge was received
until a final decision was made by the EQB.

Local governments often expressed resentment that
their decisions could be appealed to the EQB. Likewise,
the EQB was often overburdened with examining issues that
were clearly appeals of local land-use decisions and did
not involve any environmental issues of statewide concern.

The EQB staff also had its own criticisms of the
language and procedures of the existing rules and law.
Primarily, the staff was frustrated by the lack of
direction and definition in the process. Although the law
and rules stated that EISs were required on "major
actions" having the "potential for significant
environmental effects," these terms were not clearly
defined and no goals or standards were provided by which
to evaluate the significance of a particular impact. This
made it difficult to determine which projects warranted
EIS review and, if an EIS were ordered, on what basis it
would be evaluated.

Two other major flaws in the procedure added to the
frustration of the EQB staff. First, the law specified
which issues must be addressed in every EIS ordered.
However, it was discovered that in nearly every project
reviewed, usually only two or three main issues warranted
further study. The board lacked the flexibility to order
studies on just the issues of concern and, thus, often
ordered no study at all rather than ordering a full EIS.
Second, citizens could become involved in the decision on
the need for an impact statement only through the
petition/challenge process. This immediately set the
stage for a confrontation situation between the project
proposers, the citizen petitioners, and the government
agencies. The 1976 rules provided for no peaceful,
nonadversarial method for citizen involvement in the
decision on EIS need.

Adding to this chorus of criticism, the EQB members
and the governor's office expressed concern that the

demands of the EIS program still claimed too much of the
board's time. They felt that the board should be relieved
of its EIS responsibilities in order to devote more time
to directing environmental policy in the state. A number
of policy-directing activities were given to the board in
the 1973 legislation but, partially due to the demands of
the EIS program, the board had been unable to pursue these
other activities. Board members also felt that state
environmental policy was not adequately directed through
EIS decisions and that such policies could be better set
through other methods.

A SOLUTION

These and other problems with the process were well
known to the staff. Early in the 1979-80 legislative
session, the EQB staff proposed legislation that would
have made a number of changes in the program. This
proposal included granting authority to use scoped EISs
and establishing categories for projects that would
automatically require EISs. However, this proposal was
rejected by the governor's office and was never presented
to the legislature.

Despite this setback, the staff continued to search
for a solution to the problems. That search included the
investigation of other states' processes to see if they
encountered similar problems and how they were resolved.
In this search, I discovered that the environmental review
program in Massachusetts had recently been revised. The
new program used a number of features that we had
considered for our program--scoping and a listing of
thresholds of actions requiring environmental review.

After examining the Massachusetts rules and
discussing the process with staff by phone, I visited
Boston and spent two days in the Massachusetts
Environmental Protection Act (MEPA) offices. Sam Mygatt,
Director of the MEPA Unit, patiently answered my questions
about the program's methods and problems and provided
files and staff people to explain the process further.
The results were exciting; here was an environmental
review program that seemed to function efficiently and
effectively. Although the basic organization was
significantly different from the Minnesota situation
(Massachusetts had the EIS authority centralized under one
person, the Secretary of the Executive Office of
Environmental Affairs), many elements of the program could
be adapted for Minnesota. Moreover, Massachusetts had
provided a proving ground for many of the elements that we
had previously proposed. Some of these "innovations"
could now be justified by reference to the Massachusetts
experience.

Now that we had the example by which to refine and
justify our ideas for improvement in the process, the
problem was how to get these ideas into legislation.

Unexpectedly, that opportunity soon arose. After our initial legislation was rejected, the agency proposed another amendment that would relieve the EQB of its EIS program burden (putting the decision on need and adequacy in the hands of the "responsible agencies") but did nothing to solve the other problems in the EIS program. Two other amendments to MEPA were also proposed. The first, offered by the Minnesota Association of Commerce and Industry (MACI), proposed strict time limits on the process. The second, offered by a law firm representing the Sierra Club and other environmental interests, proposed alternative forms of review and increased citizen access to the process. State Senator Robert Dunn, who would eventually become one of the authors of the legislation, handed the three proposals back to the EQB staff with instructions to work out a compromise proposal within a week.

This was the opportunity we needed. Rather than working out a line-by-line compromise between the three bills, we rewrote the entire proposal. Many of the elements contained in the original rejected proposal were reinserted, but they were now refined and justified by reference to the Massachusetts experience.

THE PROPOSAL

Some of the main elements contained in the proposed compromise bill included:

1. The EIS process would be further decentralized by giving other governmental units the authority to make final administrative decisions on the need for and adequacy of an EIS. The EQB would retain the authority to make rules governing the review process and could intervene in EIS review at certain specified times during the process. However, administrative decisions could no longer be appealed to the EQB. Such appeals would have to be filed directly with the district court.
    Decentralization may be the most sensitive element of this new law. On the one hand, this provision would force individual agencies to assume greater responsibility for protecting the resources within their jurisdiction. For some local governments, this would mean that they could no longer avoid making environmental evaluations and decisions by referring them to the EQB. It would also allow more review on projects that might have environmental impacts of local significance, but which might not warrant statewide review (and, under the 1976 rules, would not require an EIS). On the other hand, there was the possibility that some governmental units might not provide adequate review of

proposed projects, either through indifference or
lack of information. The fact that agencies
would determine the adequacy of their own
documents was also a potential problem. However,
if the rules for this procedure were written well
enough, including specific criteria for
determining need and adequacy of environmental
review, these potential problems should be
avoided or minimized.

As decentralization would shift the
responsibility for environmental decisions onto
individual government units, it would also take
most of the project-specific decision authority
away from the EQB. This shift of authority was
supported by the EQB because it was believed that
this would free the board to pursue other policy-
directing activities. However, without this
project-specific authority, the board would have
to make an imaginative and well-organized effort
to direct environmental policy through other
means.

2. The EQB would be authorized to establish
    thresholds for projects and impacts that would
    automatically require preparation of an EIS or an
    EAW. The EQB would also have to establish
    categories for projects exempted from review.
       This would, in most cases, streamline the
    cumbersome process of deciding the need for an
    EIS. Further, the categories would give an
    indication of the types of resources and the
    types of impacts that the state considers
    significant. This would essentially establish
    the beginning of a state environmental protection
    policy.

3. The new amendments would impose strict time
    limits on the preparation and review of
    environmental documents. This would enhance the
    predictability to the process.

4. An amazingly simple change was proposed for the
    preliminary environmental assessment process that
    would change citizen involvement from one of
    inherent conflict to one of cooperation. Under
    the existing system, the responsible agency
    prepared the EAW and made a decision on the need
    for an EIS. That decision then underwent a 30-
    day review period. Any citizen or agency could
    informally comment on the worksheet but the only
    official response to a worksheet was via a formal
    challenge to the decision.
       The new legislation would reverse the
    process somewhat. A governmental unit would
    prepare the EAW and that worksheet would be
    distributed for comment and response. At the end
    of 30 days, the governmental unit would review

the comments received and then make its decision on the need for an EIS. That decision could then be appealed to a court, if necessary. Based on the Massachusetts experience with a system very similar to this, these decisions are rarely appealed. Massachusetts has found that during this review period many compromises occur and many problems are resolved without resorting to legal confrontation.

5. Citizens would also be able to initiate environmental review for projects not covered under any mandatory inclusion or exclusion categories. A petition signed by 25 or more persons could request that an EAW be prepared for a particular project. If an assessment were then prepared, the process for assessments, as described above, would be followed.

6. The amendments would provide flexible content requirements for EISs. As a first step in EIS preparation, an "early and open process" would have to be used to determine the form, content, and level of detail. The new language also urged that the EIS be clear and analytical and that economic and sociological impacts be considered. We had realized long ago that flexible content requirements were needed, and the scoping experience of Massachusetts and the federal government gave us the added justification to include it in the amendment.

7. During the scoping process, the permits needed for the project would be identified. Where appropriate, the information needed for these permits would be gathered concurrently with the conduct of the EIS. This was included to avoid duplication in the processes. Ever since the EIS process was first established, there had been confusion concerning the relationship between permits and environmental review. Although the environmental review procedure was designed to aid decision makers (including, of course, permitting agencies), it has never been resolved how this could be accomplished without considerable overlap in the two processes.

8. The amendment would provide alternative forms of environmental review to be used in lieu of EISs. These alternative forms would have to address the same issues and use procedures similar to the EIS process. Although the legislation did not specify any particular alternatives, it was assumed that some comprehensive land-use plans or actions that would require special review and approvals under other regulations could be included under this provision.

The staff believed that this proposal represented a compromise of the spirit, although not the exact wording, of the other proposals. For business and industrial interests, it provided predictable time frames and shorter review periods. For environmental groups, it provided the opportunity for greater citizen access to the process, more review options, and more useful review documents. It also provided more flexibility and clearer definitions, much to the pleasure of the staff.

COMPROMISE

As it turned out, our belief that this represented a true compromise of the various interests must have been correct because the proposal was enthusiastically received. The only disagreements involved one detail concerning court appeal requirements and some specific wordings. The rather tedious process of arguing about wording continued in informal gatherings while the amendment proceeded through the legislative committees. During this process, several other persons representing utilities and other business interests joined in on the dissection of the language, but compromises acceptable to nearly everyone involved were finally reached.

As the end of the legislative session approached, our main worry no longer was that an agreement could be reached but rather that the bill would not reach the House and Senate in time to be heard. The compromise had been so carefully balanced between so many parties that any last-minute change or even a clerical error could doom the proposal's chances for passage in the session. But despite all our worry and initial pessimism, the bill was approved within the last three days of the session.

RULE MAKING

Now that the euphoria of legislative approval is waning, the difficult and unglamorous task of writing rules to implement the law begins. Now the hard questions that could be answered with generalities in the law will have to receive specific answers. Specific thresholds for review and definition of terms will have to be devised.

Anticipating that this will not be an easy process, we have already begun meeting with some of the same people who were involved in negotiating the legislation. As the rules are formulated, these same people will be continually consulted in order to resolve conflicts as early in the process as possible and to produce a process that is balanced between business and environmental interests.

CONCLUSION

Minnesota has had an EIS process for about seven

years. This has been enough time to try out the process, realize its weaknesses, and experiment with improvements. As the process matured, the law and procedures have been manipulated to accommodate new situations. But we realized that the old law could not be pushed and contorted any further to accommodate the needed changes. It is a tribute to the original law and the concepts of an environmental review that the process did survive its difficult infancy and could be revised without being destroyed.

With this maturing process, however, has come the realization that more compromise between business and environmental interests must occur. When MEPA was originally passed (1973), the climate for environmental concerns was more favorable. As energy and economic pressures increase, there seems to be less sympathy toward environmental issues. Environmentalists are realizing that, in order to maintain any sort of control over the use of our natural resources, the processes for such control must be efficient and effective. The days of the endless studies producing virtually useless information are numbered. In order to maintain any sort of rational control, the review process must be predictable, rapid, and produce usable information. Although it may be uncomfortable, this pressure can be healthy for environmental protection if it can strip the excess from the often ponderous procedures.

The new legislation in Minnesota reflects this maturing process and its pressures. The challenge now is to ensure that only the excess and not the power of the process is removed and that the end product is a lean, efficient, and effective system.

NOTES

¹The opinions expressed in this article are solely those of the author and do not necessarily reflect the opinion or policies of the Minnesota Environmental Quality Board.

PART 5

Recent Changes and Conclusions

INTRODUCTION

This final chapter examines recent changes in the EIS process and then presents the editors' concluding observations on the overall project, NEPA, and the EIS process. Nicholas Yost, former General Counsel of the Council on Environmental Quality, examines the intent, scope, and workings of the 1979 changes in CEQ regulations regarding the implementation of NEPA through the EIS process. He notes that the main intents of these changes were to reduce delay, reduce paperwork, and improve decision making. The purpose of these binding regulations is the improvement of the quality of EISs, with many of these changes potentially addressing the issues raised by the authors in this book's previous chapters. The overarching goal of the CEQ regulation changes is the removal of emphasis from the EIS document and placement of emphasis on improved decision making.

Following Mr. Yost's paper, the editors present their concluding overview of prospects for enhancing the quality and utility of the scientific and technical content of EISs. In reviewing all this book's authors' presentations, the editors also summarize other implications for improving the EIS process as a means of enhancing environmentally sound decision making. The chapter concludes with the editors' sense of what the future holds for the National Environmental Policy Act and its implementation.

23. The 1979 CEQ NEPA Regulations

Nicholas C. Yost

On January 1, 1980, President Carter issued a
proclamation celebrating the tenth anniversary of the
National Environmental Policy Act (NEPA). In it he said,

> Ten years ago, the United States turned over a new--
> and greener--leaf. On the first day of the decade,
> the National Environmental Policy Act became the law
> of the land. This law is one of our nation's
> fundamental charters: it is a pledge from each
> generation to the next to protect and enhance the
> quality of the environment.

What has happened with NEPA during this past decade?
NEPA has taken hold. The basic message of the law--you
look before you leap--is now assumed by everybody. Today
one cannot readily imagine building a highway or a power
plant or embarking upon a timber harvesting program
without first publicly examining the environmental
consequences. We may argue about when to prepare which
document, in what detail, and within what time. But we
all assume and agree that we must examine the
environmental consequences before we act. That was NEPA's
intent. That is NEPA's record. And that is NEPA's
success.

We are now engaged in perfecting a system that
works--in making NEPA work better. All our efforts at
improving the relevance and utility of scientific and
technical information in Environmental Impact Statements
(EISs) will make a very real contribution to that process.

NEPA, as you recall, stated a national environmental
policy in Section 101 and in Section 102 created a series
of what Senator Jackson, one of the bill's authors, called
"action-forcing" devices to see that the goals of Section
101 are achieved. NEPA and its principal "action-forcing"
provision, the Environmental Impact Statement, have come a
long way in these ten years. Much federal decision making
was improved by this law. Environmental considerations
were taken into account where before they had often been
ignored. But other projects became bogged down in
paperwork and delay. While generally viewed as a good

law, its implementation has picked up altogether too many encumbrances.

This was the situation when President Carter came into office. Shortly thereafter, he directed the Council on Environmental Quality (CEQ) to do something about it. Speaking of NEPA, the President said,

> In the seven years since its passage, it has had a dramatic--and beneficial--influence on the way new projects are planned. But to be more useful to decision makers and the public, environmental impact statements must be concise, readable, and based upon competent professional analysis. They must reflect a concern with quality, not quantity. We do not want impact statements that are measured by the inch or weighed by the pound.

On May 24, 1977, President Carter directed CEQ to reform the act. He specified three goals: to reduce paperwork, to reduce delay, and to see that the process results in better decision making.

After a year and a half of concentrated effort, the council concluded that it had accomplished these three goals by establishing a set of new regulations. It is to those regulations that this preface is directed. The regulations were issued in November 1978 and became binding on most federal agencies July 30, 1979 and on the balance November 30, 1979. This paper addresses three separate areas:

1. The process by which the new regulations came into being;
2. The principal provisions of those regulations and the problems they were designed to resolve; and
3. The initial results of CEQ's oversight of the new regulations.

Throughout this treatment, we must bear in mind two overall factors that differentiate the regulations from the old guidelines. First, these are regulations, not guidelines. They are mandatory requirements binding on all agencies. Second, the regulations cover all nine subsections of Section 102(2) of NEPA, while the guidelines covered only the one subsection, 102(2)(C), dealing with Environmental Impact Statements. This latter change has several implications. It means that the regulations apply to the whole environmental review process--from planning to assessment to Environmental Impact Statement to decision to follow up. Further, by tying the process more closely to the decision, the regulations further the purpose of the act whereby the procedures of Section 102 are to be "action-forcing" devices to achieve the environmental policies stated in Section 101. In brief, environmental factors are to be

built into the whole process whereby decisions are made
and implemented.

I will now discuss the process whereby the
regulations were adopted, an open process that has had
much to do with the warm reception the regulations have
enjoyed. CEQ began this process with public hearings,
actively involving NEPA's critics as well as its friends.
We asked the U.S. Chamber of Commerce to coordinate the
presentation of the views of American business; the
Building and Construction Trades Department of the AFL-CIO
to do so for labor; and the Natural Resources Defense
Council for environmental groups. We also sought the
participation of state and local governments, the
scientific community, and the general public.

After the hearings, we developed a 38-page
questionnaire, reflecting not CEQ's views but the views of
all who testified, their identification of what the
problems were, and their suggestions for solving them.
This questionnaire was distributed widely and resulted in
hundreds of responses. The returned questionnaires were
then tabulated not only for good ideas but also to
determine where consensus existed among those dealing with
the NEPA process. If both business and environmentalists
agreed that something was a good idea, the chances were
that it was, indeed, a good idea.

Next, CEQ arranged meetings with all federal
agencies. (There are, I might add, over 70 of them.) I
then undertook the process of drafting new regulations in
collaboration with my colleagues at the council. This
draft underwent six months of interagency review and
revision. Throughout this process we arranged meetings
with all who showed concern. We at the council met with
every group that expressed dissatisfaction with either
NEPA or the regulations. We asked the staffs of
congressional committees with NEPA oversight
responsibilities to let us know if they received any
complaints. We then sought out those people, listened,
and attempted to accommodate any legitimate concerns. If
we could not accommodate them, we explained why.

The council succeeded in its effort. Every major
group in the United States concerned with implementation
of NEPA told us they supported the new regulations. The
United States Chamber of Commerce "congratulated" the
council, finding the regulations "a significant
improvement over prior EIS guidelines." The National
Governors' Association commended the council for "a job
well done." The Natural Resources Defense Council wrote
to "welcome" the regulations as an "important improvement"
over the guidelines, saying they "cut the wheat from the
chaff" and promised to make the process "much better" for
citizens and produce "better decisions as well."

Here are the principal provisions of the new
regulations. First, there is an emphasis on shorter
documents. The new regulations require reducing the

length of Environmental Impact Statements so that they normally do not exceed 150 pages; in the case of complex proposals the limit is 300 pages.

A second major concept is that of "scoping," which is identifying everybody who will ultimately be involved in the process, involving them early, and getting everybody's views as to what constitutes the important issues. As a result, the truly significant issues will be given adequate study while those that are not significant will not need to be analyzed at length. The results will be both a better, more rounded draft Environmental Impact Statement and a reduction in delay by diminishing the need to object to an EIS and send it back for restudy before proceeding with an action.

A third major development is the emphasis on interagency cooperation before the EIS is drafted; this reduces the likelihood of adversary comments on a completed document that prolong the process. With the advent of the regulations, an agency other than the lead agency with jurisdiction or expertise will not just sit back and criticize somebody else's EIS. It will help write it in the first place. This will produce a better draft document and will reduce the occasion for later delays.

Fourth, the regulations stress interdisciplinary preparation. They place a new emphasis on the statutory command to "utilize a systematic, interdisciplinary approach" to decision making.

Fifth, the regulations emphasize options among alternatives rather than extensive accumulations of background material that is not useful to the decision makers or to the public.

Sixth, several innovations may be summarized under the general heading of "streamlining the process." There are, for the first time, mandatory time limits on the NEPA process set at the request of the applicant. Several provisions are designed to make the permit process move more smoothly. To start with, the lead agency must identify other permits and reviews that will be necessary before a project is to proceed. Then, interagency cooperation rather than confrontation is fostered by making commenting agencies into cooperating agencies. Next, agencies are specifically directed to develop procedures to aid applicants. Then, the regulations try to use the EIS process to make environmental reviews run concurrently rather than consecutively. They use the EIS to rope together all the different reviews required by law so that all the reviews take place at the same time; the EIS serves as the unifying document. In addition, any necessary information and mitigation are to be identified early. The regulations use the EIS to force other permitting agencies to identify any information they will need to pass upon the project and to identify any mitigation measures necessary for their approval of the

project; thus, all the information can be developed
concurrently rather than consecutively. To a great
extent, when the EIS is complete, all agencies with permit
or review authority over the action will be in a position
to take the appropriate action without further study or
delay. The regulations placed a repeated emphasis on
eliminating duplication. With respect to federal agencies
and those states that have their own Environmental Impact
Statement requirements (about half the states), the
federal agencies are directed to work jointly with their
state counterparts to produce one document that will
satisfy both laws. With the cooperation of the Council of
State Governments (CSG), a CEQ-drafted state counterpart
provision was made part of the CSG's 1979 "Suggested State
Legislation." This provision, when adopted by a state,
directs the state or local agencies to work with their
federal counterparts to eliminate duplication. With
respect to federal agencies duplicating the work of other
federal agencies, through the concept of "adoption"
provision is made for one agency to adopt, with certain
safeguards, the work of another.

After all is said and done, better decisions are what
we are seeking. In the words of the regulations:

> Ultimately, of course, it is not better documents but
> better decisions that count. NEPA's purpose is not
> to generate paperwork--even excellent paperwork--but
> to foster excellent action. (50 C.F.R. Section
> 1500.1[c])

The original congressional purpose in enacting NEPA
was to see that all federal agencies build environmental
considerations into their decision making. Often in the
implementation of NEPA this purpose has been forgotten.
Instead, interest has focused on the adequacy of a
document more than on the underlying concerns--whether or
not the action should go forward as proposed or be
rethought in terms of approach, content, or intent.

These new regulations attempt to redress the
misemphasis on the document and place the emphasis back
where it was supposed to be in the first place: is the
decision sensitive to environmental considerations? The
principal devise to be used is the record of decision that
requires the decision maker briefly to record what the
environmentally preferable alternative (or alternatives)
was and then to describe how he or she balanced this with
other "essential considerations of national policy" in
making the decision. The regulations do not mandate the
choice of the environmentally preferable alternative in
every case. Quite the contrary. They explicitly refer to
other essential considerations such as economics or
congressionally determined agency mission. What the
regulations do require is that the decision maker pay
attention to the bottom line of the EIS--they make the

decision maker at least think about why not to proceed in what the EIS has shown to be an environmentally sensitive manner. We hope that by making the decision maker think about the environment he or she will make better, more environmentally sensitive decisions. The decision maker's decision remains his or hers to make, subject, of course, to judicial review for compliance with the substantive and procedural requirements of Sections 101 and 102 of NEPA.

Finally, the regulations emphasize follow-up and post-verification. Sometimes, in the past, the NEPA process has ended with the EIS or the decision. CEQ wants to ensure that what the EIS has discovered is reflected in the decision and what the decision concluded about environmentally protective measures is, in fact, implemented. For this reason, there will be new emphasis on mitigation and monitoring and, where appropriate, reports on the progress of such measures.

An examination of the results of the new regulations to date is illuminating. First, in the courts a fascinating thing happened to the regulations; it was a draftsperson's dream. The regulations were relied upon in a unanimous U.S. Supreme Court opinion before the regulations' effective date. The court's opinion in Andrew v. Sierra Club was such that the Environmental Law Reporter concluded,

> The new CEQ NEPA rules now go into effect with what amounts to an unrestrained stamp of approval from the Supreme Court, a most auspicious beginning for these ambitious and promising refinements of the NEPA process.

Second, in practice CEQ has been engaged in a massive effort to see that all agencies are, in fact, following the mandates of the new regulations--reviewing each agency's procedures, reading the EISs, reading records of decision, holding meetings, conducting a study of scoping, writing letters to and conducting meetings with agencies, and holding briefings in both Washington and the ten federal regions.

Here is an outline of the results of CEQ's review of EISs prepared under new regulations. This review was undertaken, I note with caution, based only on the face of the EIS--not on its adequacy or scientific accuracy. Overall, agencies are not presently preparing EISs that adequately inform decision makers and the public of the environmental consequences of an action in a way that can assist and guide decisions. While most EISs follow the CEQ format, they still tend to be more encyclopedic than analytic. However, the groundwork has been laid by many agencies to improve their documents; the recent trend has been toward more analytic EISs.

With respect to page limits, agencies are generally complying with requirements. The agencies have complied

with the requirements for a cover sheet but still fail to
include abstracts. Recently filed draft EISs have
improved considerably in writing style and clarity. With
respect to the recommended format, the agencies have
generally followed the CEQ outline. The majority of
agencies have written fairly good and clear summaries that
lay out the alternatives, summarize major impacts, and
present conclusions in a readable and understandable
fashion without unnecessary detail. The majority of
agencies clearly lay out the purpose and need for action.
However, a number of agencies seem to weight this section
heavily in favor of construction or development
alternatives.

Much improvement is needed in the quality of the
section dealing with "alternatives including the proposed
action." It is often not the focus of the draft EIS, even
if the CEQ-recommended format is used. In some instances,
the old format is used. In it, a very poor, nonanalytical
section on alternatives follows a detailed description of
the affected environment. Many EISs also obscure the
range of alternatives. Another major problem is the
failure to analyze adequately the no-action alternative or
alternatives outside the jurisdiction and control of the
lead agency. Many EISs do not emphasize mitigation
measures as much as they should and do not cross-reference
sections on the affected environment or environmental
consequences. There are no EISs that specifically state
how the alternatives will or will not advance the
requirements of Sections 101 and 102(1) of NEPA.

Agencies still place too much detail in the section
dealing with the affected environment by including
statistics and charts that are more properly presented in
the appendix. However, presentation of the affected
environment is well done when EISs follow our recommended
format. Similarly, the section on environmental
consequences is usually better presented when the EIS
follows CEQ's recommended format and focuses on the
analysis of alternatives.

With respect to the list of preparers, most agencies
include it, but they merely list names and titles; they
offer very little information on educational background or
experience and include virtually no identification of the
preparers' areas of EIS responsibility. This inadequate
treatment makes it difficult to tell whether a systematic,
interdisciplinary approach has been used.

Most EISs include an appendix that is generally
analytical and substantiates the EIA conclusions. Most
EISs also list sources and material relied upon; these are
also cited in the text of the discussion. Instances of
incomplete or unavailable information are rarely even
addressed in the impact statements. Most agencies
apparently assume that all relevant data have been
gathered. Where relevant, the list of federal permits and
approvals in identified in the EIS, although often not as

a formal section.

Very few records of decision have been prepared thus far. The ones reviewed by CEQ range from lengthy decisions to brief documents. CEQ will develop and circulate models after reviewing a larger sample.

Next, let me turn to the results of our scoping study. Only the most preliminary results are available so far; only 19 of 94 surveys have been returned. Most agencies are using the "open forum" type of meeting. Some agencies are contacting other agencies or scoping only by mail. This, clearly, is neither a very helpful nor desirable way of doing things. The following are some of the points made by respondents:

- Early scoping cuts the time needed for additional analysis after the draft and before the final EIS.
- The comment evaluation stage was sharply cut.
- It (the new scoping process) makes agencies cooperate more than they would have otherwise.
- It (the new scoping process) helps early public involvement.

Other comments include:

- Applicants pack the meeting with people saying do not do an EIS at all.
- Agencies are not prepared to comment.
- The public is not ready to use the process.
- Public involvement does not change anything.
- Agencies lack funds to attend meetings.

It must be stressed that these comments, both pro and con, are only individual responses; they do not represent consensus or general conclusions. When the scoping study is completed, CEQ will makes its results public.

At the beginning of his term, President Carter charged the council with streamlining the NEPA process-- with reducing paperwork, reducing delay, and returning to the original congressional purpose of ensuring better decisions. After a year and a half of highly detailed consultations with all concerned interests in America, those associated with CEQ think we have succeeded. The major concerned groups, from the U.S. Chamber of Commerce to the National Governors' Association to the National Wildlife Federation and the Natural Resources Defense Council, agree. All of us working together have changed the process. But our working together cannot stop there. The job of implementation is now underway. Professionals in the field of environmental impact analysis today have a special obligation. In their hands the implementation of the process will in good part lie. This obligation carries great responsibility. It is now up to all of us to work together to make the new process work and work well.

24. Concluding Observations and Future Directions

The National Environmental Policy Act, like other pieces of major legislation, created opportunities for political leverage and catalyzed change that the initial authors never envisioned. Indeed, given the broad, interdisciplinary nature of the program goals and objectives, it has been extremely difficult to define operationally what the purposes of NEPA are, let alone a technique for determining whether or not those purposes are being achieved. The extensive body of legal, as well as administrative, interpretation of NEPA is indicative of this problem.

In many ways, it is useful to think of NEPA as a handful of policy "seeds" cast on the "fertile soil" of national concern and nurtured by a beneficent implementation "climate." To be sure, NEPA was formulated within the context of widespread political and popular consensus regarding the mishandling of natural resources and abuse of the environment. There was, however, little initial discussion of such things as action-forcing provisions, citizen participation, or judicial review of agency action—themes that have come to characterize NEPA. No one can say precisely what the intent of Congress was regarding the act; indeed, unless a policy matter is narrow and uninteresting (i.e., routine), the policy statement will never be able to contain its own consequences.[1]

Thus, NEPA has evolved through the collective actions of those attempting to implement or influence it. Numerous circumstances also greatly influenced the development of the initial, rather vague NEPA seeds. These circumstances included the explosion of the environmental movement in the early 1970s (coupled with the emergence of environmental law firms at a time of growing judicial activism) and presidential endorsement of a strong role for the newly established Council on Environmental Quality vis à vis NEPA implementation. The result of all this has been a tremendous metamorphosis and proliferation of the perceived purposes of NEPA and the EIS process. A highly active public demanded increased access to federal decision making; the courts, sympathetic to the cause of citizen activists, established a standard of strict compliance with the procedural provisions of the act. This resulted in the emergence of the EIS as a comprehensive, full-disclosure document and the judicial tests of good-faith consideration of environmental data and a balancing of environmental factors against economic and technical ones. Further, several states followed the federal lead by establishing impact statement requirements for state and, in some cases, local action (Hart and Enk, 1980). In short, when Congress passed NEPA in 1969, it created a catalyst rather than a policy, and any attempt at analysis must necessarily adopt a "motion picture" image rather than a "snapshot" approach.

Many analysts have attempted to interpret the evolution of NEPA over the last ten years;[2] all agree that, for better or worse, the EIS has been the key variable in the law's application. Further, most would agree that efforts have moved from the initial implementation stage (characterized by administrative backlog and protracted litigation) to one of refinement and fine tuning. Indeed, the whole notion of improving the quality and utility of scientific information in EISs can be viewed (at least on the surface) as largely a refinement of the process. In fact, most research[3] and practical experimentation[4] has centered on either methodological refinement or procedurally oriented changes in the law's application.

Some recent research has taken exception to this trend. Using survey research methods, Caldwell and Bartlett (1981) have begun to shed some light on practitioners' perceptions concerning the effects of NEPA and the quality of EISs. Their initial findings suggest that NEPA has significantly enhanced communication within federal agencies but has had less effect on interagency communication and agency-scientific community linkages. Indeed, most respondents felt that the state of scientific information and methodology was, in fact, limiting in NEPA implementation efforts but that, by and large, the EIS was an effective tool of planning and decision making. Thus, they concluded, as the quality of decision making improved, the weaknesses of available science began to be revealed. However, while the investigators distinguish between "environmental analysts" and "managers and planners," it is difficult to determine how these distinctions were made; given the lack of explanatory power of this variable in the analysis, the study seems lacking when it comes to identifying the fine-grained differences between those who prepare environmental analyses and those who purport to make decisions with them.

On another front, work initiated by Bissett (1981) has begun to stress the importance of post hoc audits in order to assess the accuracy of EIS predictions during the development stage and beyond. Following in the footsteps of Holling (1978), Bissett emphasized that environmental assessment should not stop with the decision to undertake

a project. Instead, it should continue through the
construction and operation stages in order to test initial
impact predictions (with an eye toward improved predictive
techniques) as well as identify emerging problems and
their associated mitigative measures. While both of these
objectives are important additions to the existing
environmental assessment approach, we sense that
preoccupation with predictive accuracy may lead analysts
and decision makers down the wrong path. Given that most
EISs address issues that range from empirical to value-
oriented, the key question is how complexity and
uncertainty are dealt with in the context of the proposed
action. Indeed, the most compelling EISs may have the
least predictive accuracy from a scientific point of view.
Conversely, it is possible to imagine a predictively valid
EIS analysis that is never heeded by decision makers.
Clearly a blend of these perspectives is required.

An innovative analytical approach can be found in the
recent work of Culhane, Armentano, and Friesema (1981).
In this research, the "scientific quality" of EISs was
assessed in terms of the extent to which discussion of any
given topic reflects the scientific state-of-the-art
understanding of that topic. The topic chosen for
analysis was that of acid rain; given that power plants
constitute a major source of acid-rain precursors, the
authors examined all power plant EISs issued by the
federal government for the period 1970-1980. The quality
of the discussion about acid rain in each of the EISs was
judged by comparison to "milestone developments" in the
scientific understanding of acid deposition as determined
from the literature and experts in the field. It was
initially expected that the lag time associated with
scientific progress and eventual inclusion of such
discussion in EISs would follow predictable patterns; this
turned out not to be the case. In fact, the results
indicated that most EISs did not mention points that
constituted the state of the art and that the best
predictors of acid-rain coverage were institutional and
political factors (especially the number of comment
letters sent by outside parties).

While many may be quick to point out that there are
problems with aspects of the above research design (e.g.,
the selection of such a large-scale, long-term issue as
acid rain may not be generalizable), it nonetheless
constitutes an interesting, new, more rigorous approach to
understanding and evaluating the NEPA/EIS experience.
Future analysts may extend the approach by applying it to
other types of benchmarks. Such studies could, for
example, be conducted on the extent to which EISs reflect
the state of the art from a methodological or even
procedural point of view. Extending this even further, it
might be desirable to assess those situations where EIS
analysts have actually led, rather than followed, the
existing state of the art. Given that EIS preparers are

426

in a unique position (in between the world of practice and theory), they possess real capabilities either to discover new issues or apply existing techniques in new ways. Such a creative approach can be found, for example, in the paper by Carl Petrich in this volume. By extending an existing visual assessment methodology and corroborating the analysis with other approaches, Petrich actually advanced the state of the art. We sense that this indicates potential for other areas and deserves further attention.

Despite such innovation in the research community, however, government handling of NEPA has continued to be largely procedural in nature. The latest CEQ NEPA regulations, for example, define three objectives: (1) reduce delay, (2) reduce paperwork, and (3) ensure that EISs result in better decisions.[5] Thus, ten years after NEPA's passage, two-thirds of the discussion is still predominated by strictly procedural issues--the timing and size of the statement. Furthermore, despite much discussion about the need to make EISs better decision tools, little has been done to define or dimensionalize the criteria for determining what constitutes better decisions. Viewed in this light, it is possible to conclude that the biggest single innovation of the NEPA experience was the passage of the act itself and its initial, explosive implementation. Indeed, at least one analyst[6] has suggested that the entire EIS experience has been counterproductive--a waste of the prodigious popular sentiment and government concern of the early 1970s. We propose, however, a substantially different interpretation of the EIS experience--an interpretation that views the cumulative modifications and refinements in the process as potentially system transforming rather than mere increments of technical fine tuning.

The initial image of EISs as a means to add environmental quality concerns to the list of existing planning and development criteria resulted in a perceived conflict with the institutionalized notions of economic efficiency, political expediency, and engineering effectiveness.[7] This is best epitomized by the image of the EIS as a supplemental document intended to apprise decision makers of this new area of social concern; operating with this model, the EIS becomes simply an additional piece of data to be fed into the traditional economic and technical framework of administrative decision making. While the dynamics of the law's implementation resulted in the production of long, justisficatory documents (which were used more as court exhibits than as additional data), it is our perception that over time (and spurred by extensive litigation) the EIS has come to assume a much broader and very different character.

Indeed, EISs have had more of a conceptual than instrumental effect on decision making. That is, while

decision makers generally have not turned to EISs in the
expected ways--for specific data, evidence, or policy
implications--many have been affected by and begun to
adopt the larger intellectual framework or paradigm of the
analyses.[*] Thus, while the information contained in
individual impact statements has rarely seemed to affect
policy decisions, the desire to prepare legally defensible
documents has succeeded in jarring the consciousness of
many decision makers and administrators. Many
practitioners have become more sympathetic toward NEPA-
style analysis as well as more sophisticated in its
interpretation and use. The process has also become more
receptive to the needs of decision makers--both the 1979
CEQ regulations and this book serve as testimony to this
fact.

   Further, the EIS process has steadily come to embrace
the total human environment. Consideration of social,
economic, aesthetic, historical, and cultural factors is
gradually becoming accepted in the environmental review
process. Practitioners, it appears, are also beginning to
accept and use many methods and approaches previously
discussed only in academic circles; such considerations
have also become persuasive decision criteria (witness the
papers by Petrich and Peelle in this volume).

   In addition to this accretion of concerns regarding
environmental impact (i.e., increased breadth), a greater
depth of analysis has also begun to characterize the
public policy arena: psychological theory has provided
important insights into the practical use of visual
information in assessing environmental preferences; the
papers by Rachel and Stephen Kaplan serve as examples
here. Computer technology has provided the practitioner
with a powerful arsenal of tools for the collection of
baseline information as well as the systematic storage,
retrieval, and display of impact information (see the
discussion by McLeod in this volume). Finally, the
application of classical experimental designs to impact
assessment can be a great aid in both simplifying the
analysis and providing information on key causal chains
and assumptions more efficiently than long descriptive
studies; the contribution by Diana Valiela to this book
serves as a good example of this growing concern for
scientifically rigorous yet practical approaches to
assessment and monitoring.

   While many authors' have rightfully criticized the
overemphasis on procedural issues that characterized the
early years of NEPA (largely through citizen suits and
judicial interpretation), the net effect of such legal
refinements (in conjunction with the other trends noted
above) appears to be a much closer alignment of the EIS
process with the governmental decision process. In this
sense, the EIS process has gradually become more
substantive since it now plays a greater role in providing
the information and process for determining the allocation

of society's resources.[10] Indeed, in the final analysis, the EIS's ultimate utility will be determined by the extent to which social decision makers demand such information and not by the extent to which the legal system determines the supply of analysis through litigation.

By widening the number of actors in the process (through citizen input and interagency/intergovernmental participation) and supplementing the traditional adversarial nature of the administrative process (through scoping and other consultation procedures), the evolving EIS process offers the potential for both more creative and acceptable agency decisions. Similarly, by involving decision makers in the process from the outset (through interactive scoping and other participatory sessions), their commitment to the outcomes of the process can be greatly heightened. In short, by embracing the idea that not only analysts but also decision makers and representatives of the interested and affected publics all are "knowers," the diversity of perspectives garnered can serve as raw material for a larger synthesis than would be possible with the traditional consultant-prepared EIS. Equally important, however, is the recognition that, during the process, all parties must also be "learners" and, by instituting numerous iterations of input-review-revision (e.g., scoping, draft EIS, final EIS, and record of decision), the opportunity to learn as the process advances greatly enhances the possibilities of adaptive programs and project design.

Further, by moving toward a more usable yet self-recording style, the entire environmental assessment process can become more of a "learning system." Such a system learns from past mistakes and draws upon its experience bank but is not locked into performing analysis in any particular way. Rather, it allows each unique situation to determine the best configuration of approaches. In this sense, the process becomes resilient--that is, able to be open and responsive to input from all parties who can affect or be affected by a given proposal or change.

Such a process can help to frame better both the nature and extent of a given problem and scope the amount and type of analysis to be done for a particular EIS. As Donald Schon (1980) noted in a recent manuscript, "the construction of well-formed problems is not itself a well-formed problem." Indeed, what practitioners usually encounter are not problems at all but problematic situations; converting problematic situations to problems requires that the complexity and uncertainty of the situation be reduced by focusing on particular elements and relations.

Three broad classes of uncertainty can be defined for this purpose as follows:[11]

1. Factor UE; uncertainty in knowledge of the environment--"we need more research;"
2. Factor UV; uncertainty as to appropriate value judgments--"we need more outside input;" and
3. Factor UR; uncertainty as to intentions in related fields of choice--"we need more governmental coordination."

Formal scientific research thus constitutes only one route among several for dealing with the uncertainties surrounding social decisions. The EIS process provides an ideal forum for simultaneously framing (i.e., scoping) the problem and establishing (and, to some degree, gathering) the appropriate mix of formal analysis, value preferences, ordinary knowledge, and political coordination to suit the given situation. In this way, the information gathered (and the scope and configuration of the "solution space") are determined collectively by both experts and stakeholders. The EIS process can thus be envisioned as the social process by which the supply of information for decision making is brought into alignment with the demand for analysis or consideration. Indeed, Michael O'Hare (1980) has taken this a step further by calling for "the abandonment of the supply-side impact statement process." Instead, the interested and affected parties themselves would be expected and enabled to get their own "facts;" the impact statement would then simply be a record of the debate that ensued. Participants would thus use a collective and inclusive process as a decision tool, rather than rely on the product of an exclusive and selective process (i.e., the consultant-prepared EIS).

Such a market approach would also indirectly resolve the perennial NEPA problem of goading agencies into serious consideration of alternatives.[12] Rather than badgering agencies into analyzing a handful of present alternatives complete with a balancing statement of environmental vs. economic or technical considerations, the emerging interactive approach decomposes the problem into its constituent parts and then builds the preferred option from the ground up. In so doing, it enables a much more fine-grained response to public preferences than does the force-fitting of preselected alternatives with mitigative measures. Such an approach is also much more efficient than the old-style alternatives approach; it is akin to comparing the old-fashioned eye doctor who asked you about your sight and then ground five alternative pairs of glasses (none of which was quite right) with the modern optometrist who uses lens diagnostics to determine interactively the proper prescription before grinding the glasses. Recent developments in the related fields of technology assessment[13] and innovation[14] provide examples of similar notions such as the "creation of preferred futures" and the design of "custom-made" solutions to fit particular situations.

Thus, framed in its broadest social context, the EIS process offers the opportunity to move beyond the provision of supplementary technical data or elaborate legal justification toward a self-contained decision process--a new and innovative "social technique" to foster better administrative decisions, to use the words of Dahl and Lindblom (1976). Through the alignment of preferences and data needs, it is feasible to begin to think of a decision process that yields results that more closely approximate the social optimum in the Pareto sense[15]--that is, a configuration of policy instruments that makes as many people better off as is practical without making anyone worse off. Since the ultimate configuration is arrived at interactively, the optimization proposed here does not assume that people's preferences are fixed and known a priori (as in classical decision and utility theory).[16] Rather, individual and group preferences are sequentially discovered, influenced, and reformulated by the process of exploring alternative combinations of policy approaches. In short, the size of the solution pie need not be fixed, and it is possible first to enlarge the pie before slicing it.

The ultimate pattern of the social response thus reflects a sense of consensus that would be unattainable in the traditional world of adversarial administrative decision making and is defined as the point at which the collective cannot improve the outcome. The real concern thus shifts from the scientific quality and utility of a document to the acceptability of a social process. As such, the central focus is no longer legal defensibility, procedural compliance, or even research design and predictive validity; rather, the real goal is an improved or enhanced social decision as reflected by the support of all legitimate parties to the outcome.

Acknowledging past trends and identifying future potentials, however, are quite different from charting a course to implementation. Indeed, just as the fertile soil of the 1970s nurtured the EIS process, so the soil of the 1980s may weather and lose its fertility, thus transforming the process in unforeseen ways. In this regard, Buttel and Larsen (1980) examine the possible future paths of environmental policy. Characterizing the growth of environmentalism in the 1970s as an extension of the liberal democratic state (characterized by interest group politics) so eloquently described by Lowi (1979), the authors suggest that the continuation of such a centrist strategy would be quite vulnerable to any number of increasingly likely resource crises (e.g., a protracted energy supply shock). Centrist environmentalism thus will probably shift toward the right or the left as incidents of resource scarcity emerge.

In brief, environmentalism of the right would place control of scarce resources in the hands of a few and "solve" environmental problems by drastically reducing the living standards of the working class; alternatively, environmentalism of the left would attempt to enhance ecological and organizational sustainability while simultaneously striving for greater social equity. While such a dichotomy is obviously an oversimplification, it serves to portray the two most likely directions that the policy climate might take in the 1980s.

While we have shown signs of moving toward the left in the last decade (e.g., greater public involvement in decisions, emphasis on health requirements in the workplace, and regulation of toxic materials), there have also been mixed signals from the right (e.g., the "lifeboat ethics" of Garrett Hardin[17] and the proposed Energy Mobilization Board). Further, the Reagan administration appears to be moving increasingly toward an environmentalism of the right (witness the shifts in policy concerning environmental and workplace standards, use of pubic lands, and the regressive effects of current budgetary and tax policies).

It is thus within the above context that the EIS process must assert itself as a pragmatic policy tool. It has long been known that, when the social situation is changing rapidly and there are divergent and often conflicting images of the situation, organizations should open themselves to the external environment (interested, affected, and expert parties) in order to understand better and structure appropriate responses to problems.[18] Given the expected turbulence of the decade and the recent trends toward fiscal retrenchment, the EIS process must demonstrate its ability efficiently and effectively to structure appropriate and equitable social responses to complex problems and situations. In large measure, such an accomplishment depends upon the existence of sensitive decision makers in agencies capable of asking the right questions before deciding what the answers are. By approaching problems in a collaborative, participatory, and multi-perspective way, the EIS process might prove itself to be a social process that will not only survive but thrive in the coming years of economic slowdown and international turbulence. The call is for nothing less than a process that both resolves conflict resulting from wider involvement and helps structure the situation to make it manageable. Anything less will cause even the best intentioned governmental decision makers to turn solely to their own organizations to make decisions since complexity and conflict can quickly lead to overload of information. During the coming period of societal change, such a myopic approach to decision making can only lead us down a path to inappropriate, unadaptive, and inequitable public policies.

REFERENCES

Ahmad, R., and Christakis, A. (1979), "A Policy-sensitive Model for Technology Assessment." Washington, D.C.: Battelle.

Andrews, R. (1976), Environmental Policy and Administrative Change. Cambridge, Mass.: D. C. Heath and Co.

Andrews, R., et al. (1977), Substantive Guidance for Environmental Impact Assessment. Indianapolis, Ind.: The Institute of Ecology.

Bardach, E., and Puglioresi, L. (1977), "The Environmental Impact Statement and the Real World." Public Interest, 49.

Baumol, W. (1965), Economic Theory and Operations Analysis. Englewood Cliffs, N.J.: Prentice Hall.

Bissett, R. (1981), Problems and Issues in the Implementation of Post-development Audits. Aberdeen, Scotland: University of Aberdeen (draft manuscript).

Buttel, F., and Larson, O. (1980), "Whither Environmentalism? The Future Political Path of the Environmental Movement." Natural Resources Journal, 20(2), 323-344.

Caldwell, L. (1978), "Is NEPA Inherently Self-defeating?" Paper prepared for the annual Environmental Law Institute Conference, Indiana University, Bloomington, Indiana.

Caldwell, L. K., and Bartlett, R. B. (1981), The Cybernetic Effect of NEPA: The EIS Links Science, Management, and Policy in a Feedback Loop. Study under National Science Foundation Grant No. PRA 79-10014. Bloomington, Ind.: Indiana University.

Council on Environmental Quality (1976), Environmental Impact Statements: An Analysis of Six Years' Experience by Seventy Federal Agencies. Washington, D.C.: Council on Environmental Quality.

Culhane, P. J., Armentano, T. V., and Friesema, H. P. (1981), State-of-the-Art Scientific Understanding of Acid Deposition in Environmental Assessments of Fossil-fuel Power Plants. Study under National Science Foundation Grant No. PRA 97-10014. Report to the Center for Advanced Studies in Technology and Public Policy, Indiana University. Indianapolis, Ind.: The Institute of Ecology.

Dahl, R., and Lindblom, C. (1976), Politics, Economics, and Welfare. Chicago, Ill.: University of Chicago Press.

Downs, A. (1967), Inside Bureaucracy. Boston, Mass.: Little, Brown and Co.

Emery, F., and Trist, E. (1965), "The Causal Texture of Organizational Environments." Human Relations, 18.

Fairfax, S. (1978), "A Disaster in the Environmental Movement." Science, 199, 17.

Federal Register (1978), November 29, 55978-56007.

Friend, J. K., and Jessop, W. N. (1977), Local Government and Strategic Choice. New York: Pergamon Press.

Hardin, G. (1972), Exploring New Ethics of Survival: The Voyage of the Spaceship Beagle. New York: Viking Press.

Hart, S. L., and Enk, G. A. (1980), Green Goals and Greenbacks: State-level Environmental Review Programs and Their Associated Costs. Boulder, Col.: Westview Press.

Hill, W., and Ortolano, L. (1978), "NEPA's Effect on the Consideration of Alternatives: A Crucial Test." Natural Resources Journal, 18, 2.

Holling, C. S. (Ed.) (1978), Adaptive Environmental Assessment and Management. New York: Wiley-Interscience.

Katz, D., and Kahn, R. L. (1978), The Social Psychology of Organizations. New York: John Wiley and Sons.

Lawrence, P., and Lorsch, J. (1967), Organization and Environment. Homewood, Ill.: Richard Irwin.

Lindblom, C., and Cohen, D. (1979), Usable Knowledge. New Haven, Conn.: Yale University Press.

Lippitt, R., and Lindaman, E. (1979), Choosing the Future You Prefer. Ann Arbor, Mich.: Human Resource Development Associates.

Liroff, R. (1976), A National Policy for the Environment. Bloomington, Ind.: Indiana University Press.

Liroff, R. (1980), "NEPA--Where Have We Been and Where Are We Going?" American Planners Association Journal, April.

Lowi, T. (1979), The End of Liberalism. New York: W. W. Norton and Co.

Lundquist, T. (1975), "Substantive and Procedural in the NEPA Context: Suggested Definitions and Some Further Thought." Working paper of the Economic and Environmental Studies Center, The Institute on Man and Science. Available from the Research and Decision Center, Medusa, New York, 12120.

March, J., and Simon, H. (1958), Organizations. New York: John Wiley and Sons.

McKenna, C. (1980), Quantitative Methods for Public Decision Making. New York: McGraw-Hill.

Merewitz, L., and Sosnick, S. (1971), The Budget's New Clothes. Chicago, Ill.: Markham Publishing Co.

O'Hare, M. (1980), "Improving the Use of Information in Environmental Decision Making." Environmental Impact Assessment Review, 1, 3.

Pelz, D., and Munson, F. (1982), "Originality Level and the Innovating Process in Organizations." Human Systems Management, 3, 173-187.

Pressman, J., and Wildavsky, A. (1979), Implementation. Berkeley, Cal.: University of California Press.

Raiffa, H. (1968), Decision Analysis. Reading, Mass.: Addison-Wesley.

Schon, D. (1980), The Reflective Practitioner. Cambridge,

434

Mass.: MIT, draft manuscript.
Steck, H. (1975), "NEPA after Five Years: A Second Look."
Paper prepared for the annual meeting of the Society
for Study of Social Problems. Cortland, N.Y.: State
University of New York-Cortland.
Tryzna, T. (1974), Environmental Impact Requirements in
the States: NEPA's Offspring. Washington, D.C.:
U.S. Environmental Protection Agency.
Warner, M., and Preston, E. (1974), A Review of
Environmental Impact Assessment Methodologies.
Washington, D.C.: U.S. Environmental Protection
Agency.

NOTES

[1]See the chapter "Implementation as Evolution" in
the latest edition of Pressman and Wildavsky (1979).

[2]For example, see Andrews (1976), Bardach and
Puglioresi (1977), Caldwell (1978), Fairfax (1978), and
Liroff (1976).

[3]For example, see Council on Environmental Quality
(1976), Hart and Enk (1980), Tryzna (1974), and Warner and
Preston (1974).

[4]Most of the current elements of the EIS process
fall into this category--for example, the "draft" and
"final" document distinction, early "scoping" meetings,
and official "records of decision."

[5]These were published in the Federal Register,
November 29, 1978.

[6]See Fairfax (1978).

[7]The extensive litigation that pervaded NEPA's
implementation for many years is testimony to this.

[8]See Lindblom and Cohen (1979) for a discussion of
this idea.

[9]For example, Andrews et al. (1977), Fairfax (1978),
and Steck (1975).

[10]For an interesting discussion of the "substantive"
and "procedural," see Lundquist (1975).

[11]Abstracted from Friend and Jessop (1977).

[12]See Hill and Ortolano (1978) for a discussion of
this problem.

[13]For example, see Ahmad and Christakis (1979).

[14]For example, see Pelz and Munson (1982) and Lippitt
and Lindaman (1979).

[15]For a discussion of this concept, see Baumol
(1965), Dahl and Lindblom (1976), and Merewitz and Sosnick
(1971).

[16]See, for example, McKenna (1980) and Raiffa (1968).

[17]See Hardin (1972) for details on this matter.

[18]Numerous scholarly works support this claim; these
include Downs (1967), Emery and Trist (1965), Katz and
Kahn (1978), Lawrence and Lorsch (1967), and March and
Simon (1958).

Contributors

DR. SELINA BENDIX is President of Bendix Environmental Research, Inc. Her firm specializes in advising consultants on how to write effective EISs and in writing EISs for projects involving toxic substance issues. She has published over 100 articles on environmental and consumer issues.

MS. SHARON DECKER is currently Project Manager for hazardous waste processing for the Minnesota Waste Management Board. Prior to this, she worked with the Minnesota Environmental Quality Board and the Hennepin County (Minnesota) Department of Public Works. She is the author of many environmental review documents and has published articles on environmental review and hazardous waste management in Minnesota.

DR. STUART L. HART is currently Project Director at the University of Michigan's Institute for Social Research and consultant to Gordon Enk and Associates. He was formerly Research Associate at the Institute on Man and Science and has worked extensively in the areas of environmental and social impact assessment. His most recent publications in these areas have included Beyond NEPA Revisited (1978) and Green Goals and Greenbacks (1980).

DR. ROBERT E. HENSHAW has been Associate Aquatic and Terrestrial Ecologist with the New York State Department of Environmental Conservation since 1974. After his early involvement in review of the transAlaska pipeline system EIS, he directed environmental consulting firms writing EISs, advised utilities during the scoping of EISs, and, in his present position, has reviewed and testified on numerous EISs on diverse projects.

DR. BENJAMIN F. HOBBS is currently Assistant Professor at Case Western Reserve University. He was a Wignor Fellow at Oak Ridge National Laboratory, having obtained his Ph.D. in Environmental Systems Engineering at Cornell University. He has done impact assessment work as a consultant to the U.S. Air Force and as an intern at the President's Council on Environmental Quality, the Salt River Project, and Northeast Utilities. He also served as

a member of the governing board of the South Dakota
Environmental Coalition.

DR. MARGARET S. HREZO has taught Political Science at
Radford University and Virginia Polytechnic Institute and
State University. Presently she is Senior Research
Associate at the Virginia Water Resource Research Center
in Blacksburg, Virginia.

DR. WILLIAM E. HREZO received his Ph.D. in Political
Science from the University of Maryland in 1977. He is
presently Assistant Professor of Political Science at
Radford University, Radford, Virginia, where he teaches
Public Administration, American Government, and State and
Local Government.

DR. ERIC L. HYMAN is an Evaluation Economist at
Appropriate Technology International in Washington, D.C.
He is co-editor of Economic Valuation of Natural Resources
and Environmental Aspects of Development, published by
Bowker Press, and author of numerous articles dealing with
environmental impact assessment.

DR. LLOYD C. IRLAND is an economist with the State
Planning Office in Maine and principal advisor to the
Governor. He served five years in the Maine Department of
Conservation and at the Yale School of Forestry and
Environmental Studies after an early stint with the
U.S. Forest Service. He is the author of two books and
over 50 articles and bulletins on forest economics and
policy.

MR. JAMES J. JORDAN is President of Resources in Balance,
Inc., South Lake Tahoe, California. He served as
Executive Director of the Tahoe Regional Planning Agency
(1977-79) and formerly was Chief of its Environmental
Division (1975-77). Prior to that, he held various
environmental planning positions with the U.S. Army Corps
of Engineers (1968-75). He currently is directing the
development and implementation of a national
transportation plan for Nigeria.

DR. RACHEL KAPLAN is Professor of Environmental Psychology
in the School of Natural Resources and the Doctoral
Program in Urban and Regional Planning at The University
of Michigan, where she is also Associate Professor of
Psychology. She has made numerous contributions to the
research literature in the areas of visual assessment,
public participation, and the psychology of natural
environments.

DR. STEPHEN KAPLAN is Professor of Psychology and of
Computer and Communication Sciences at The University of
Michigan. He has published extensively in the areas of

environmental psychology and cognitive functioning. His theoretical work has focused on the integration of evolutionary, behavioral, and adaptive perspectives.

MS. SUSAN KORRICK is a Research Associate in the Division of Environmental Sciences, School of Public Health, Columbia University. She is a graduate of Harvard College in Biology and has a particular interest in the biomedical sciences.

MR. DENNIS LUNDBLAD is the Supervisor of the Office of Operations and Enforcement in the Washington Department of Ecology in charge of environmental impact reporting, state coordination for the review of NEPA documents and major federal proposals, implementation of the state master application process for permits, and major issue analysis. Mr. Lundblad's background is in resource planning and management, engineering geology, and construction. He has worked with the state and national environmental policy laws since their inception.

MR. RONALD G. MCLEOD is a senior staff member at the Jet Propulsion Laboratory's Image Processing Lab. He is currently pursuing research in Landsat digital mosaics for land resources assessment and defining methods to apply geographic information systems to environmental problems.

DR. PETER M. MEIER is a senior scientist at Brookhaven National Laboratory and holds faculty appointments at the Polytechnic Institute of New York and the State University of New York at Stony Brook. He is involved in numerous environmental and regional assessments for the U.S. Department of Energy and the Nuclear Regulatory Commission, and he has served as advisor and consultant to many organizations, including the United Nations, the International Joint Commission, and the National Commission on Air Quality.

MS. RUTH-ELLEN MILLER serves as Consulting Policy Analyst and Project Facilitator to several research organizations and futures-oriented community groups in the northwestern states. She is author of several papers on the use of intuition in social systems research and design, lectures on problems of technology and society, and edits the newsletter Critical Paths: Strategies for the Intervening Futurist.

DR. DAVID H. MOREAU is Professor of City and Regional Planning at the University of North Carolina, Chapel Hill. He is principal investigator of the environmental indicators research upon which Hyman, Moreau, and Stiftel's paper is based.

MR. SAMUEL G. MYGATT is Executive Director for
environmental impact review in the Executive Office of
Environmental Affairs, the Commonwealth of Massachusetts.
In the past three years he has reviewed some thousand
projects, conducted 150 scoping exercises, and reviewed as
many Environmental Impact Reports.

DR. JAMES R. PEASE is an Associate Professor of Resource
Planning and Extension Specialist in Resource Management
at Oregon State University. He has done research and
community service work in land use planning and
environmental impact assessment. His special interests
include techniques for resource analyses and land use
planning implementation.

DR. ELIZABETH PEELLE is an environmental sociologist at
Oak Ridge National Laboratory. She helped initiate the
field of social impact assessment with her work on the
proposed Mendocino, California, nuclear power plant for
the Atomic Energy Commission in 1972. She was one of
several Oak Ridge National Laboratory social impact
assessment staff who worked on the various environmental
impact statements for the proposed Greene County, New
York, nuclear plant.

MR. CARL H. PETRICH is a Research Associate in the Energy
Division at Oak Ridge National Laboratory. He has been
working at Oak Ridge since receiving his master's degree
in landscape architecture from The University of Michigan
in 1976. He is presently studying the visual quality of
alternative schemes for surface mine reclamation in the
country's coal regions and methods for determining and
implementing innovative postmining land uses.

MS. BARBARA L. PIERCE is an Environmental Science
Associate at Brookhaven National Laboratory. She has
examined nuclear power plant siting methodologies for the
Nuclear Regulatory Commission and has assessed
environmental impacts of energy production for the
Department of Energy. She is currently using optimization
techniques to analyze energy use and conservation in
several industries.

DR. MICHAEL D. ROWE is a policy analyst at Brookhaven
National Laboratory. He specializes in assessing health
and environmental impacts of energy policies and
developing energy technologies for the U.S. Department of
Energy.

DR. GRANVILLE H. SEWELL is Associate Director of the
Division of Environmental Sciences, School of Public
Health, Columbia University. He has directed or
participated in environmental assessments of projects in

more than a dozen countries and written widely on environmental and energy problems.

MR. RICHARD C. SMARDON is a Research Associate and Coordinator of Research at the School of Landscape Architecture, College of Environmental Science and Forestry, State University of New York-Syracuse. He is also an Associate with the Graduate Program in Environmental Studies and an environmental planner with the U.S. Geological Survey in Reston, Virginia. He has published numerous articles on environmental impact assessment, visual analysis, and environmental administration.

DR. SHELBY J. SMITH-SANCLARE is currently Coordinator (Environmental Matters) with the Division of Land and Forest Resources, Tennessee Valley Authority. Prior to coming to TVA she was the Environmental Evaluations Coordinator for Los Alamos National Laboratory, New Mexico. She taught environmental planning and ecological design at the Universities of New Mexico and Georgia and was the Assistant Director, Center for Environmental Research and Development, at the University of New Mexico. She developed the Environmental Coordinating role at Los Alamos and was a management team member who originated and developed the TVA Environmental Quality staff.

DR. NELLIE M. STARK is a Professor of Forest Ecology at the School of Forestry, University of Montana. She has studied nutrient cycling in coniferous and tropical forests. Much of her work has dealt with minimizing the impacts of harvest and burning and predicting nutrient losses.

DR. BRUCE STIFTEL is currently Assistant Professor of Urban and Regional Planning at Florida State University. He was formerly at the University of North Carolina. His research interests concern citizen participation and institutional aspects of natural resource planning.

DR. DIANA VALIELA is currently Head, Water Quality Objectives Division, Environment Canada, Vancouver, British Columbia. During this project she was Research Associate at the Westwater Research Centre of the University of British Columbia, Vancouver, B.C., Canada. She has done extensive work in environmental impact analysis methods, coastal resource management, aquaculture, ecosystem impacts of pesticides, and water quality management, and she is author of Biological Environmental Impact Studies: Theory and Methods (Academic Press, 1978).

MR. NICHOLAS C. YOST is a legal staff member at the Center for Law in the Public Interest in Washington, D.C. From

1977 to 1981 he was General Counsel of the Council on
Environmental Quality and had lead responsibility for the
development of the CEQ NEPA regulations. Prior to that,
as Counsel to the State Environmental Quality Study
Council in California (1969-1971) and as Deputy Attorney
General in charge of the Environmental Unit of the
California Justice Department (1971-1977), he had major
responsibility for the development of California's "little
NEPA."